Independence
LOST

Independence
LOST

Lives on the Edge of the American Revolution

Kathleen DuVal

RANDOM HOUSE

NEW YORK

Published in the United States by Random House, an imprint and division
of Penguin Random House LLC, New York.

Random House and the House colophon are registered
trademarks of Penguin Random House LLC.

ISBN 978-1-4000-6895-1
eBook ISBN 978-1-58836-961-1

Printed in the United States of America on acid-free paper

atrandom.com

2   4   6   8   9   7   5   3   1

First Edition

Book design by Christopher M. Zucker

For Marty

CONTENTS

LIST OF ILLUSTRATIONS AND MAPS

List of Illustrations

List of Maps

INTRODUCTION

AS THE SKY LIGHTENED in the early morning hours of March 9, 1781, British sailors on a frigate floating at the mouth of Pensacola Bay spotted a fleet heading straight for them. One sailor scrambled high on the mast, straining to see the flag flying over the lead ship. Hoping to see the red, white, and blue of the Union Jack, instead the lookout recognized the bold red and gold stripes of Spanish King Carlos III's naval flag. The British frigate fired seven shots, whose thunderous sound warned the people of Pensacola of imminent invasion.

These sailors were not surprised at the Spanish invasion—Pensacola was the capital of British West Florida and the last line of defense against Spanish conquest of the entire colony. The sailors had only hoped that the Spanish would not arrive before reinforcements. However, readers today might be surprised by this North American battle adjacent to battles of a better-known war—the American Revolution. While histories of the American Revolution include the Marquis de Lafayette and the French fleet at Yorktown, most Americans and even many historians do not know that the Spanish were fighting

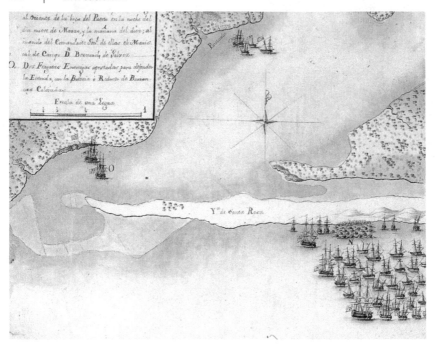

Pensacola, March 9–10, 1781, with the Spanish fleet off Santa Rosa Island and the British *Mentor* and *Port Royal* guarding the Bay. (*Toma de la plaza de Panzacola y rendición de la Florida Occidental a las armas de Carlos III*, Ministerio de Defensa, Archivo del Museo Naval, Spain).

their own battles against the British at the same time. As Britain tried to put down the rebellion in thirteen of its colonies, it was also defending its other thirteen colonies on the North American mainland and in the West Indies against the Spanish and the French. By invading West Florida, Spain was taking advantage of the distraction of the rebellion to expand eastward along the Gulf of Mexico. For Britain, now on the defensive on two fronts, the prospect of Spanish expansion raised the stakes of the war.

Forgotten Stories

The American Revolution on the Gulf Coast is a story without minutemen, without founding fathers, without rebels. It reveals a different war with unexpected participants, forgotten outcomes, and surprising winners and losers.

Although the Revolutionary War was a global war with global causes and consequences, two circumstances following the rebels' victory led their story to take center stage as the standard history of the Revolution. The first was the Treaty of Paris, in which the United States and Britain divided the eastern half of the continent—and excluded other Europeans and Indians. The second, following the treaty, was the large numbers of Americans settling on lands claimed by Spaniards, Creeks, Chickasaws, Cherokees, and others. The kings of France and Spain entered this global war not because they loved rebellion (much the contrary) but for the same kinds of imperial objectives that had propelled them into previous wars. Although both worried that the rebellion could set a bad example for their own colonies, they were more interested in reversing Britain's victories from the Seven Years' War of the 1750s and 1760s and protecting and expanding their global empires.[1]

On the Gulf Coast, and indeed for most people, the Revolution seemed to be just another imperial war, another war fought for territory and treasure. As different alliances competed for power, Spanish, British, and French colonists, black slaves, and Indians of many nations were drawn into this multifaceted war. The narrative of the Revolutionary era is more true to its people and more fascinating in its complexity if it includes less familiar regions and peoples and if it encompasses the war's experiences and results in all their diversity.

The war on the Gulf Coast proves two truths often buried by common narratives of the Revolutionary War: that most people chose sides for reasons besides genuine revolutionary or loyalist fervor and that non-British colonists exercised a great deal of influence over the war's outcome. In Virginia, slaves rushed to British lines seeking freedom from their American masters. Near the border of New York and Canada, Mohawk Indian Molly Brant spied for the British, sheltered loyalists in her home, and persuaded men of the Iroquois Confederacy to fight on the British side. She hoped that by supporting the British she could maintain the Iroquois-British alliance and stem the tide of settlers into Iroquoia. Sometimes support was merely for self-preservation. In Vincennes (present-day Indiana), French families came out to welcome American George Rogers Clark with a bottle of

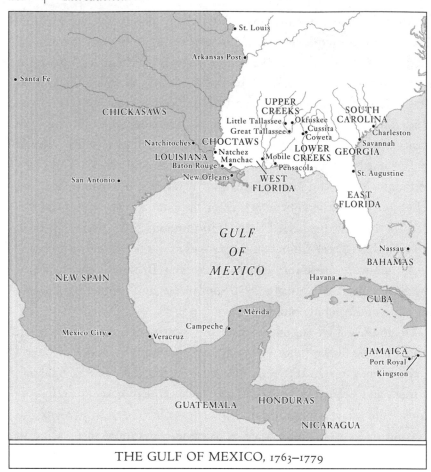

THE GULF OF MEXICO, 1763–1779

wine when he took their town from the British, assuring him of their love of the American rebels. They did the same for the British when they retook Vincennes a few months later, and again brought out the wine when Clark returned, each time hoping to curry favor with whatever military power was ascendant.[2]

This book focuses on the Gulf Coast, from Florida to Louisiana, because of the astounding number of competing interests that came into conflict there. The Gulf Coast was the only site of Revolutionary War battles that was outside the rebelling colonies during the war but soon became part of the United States. The Gulf Coast's war included participants that most people do not think of when they consider the American Revolution: the French and Spanish, who had a centuries-long history in the region; Creeks, Chickasaws, and Choctaws, whose lands spread from the coast deep into the interior of the continent; and people of African descent, whose experiences of enslavement and freedom differed widely and, with the introduction of large-scale plantation slavery, would be changing faster than ever.

The People

To make sense of the dizzying complexity of the Revolutionary War on the Gulf Coast, this book centers on eight individuals. These characters stand in for larger peoples but also illustrate that imperial relationships were almost always personal and that the most complete history is a multi-perspectival one. Today, their names are obscure, but some were famous in their time. Oliver Pollock, Alexander McGillivray, and Payamataha, for example, were names that George Washington and Thomas Jefferson came to know well.[3]

Less known was Petit Jean, who grew up a slave in Mobile. As he tended his master's cattle, he would never have imagined that he would become a trusted spy and courier for Spain. Yet right before the Spanish fleet left Havana for Pensacola, it was Petit Jean who transported Spanish orders for New Orleans to prepare the local militias to aid the naval forces. The Revolutionary War brought Petit Jean this opportunity, and his operations helped the Spanish cause.

Another man assisting the Spanish invading force was a young Cajun militiaman named Amand Broussard. A refugee from the last war between France and Britain, he hated the British for forcing his family out of their Acadian homeland in eastern Canada and was glad to get the chance to fight again.

Eagerly awaiting news in New Orleans, Oliver Pollock, a merchant, had garnered financial support for the war effort. The Continental Congress had appointed Pollock as its agent in Louisiana, where he fostered an unofficial alliance between the rebels and the Spanish crown. Pollock hoped soon to send news of Pensacola's fall to Congress and to General George Washington. Waiting with him was his wife, Margaret O'Brien Pollock, whose Irish Catholic family had long fought against the British and whose husband's wartime decisions would create opportunities and perils for their growing family.

A pressing question on the minds of those defending as well as those hoping to take Pensacola was whether the region's Native peoples would show up for the battle. The vast inland of North America was Indian country, and its people far outnumbered the Europeans clashing on the Gulf Coast. North of Pensacola was the Creek Confederacy, a loose confederation whose towns ruled themselves separately, needed interpreters within the Confederacy, and had occasionally even joined opposite sides in war. Alexander McGillivray, the son of a Creek mother and a Scottish trader, blamed the rebels for threatening his parents' lands and livelihoods. During the war, he tried to rally Creek fighters to aid the British. His frustrations coordinating war parties later inspired him to try to centralize the Creek Confederacy into a nation and to unite all southeastern Indians into a "Southern Confederacy."

In contrast to Alexander McGillivray, the Chickasaw leader and diplomat named Payamataha influenced the war by inaction. The British considered Payamataha and the Chickasaws "absolutely at our disposal" and believed that Payamataha was rallying his people to ride the four hundred miles from their towns near the Mississippi River to rescue Pensacola.[4] Payamataha had different plans. He was a leader in a growing movement among Indians to stay out of European conflicts, a movement that, if it succeeded, might doom the British effort to retain the Gulf Coast and to quell the rebellion to the north.

Within all of the groups involved in the Revolutionary War, both familiar and unfamiliar, there were tremendous differences in background and opinion. "British" soldiers came to the Gulf Coast from not only England, Scotland, Wales, and Protestant Ireland but also Jamaica, the German principality of Waldeck, and German-American communities in Pennsylvania. People of African descent included Malike-speaking Bambara people from the inland tributaries of the Senegal River, Wolof speakers from the lower Senegal Valley, and Yorubas from the Bight of Benin. They had lived through the horrors of the Middle Passage and found themselves enslaved in the towns and plantations of the Gulf Coast. Other people of African descent had been in the Americas for generations. Some of them were enslaved, some had gained their freedom, and others had been free all their lives. The invading Spanish force included soldiers from, in addition to Spain itself, Catholic Ireland, Cuba, France, Flanders, Mallorca, Catalonia, and the Canary Islands.

Although diverse, the people of the Gulf Coast had more in common than their ethnic or racial labels imply. Europeans and Africans had been coming to the Americas for nearly three centuries, and they and Native Americans had changed one another. Indians and Africans had readily established trade with Europe, and they had acquired metal tools and new kinds of cloth and weapons. Trading partnerships and alliances had in turn affected regional wars. Although the Declaration of Independence accused King George III of inciting "merciless Indian savages" against the thirteen colonies, Indians worked for their own interests and indeed had demanded the king's restrictions on westward expansion. They were not simply pawns of the British king. Like Europeans and Africans, American Indians had their own policies, disputes, and agendas. Natives, Europeans, and Africans knew one another well by the eighteenth century, and their lives had been changed by the same global forces. The natural resources and labor of Europe's colonies fed an industrial revolution in England, which was changing the material lives of people all over the world.

This book's characters lived more than a thousand miles away from where the war began. Most had no interest in Britain's attempt to tax and regulate its colonies and little in common with Boston's famously raucous protesters. Still, when war came, it presented them all with opportunities and dangers, and they worked to profit from the squabble among the English speakers to the north. They tried, in dramatic and innovative ways, to use the war to forward their own ambitions for themselves, their families, and their nations.

Interdependence

When James Bruce, a member of His Majesty's Council for West Florida, and his wife, Isabella, heard the cannon fire and saw the smoke rising from the extinguished fire of the lighthouse to signal the arrival of the Spanish ships, they gathered their children, some provisions, and a few belongings. Along with Pensacola's other government officials and several hundred European, African, and Native women and children, the Bruces rushed into the town's main fort. Natives of Scotland, their fortunes lay with the British empire. If the Spanish or the rebels prevailed, they were likely to capture the Bruces and their children and send them into exile—or worse.

Every July 4, Americans celebrate the independence the Revolution created, the political separation from Britain and the creation of the United States of America. On such occasions, Americans might imagine that independence was a universal and uniform goal in the eighteenth century. But as the story of James and Isabella Bruce would remind us, the Revolutionary War was not fought solely for the independence of the United States. The war's conclusion did not bring freedom to all of those who became part of the new republic. Some people fought hard against joining the new nation that Jefferson called "the only monument of human rights, and the sole depository of the sacred fire of freedom and self-government."[5]

Stories of competing colonial groups, strong Native confederacies and nations, and overlapping systems of slavery reveal that the Anglo-American nation that arose from the Revolution was not inevitable. In fact, both the defeat of the most powerful empire in the world and the creation of a lasting republic were highly unlikely outcomes. Scholarship and popular memory have long portrayed late eighteenth-century Spaniards and Indians as people out of time—Spain as a crumbling empire and Indians living in ways incompatible with the agrarianism to come. In this view, both were incapable of change, destined to be overrun by settlers from the United States. But in fact, they had ambitions that were reasonable at the time, and they came close to realizing their goals, goals that if achieved would have spawned a very different nation or (more likely) multiple polities.[6]

Being independent would have been unwelcome to most people in eighteenth-century North America. Men and women depended on a web of economic, social, and political connections that provided stability and opportunity even as they limited complete freedom of action. Indeed, empires worked in part because they incorporated diverse and unequal populations into a system of beneficial, if also coercive, connections. An individual or society that tried to act completely alone had no chance.[7]

For most, *advantageous interdependence* was a more logical goal. Leaders of all kinds of polities struggled to establish a balance in which they might have more control over dependent relationships. Sovereign states involved networks of dependency. Families and individuals measured their freedom according to how much less dependent they were on others than others were on them. Colonists might feel that their empires took advantage of them, restricting their trade and limiting their production. Still, it was empire that delivered manufactured goods, created a market for colonial produce, and secured property rights. It was empire that protected them from the military might of other empires and powerful Indians who might otherwise expel or kill them. Even propertied Britons like James Bruce, who believed themselves the most independent subjects in the world, were part of a hierarchy of reciprocal dependencies that extended from the king at the top to slaves at the bottom.[8]

Throughout the early modern world, dependence meant security, while independence could mean vulnerability and even slavery. Being captured and enslaved meant that a man, woman, or child was ripped from the interdependent relationships of kin and community to face a cruel world without protection. A slave like Petit Jean might work for freedom from literal enslavement, but he also wanted ties of community and patronage that would make his life more secure. Other freedoms might be more pressing than freedom from slavery— freedom from violent abuse, freedom to reunite with family members, or even some measure of independence of daily life within the legal strictures of enslavement.[9]

The only people involved in the war on the Gulf Coast who fought for sovereign independence were Native leaders. Through the early nineteenth century, independent Indian polities ruled the vast interior of North America, although they too operated within a complicated set of interdependencies. The basic unit of southeastern Indian politics was the town, but towns were not fully independent. People were born into matrilineal clans that united people of different towns and could make decisions of war and peace that might not align with the desires of particular town leaders. And towns and clans were then part of even larger polities. The Chickasaws exercised sovereignty as a nation (in the eighteenth-century sense of "a numerous people inhabiting a certain extent of land, enclosed within certain limits, and under the same government").[10] In contrast, the Creek Confederacy was a much looser collection of towns. Each major Creek town ruled itself and lesser towns and farms in its jurisdiction, while the Creek Confederacy tried, but often failed, to unite the towns' foreign policy. Like European monarchs, Native leaders were bound by reciprocal obligations. While men conducted most of the diplomacy, Creek and Chickasaw women had some say in community decision-making. More important for daily life, women owned the houses and fields and therefore did not depend on marriage for economic security. Women's and men's reciprocal responsibilities together established and protected family and community.

Although politically independent, Indian polities still needed external connections for trade and security. Historians have at times argued that American Indians and other colonized peoples became subject to imperial powers because they became dependent on European goods, thereby debilitating their economies. But dependency is a tricky concept—each side in an exchange relationship trades because the other has what it wants. Europeans needed the products of the fur trade and Indians' cooperation in everything from allowing a post on their lands to providing transportation and information. And European trade did not end Indian control over their economies, their land, or their internal governance. Indeed, Indians had participated in both local and long-distance trade with other Indians long before the arrival of Europeans and Africans, and they incorporated European trade into old networks and old practices based on reciprocity. Being part of a world economy had made the lives of Payamataha and Alexander McGillivray more cosmopolitan than those of their Native ancestors, but in most cases Indians had shaped their own participation and understanding of that change more than Europeans had.[11]

Yet as the British population in North America grew, some leaders of both Native and colonial communities began to advocate for more independence from empire, although for quite different, indeed often conflicting, reasons. In the 1760s and 1770s, some British colonists began to see the British empire as a force of tyranny more than opportunity, as an empire that did not allow the colonies enough say over taxes or access to western lands. At the same time, fearing dependence, some Indian leaders sought ways to end or diversify their trade with Britain. And some advocated military solutions against the colonial settlers infringing on Indian lands, the very settlers who protested their empire's efforts to hold them back from expansion.

Nations used some dependencies to free themselves from others. Chickasaw leader Payamataha promoted Chickasaw independence from British dictates by increasing connections to other Indians and the Spanish empire. After the war, Creek leader Alexander McGillivray sought to persuade other Indians to cede some sovereignty to a centralized structure that would be led by Creeks. But a Creek-led confederacy was not at all what Payamataha had in mind. For its part, Spain hoped to preserve and expand its empire by offering various communities—both Indian and non-Indian—military protection and the economic opportunities of empire. For the thirteen colonies that declared political independence from King George III, recognition by and relations with other nations were essential to operating an independent state, particularly one begun in rebellion. As the Declaration of Independence put it, the new nation wanted to take its place "among the powers of the earth."[12]

A Lost World

In colonial and Indian towns along the Gulf Coast and in the interior, the surprising surrender of the British in 1783 seemed parallel to the French surrender at the end of the Seven Years' War twenty years earlier. People expected that the borders of European empires might shift and that imperial officers might speak Spanish instead of English, but borders had changed in the past. However, the Revolution was not like the wars that had come before. Its importance for the Gulf region lay not in immediate changes but in the new empire it created—a land-based "empire of liberty," in Thomas Jefferson's words. With a population doubling every twenty-five years, the land base of the United States also needed to double every twenty-five years if it were to follow Jefferson's ideal of independent and small family farms. Ultimately, the independence of the United States was built on refusing to share the continent with empires or with sovereign Indians.[13]

In winning the Revolutionary War and eventually revolutionizing power relations on the continent of North America, American rebels forwarded their own varieties of independence at the expense of others. The eventual transition to one sovereign state—the United States—over all others meant the loss of earlier kinds of interdependence. At the same time, as an empire of its own, the nation's expanding plantations and farms robbed Indians of their lands and enslaved millions of men and women to grow the cotton that fed a new industrial economy. The longevity and power of an independent United States depended on the land and labor Americans took by force.

Beginning in the 1970s, historians challenged the standard litany of inevitabilities in early American history: British colonial success, the rise of an English-speaking American republic on the Atlantic coast, the expansion of that republic across the continent, and the entrenchment of a plantation economy in the South. Women, Native Americans, non-English Europeans, and Africans are becoming as prominent in our histories of early America as they were in its reality. At its best, this approach to history is multi-perspectival. That is, it not only includes people who were once left out of the history books but also acknowledges their full humanity, including their motivations, diversity, resourcefulness, successes, misjudgments, and mistakes.

More recently, a new narrative of colonial history has evolved from this approach, one that emphasizes cross-cultural encounters, variations and changes in slavery practices, and the changing power dynamics of the entire continent, not just the thirteen British colonies that eventually rebelled. The story of early America in textbooks and classrooms today usually presents a broad view of colonial America, but because scholarship on the Revolution in particular has been slower to move beyond the thirteen colonies, around 1770 the story sharply narrows its focus and disconnects the Revolution from previous history. This narrowing then sets up the early republic as the era when the United States expanded into regions whose past histories are oddly disjointed from their nineteenth-century fates. In reality, the shift from multiple empires and powerful Indian nations to one dominant United States is part of a centuries-long narrative of changing power relations.[14]

The Gulf Coast, far from the traditionally recognized centers of the Revolution, sheds new light on some of the major themes that would dominate the development of the young republic for the next century and still have relevance today. In this region, we see the burgeoning system of the Deep South's plantation slavery. We observe the continued negotiation between colonial settlers and Indian tribes as well as settlers' earliest and increasing efforts to remove these tribes wholesale from their native lands. And we witness the definition of U.S. citizenship hardening around the white male individual. These changes replaced the eighteenth-century world with its diversity of polities, shifting networks of interdependency, and more inclusive (and often more hierarchical) definitions of belonging.[15]

As the Spanish fleet approached Pensacola in 1781, people's hopes and fears were the usual ones in an imperial war. James and Isabella Bruce feared that Catholic Spain would take their home. Amand Broussard looked forward to a chance to humiliate the British. Alexander McGillivray hoped for personal glory and Creek victory. They might have foreseen a new regime controlling West Florida, but what they could not have imagined was that an entire system of imperial and Native interdependence would be utterly overtaken by the rise of the United States.

PART I

The Place and Its People

IN 1774, West Florida Governor Peter Chester opened a letter from men in Philadelphia calling themselves "a general Congress of deputies, from the colonies of New-Hampshire, Massachusetts-bay, Rhode-Island, Connecticut, New-York, New-Jersey, Pennsylvania, the lower counties on [the] Delaware, Maryland, Virginia, North-Carolina, and South-Carolina." The letter asserted that "so rapidly violent and unjust has been the late conduct of the British Administration against the colonies," that each colony must either resign itself to losing its "ancient, just, and constitutional liberty" or join the opposition. They hoped West Florida and the other British colonies in North America would join them.[1]

There were not just thirteen British American colonies in 1774. From Nova Scotia to Jamaica, the actual count was at least twice that. People all across the British colonies would have to decide how to respond to this protest and, later, to the war and the independence movement it would become. Local people would decide whether or not to rebel, and then they and their adversaries would try to recruit others. Allegiances were complicated, seldom tied to simple national or imperial loyalties. Familial or community ties often trumped more abstract identities, and allegiances could shift depending on who promised what and who seemed likely to prevail. As the Spanish and French kings watched this rebellion from Europe, they hoped that it would prove disastrous for their British rival and would revise British gains from victory in the Seven Years' War just a few years earlier. For now, though, most people on the Gulf Coast remained focused on local matters. Governor Chester shoved the letter into his pocket and did not tell anyone about it.

Part I introduces the region of the Gulf Coast and the book's eight central characters, showing how their personal backgrounds and the histories of their peoples brought them to the Gulf Coast and its interlocking dependencies. The book's subsequent parts will weave together these people's stories and show how they influenced the course of the war and the shape of the world to come.

CHAPTER ONE

The Gulf Coast

WHEN THE LETTER from Congress arrived, West Florida Governor Peter Chester was building himself a new house. Most of Pensacola's buildings had log frames with sides of bark and plaster and thatched roofs made of palmetto leaves, but the governor's would be made of brick with a balcony and a shingle roof. It was a sign of British permanence in their relatively new colony, and West Florida's leaders hoped that more development would follow.

From their town, Pensacolans could look out onto a place of striking colors—white sand beaches, water in hues from icy blue to gelatinous green to deep indigo, dark green sea grasses, and tall yellow sea oats. To European explorers in previous centuries, this coast had been a confusing array of inlets and barrier islands, but eighteenth-century merchant sailors knew the region well and skillfully navigated its shoreline to enter its harbors and approach its port towns. Pensacola Bay was a large deepwater port, its narrow entryway well protected by the Santa Rosa barrier island. Nearby Mobile Bay was much shallower, so ships had to unload at Dauphin Island onto smaller sailboats and canoes, which then traveled the forty miles across the

Note how this French mapmaker wrote colonial names across the map, such as *Louisiane* and *Floride* but still showed the dominions of Indian nations, including the "Chicachas" (Chickasaws). Rigobert Bonne, *Carte de la Louisiane et de la Floride*, c. 1750. (Guillaume Thomas François Raynal, *Atlas de toutes les parties connues du globe terrestre*, 1780, Geography and Map Division, Library of Congress)

bay to the town of Mobile. In the same manner, large ships approaching New Orleans stopped at Balize at the mouth of the river to unload onto smaller vessels to reach the coast's largest and busiest port.

New Orleans was more physically impressive than either Mobile or Pensacola, and its buildings tended to be of higher quality than those found in most colonial towns. That city's several thousand residents lived in the low-lying flatland now called the French Quarter, protected by levees from the unpredictable Mississippi River. The better buildings were built of plastered and whitewashed wood planks with glass windows and stone foundations and chimneys, but most houses were single-story log-framed buildings that sat directly on the sand, with windows covered in linen cloths. As in Mobile and Pensacola, houses were hot in summer and cold and drafty in winter. Slaves, as usual, had the worst accommodations. Hurricanes and smaller storms caused frequent damage, and buildings had to be perpetually repaired and rebuilt. As the capital of the colony of Louisiana, the city had a cathedral, an Ursuline convent, government buildings, several schools, and many taverns. In and around the central market of New Orleans, vendors sold goods to the city's white, black, Indian, and mixed-ancestry customers. Pigs, chickens, goats, and vegetable gardens were ubiquitous, and on the edge of town, herds of cattle roamed.

Trade had made the region cosmopolitan. Most of the people and goods on the Gulf Coast came from somewhere else: Indian towns to the north, other colonies, Europe, or Africa. The fur trade of the lower Mississippi Valley was the lifeblood of Gulf Coast commerce. Indian and European traders carried skins, furs, and tallow down the region's rivers in huge canoes and flatboats to the port cities. At the ports, dockworkers loaded the products of the hunt onto ships, as well as timber cut from nearby forests, barrels of tar processed from pine trees, and baked hardtack and other provisions for sailors. Enslaved men and women on plantations along the lower Mississippi and its tributaries grew and processed tobacco, rice, and indigo, which were sailed from Gulf ports to markets around the Atlantic. In return, merchant ships arrived with cotton, linen, taffeta, silk, wool, rum, candles, soap, hats, wine, kettles, knives, needles, flour, sugar, fruits, spices, muskets, gunpowder, ammunition, and other products from Europe, Africa, Asia, and the Americas. They also brought human beings to sell in the slave markets of the major Gulf ports.

Despite their involvement in global networks of trade, the people in and around the Gulf Coast still lived in the early modern world of small communities where kin relationships dominated and information traveled only as quickly as a horse, canoe, or sailing ship dependent on winds and currents could carry it. Parents understood that if they had several children, it was unlikely that all would survive the treacherous years of early childhood.

The colonial posts of the Gulf Coast had changed hands several times, most recently in the Seven Years' War. Because that war began in the Ohio Valley, where British settlers pushing west from Virginia and Pennsylvania clashed with the Indians and their French allies, British colonists called it the French and Indian War. Soon, however, the war spread to Europe and beyond. Spain joined the war late, and its help was not enough to prevent France from surrendering.

The Treaty of Paris of 1763 dramatically reshuffled colonial possessions. France surrendered all of Canada to Britain as well as the half of Louisiana that lay east of the Mississippi River, including Mobile and the smaller inland posts of Baton Rouge and Natchez. The British renamed this region "West Florida." Spain was eager to regain Havana, seized by Britain during the war, so Spain traded Britain the Florida peninsula, which the British called "East Florida." To compensate Spain for being dragged into the losing venture, France gave Spain the western half of Louisiana, including New Orleans. Thus France lost all of its colonies on the North American continent.[1]

Because of European protectionism, including Britain's Navigation Acts, direct trade between now-British West Florida and now-Spanish Louisiana—which had all been French Louisiana before the treaty—was suddenly illegal. Commerce thrived anyway. British traders had better and cheaper goods, so they rowed canoes (or "floating warehouses," as Louisianans called them) into the middle of the Mississippi River or its lakes to sell British-manufactured goods to consumers in the New Orleans market. Louisianans paid with rum and wheat as well as gold and silver dug from the mines of Spanish Mexico, precious metals that the British empire sorely lacked.[2]

The vast interior of both sides of the Mississippi Valley was Indian country. A few small European settlements and trading posts—Natchez, Baton Rouge, Manchac, Natchitoches, Arkansas Post, St. Louis—hugged the Mississippi River and its large tributaries, but, despite claims on paper, Europeans controlled fewer than one hundred square miles of territory in Louisiana and West Florida. In contrast, Indians of various nations held some three hundred thousand square miles. Until the 1760s, the Indian population of the region outnumbered the colonial population (counting Europeans, slaves, and free people of color) by a factor of ten, even after Indians had suffered for almost three centuries from diseases the newcomers had brought. As the British in West Florida quickly learned, they were "surrounded with ten thousand Indians capable of bearing arms." When the Revolution began, that was still approximately the ratio west of the Mississippi River, but the massive immigration of British settlers and their slaves since 1763 was bringing the colonial population of British West Florida closer to the size of its neighboring Native population.[3]

Indians themselves were not one people, any more than the colonial newcomers were. They spoke dozens of languages, had diverse economic and political systems, and were every bit as motivated by commerce as the Europeans. Three large groups dominated the Gulf South: the Creeks, Choctaws, and Chickasaws. The Creeks, a fairly new confederacy of smaller groups, lived in the river valleys of the region that would become the states of Alabama and Georgia. The Choctaws controlled the territory to the west, north of Mobile. And farther north, the Chickasaws lived in what is now Mississippi and Tennessee. Like colonists, southeastern Indians built their towns on waterways and trading paths. Women farmed corn, beans, squash, and tobacco, and men tended cattle and pigs for the town's consumption and for sale. They built private homes, public gathering spaces, and workshops for processing deerskins or pottery with vertical wood or cane frames interlaced with horizontal small branches, covered with mud, and thatched with palmettos.

Even as commerce abounded in the Gulf Coast, only a careless observer would fail to see evidence of recent wars and fear of war. Each colonial town was nestled near a fort, into which the townspeople could flee when trouble approached. To the north, Native towns were surrounded by wooden stockades. From the south, trading ships protected themselves with cannons and were outfitted with sails designed for quick maneuvering into or out of a conflict on the seas. Watchtowers with cannons protected forts and stockades. Travelers carried muskets, bows, hatchets, and knives and knew how to use them.

In the early 1770s, trade was more common than warfare on the Gulf Coast, but the balance was about to shift again. Soon the new house that the governor of West Florida was building would become a barracks for British troops. Warriors on the march and refugees in flight would soon tread ancient trading paths. In a few years, men would lie dying outside and inside Mobile and Pensacola. More than battle wounds, disease spread by traveling armies and famine caused by interrupted commerce would claim the lives of Natives and colonists on all sides.

The aftermath of the Seven Years' War shifted relationships between European empires and people living in North America. Indians and colonists alike learned that protecting autonomy and economic opportunity might necessitate violence to rein in the new (or newly confident) empire. Indians throughout the eastern half of North America would insist that Britain's victory did not give it control over Indian lands nor make Indians into British subjects, and some of them around the Great Lakes and the Ohio Valley would prove their point in Pontiac's War in 1763–1764. French residents of New Orleans would gain concessions by rising up against Spanish rule in 1768. And, of course, taxpayers in Boston and other parts of the British colonies would protest Parliament's attempts to pay for the war with new taxes.

The following chapters introduce people who lived through these changes and would react to the next war as people usually do, by applying the lessons learned in the last one. Perhaps the greatest lessons were that empires come and go, and the burdensome strictures of one empire might be cast off for the promises of a more beneficial order.

CHAPTER TWO

Payamataha

DECISIVE BATTLES WOULD soon take place near the Gulf
Coast, but the region's fate would depend mostly on decisions made
elsewhere: by Spanish military commanders in Havana, British ministers in Whitehall, and town assemblies across North America's interior in which Native men and women debated how their peoples
should respond to the conflict. Mapmakers in Europe might write
"Louisiana" or "West Florida" across wide swaths of the continent,
but the vast majority of the land was Indian country. The outcomes of
the war between the British and Spanish as well as of the conflict
within the British empire would depend on the decisions of Native
populations to fight or stay home. Among the Chickasaws, the man
with the leading role in the decision would be Payamataha.

British expectations of Chickasaw military assistance had a long
history. Starting decades before Payamataha's birth in the mid-1720s,
Chickasaws and Britons had fought together against the French and
various mutual Indian enemies. As the Revolutionary War began, the
British again expected Payamataha's people to help defeat the rebels
and any others who joined their side. In the Revolutionary War, how-

ever, Chickasaws would decide differently. The history of British allegiance caused officials and even recent historians to classify Indians who fought against the American rebels as "loyalists" to the British empire, but in fact their decisions to fight stemmed from their own goals, including political independence. While much of North America and Western Europe prepared for war, Payamataha and most of his people broke from precedent and chose peace.[1]

War and the Chickasaws

Payamataha began his career as a warrior, which was the standard path to leadership among the Chickasaws. Like most of their neighbors, they descended from a powerful Mississippian chiefdom, but while others had splintered into small towns and bands by the late 1600s, the Chickasaws remained a cohesive group of towns. They still centralized leadership in a principal civil chief, who was chosen by a combination of heredity and proven merit. He shared power with a chief in charge of war and diplomacy as well as with town and clan civil and war chiefs, and he depended on persuasion and goods distribution for his influence. When major issues arose, large assemblies of Chickasaw women and men met to discuss and debate the course of action to be taken.[2]

Like most southeastern Indians—indeed, like most of the world—the Chickasaws in the past had captured enemies in battle and turned some of them into slaves. Throughout the ancient and medieval world, slaves were low-ranked members of society forced to labor for others, often far from home and at risk of being sold or killed if found wanting by a master. But in most cases, a slave's children would not necessarily be enslaved, and slavery was not confined to a particular race. In some societies, there were opportunities for skilled slaves to improve their status or even gain their freedom. Antebellum southern plantation slavery is an anomaly in the long history of slavery in the Americas, Europe, Africa, and Asia.[3]

Beginning in the 1600s, with the new English market at Charleston

(Charles Town, as it was known then), Chickasaws accelerated their slave-raiding. They found that human captives were easy to transport, did not require the processing that deerskins did, and fetched a higher price in England's Caribbean colonies, which were eager for enslaved labor. Chickasaws became the primary raiders over hundreds of square miles east and west of the Mississippi. Chickasaw warriors attacked traveling parties or undefended towns of Choctaws, Quapaws, Tunicas, Taensas, Colapissas, Caddos, various Illinois peoples, and occasionally Creeks and Catawbas to sell in Charleston. The Chickasaw population was about five thousand in the early 1700s, in contrast to probably twenty thousand Choctaws and some ten thousand people in the Creek Confederacy. But their strikes and retreats were rapid and well coordinated, and they maintained good relationships with key Indian towns that traded with the British. By the early 1700s, their reputation for ferocity was widespread. Neighbors called them "the most military people of any about the great river," meaning the Mississippi.[4]

Although the British market for Indian slaves declined when Carolina colonists began to import more African slaves after the 1715 Yamasee War, Chickasaw warfare against the Choctaws, Quapaws, Catawbas, and some Illinois peoples continued and drew the Chickasaws into enmity against the French. Persistent reasons for warfare included various unresolved grievances, a continuing (albeit depressed) market in Indian slaves, and the Chickasaws' use of captives to supplement their declining population. Starting in 1729, the Chickasaws engaged in a series of wars against the French, which bolstered the Chickasaw alliance with the English, who were already competing with the French for imperial territory and trade.[5]

Warfare changed how and where the Chickasaws lived. At the start of the 1700s, the approximately five thousand Chickasaws lived in small towns dispersed across the upland prairie. As war decreased security, they moved to clusters of fortified towns on a ridge overlooking the region. War and disease decreased the population. The dangers of war persuaded many Chickasaw families to leave Chickasaw country and live as refugees. As a result, there were only about 1,600

Chickasaws living in Chickasaw country by the time of the Seven Years' War, all in a single fortified town known as Big Town.[6]

Payamataha the Warrior

The man who came to be known as Payamataha, meaning *war leader* or *war prophet,* grew up in the fortified Chickasaw towns during this era of escalating warfare. Chickasaw boys had nicknames and would acquire adult names only once they showed their character and achievements. As a child, the boy who would become Payamataha saw his mother and aunts keep a watchful eye for enemies riding across the plain as they farmed or collected drinking water from wells near their town. Like most Chickasaw children, he would have enjoyed bear bacon, the annual crop of strawberries, and another Chickasaw favorite, a milkshake of hickory nut milk and sweet potatoes. He learned to play stickball (a game similar to lacrosse) on his town's ballfield. As he grew older, he learned to hunt. Like other boys, he made his own deer decoy by carefully carving out the interior of a deer's head, stretching the dried skin back over the frontal bone, and scooping out the interior cartilage of the horns so that the decoy would be light enough to carry easily and to maneuver like a puppet on his left hand, in imitation of a live deer's motions. Once close enough to the unsuspecting deer, a hidden partner would aim and shoot.[7]

The young Payamataha showed no sign of his future as a peacemaker. He earned his war titles, filled his amulet bag with scalps of his fallen enemies, and received white arrows to wear in his black hair, signifying his battle honors. By the time he retired as a warrior, he reportedly had killed over forty men on his own. On one spring night in the late 1740s during the wars against the French, he led Chickasaw and Creek warriors to cypress bark canoes parked along the east bank of the Mississippi. Under cover of darkness, they paddled across the great river. At the first light of day, the warriors left their canoes and quietly sneaked to the edge of the small French Arkansas Post. To the sound of Chickasaw women singing their usual songs of encourage-

George Catlin, *Ball-play of the Choctaw*, 1840s. (Smithsonian American Art Museum)

ment, they attacked the post with arrows. In the melee, grapeshot from a French gun wounded Payamataha. According to James Adair, an Irish trader living with the Chickasaws who heard the story on their return, Payamataha's men thought he would die, and in their rage they killed their French prisoners and "overspread the French settlements, to a great distance, like a dreadful whirlwind, destroying every thing before them." Payamataha survived to tell the story back in Chickasaw country.[8]

Hatred of the French kept the war chief Payamataha firmly allied with the British. Once, on the road to sell captives in Charleston, he and his men fell in with a traveling party of Creeks, one of whom told the Chickasaws that a good number of Creeks had decided that the British were the region's biggest problem. The Creek man pointed out that British colonists encroached on Indian lands far more than French people. Recalling the bloody Chickasaw wars against the French, Payamataha exploded in anger. Had it not been for English help, Payamataha said, "the artful and covetous French, by the weight of presents and the skill of their forked tongues, would before now, have set you to war against each other, in the very same manner they have done by the Choctaw." It was true that the Choctaws were embroiled in a civil war, caused in part by arguments over whether to fight against or ally with the French. Payamataha promised that the Chickasaws "are born and bred in a state of war with" the French.[9]

Chickasaw war against the French continued through the Seven Years' War. When Upper Creeks advised the Chickasaws that all Indians "should be united and stand together" against the British, Payamataha responded that the Chickasaw-British friendship "was steady and invariable." The Chickasaws "would not be idle lookers on; the cause of the English should be theirs, in opposition to French, Cherokee, and all other enemies," which could certainly include Creeks.[10]

In the 1740s and 1750s, Payamataha met with British officials at Charleston and sent official diplomatic messages to London. Although his name is not recorded, the Chickasaw leader who traveled to England and met with King George II may have been Payamataha. In a letter to the king in 1756, Payamataha and other Chickasaw headmen and warriors proclaimed that "we look upon your enemies as ours and your friends as our friends. The day shall never come while sun shines and water runs that we will join any other nation but the English."[11]

Just a few years later, though, something happened that was almost as astonishing as the sun ceasing to shine or the water drying up: France abandoned its claims to the North American continent.

Payamataha the Diplomat

In the summer of 1763, rumors arrived in Chickasaw country that the French had surrendered, ending the Seven Years' War. The rumors were true, and the British would take over the French posts east of the Mississippi, while the Spanish would occupy those west of the Mississippi plus New Orleans at the river's mouth. Payamataha would need to decide how to deal with the new Spanish officials who would come to the Mississippi Valley.

By this time, Payamataha had risen to the position of Chickasaw headman in charge of war and diplomacy, a role Chickasaws described as "head leading warrior of the nation, to treat with all nations." Slave-raiding and warfare had become so dominant among the Chickasaws by the early eighteenth century that even the civil or "peace chiefs" at times got caught up in the violence, forgot their role, and "turned warrior" too. Yet Payamataha, despite being in the office called "head leading warrior," decided to end Chickasaw warring. He figured that if the Chickasaws wanted to avoid further devastating war and population loss, the time to change had come. With the French empire gone from North America, perhaps the Chickasaws could turn warpaths back into trading paths and make peace with all Europeans and Indians.[12]

As the Chickasaws' chief diplomat to other nations, Payamataha strove to maintain Chickasaw independence through a pragmatic course of peaceful coexistence. The Chickasaw population had declined by more than half from 1700 to the end of the Seven Years' War. More war, even if victorious, would further erode the Chickasaw population. Late in 1758, Payamataha began meeting with Choctaw leaders from the towns closest to the Chickasaws to discuss ending their decades of war. Payamataha made the peace offer attractive by directing British goods to his new Choctaw friends. In May 1759, the Chickasaws accepted an official Choctaw peace delegation. The Choctaw-Chickasaw peace became one of the most successful diplomatic initiatives in history, turning decades of war into a permanent peace.[13]

It is impossible to know what went on in most Chickasaw councils, much less in Payamataha's head; what we do know is that in the 1760s and 1770s he led the Chickasaws in systematically making peace with a startling array of old enemies: Choctaws to the south, Cherokees and Catawbas to the east, Creeks to the southeast, and Quapaws to the west across the Mississippi River. As Choctaw leader Chulustamastabe later explained to the British, "There were formerly great discord & enmity subsisting between the Chickasaw & Choctaw Nations, which I hope are now all removed & that friendship & peace will be established."[14] Chickasaw women made diplomacy possible by hosting the negotiations and preparing the feasts. Had most women opposed his peacemaking efforts, he would have failed.

Payamataha was a spiritual as well as a diplomatic leader, roles that were inseparable to the Chickasaws. Choctaws referred to Payamataha as "a witch" or "an oracle." Payamataha's power came in part from the spiritual world, and his exhortation to make peace was based on a spiritual calling to avoid war.[15]

In congresses of Indian nations in Augusta, Georgia, in 1763 and Mobile, West Florida, in 1765, Payamataha contrasted his position with that of other Indians. He told British Superintendent of Indian Affairs John Stuart that he wanted "not to imitate other Indian nations" that try to be totally independent. Speaking through an interpreter, Payamataha declared that the Chickasaws knew they "cannot do without the white people" and that "it is the same case with all the red people."[16] In accentuating Chickasaw dependence, Payamataha was purposefully contrasting Chickasaw foreign policy with that of Indian Nativists.

Beginning in the 1730s among Indian refugees in the Ohio Valley, Nativist prophets preached that all Indians had a history and culture in common with one another and different from Africans and Europeans. According to Nativists, Indians should unify in military opposition to Europeans, particularly the British. Immediately following the Seven Years' War, the Delaware prophet Neolin and the Ottawa war leader Pontiac led people to war under the ideology of Nativism. Today it is hard to see the idea that Indians had a common past and a common future as radical, but rigidly race-based antebellum slavery, forced Indian removals of the 1830s, and scientific racism had not yet hardened beliefs about racial difference. Even today most Indians see their particular tribal citizenship or community as at least as important as their American Indian identity, and a pan-tribal identity was hard for most Indians even to imagine two centuries ago.[17]

Payamataha agreed with Nativists that Indians should not fight one another, but he disagreed that the solution was to fight Europeans. Payamataha's movement focused on getting along with everyone no matter their history. This position was less risky than in the Ohio Valley because British settlers had not gotten as far west as Chickasaw lands. Payamataha still followed his ancestors' assumptions that the world was divided not into a few "races" but into thousands of different peoples—the big divide was between Chickasaws and all non-Chickasaws, not between Indians and non-Indians.[18]

Payamataha also portrayed himself as leading other Indians— particularly former French allies—to peace with the British. British officials recognized that Payamataha's peacemaking complemented their mission to promote a stable empire, and British rhetoric emphasized security and opportunity for Indians if they chose not to stand alone. Knowing that land was the key issue for Indians bordering British colonies, British officials repeatedly assured Indians that "no land can be settled without your consent."[19]

Despite the British assumption of their own centrality, confirming Chickasaw peace with the Choctaws, Cherokees, and Creeks was more important to Payamataha at Augusta in 1763 and Mobile in 1765. Lingering fears of violence are evident in the fact that Chickasaws worried about sending a delegation across Creek country to get to Augusta. But at Augusta, Payamataha and Upper Creek headman Emistisiguo worked on Chickasaw-Creek relations. Emistisiguo even asked the Chickasaws for their approval before the Creeks would agree to sell the Georgians a bit of land between the Savannah and Ogeechee rivers, a precondition that foreshadowed both continuing Chickasaw-Creek peace and cooperation across Indian nations regarding land sales and preservation.

At the 1765 Mobile congress, Payamataha confirmed his personal connection to the British, attesting that "it is well known I never deserted the British interest and I never will." White was the symbolic color of peace (signifying the absence of blood) among southeastern Indians, and Payamataha played with the multiple meanings of *white* in his assurance that "though I am a Red Man my heart is white from my connections with and the benefits I have received from the white people, I almost look upon myself as one of them." Then he turned his attention to the Choctaw delegation, whom he addressed as "my younger brothers." "Let what is past be buried in oblivion," he offered, "and let us only now think of what is to come."[20] Choctaw Chief Chulustamastabe agreed that "Payamataha is much [my] superior, but [I am] equally well inclined to hear good talks."[21]

Making Peace

Payamataha encouraged the British belief that the Chickasaws were their staunchest ally and that he was working solely for British interests, but in reality Payamataha's model for Chickasaw independence and stability in the region was to expand connections to as many European and Indian neighbors as possible. Chickasaws had no desire to create a new European enemy out of the Spanish just after celebrating the departure of the French. Instead, Payamataha defied British expectations and established Chickasaw alliance and trade with Spanish Louisiana.[22]

In the past, Chickasaw enmity against the French and against Indians allied with the French had been mutually reinforcing. Now, Payamataha's peace efforts with Europeans assisted his peacemaking with Indians and vice versa. In 1765, the Chickasaws asked British officials in the Illinois country to provide the goods that would allow them to make peace with people who had been allied with the French. The following May, the Chickasaws made peace with the Kaskaskias, the Michigameas, and other Illinois peoples, although that peace proved more fragile than the others that Payamataha was forging.[23]

One of the Chickasaws' most important new alliances was with the Quapaws, who could help the Chickasaws make peace with Spain and with Illinois Indians. Living west of the Mississippi near its confluence with the Arkansas River, the Quapaws had quickly established good relations with the Spanish after 1763. In the spring of 1770, Quapaw chiefs introduced Payamataha to the Spanish commandant at Arkansas Post. Payamataha accepted a Spanish flag and medal, signifying, misleadingly, to the Spanish that he had abandoned his British alliance in favor of a Spanish one. The Spanish commandant in turn provided food, brandy, and gifts, which helped to seal the nascent Chickasaw-Quapaw peace.[24]

In return, Payamataha assisted the Quapaws in diplomacy with the British and the Choctaws. In March 1771, a delegation of Quapaws went to Natchez and Pensacola declaring their new friendship with Payamataha and the Chickasaws and their desire for alliance with the British and the Choctaws. British officials specifically asked Payamataha not to bring the Quapaws to any more congresses for fear of antagonizing the Spanish. Nonetheless, Payamataha escorted several Quapaw representatives to a 1772 Mobile congress and presented the Quapaws' eagle feather calumet for the British to smoke, declaring, "this Calumet was given me by the Quapaw Chief . . . in token of friendship." At that congress, he also brokered peace between the Quapaws and the Choctaws and even threatened the Choctaws that the Chickasaws would fight them if they did not make peace with the Quapaws. The Choctaws agreed to peace, and the three-way agreement helped to strengthen all of its parts.[25]

Because the British ended Pontiac's War by compromising with Nativists, Chickasaw and Nativist strategies could align. In 1772, Nativist messages circulated through the south, urging that if "the English, France and Spain are at war[,] all the red people is to be at peace." Shawnees in the Ohio Valley sent a wampum belt—an elaborate message written in beads—that was white on each end with a small black piece in the middle. They explained that "the black in the middle signified the Chickasaw nation, the white on each side the Choctaws and Creeks, and that they wanted them to be all of one mind and of one color." Certainly Payamataha agreed.[26]

Although Payamataha's successful diplomacy with Europeans and other Indians helped him to gain Chickasaw support for peace, he did not rule his people. The Chickasaws' principal chief was a younger man named Tascapatapo, usually called Mingo Houma (Red King). At the 1772 congress, Mingo Houma tried to explain to the British that he was "the King of my Nation and Payamataha is my warrior."[27] The Chickasaws referred to Mingo Houma as their "king" and explained that the word *mingo* meant *king*. Nonetheless, the fact that Payamataha represented the Chickasaws in foreign relations confused Europeans. They could have paralleled Mingo Houma with King

George and Payamataha with the Earl of Hillsborough's role as secretary of state for the colonies, but Europeans tended to assume that whichever Chickasaw met with them must be the most important.[28]

Like most southeastern Indians, Chickasaw leaders established and maintained their positions through obligations of interdependence, including a leader's redistribution of goods. Many of Payamataha's speeches to the British concerned goods. At the 1772 congress in Mobile, Payamataha reminded British Superintendent John Stuart that at the last congress they had agreed on fixed prices and tariffs and that Stuart "gave me a yard to carry with me as a standard by which measure of all goods sold in our nation was to be regulated."[29] Payamataha and Stuart had a common interest in controlling trade to enhance their own influence. The British victory over the French had sparked an influx of unlicensed British traders, who undermined both Stuart and Payamataha by trading directly with other Chickasaws, including Principal Chief Mingo Houma. At Payamataha's urging, Stuart repeatedly reminded both Britons and Chickasaws that all trade was supposed to go through Payamataha.[30]

Toward the Revolution?

By the early 1770s, Payamataha had succeeded in making the Chickasaws more interdependent with their neighbors, especially other Indians. Peace was paying off. Chickasaws had moved out from Big Town and had spread back over Chickasaw lands in smaller towns and farms. They no longer lived within fortifications, in part because they felt more secure but also as a sign to former enemies that they had changed their ways. With the safety of peace and the return of Chickasaws who had fled war, the Chickasaw population grew from its low point of around sixteen hundred to more than two thousand and rising by the mid-1770s. They could allow their horses to enjoy the grasses growing outside their towns without fear that they would be carried off in an enemy raid. The hunters ranged far, a hundred miles east to the Tennessee River, north to the Ohio River, and south to the hunting grounds they now shared with the Choctaws. Payamataha took advantage of his prominence among the Chickasaws and the British to profit from trade and even to establish his own cattle ranch near the British trading post in Chickasaw country.[31]

After these diplomatic successes, troubles within the British empire were far from Chickasaw minds. The future promised a continuation of Payamataha's diplomacy with the Chickasaws' growing collection of European and Native allies. Instead, the rebellion within the British empire would eventually expose Payamataha's contradictory promises and imperil the networks that he had built.

CHAPTER THREE

Alexander McGillivray

BORN IN DECEMBER 1750 in the town of Little Tallassee in
Upper Creek country (north of present-day Montgomery, Alabama),
Alexander McGillivray would occupy an important position in the
revolutionary conflict and its aftermath. The Creeks were a matrilineal society, and the boy's mother, Sehoy, and maternal uncle, the influential headman Red Shoes, belonged to the powerful and prestigious
Wind clan. Sehoy was probably the daughter of a French soldier,
which by European reckoning would mean the boy was only one-
quarter Indian. However, the Creeks interpreted inheritance entirely
through the mother's line, so to them he was fully Creek and a full
member of the Wind clan. He described himself in his adult years as
"a Native of this Nation and of rank in it."[1]

We do not know what he called himself when with his mother's
family, but when he signed his name, he wrote "Alex. McGillivray."
His father, Lachlan McGillivray, was born in the Scottish Highlands
to the McGillivray clan. It is because of Lachlan that historical documents tell us much more about Alexander McGillivray's lineage than
they do about Payamataha's. Like Sehoy's Creeks, Lachlan's Highland

Scots had long confronted European imperial ambitions. In the 1540s, at the same time that Sehoy's ancestors met Spanish conquistador Hernando de Soto, Lachlan's ancestors began fighting the expansionist English. In 1745 and 1746, English forces drove back those of Charles Stuart, "Bonnie Prince Charlie," including the McGillivray clan, and inflicted the final defeat of the Scottish uprising at the Battle of Culloden. In the late decades of the conflict, thousands of Highlanders left the chaos of their homeland for opportunities in the very empire that they had fought. In 1735, Lachlan came as an indentured servant from Scotland to Georgia, where his fellow Highlanders were settling James Oglethorpe's colony and entering the deerskin trade business. Lachlan gave his son the name Alexander to honor the chief of the McGillivray clan who fell at the Battle of Culloden. As the Revolutionary War approached, being Creek and Scottish would give Alexander McGillivray strong connections among both the Creeks and the British.[2]

The Rise of the Creeks

While the Wind clan was ancient, the Creeks were a fairly new confederation of clans and towns. At least some Creeks descended from Mississippian chiefdoms. After the chiefdoms' decline in the sixteenth century, the people who would become known as Creek Indians settled in two large clusters totaling about sixty towns. Alexander McGillivray's ancestors lived in towns that would become part of the Upper Creeks along the Alabama, Coosa, and Tallapoosa rivers in present-day Alabama. On the Alabama River south of the Upper Creeks lived the Alabamas, Creek allies. To the east, the Lower Creeks were near the Chattahoochee River, the present-day border between Alabama and Georgia. Most Creek towns spoke related languages, had similar cultural practices and beliefs, farmed on a smaller scale than in the past, and spread governance more broadly than their Mississippian ancestors.[3]

Gradually these towns confederated. Unlike the Chickasaw nation, the Creek Confederacy did not influence its towns' domestic gover-

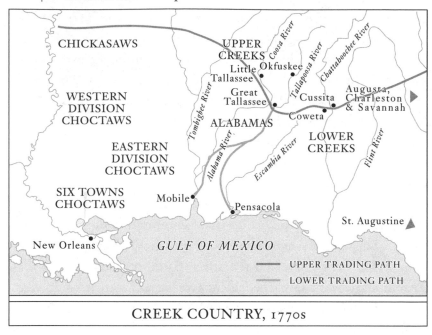

CHICKASAWS

UPPER
CREEKS
Little Okfuskee
Tallassee
Great
Tallassee   Cussita
Coweta
Augusta,
Charleston
& Savannah

Coosa River
Tallapoosa River
Chattahoochee River

WESTERN
DIVISION
CHOCTAWS

ALABAMAS

LOWER
CREEKS

Tombighee River
Alabama River
Escambia River
Flint River

EASTERN
DIVISION
CHOCTAWS

SIX TOWNS
CHOCTAWS   Mobile

Pensacola

St. Augustine

New Orleans

GULF OF MEXICO

—— UPPER TRADING PATH
—— LOWER TRADING PATH

CREEK COUNTRY, 1770s

nance. The confederated towns consulted on foreign policy and defense, but even this coordination was limited. Each town or clan made
its own decisions about going to war. The founding of Spanish St.
Augustine in 1565 and English Charleston in 1670 brought new opportunities for trade but also gradually increased the Creeks' need for
a common defense. Indian raiders arrived from the east armed with
Spanish and English weapons beginning in the mid-1600s, and soon
Chickasaws and others began raiding neighboring towns. The Creek
population declined because of these raids and also from diseases that
spread from town to town.[4]

The Creeks' less centralized governance allowed for more autonomy of individual groups within the confederacy and allowed them to
grow by incorporating new towns that might have little in common
with other Creeks. When the Indian slave trade declined after the
1715 Yamasee War, Creek numbers began to rise as they suffered
fewer raids and also invited refugees from war and disease to settle on
Creek lands and join the confederacy as incorporated towns. They
also adopted individual escaped slaves, both Indian and African.
Brims, headman of the Lower Creek town of Coweta, worked to build
a stronger Creek Confederacy through neutrality toward all Euro-

pean colonies, somewhat the way Payamataha did several decades later and in contrast to Nativists who rejected European alliances. Beginning in 1718, Creek diplomats journeyed to French and Spanish posts and even to Mexico City.[5]

Different Creek towns took responsibility for diplomacy in their regions, creating physical and diplomatic links with all Europeans as well as with other Indians in the region. For southeastern Indians, "paths" were both literal and metaphorical links between peoples, both the actual ways to get places and the language of good relations. Within the confederacy, Upper Creeks and Alabamas established new paths of trade and diplomacy to Spanish Pensacola and French Mobile and New Orleans. Lower Creek towns took responsibility for the paths to Spanish St. Augustine and the British colony of Georgia once it was founded in the 1730s. In 1717, the Upper Creeks allowed the French to build Fort Toulouse in the heart of their territory to gain convenient access to trade. Most versions of Alexander McGillivray's ancestry claim that his grandparents, a French soldier and a Creek woman, met at Fort Toulouse.[6]

An epidemic among European cattle created an urgent market for leather, and by midcentury Creeks were processing and selling hundreds of thousands of deerskins per year. French and Scottish traders and their servants and slaves transported hides to New Orleans, Charleston, and the new post of Augusta for export to other colonies and Europe. One of the Scottish traders operating out of Augusta was Lachlan McGillivray.[7]

Alexander McGillivray's mother, Sehoy, lived in her mother's house in the Upper Creek town of Little Tallassee where the Coosa River met the Upper Trading Path. Growing up in a prominent family and clan, Sehoy's brothers aimed to be warriors and eventually part of the town's or confederacy's leadership. In this matrilineal society, having a French father did not cause Sehoy and her siblings to be treated differently from other Creek children. Sehoy would grow to become a prominent Creek woman with authority over agriculture, land use, deerskin processing, and her family's home. Like all Creek adults, she would have a say in her town's important decisions. When the British trader Lachlan McGillivray showed up, Sehoy may have been attracted to his worldliness or his interest in Creek ways of life. She may have married him to please her family so that they would have access to British trade goods to support their authority within their town, as other Indian women did before and after her. Whatever Sehoy's motivations, the connection was good for their interests and for Lachlan's.[8]

Sehoy and Lachlan's Son

Like most Creek boys, the son of Sehoy and Lachlan was born into the fur trade business, but having Lachlan as a father meant that he was also born into a world of European merchants. Growing up in the rolling hills of the Coosa River Valley, young Alexander joined men on the hunt and in helping the women in the fields at planting and harvest time. Creek men were some of the best hunters in the southeast, and Lachlan exported hides from their hunt and imported European goods through his trading post on the Coosa River. Alexander's maternal uncles may have groomed the young man to be a Creek leader, modeling for him the ways of Creek speechmaking and governance as well as hunting and warfare, while his father taught him the intricacies of international trade.[9]

During the Seven Years' War, when Alexander was six, his father took him and his ten-year-old sister, Sophia, to Georgia from Creek Country. The children were accustomed to their father as a sporadic presence, coming for months at a time for business or diplomacy. Now they settled into his plantation and trading post just north of Augusta, an important crossroads in the global fur trade, near the paths that led to the Cherokees in one direction and the Creeks in another. At Lachlan's post, his son talked with visiting Creek and Scottish relatives. McGillivray learned the life of a white master as his father acquired more land and slaves, who worked the fields, processed cornmeal in the mill, and served as boatmen and skin dressers in the fur trade. Lachlan put two of his plantations in Alexander's name, so now the young man was a landed planter himself.[10]

Alexander McGillivray also spent time in Charleston, living with

Lachlan's brother and his family to improve his writing and math and
to learn to read Latin and Greek. By 1765, he moved with his father
to a new plantation, Vale Royal, just outside Savannah on the road to
Augusta. There, dozens of slaves grew rice and raised horses. At Vale
Royal and in Savannah, as an apprentice to the merchants Inglis and
Hall, Alexander McGillivray learned the shipping side of the fur
trade business.[11]

Alexander McGillivray could write and keep accounts like a colonial British businessman, yet he was born to be a Creek leader. His
knowledge of multiple languages and his connections across the
southeast would make him valuable to both Creeks and Europeans.
His birth as a prominent Creek man coupled with his colonial education and business training placed him in an unusual position—
powerful in his own right and a valuable leader and contact for Creeks
and Europeans.

Dealing with the British

At the same time that McGillivray came of age in two societies, the
Creeks dealt increasingly with settler incursion in their territories. In
the 1750s and 1760s, many a Creek band hunting to the east came
across a settlement that had not been there the last time through, and
Creek warriors repeatedly drove settlers back into Augusta or Savan-
nah. As among the Chickasaws, Creek opinions varied about the
Seven Years' War and the Cherokee-British War of 1760–1761. Many
Creeks rallied to fight alongside the French and Cherokees against
British incursions, especially in Georgia. But most Creeks interpreted
the lessons of the previous decades as an argument against fighting
Europeans. The pre-1715 era of war had done great damage, while
Brims's policy of neutrality had brought prosperity. In 1759, Creeks
recalled Brims as advising "hold fast all three, English, French, &
Spanish" and "take care and never quarrel with any of them." Some
Creeks also extended the philosophy to include Indian nations and,
like Payamataha, began to make peace with Choctaws and Cherokees
in the 1750s.[12]

When news reached them that the French had lost the Seven Years' War, Creeks realized Brims's strategy would be useless if the British had the power to dominate everyone else. The French had surrendered without consulting their Indian allies and were leaving North America entirely, and the Spanish were giving Pensacola and St. Augustine to the British. Rumors circulated that British troops intended "to kill your men, enslave your women and children, and settle your lands without leave." The French evacuation of Fort Toulouse left the Creeks without an official European trading post in Creek country and therefore without a dependable local source of trade and diplomatic gifts.[13]

Alexander McGillivray was still a teenager when Creek representatives assembled in Augusta in 1763 with Chickasaws (including Payamataha), Cherokees, Catawbas, Georgians, Carolinians, and Virginians to agree on boundary lines between British settlements and Indian lands. Creeks had never needed clear borders to ensure their sovereignty against the sparse Spanish and French settlements, but they knew that the British had thousands more people who wanted Indian land for their farms. At Augusta as well as in meetings at Mobile and Pensacola, Creeks explicitly and repeatedly instructed the British that West Florida settlements could extend no farther than three hundred yards from the coast, a boundary that barely included the forts of Mobile and Pensacola. Creeks enforced their border by killing uninvited people and cattle found inland.[14]

Creeks were savvy about power dynamics in the region. The few British troops stationed in the region could not counter the Creeks' thousands of warriors. British negotiator Major Robert Farmar spoke paternalistically of the king's "love and affection" while standing in front of Mobile's fort, which was in such a "ruinous condition" that its very gate was off its hinges.[15] Any Creeks looking in Farmar's direction could have noticed the discrepancy between rhetoric and reality. The British were, as the governor of West Florida admitted, "incapable of protecting the country against such powerful tribes, being hardly sufficient to defend the pitiful fortresses if attacked."[16] For their part, the Creeks "firmly believe they are now more powerful than any nation that might be tempted to invade them."[17]

Surprisingly, Creek relations with the British improved after the Seven Years' War. In an effort to control violence on the frontier, the British crown limited settlement west of the Appalachians. From his father, Alexander McGillivray could hear news of the "Proclamation Line" that the crown created in October 1763, beyond which settlement was restricted. When settlers violated the ban, the British government and the Creeks found themselves on the same side in seeking to contain settlement. At a congress in Pensacola in May 1765, Upper Creeks gave the British a more generous slice of land than they had two years earlier, from the coast to fifteen miles inland, but no more. In return, they received presents and guaranteed prices for trade. The Creek delegation explicitly retained the right to hunt in those lands. Their continued power is evident in a pledge the governor had to make that "if any white people settles beyond" the fifteen-mile zone, British officials "shall never enquire how they came to be killed."[18]

The British would not be the Creeks' only ally. Creeks had long traded at Spanish Pensacola and St. Augustine and even sent delegations to Havana and Mexico City. Making peace with other Indians would be harder. Some Creeks apparently blamed the Chickasaws and even the Cherokees and Choctaws for the British victory in the Seven Years' War. Payamataha's efforts at Augusta in 1763 paved the way for a Chickasaw-Creek peace, but a full-blown war broke out between the Creeks and Choctaws. Part of the reason was the desire of each for a monopoly over trade at Pensacola and Mobile.[19]

Lachlan's Loyalties

When Lachlan McGillivray's Georgia neighbors began to protest British taxes and land policies, his allegiances were complicated. In 1765, British Parliament passed the Stamp Act, which required that colonists pay a tax (signified by a stamp) on all printed documents, including newspapers, pamphlets, wills, playing cards, and royal land grants. The Seven Years' War and Pontiac's War had been costly, and Parliament needed revenue to retire the war debt. Parliament had levied new taxes in England on stamps, windows, malt, and cider, piling new taxes on one of the most heavily taxed populations in the world. In contrast, Britons living in the colonies paid only import and export duties but no direct taxes to the empire. Surely they could share some of the pain—or so went the logic of Prime Minster George Grenville. But the Stamp Act of 1765 sparked dissent among colonists already unhappy about the Proclamation of 1763's restrictions on settlement west of the Appalachians. The ten thousand soldiers patrolling the line seemed an affront to all the reasons British colonists had fought the French in the Seven Years' War. In 1766, British subjects throughout the empire were relieved when Parliament repealed the Stamp Act and then were disgruntled again a year later when Parliament enacted duties on tea and several other imported goods. While many people found these import duties more palatable than the Stamp Act's direct tax, boycotts of the goods in question began in Boston, Philadelphia, New York, and more than a dozen other cities.

By the 1770s Lachlan McGillivray was an elected member of the Georgia legislature representing constituents who deplored both Parliament's taxes and the Proclamation Line. Lachlan opposed the taxes, but he had no interest in western lands. His plantation was safely near Georgia's border with South Carolina, and his fur trade and kin interests inclined him to support Creek land rights. Like many people who became loyalists, Lachlan supported the early tax protests but not rebellion and revolution. When shots were fired at Lexington and Concord in April 1775, Lachlan chaired a meeting to discuss Parliament's refusal to repeal the Coercive Acts, enacted to punish Massachusetts after the Boston Tea Party. The Georgia meeting passed resolutions that "the present acts of Parliament tending to raise a revenue in America are grievances" and that "we will do all that we legally and constitutionally may to obtain redress of those grievances." That fall, Lachlan's neighbors elected him to Georgia's provincial congress, an extralegal body called to decide whether to send representatives to the Continental Congress. Lachlan and his fellow delegates chose not to, so representatives from only twelve colonies met in Philadelphia as the Second Continental Congress and in 1775 created an army.[20]

Needing the empire for security and markets, Georgia could easily have joined East and West Florida in staying out of the rebellion. But enough Georgians grew radical that Georgia moved toward revolution. Lachlan's support of protest by legal and constitutional means began to seem suspiciously pro-British. Indeed, his business interests depended on ties with Britain, and he had good friends among crown officials. He could see violence escalating around him. In July 1775, a mob dragged a man to Savannah's town square for supposedly drinking a toast damning the rebel cause. The mob poured hot tar on the man, covered him in feathers, and carted him through the streets for hours, forcing him repeatedly to toast American liberty. Lachlan soon became a target, too, for arguing against Georgia's participation in the boycotts and revolution. His neighbors seized his property and arrested him. When British ships entered Savannah's harbor in 1776, Lachlan escaped and boarded a British ship along with Georgia's royal governor.[21]

As their father sailed away, Alexander and Sophia McGillivray headed the other direction. Their father's slave, a man by the name of Charles, led them home. Leaving Savannah on a tributary path, they joined the Upper Trading Path as it came south from Augusta and Charleston. For a month, they rode through forests of fir and crossed the Ogeechee, the Oconee, and the Altamaha. The small party rested in the Lower Creek towns before continuing northwest to Little Tallassee.[22]

Toward the Revolution?

By the time the Revolutionary War broke out, Alexander McGillivray's relatives in the Creek Wind clan and the Scottish McGillivray clan both had more reason to oppose the rebellious American colonists than to overthrow the empire that claimed them all. The empire could protect Creek independence against encroaching colonists and provide economic opportunities to ambitious Scotsmen in imperial trade. This child of Creek and Scottish ancestry would fight wholeheartedly for the British. After the war, he would promote Creek national independence and a confederation of Indian nations committed to protecting their common territorial independence. He would become a leader who, like Payamataha, had a clear vision of who he was and what he wanted for his people. But in 1777, Alexander McGillivray was a young man eager to fight and motivated far more by anger at the rebels for the loss of his father's land and business than allegiance to the Creeks.[23]

CHAPTER FOUR

Oliver Pollock and Margaret O'Brien

OLIVER POLLOCK AND MARGARET O'BRIEN would not have married in their native Ireland. The Pollocks were a Protestant family whose ancestors had settled in northern Ireland as part of England's colonization. Living in the town of Coleraine, the Pollocks had benefited from English rule over Ireland's native Catholic population. In contrast, the O'Briens were Irish Catholics. At home in County Clare on Ireland's western coast, they deeply resented English colonization of their homeland. The British empire sparked both the Pollocks and the O'Briens to leave Ireland, but for very different reasons. Oliver Pollock's family sought opportunity in another British colony, while Margaret O'Brien's family left to join the global Catholic fight against Protestant Britain.

Margaret O'Brien and Oliver Pollock could have ended up on opposite sides of the American Revolutionary War, but instead Margaret's family's resistance to British colonialism combined with Oliver's opposition to British trade restrictions. Through back channels in New Orleans, Oliver Pollock would be more successful than Congress's official representatives to the court of Spain in encouraging

Spanish financial and military assistance. And he lent the family's private money to the revolutionaries. For the Pollocks, the American Revolution was a true investment—they had everything to gain or lose.

Becoming a Merchant

Around 1760, when Oliver Pollock was in his twenties, he moved with his father and brothers to Carlisle, Pennsylvania, where immigrants from northern Ireland had settled before them. They established farms, and some of his brothers became mill operators and small-town tavern keepers. However, the Pennsylvania frontier did not suit the ambitious young Oliver Pollock, who decided to enter the merchant trade. Two years after coming to Carlisle, he backtracked to Philadelphia, the port where he and his family had arrived, and introduced himself to the shipping and banking firm of Willing and Morris. The merchants agreed to Pollock's proposal to lend him a load of flour they wanted to sell, and Pollock hired a ship and crew to sail to Spanish Cuba. He successfully sold the goods and soon was importing molasses, tea, coffee, spices, and sugar for the company to sell in Philadelphia in return for Pennsylvanian flour, rum, and lumber.[1]

After several profitable trips, Oliver Pollock established his own base in Havana, taking advantage of loopholes in European protectionism. Pollock managed to define himself as both a British and Spanish merchant in the eyes of each government. According to the British Navigation Acts, Spanish ships could not trade directly with British ports such as Philadelphia, Kingston, New York, and Baltimore. Yet, because Pollock was a British subject, his ships were British in the eyes of British colonial port authorities, allowing him to continue his Philadelphia trade. At the same time, his permanent base in Havana and good relations with authorities there let him skirt Spanish protectionist policies and trade directly with Spanish and French ports in the Caribbean and the Gulf of Mexico, including New Orleans.[2]

A New Orleans Family

On one of his trips to New Orleans, Oliver Pollock met Margaret O'Brien. Margaret's father had chosen the path of many "wild geese," the term for Irishmen who dispersed from Ireland to fight for Catholic empires and dreamed of retaking Ireland from Protestant Britain and making it independent again. When Margaret was a girl, her father fought in France's Irish Brigade while she attended school in France. When the French crown posted him to the Americas, she accompanied him. Oliver Pollock and Margaret O'Brien had in common an Irish past and a cosmopolitan present. Both were well traveled and fluent in English, French, and Spanish.[3]

Individual European and colonial men and women tried to better their opportunities by exploiting and improving their places within hierarchical dependencies. Ambitious young men like Oliver Pollock cultivated powerful patrons who could assist their advance. For all men below the king, status depended on impressing and showing deference to more powerful men. In Havana, Pollock had gained the favor of the famous Spanish general Alejandro O'Reilly, a "wild goose" like Margaret O'Brien's father. Independence was even less tenable for women in early modern Europe and its colonies. For an eighteenth-century European woman like Margaret O'Brien, dependence on a decent and economically successful husband was the most likely path to a good life for herself and her children.

Alejandro O'Reilly's patronage would pay off for the Pollocks. In 1768, after Spanish officials tried to enforce their empire's trade restrictions, French Louisianans rose up against Spanish rule. The crown sent General O'Reilly from Havana to restore order. O'Reilly awed the French rebels with a massive show of force. However, he knew he would soon have trouble feeding his troops. Forcing the locals to feed them would have caused more strife, as forced quartering of British redcoats did in some British colonies. To O'Reilly's great fortune, his old friend Oliver Pollock arrived at the port of New Orleans just in time on a ship with the very British name *Royal Charlotte*.

O'Reilly was delighted to learn that the ship was full of flour loaded in Baltimore. By then the initial upheaval and the arrival of hungry troops had inflated the price of flour, but Pollock sold his barrels to O'Reilly at the former, un-inflated price.[4]

As a reward for Pollock's help, O'Reilly granted him free trade privileges in Louisiana as well as the contract for provisioning New Orleans troops. Free trade was a particularly valuable concession. It was illegal for just about everyone but Pollock to trade directly across the Mississippi River without first sending goods several thousand miles across the Atlantic to England or Spain and back. Although smuggling between British and Spanish colonies increased throughout the Americas after the Seven Years' War, there was more profit and security in legal trade.[5]

Pollock moved his headquarters to New Orleans, where he and Margaret O'Brien married. Oliver converted to Catholicism, and he and Margaret settled into a prosperous life as part of the New Orleans elite. They and their growing family lived in what is now the French Quarter in a house on Chartres Street conveniently within two blocks of the wharf and the Cabildo, which housed Louisiana's government.[6]

The Pollocks reaped the benefits of belonging to multiple empires, raking in considerable profits transporting goods among ports that officially did not trade with one another. The 1770s and 1780s were a time of extreme tropical storms and drought in the Caribbean, which decreased trade within the Spanish empire, opening opportunities to a few merchants operating beyond imperial borders. Oliver Pollock's background, connections, and good luck brought him profits throughout the Mississippi Valley, Caribbean, and Atlantic, and he amassed one of the greatest personal fortunes north of Mexico. He expanded his own trade in Spanish Louisiana and served as the New Orleans agent for Willing and Morris as well as other Atlantic coast firms. He exported rice from Louisiana and corn and wheat from Illinois. His ships would arrive in New Orleans with a wide variety of goods for colonists and Indians. Men and women in New Orleans must have delighted in his cargoes of sugar, coffee, tea, wine, rum, glasses, frying pans, shoes, cotton, linen, and silk.[7]

While benefiting from Spanish trade privileges, Oliver Pollock used his continuing status as a British subject to establish trading posts and plantations in West Florida. He transported tobacco from Louisiana plantations into West Florida and deerskins and beaver pelts from Choctaw country out through New Orleans. He acquired lands along the east side of the Mississippi, near British Baton Rouge, Manchac, and Natchez, for himself and for his Philadelphia business associates Robert Morris and Thomas Willing. There, enslaved men and women grew rice, indigo, tobacco, corn, and vegetables to sell in New Orleans, Pensacola, and beyond.[8]

The Pollocks' wealth and position depended on the slave trade. As Oliver later blithely recalled, "I was supplied dry goods from London, Negros from Africa, and flour from Philadelphia." In the 1770s, he unloaded shiploads of African men, women, and children into the lower Mississippi Valley, selling them for hundreds of dollars each. He also profited from the domestic slave trade when owners wanted to sell enslaved people who already lived in Louisiana or West Florida. In a cash-poor region where most of his dealings were on credit, the bodies of enslaved men, women, and children served not only as labor but also as capital.[9]

Margaret Pollock did not own plantations or run the family business. She did not have audiences with governors, although she might catch one's ear at a dinner party. Yet, while we might focus on the fact that women lacked the right to vote or hold office, Margaret Pollock almost certainly did not see herself as what we today might call a "second-class citizen." There were no citizens in the American colonies, only subjects, foreigners, and slaves, and she was now a Spanish subject. She had considerable power within her household and in New Orleans society. She helped to entertain the patrons and other connections that Oliver's business needed. Her family's background and her language skills gave her commonalities with O'Reilly and other Spanish and French officials and their families and helped Oliver to establish himself in this alien empire. She cared for the children and managed the enslaved staff of her elite household. Oliver Pollock and Margaret O'Brien built their prosperity on the border of empires and thrived.

A Revolution for Free Trade

The Pollocks would risk all they had built to support the Revolution. Their Irish upbringing and opposition to British trade restrictions combined to make them a ready audience for the rebels' accusations that, as the Declaration of Independence put it, King George III was "imposing taxes on us without our consent" and "cutting off our trade with all parts of the world." However, the Pollocks' support had little to do with the rebel colonies themselves. Before the Revolution, Oliver had lived only two years in the thirteen colonies and Margaret none at all. But they had no love for the British empire, and they saw economic opportunity in the rebellion. If West Florida freed itself from the British empire, either by joining the thirteen rebelling colonies or by Spanish takeover, Oliver Pollock's tolerated smuggling between that colony and Louisiana could become a legitimate trading bonanza. Like many ambitious revolutionaries in the thirteen colonies, Pollock believed that separation from Britain could create a more commercialized society that would liberate his enterprises from imperial restrictions.

The Pollocks realized that the revolutionaries would need the support of Spain to defeat the British empire and that Oliver was in the perfect position to lobby for that support. Although he might lose his British connections and property in the short run, he could increase his trade with the Spanish empire and the rebels during the war and with the new American nation if it gained its independence. He began to pressure O'Reilly's successor, Governor Luís de Unzaga y Amezaga, to allow and even to protect American trade at New Orleans. Unzaga demurred, but his interest was piqued, and he dispatched a Spanish spy to see if this independence movement was truly serious.[10]

In the late summer of 1776, several men calling themselves traders arrived in New Orleans from Virginia via the Ohio and Mississippi rivers. They asked the way to Oliver Pollock's house. Once there, the leader introduced himself as Captain George Gibson, the bearer of a letter from Continental Army General Charles Lee, George Washington's second-in-command. On behalf of the Continental Congress and the state of Virginia, Lee requested Spanish assistance in the war, including trade, financial aid, and supplies. The letter promised an invasion of West Florida in the spring of 1777 to take Pensacola, Mobile, and the other British forts of West Florida. Lee's idea was one of countless grandiose proposals that Americans introduced throughout the war, despite their chronic shortage of men, money, and supplies that made these geopolitical imaginings entirely impractical. Nonetheless, Pollock believed that Spanish support could extract West Florida from the British empire and transform his own prewar smuggling into unprecedented postwar trading opportunities. He translated the letter into Spanish and, accompanied by Gibson, carried it to Governor Unzaga. Gibson reported news of the Declaration of Independence to Unzaga and expressed the American willingness to hand Pensacola over to the Spanish once it was taken (a rumor that reached Pensacola as well).[11]

Pollock was responsible for Spain's first direct aid to the rebels. As he later recalled, "after many solicitations I prevailed on the Governor to grant a Batteaux load of the King's Powder, and then I purchased fitted out and dispatched a vessel with the powder." The American representatives paid for the gunpowder with IOUs from the newly declared state of Virginia, and Pollock sent it up the Mississippi and Ohio rivers to Fort Pitt, where it arrived in May 1777. Because merchants in New Orleans and traders at the posts up the Mississippi where the barge docked doubted Virginia's ability to pay, Pollock backed the loans with his own good name and provided the transportation. On hearing of this event, Spanish Minister of the Indies José de Gálvez instructed Governor Unzaga to encourage the Pensacola plan and to find an agent to funnel support to the rebels. Oliver Pollock was the obvious choice. Unzaga sent more supplies from the port of New Orleans to Philadelphia on one of Pollock's ships.[12]

As the war continued, Oliver Pollock changed from a self-proclaimed advocate to an official promoter of American interests. The Continental Congress appointed Pollock as its commercial agent in Louisiana, and, as he put it in October 1776, he looked forward to "exerting my utmost endeavors for the glorious cause" of "the country I owe everything but birth." He also mentioned, "I have often been obliged to advance money for the benefit of the cause," but he nonetheless spent another thousand dollars chartering a ship to deliver his acceptance of the appointment and congratulations to Congress for declaring independence.[13] Congress, delighted to get the news, immediately asked Pollock to buy and ship at least thirty thousand dollars in goods for the Continental Army and potential Indian allies. Pollock got to work and by the end of the year had packed one of his ships with over 300 shirts, 750 handkerchiefs, 60 pairs of stockings, 360 shoes, nearly 500 hats, thread, fabric ranging from heavy-duty cambric to silk, and some goods especially for the officers: barrels of brandy and Málaga (a fortified wine) and trunks packed with silver bread plates, eating utensils, combs, and candles.[14]

Toward the Revolution?

Margaret and Oliver Pollock's experiences before the Revolution would shape Oliver's decision to lay his reputation and fortune on the line for the American cause. He had built an independent fortune for himself and his family by finding ways around the rules and by closely affiliating himself with Spanish officials. Spain's trade laws were every bit as restrictive as Britain's Navigation Acts, but Spanish officials had granted Oliver Pollock exemptions. In his experience it was Spain that effectively promoted inter-imperial trade. If the British colonies gained their independence, the Pollocks might have the best of all worlds: plantations on the Mississippi and businesses in New Orleans, strong ties to the expanding Spanish empire with its vast markets, and the gratitude of a new country whose Congress promoted free trade among its states and with the Spanish, French, and Dutch empires. Once he bet against Britain, he was all in.

Whether Margaret agreed with the risks her husband was taking is unclear. Certainly her family's history put her on the side of Catholic empires against Protestant Britain. It is possible that she was a force behind her husband's financial support for the rebels. On the other hand, she may have worried that her husband was stretching himself too thin. Whatever she thought, it was Oliver who owned the business and Oliver who would decide. Women's ineligibility for military service or government office and lack of opportunity in business severely limited their ability to exercise opinion on matters of war.

Although nearly half of North America's population was female, few women appear in tales of war and nation-building. Surviving documents tend to focus on what the men were doing: fighting, strategizing, and writing. Wars of the past often seem the realm of men—of kings, politicians, and soldiers—but wars are domestic too, as the women who lived through them knew very well. While choosing loyalties at the onset of revolution was as often a matter of personal interest as political principle, for half the free population, following the tide of history was seldom about choices at all. Still, the outcome would be just as important to their personal safety and their ambitions for their families.[15]

CHAPTER FIVE

James Bruce
and Isabella Chrystie

IN CONTRAST TO Margaret O'Brien and Oliver Pollock, Isabella Chrystie and James Bruce knew their interests lay firmly within a single empire, the British. As Protestant Lowland Scots, their families had long accepted being part of Britain. Unlike the Irish O'Briens or the Highlander McGillivrays, rebellion was a distant memory for their Lowland families. Their rebellions had ended with James Bruce's distant ancestor Robert the Bruce nearly five centuries earlier. The British colony of West Florida brought James and Isabella Bruce opportunities for economic and social advancement, the kinds of opportunities that attracted hundreds of thousands of European men and women to the Americas.

James Bruce chose to seek his fortune in West Florida and became a leader in local government and the owner of a house in town and several plantations, but Isabella Chrystie had little choice when her husband brought her there in 1769. The price for moving to the colonies was high: leaving behind family, friends, and all she had ever known to go to a place that seemed to her a wilderness. Like Margaret Pollock, Isabella Bruce had no expectation of equality with her husband. Dependence on a successful husband brought security and prestige that she would not have wanted to lose. The American Revolution threatened the empire and the husband to whom she had committed her future. Isabella Bruce's sacrifices in leaving Scotland were supposed to make a better life for her children someday, but war would bring the dangers of violence, famine, and disease to herself and her children. When revolution came, men and women like the Bruces would have to decide whether to stick by the empire for which they had already risked all by simply making the journey.

James Bruce

In August or September 1769, James and Isabella Bruce boarded a ship in Britain and set sail for the colonies. This was Isabella Bruce's first trip across the Atlantic, but James had lived in Pensacola for five years before returning to Scotland and marrying her. He had served as a low-level officer in the British Navy's triumph over French Canada during the Seven Years' War and earned a land grant of four thousand acres. Royal land grants to award service in the war ranged from fifty to five thousand acres, so his was quite large. However, it was not in a developed colony but in Britain's recent acquisition of West Florida. The crown also appointed him Collector of His Majesty's Customs and a member of His Majesty's Council for the Province of West Florida, the body that advised the governor. Through a combination of his military pay, family, and past investments, Bruce had a "considerable sum of money" with which to begin developing the land.[1]

It was a good opportunity. Across the British empire, land was the basis of wealth and family independence, and one could not simply go out and acquire it in rural England. In the English colonies, land ownership and relatively independent farming had been reasonable, if not guaranteed, ambitions. By the time of the Seven Years' War, arable and uncontested land was scarce in Britain's Atlantic Coast colonies, but now the new colonies acquired from France and Spain beckoned. When the Proclamation of 1763 declared that most land west of the Appalachians belonged to Indians, it encouraged settlement in the newly British colonies of West Florida, East Florida, Quebec, and Grenada. West Florida promised both land and security. The coastal Native inhabitants belonged to small tribes, and most of them had moved either to Spanish Louisiana or inland. The powerful Choctaws and Creeks claimed coastal lands but lived inland and allowed European development near the Mississippi River, if they were paid with goods and if the colonies respected the borders they set.[2]

British leaders knew that the Spanish and French had never made money from these lands, but their patriotism persuaded them that Britons could succeed where lazy Catholics had failed. As the new British governor of East Florida wrote in 1763, "the indolence of the Spanish" kept them from making use of "what the soil and climate are capable of producing."[3] Whereas the French and Spanish failed to take advantage of the Floridas' location on the Gulf with ample land and easy connections to the West Indies and the Atlantic beyond, the British were confident they could make them the next Jamaica. West Florida Governor George Johnstone argued that "Nature seems to have intended to place the seat of commerce" on Pensacola Bay. From there, the British could export indigo, hemp, cotton, rice, and flour not only to their own colonies but also through New Orleans, whose conquest would "deliver to us the keys of the wealth of Mexico." West Florida could be "the emporium, as well as the most pleasant part of the new world."[4] For five years, James Bruce worked to build his business and prominence within these West Florida imperial dreams before heading back to Scotland.

Isabella Chrystie

As a woman, Isabella Bruce is harder to find in the documentary record. We can only guess the details of her life before she married James Bruce and moved to Pensacola in 1769. Following the patriarchal system of British common law, the West Florida records always refer to her as "Isabella Bruce" or "Mrs. Bruce," so we cannot be sure who she was before she married. It appears that she was born Isabel Chrystie in Aberdeenshire in northeastern Scotland in 1742 into a household already crowded with brothers and a sister. In her mid-twenties, she met James Bruce when he was back in Scotland on leave, with a handsome payment from the Seven Years' War and good prospects in the colonies. Parents of daughters knew he was a catch. Isabella Chrystie married James Bruce in Auchterless, Aberdeenshire, on August 8, 1769.[5]

Now Isabella Bruce, she lived on a ship with her new husband for more than a month as it followed the trade winds to the West Indies. The newlyweds had plenty of time to get to know each other and wonder what their life together would bring. If they wrote letters home describing their journey, they are lost; however, other people who made the same trip around the same time help us to imagine what they saw. Crossing the ocean for weeks, possibly seasick and probably terrified as storms came and went, they felt the weather grow increasingly warmer as their ship approached Jamaica. The tropical heat was always shocking to Scots on their first trip to the Caribbean.[6]

Kingston surely impressed them, as it did other travelers with its three thousand mostly brick houses nestled under verdant mountains. Finally freed from her stale ship cabin, Isabella Bruce saw black women rowing small boats from ship to ship in Kingston Harbor. They were an unfamiliar but welcome sight, as they sold their wares of fresh cucumbers, carrots, oranges, lemons, pineapples, bananas, coconuts, yams, fish, and bread. Enslaved men on the docks loaded coffee, sugar, chocolate, ginger, potatoes, pineapples, pomegranates, and melons to send to the mainland British colonies and beyond. These people were Isabella Bruce's first introduction to the enslaved Africans she would come to know intimately in West Florida. If her reactions resembled those of other Britons upon seeing a slave society for the first time, she was likely intrigued and appalled at the same time. Perhaps, like diarist Janet Schaw, who also traveled from the Scottish lowlands to the West Indies, she believed that enslaving human beings was abhorrent in theory but that colonies required different kinds of labor and that slavery was acceptable under a good master. Whatever Isabella Bruce thought, slavery would be central to her husband's ambitions.[7]

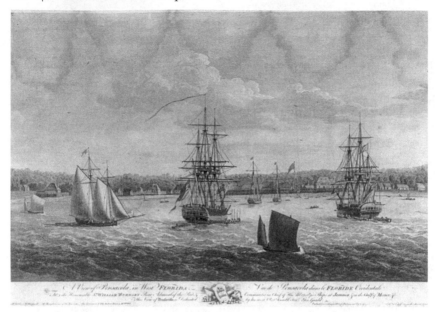

George Gauld, *A View of Pensacola in West Florida, 1770s.* James and Isabella Bruce's house may be one of those pictured. (Prints and Photographs Division, Library of Congress)

If Isabella Bruce expected Pensacola to resemble Kingston, she was disappointed. In 1769, it was still not Governor Johnstone's imagined "emporium of the New World." Approaching from the Gulf, she could see the blinding white sand that "lies low and flat and seems to have swum out of the sea" and the "small and scattered" town of Pensacola. One visitor wrote that "anywhere else that one might enter a port, he would be curious to see the city. Here, however, one could already see from the ship that this must be a miserable place." Disembarking would not have changed the impression. "The streets, if they can be called that," one arrival wrote, "are full of sand in which one walks with the sand, like snow in Germany, over the shoes, and in summer, so hot that the shoe soles and feet are burned." Pensacola's main square was "the only place where a person can go without getting his shoes full of sand." The "wretched habitations" were "built with pieces of bark, covered with the same materials, and most of them without floors; so that in the summer they were as hot as stoves, and the land engendered all sorts of vermin." The "place which is called the fort," one British officer remarked, was really just "half a mile of ground in circumference, surrounded with a rotten stockade" and was "so defenceless that any one can step in at pleasure." Most of Pensacola's Spanish settlers had fled for Cuba and New Spain, leaving little behind, but British settlers like James Bruce had come and begun improvements. A few years earlier, in 1764, British civil engineer Elias Durnford had replanned the city. Now its streets were laid out in a grid around the large public square. West Florida had nearly two thousand settlers and was growing. Chickens, goats, and pigs were underfoot throughout the town of Pensacola, and their waste, as well as that of the horses, made Pensacola smell much like other colonial and European towns.[8]

Isabella Bruce moved into the house James had built in Pensacola. It was right on the water, on a lot that was free as long as they paid their annual taxes. To Scots, it must have seemed strange to live so close to the sea, which could flood homes and lands and, at least in Scotland, make residents miserable with cold, howling winds. However, the forests that rose up behind the town discouraged inland settlement with their unseen dangers: animals, Indians, and Catholics. In her new home, Bruce became familiar with Africans and Afro-Floridians as well as the Creeks, Chickasaws, Choctaws, and other Indians who crowded into Pensacola and Mobile, several hundred at a time, for diplomacy and trade.

It was winter when Isabella Bruce landed, so the nights were not as chilly as Scottish nights, and the days were warmer, reaching into the 60s. Her first Florida summer must have been a shock, with its relentless heat and humidity and frightening thunderstorms that could crash in on the sunniest days. The most striking differences between Pensacola and Isabella Bruce's home in Presbyterian Scotland were what was missing. Pensacola had no church and only visiting clergymen. There were no schools, few shops, no libraries, no assembly room, and, of course, none of her extended family.[9]

No letters of Isabella Bruce's survive, but most women of her class and era wrote letters that were not preserved. Travel was difficult, dangerous, and expensive, so letters were the only way to keep in touch with family and friends far away. Ships sailed from Pensacola to the British Isles often enough to make regular correspondence possible. Bruce could usually receive a reply to a letter within a few months. If her letters resembled those of similar women, she first assured the recipient of her family's health or recovery if she had reported any sickness in the previous letter and then wrote of her children's progress, local politics, the pains and pleasures of child rearing, her management of the household's expenses and credit, and rumors of war. Letters made extended family connections possible in a world with extreme dislocations.[10]

For meals, Isabella Bruce served local oysters, fish, duck, or deer alongside bread and homegrown vegetables. She likely served them on a set of imported cream-colored Staffordshire ware, brought by the same globalization that had brought her to Pensacola. This pottery was so ubiquitous that it has been called "the Coca-Cola of the eighteenth century." In her generation, elaborate tea service had become popular. When women came to visit, she would have laid out on a tea table a complete spread, including cups, saucers, and a sugar bowl and cream pitcher, all probably of blue and white porcelain, along with silver tongs and a strainer. When a ship arrived she would go to the docks with her neighbors to see what exciting goods had come—maybe shoes she had ordered, the latest novel, cheese from Philadelphia, Madeira rumored to cure heat-related ills, or West Indies rum. And she could take her children to see the boat reload with lumber, deerskins, furs, tallow, and an occasional novelty—a sea turtle or alligator—for the folks in Philadelphia or Bristol.[11]

Isabella soon became pregnant. For all women of her era, childbirth was life-threatening, and with her firstborn she likely labored long, perhaps for days, under the watch of neighborhood friends. She bore a healthy boy who was christened Archibald Scott Bruce on December 23, 1770. As she nursed her tiny newborn, Isabella Bruce knew how precarious his life was. In the weeks just before and after his christening, three neighboring families suffered the death of small children. Within the small colonial population of Pensacola, twenty-three children died in the six months before Archibald was born, most of them infants. And getting through the first year was no guarantee that the child would live. One-year-old Anne Creek, whom Isabella Bruce had probably seen toddling across the square, went into convulsions and died when Bruce was eight months pregnant; four-year-old Mary Porter fell to "dropsy & scurvy" when Archibald was approaching his one-month birthday; and two children died the following April from what the rector could only record as "teeth." In April, Isabella Bruce may have attended the birth of Dorothy, the daughter of a man on His Majesty's Council with James Bruce, and she was surely there to grieve when Dorothy died of fever and flux (dysentery) that June. The Bruces saw death all around them. Adults died of consumption, asthma, drowning, and other accidents, and a neighbor, also named Isabella, died of "a violent contusion from her husband."[12]

But life abounded too. The grieving Elizabeth Creek named a new daughter Anne that June. And, most important for the Bruces, hearty young Archibald survived, and a year or two later, the family added a daughter, Charlotte May Bruce. Over the years, Isabella and James Bruce worried over their children's health as they suffered through but recovered from childhood diseases, such as whooping cough and even smallpox. Many eighteenth-century Britons believed that quick changes in the weather and extremes of temperature were unhealthy, so Pensacola's climate added to the young parents' worries, although colonists also believed that the sea breezes moderated the ill effects. If the children remained healthy and James Bruce continued to grow his fortune and social standing, Archibald would someday be a prominent planter and Charlotte a marriageable young woman who could one day be the wife of a landowner.[13]

Tyranny

As with plantation owners throughout the colonies, Isabella and James Bruce's family independence depended on the forcible dislocation of West Africans. Under the strange and terrible power relations of colonialism, black men called Glasgow, Aberdeen, Dublin, and Caithness worked for the Bruces in the fields and on the docks of the Gulf Coast, thousands of miles from both their ancestral West African homelands and the Scottish places for which their masters had named them. Some of the Bruces' slaves worked for the family in town. The women and Isabella Bruce washed clothes or baked bread side by side. On a lot in the northern part of town farthest from the sea, they grew pumpkins, watermelons, cabbages, lettuces, carrots, turnips, beans, and peanuts to the cries of the gulls and the roar of the waves. Although they worked closely, it is impossible to know if their relationships were friendly or distant. In either case, her husband owned them, and when a creditor wanted reassurance, it was Glasgow and his fellow slaves who served as collateral.[14]

The names of the Bruces' slaves tell us nothing about them beyond whether they were male or female, but they grant some insight into the Bruces. The men's names recalled for them the places they were unlikely to see again—the barren flatlands of Caithness, the cliffs of Aberdeen, the bustling lowlands city of Glasgow. On the other hand, the women's names—Chloe, Roxana, Statira—reflected the literary tastes of many British women of their day. Isabella Bruce may have named them, as the lady of the household, either at their birth or as they entered the household with names that were West African, French, or Spanish. In any case they surely echoed her literary knowledge. "Chloe" was the heroine of *Daphnis and Chloe,* a Greek novel translated into English in 1657 and popularized in the eighteenth century as "A Most Sweet, and Pleasant Pastoral ROMANCE for Young Ladies." "Roxana" was the eponymous heroine of Daniel Defoe's 1724 novel, and "Roxana and Statira" were known jointly as the dueling wives of Alexander the Great from Nathaniel Lee's 1677 play *The Rival Queens, or the Death of Alexander the Great.*[15]

The major theme of *The Rival Queens* is tyranny, including the potentially unjust rule of men over women. Within the British empire, the legal system of coverture made James the representative of his dependents' interests—from his wife to the slaves Glasgow and Roxana to baby Charlotte. Indeed, his status as an independent Englishman depended on the dependence of his wife, children, and slaves. Under coverture, married and unmarried minor women in Britain and its empire had no legal standing to own property or exercise other privileges guaranteed to men. Margaret Pollock and other married women in Spain, France, and their colonies held property rights separate from their husbands, and by law they inherited the property they brought to the marriage as well as half the property amassed during the marriage. In contrast, when a British man died, his will might grant his widow some of the land, but under British common law, the bulk would go to his male heirs. When James Bruce and other men of West Florida considered whether they would join the rebellion against British tyranny or stand with their empire, the question of men's tyranny over women or slaveholders' tyranny over their male and female slaves did not come up.[16]

Interrogating women's place in society would not have been alien to Isabella Bruce. Her homeland was deep into what scholars call the Scottish Enlightenment, and the nature and role of women was a central topic of discussion. Many thinkers believed that women had once been basically slaves to their husbands but that European culture had raised its women gradually to liberty. This cultural development went both ways. According to Gilbert Stuart and other Scottish Enlightenment writers, women had helped men to become civilized, leaving behind their brutally hyper-masculine past. Now women were companions and participants in advancing civilization—but not equal participants. Whatever women's place culturally, economic developments had pushed them further below men. Earlier in the British colonies, widows had some opportunities to own property and run businesses, but those opportunities had declined as men began to live long enough to leave their property to sons and as the colonial economy matured into one that required access to credit and capital, of which women had little. The Enlightenment's increasing emphasis on the independent individual defined that individual as male, while women were still defined in terms of their relations to fathers, husbands, and children. The Enlightenment had only begun defining the equality of men in politics as a fundamental right. The American Revolution would advance the fledgling notion that all men are created equal. The notion that all *people* are created equal would have made no sense in Isabella Bruce's world.[17]

James Bruce nearly was accused of tyranny by his fellow white West Floridians before Isabella ever arrived. The Stamp Act of 1765 required each colony to commission a distributor of stamps, and a customs collector was an obvious choice. James Bruce narrowly avoided the job. In West Florida the office went to Mobile's collector of customs, James Blackwell. Both he and James Bruce must have thanked their lucky stars that protests in West Florida did not become violent, as they did in Boston and several other port cities. Opponents of the Stamp Act did march to demand the surrender of the stamps when they arrived at the port of Pensacola and accused the ship's captain of importing "badges of slavery." West Florida's attorney general, Edmund Rush Wegg, claimed that Parliament had no right to levy taxes on the colonies without their consent, charging that "no man can be bound to any government, unless his own consent is conveyed either by himself, or representative."[18] Still, when delegates from nine colonies sent a resolution to Parliament and the king protesting the Stamp Act in 1765, West Florida did not join them. Indeed, no delegates from New Hampshire, Virginia, North Carolina, Georgia, East Florida, West Florida, the Canadian colonies, or Jamaica and the other island colonies participated in the resolution.[19]

The Bruces were even less likely to support protest than the average West Floridian. Scots like Governor Johnstone and the Bruces had accumulated power within the empire and feared the disruptions that rebellions could cause. As collector of customs, James Bruce earned a commission on duties he collected, so new duties meant more commissions. Inclined toward avoiding conflict and valuing what the empire provided, James urged his fellow West Floridians to "show our inclination of acting with the greatest moderation, in these unhappy disputes."[20] The new taxes were unpopular, but the Bruces would not support rebellion and independence. They felt they owed their newfound wealth and prominence to the British empire.

Toward the Revolution?

In the early years of the American Revolution, colonists did not define the Bruce family's choices as we tend to: the obvious choice being the heroic and resolute "Patriot" or "American" side versus the cowardly or traitorous "Tory" or "Loyalist" side. Through the 1770s, rebellious colonists were still having to defend *their* choice, one that the Bruce family, Lachlan McGillivray, and King George III saw as treason. The Declaration of Independence went to great pains to explain that it was not "light and transient causes" that prompted independence but "a long train of abuses and usurpations" aimed at instituting "absolute Despotism." In the minds of the Bruce family and many, many others, these causes were not longstanding or abusive enough to justify treason.[21]

As protest became war in the 1770s, West Florida—along with East Florida and the Canadian and island colonies—chose not to join the rebelling thirteen. As those colonies declared their independence, the Bruces and most of their neighbors recognized that their family independence depended on the connections, infrastructure, and order that the British empire provided. While speculators and settlers on the Atlantic Coast deeply resented the Proclamation of 1763's prohibition on settlement west of the Appalachians, West Floridians had land on the lower stretches of the region's rivers with access to the ports along the Gulf or the Mississippi. They were fine as long as they peacefully traded with the powerful Creeks, Choctaws, and Chickasaws and had the protection of His Majesty's troops at Pensacola, Mobile, and the smaller posts.[22]

By 1774, West Florida's population was only about 3,700 free people and 1,200 slaves, and they were far from other British population centers. Like the West Indies colonists, West Floridians understood that they received much more in services from the crown than they paid to it. The colonial administration financed the building and maintenance of the colony's defense works, provided the soldiers that protected the Bruces and their neighbors from Indians and slave revolts, and connected West Florida to the markets and products of the British empire. The Bruces and most of their neighbors had no desire to leave the most powerful empire in the world.[23]

Nor was the rebel side obviously the side of liberty. Loyalists took great pride and comfort in their constitutional rights within the British empire, which included the right to protest, and had faith that legitimate protest could be effective. A petition to the king in 1779 charged that Peter Chester, who had taken over as governor in 1770, had "violated the rights and liberties of your people" by not calling West Florida's General Assembly into session. The signatories were 130 "leading citizens" including Lachlan's cousin John McGillivray and Adam Chrystie, the speaker of West Florida's assembly and possibly a relation of Isabella's. Even in his protest, Chrystie agreed with James Bruce that, as the petition put it, "we hold in abhorrence the present unnatural and unparalleled rebellion raging in our neighboring colonies."[24]

As first-generation immigrants, the Bruces and most of their neighbors also had more reason to think of themselves as British subjects than did colonists whose families had by now been in the colonies for generations. False rumors that the rebels were secretly Catholic as well as more realistic rumors that they planned to hand West Florida back over to France and Spain, imperiling James's position and land title, added to the reasons to stick with Britain. In addition, there were logistical factors. Communication with the northern colonies was slow, and West Florida had no newspaper to stir up protest. On the contrary, the news coming with fleeing loyalists from nearby Georgia and the Carolinas was of rebel violence, increasing Floridians' reluctance to rebel. Loyalists agreed with the crown that the rebellion's leaders were reckless demagogues who would undermine the beneficial imperial relationship for their own selfish advancement.[25]

Beyond moral and political arguments, the rebels would probably lose. In 1775 and 1776, American General Richard Montgomery and Colonel Benedict Arnold failed in their attempt to take Canada, and Montgomery was killed. George Washington led his troops in desperate retreat out of New York City and across New Jersey to Pennsylvania, with British General Charles Cornwallis on their heels.

Still, the war did not seem likely to end soon, and West Floridians feared that the rebels might attack Pensacola due to its "very defenseless state."[26] From their house, the Bruces could see soldiers and slaves hard at work to improve defenses. In March 1777, the news from Philadelphia was that merchant Oliver Pollock had shipped gunpowder there for the rebels and that the rebels were making plans to attack West Florida. The colony had decided against war, but war might come anyway.[27]

CHAPTER SIX

Petit Jean

THE REVOLUTIONARY WAR put slaveholders in a dilemma. On both sides, war conditions demanded the assistance and loyalty of all members of a community, including slaves. Freedom was the obvious way to ensure their loyalty, but without slaves, the colonies' economies might fail regardless of the war's outcome. The British moved first. In 1775 Royal Governor of Virginia John Murray, the Fourth Earl of Dunmore, proclaimed that any slaves or indentured servants of rebellious Virginia masters who fled to British lines and served in the British army would thereby win their freedom. Thousands of people took Lord Dunmore up on the offer, not only men of military age but also women, children, and old men who interpreted the invitation to include themselves. On the rebel side, Crispus Attucks died in Boston protesting British soldiers. Other free and enslaved black urbanites rioted for the same reasons as the white men and women by their sides—protesting poverty and oppression as part of a long tradition of British subjects. Within the empire's hierarchical political system, only a small minority of British subjects could vote or hold office, but all had the right to protest. When the conflict first began, northern slaves who volunteered for the rebel militias were promised freedom. The Continental Congress at times encouraged enslaved and free black enlistments, especially as the war dragged on and white recruits became less enthusiastic. Ultimately, most of the states enlisted slaves and free blacks in the forces they were required to provide the Continental Army as well as in state militias.[1]

War on the Gulf Coast would offer opportunities to seize freedom in large and small ways, in addition to the dangers that wars always bring to those caught in them. In Mobile, Petit Jean would take advantage of the wartime need for his skills, expertise, and loyalty to become a go-between and increase his own independence.[2]

Slavery in French Mobile

Enslaved people were a central part of early America by any measure: sheer numbers, participation in the economy, influence on the decisions of imperial and local leaders. Yet the vast majority of them left no documents in their own writing, nor did colonial officials record their spoken words as they did with American Indian diplomats. In the colonial and revolutionary periods, enslaved people appear in the documentary record mostly as numbers on a page: age, price, and perhaps a name. These are chilling documents, and they remind us that colonial Americans bought and sold human beings, but they do little to tell the stories of the real people behind the numbers. We know more about Petit Jean because of his wartime work for the Spanish, but we have to guess at his history before and after the war from what we know about slavery in Mobile more generally. But that is more than we have for most. For example, an enslaved woman was married to Petit Jean, but we do not even know her name.

The ancestors of Petit Jean and his wife most likely came in slave ships to French Louisiana from West Africa in the early 1700s soon after Frenchman Pierre Le Moyne d'Iberville and his brother, the Sieur de Bienville, founded Louisiana. Coming south from Montreal, the brothers hoped to establish plantations in this warmer climate. Between 1719 and 1730, French settlers imported seven thousand African slaves to Mobile, New Orleans, and other Gulf Coast towns. Nearly five thousand of them came from Senegambia (present-day Senegal, Gambia, Guinea, and Guinea-Bissau) and most of the rest from the Bight of Benin (to the southeast, the present-day coasts of eastern Ghana, Togo, Benin, and western Nigeria). But in 1729, Natchez Indians destroyed the French plantations established on their lands and killed and captured hundreds of settlers and slaves. This massacre persuaded French colonial administrators to focus their plantation efforts on the Caribbean rather than Louisiana, where plantations on Indian lands could spark another Indian attack or even a united Indian-African war against the French. They cut off Louisiana's slave supply, although slaves continued to trickle into Mobile on unauthorized ships and with new French settlers.[3]

Petit Jean's French name (meaning "Little John") implies that he was born in French Louisiana and served a French master. One official referred to him as "the mulatto Petit Jean," so he may have had French or Native American ancestry as well as West African. Petit Jean was a cattle driver. He raised his master's cattle in the countryside north of Mobile, feeding them on forest vegetation. When his master wanted meat from his hundreds of cattle to sell or eat, Petit Jean either drove them into Mobile or Pensacola or killed and butchered them on the spot.[4]

Slavery in British Mobile

The Seven Years' War changed the map of North America dramatically, and Petit Jean saw the effects as British plantation agriculture took over. Short on settlers and fearful of slave rebellions and Indian wars, the French had built the colonies of New France (Canada) and Louisiana on the fur trade. The British experience in North America could not have been more different. Plantation slavery spread across most of the British colonies, raising tobacco in the Chesapeake, sugar in Barbados and Jamaica, and rice in South Carolina and Georgia. When the Seven Years' War left Britain with West and East Florida, slavery there grew.

The years following the war brought more and more African slaves to Mobile and put them to work on more and more plantations. British settlers, including James and Isabella Bruce, expected African slaves to do the labor to make their British land grants profitable. Some brought slaves with them from other colonies, and most bought slaves from ships coming from Jamaica and beyond. At least 2,500 new slaves arrived from Africa between 1763 and the Revolution. Almost all came from Senegambia and Sierra Leone. Most worked along the coast or up the Mississippi River, while some were sold illegally into Spanish Louisiana.[5]

British slavery in West Florida became more entrenched and more rigid than French slavery had been in the region. Now some tobacco and indigo plantations had over a hundred slaves. Foreshadowing antebellum restrictions after this region became the cotton South, the British slave code for West Florida restricted the right of slaveholders to manumit (free) their slaves and prohibited slaves from going farther than two miles from home without a pass; buying liquor without their masters' permission; conducting business for themselves; keeping their own pigs, cattle, or chickens; and carrying guns beyond their owners' property.[6]

Still, Petit Jean retained a role in the plantation system altogether different and more autonomous than most slaves in post-1763 Mobile. A skilled second- or third-generation slave, Petit Jean remained highly mobile and had a deep knowledge of the landscape around Mobile, including the confusing cattle paths. He knew its cane breaks, pine barrens, scrub oaks, bogs, and creeks. He carried messages from one plantation to another, bringing word of a birth, a harsh punishment, or an impending visit. He would regularly have come across groups of Indians traveling the region's roads. He may have spoken not only French but also Mobilian Jargon, a trade language based on Choctaw, which Indians used to communicate across linguistic barriers and which Africans and Europeans adopted since their arrival. His cattle fed Native diplomats who came to Mobile, including Payamataha. And importantly Petit Jean almost certainly carried a gun, a privilege forbidden to most slaves.[7]

Freedoms

In July 1776, Mobile's slaves whispered rumors to one another of a slave rebellion near Natchez. White men and women whispered too, with futile hopes that their slaves would not hear the news. Plantation owners had discovered what seemed to be a plot by several of their slaves to rebel against them. Four slaves accused of the conspiracy felt the noose that Thomas Jefferson and John Adams feared as they declared independence that same summer in Philadelphia. Another accused man drowned in the river to escape hanging. There is no way to know for certain if the accused actually planned a rebellion or if nervous planters imagined or exaggerated the threat, but the message Petit Jean heard was that swift and brutal violence would punish those who even discussed rising up.[8]

Running away was the most common way of seeking permanent or temporary freedom in West Florida and Louisiana. In July 1776, two slaves, Ketty and Bessy, ran away from one of the same plantations involved in the alleged conspiracy. Bessy's master found her that night at a neighbor's plantation, and Ketty returned home the following day, "finding it uncomfortable in the woods," according to her master. When another slave, Paul, went missing, the master assumed that he had gone to visit his wife on another plantation.[9] Ketty, Bessy, and Paul suffered punishment, probably physical, for running away, but they knew that they would not be killed, and their master's tone in recording the events implies that this kind of temporary flight was common and not particularly worrying.

This kind of running away is evidence that freedom was not the all-or-nothing proposition we might imagine. On a daily basis, it could be seized in small amounts. And no longer being enslaved did not necessarily mean full freedom. An old or sick slave might need a master's food and lodging. Indeed, French Louisiana's Code Noir required that "slaves sick from old age, disease, or any other malady, incurable or not, shall be nourished and sustained by their masters."[10] Depending on circumstances, being close to one's family, secure from military attack, or sold to a less vicious master might be as important as legal freedom. Finding community and ways of integrating into new social networks could be a primary goal for people who had been stripped from their homes and alienated from their peoples. No one wanted to be a slave, but almost no one questioned the legitimacy of slavery as an institution. Petit Jean had a great deal of autonomy in his work and certainly could see around him examples of slaves in worse circumstances than himself.

Petit Jean could have run away. Some of his fellow enslaved men and women crossed the border into Spanish Louisiana, hid in the bayous, sneaked onto ships, or blended into New Orleans's free population of color. Petit Jean had plenty of opportunity as he tended cattle alone or with other slaves in the borderlands of British West Florida, Spanish Louisiana, and Choctaw country. Starting in the late 1600s, in an attempt to undermine the English, the Spanish crown promised freedom to slaves fleeing from English colonies to Spanish ones. Slaves left Jamaica for Cuba and South Carolina for St. Augustine. However, the powers along the Mississippi River in the 1760s and 1770s were trying to keep a delicate peace. Not interfering with one another's slave system was a key point of agreement. If Petit Jean headed west to Louisiana or north to Choctaw country, he could count on being returned in the next diplomatic exchange, suffering worse conditions in the meantime, and facing punishment upon his return to his Mobile master. Worries over a master's retribution plus alligators, snakes, and starvation kept most slaves at home no matter how badly they wanted freedom. For Petit Jean, coming back to town meant returning to his wife, who presumably had less freedom of movement than her husband and would have found it hard to escape with him.[11]

Toward the Revolution?

Rumors of rebellion on the Atlantic Coast arrived with thousands of loyalists and their slaves fleeing Georgia and South Carolina. The British crown promised these refugees land in the Floridas, markets,

protection, and escape from the violence that threatened their personal liberty. The government compensated those who had abandoned substantial land holdings in the thirteen colonies with even
larger grants. West Florida's population doubled with people whose
lives had been torn apart by the rebellion.[12]

Protestors against the Stamp Act at times accused Parliament of
trying to enslave them, and their choice of metaphor makes sense. For
people who lived with slavery, enslavement was an image that came
quickly to mind when accusing others of tyranny. Slavery itself did
not strike them as unnatural, only tyranny by men they held to be
their equals. In the era of the Enlightenment, European colonists
throughout the Americas tended to believe that African slavery was a
necessary evil, and they had difficulty imagining a successful American colony (or nation) without it.[13]

Metaphors of slavery of course had particular resonance for people who were actually enslaved. In 1774 Massachusetts slaves drew on
the rhetoric of the Revolution as well as the Enlightenment and
Christianity to argue not just for individual emancipation but also for
a new goal: the complete abolition of slavery. They claimed that "we
have in common with all other men a natural right to our freedoms."
In 1777, abolitionist leader Prince Hall wrote a petition to the Massachusetts legislature arguing that slaves had "a natural and unalienable right to that freedom which the Great Parent of the universe
hath bestowed on all mankind."[14] But in Mobile, Petit Jean was unlikely to hear rhetoric that questioned hierarchy and dependence.
Probably no one in Mobile read Thomas Paine's *Common Sense* aloud
or erected a Liberty Pole, as they did in Atlantic coast cities.[15]

In war as in peace, enslaved people made different decisions based
on the circumstances of their bondage, and Petit Jean's slavery had
some freedoms within it. Petit Jean probably valued his important and
relatively independent work. Even though other people stole their
labor, some slaves took pride in skills and hard work and behaving
honorably. Indeed, those attributes could be particular points of pride
in the face of the common European belief that enslaved people had
no ambition or honor. Like all people, of course, slaves were individual human beings who thought and acted in a variety of ways. As

slaves, Petit Jean and his wife did not labor by choice in Mobile, and their loyalty was not necessarily to British West Florida or to their masters. Like many slaves and free blacks from New England to New Orleans, they would work for their own interests in white Americans' war for independence. Petit Jean would forward his family's personal independence by making others dependent on him.

CHAPTER SEVEN

Amand Broussard

AS THE REVOLUTIONARY WAR began, Amand Broussard was finally settling into a stable life. The twenty-six-year-old rancher was a respected and able-bodied young man who owned land, one hundred head of cattle, and twenty horses in the settlement of Attakapas, Louisiana. Although Broussard was a free man, his daily work was similar to that of Petit Jean in Mobile. He fed, watered, and milked the cows. When the cattle were ready to sell, he drove them into New Orleans, where he oversaw their slaughter and sale. He had done well enough to establish his own household and lay the foundation of a prosperous life for his two young sons. It was a life he was willing to risk in a fight against the British empire.[1]

Like Margaret O'Brien Pollock, Amand Broussard came from a family of rebels against British rule. Expelled with his family from Acadia (now on the Atlantic coast of Canada) by the British as a young boy, Broussard had hated the British his whole life. Living in Louisiana, he heard his parents, uncles, and aunts describe how the British had stolen his family's homeland, imprisoned them, killed people they loved, and sent the survivors into exile. This hatred trumped any desire Broussard had to be left alone in the good life he was building. When the Revolutionary War came to the Gulf Coast, he would once again fight the British alongside his Acadian (soon to be known as "Cajun") brothers and cousins. Perhaps this time he could save his home, as his father had failed to do in Acadia.

New France

Amand Broussard's father, Joseph Broussard (known as Beausoleil), and mother, Agnès Thibodeaux, met in Acadia, New France. Soon after they married in 1725, they moved to Petitcodiac on the Chignecto Isthmus, the contested border between British Nova Scotia and French Acadia (present-day New Brunswick). There the family settled with Joseph's brother Alexandre and Agnès's sister Marguerite, who were also married to each other. With their extended families, they farmed the land, fished in the Bay of Fundy, and traded with neighboring Mi'kmaq Indians. Amand Broussard was born around 1750 in a time of increasing conflict. From their base at Petitcodiac, Joseph and Alexandre Broussard joined with other French Canadians and Mi'kmaqs to fight against British forces and settlements in Acadia and northern New England.[2]

Amand Broussard's childhood was consumed by violence. The Seven Years' War turned the Acadian borderlands into an imperial battleground. In 1755, the British captured Amand's father, uncle, and older brothers during the siege of French Fort Beauséjour, on the border of Nova Scotia. In later years, Amand would hear the story of how his mother, determined to save her husband, brought her remaining children to the outskirts of the British fort and gained permission to visit the captives. In their refugee camp, as they prepared for the visit, Agnès gave five-year-old Amand and his young siblings and cousins knives and spoons to hide within their clothing. She warned the children to hold them tightly lest they drop or rattle and they all be killed. The women and children passed by the British guards and gave the men the food they had brought, along with the smuggled utensils. Slowly over the coming days, Amand's father and the other men used the knives and spoons to dig a tunnel under the fort's walls. Whether this story is accurate or not, they did manage to escape. If they had not, they would have been forcibly deported far from their families to resettlement within the British colonies, as almost seven thousand Acadians were that year.[3]

A Lost Homeland

The Broussards fled back to Petitcodiac to continue their resistance. For several more years, the Broussard men raided British forces and refused to accept incorporation into the empire. But French forces steadily lost ground, culminating in the fall of Quebec in September 1759. As the family ate the last of their provisions in the spring of 1760, Amand's parents knew that they could not hold out long. Ten-year-old Amand could see the worry on his parents' faces and feel the hunger in his belly. They decided to surrender.[4]

The British marched the men, women, and their dozens of children, including Amand, across the wooded coastal highlands onto a ship in the Bay of Fundy. It sailed around the tip of Nova Scotia (their old homeland) to the port of Halifax on the North Atlantic and dropped them in the same prison where his father had been held. There the families spent three long years as captives. After the war ended, the British forced the Broussard family onto a ship along with several hundred other Acadians, just a fraction of the fifteen thousand Acadians whom the British expelled and sent all over the Atlantic world in the process of seizing New France. From the terror of invasion and war, the Broussards headed into the terror of exile.[5]

Louisiana

For his entire life, Amand Broussard had been on the run from or imprisoned by the British. As the teenager sailed out of Halifax after years in prison, the open sea must have felt both exhilarating and frightening. After a stop at the French Caribbean island of Saint

Domingue, the Broussards sailed on to New Orleans, where they arrived early in 1765. His father and uncle had not been able to save their homes or their country, but they had led the family to safety and a new life in Louisiana.[6]

Although the war was over, the French still held New Orleans when the Broussards arrived. French Louisiana Governor Charles-Philippe Aubry welcomed the Acadian heroes with open arms. And they needed his help. Hungry and poor, they accepted the bread, rice, corn, flour, beef, and tools from the king's storehouse in New Orleans. Governor Aubry felt for their plight, "the result of their sacred attachment to their homeland and to their religion." He opened his bounty to them because, as he put it, "without these, what would become of them?" In an official proclamation, he praised the "valor, fidelity, and attachment in the service of the king" that Joseph Broussard "has given on different occasions," particularly his "efforts against the enemies of His Majesty." The governor appointed Joseph Broussard "Captain of Militia and Commandant of the Acadians."[7]

The Broussards joined other Acadians who had made their way by various routes to this last remaining French piece of continental North America. The governor granted them lands in the Attakapas district west of New Orleans. Benefiting from the population decline of the Attakapa Indians, the Acadians would have enough land for their children to have shares when they came of age. Governor Aubry set aside land for a church and lent the Broussards starter cattle: one bull and five cows. The Broussards planned to employ their Canadian ranching experience to provide cattle for New Orleans, which was chronically short of meat. Amand Broussard, now of age, enrolled in the militia.[8]

But things soon turned bad again. Amand Broussard's father as well as Uncle Alexandre and Aunt Marguerite fell ill and died soon after arriving. News came that the French crown had given Louisiana to the Spanish, who might be less sympathetic to the Acadians than their French compatriots. Although outgoing Governor Aubry realized that the Spanish would be wise to cultivate Acadian support, the new Spanish governor failed to follow through on Aubry's promises of land. In 1768, Louisiana-born French rose up against the new Spanish governor because of his efforts to regulate trade and reduce local rule. The rebellion's leaders were able to persuade Louisiana's hundreds of Acadians to join them in opposing "the injuries which are being done to them" by the Spanish.[9] When Spanish General Alejandro O'Reilly put down the uprising, he also wisely worked to prevent a future one by making concessions to locals whom the first Spanish governor had offended, including formalizing the Broussards' land grants in Attakapas.[10]

As the Acadians took up their land and settled into their new homes, Amand Broussard married a fellow Acadian refugee, the teen-aged Hélène Landry. The British had deported her family to Maryland, but they escaped poverty and discrimination in that British colony by finding passage on a ship to New Orleans. The young couple married in July 1771 and moved in with Amand's brother François in Attakapas. Amand and his cousin Pierre drove cattle from Attakapas on the trail that followed the bayous to New Orleans. Hélène lived long enough to bear a child, Joseph, a few months after the wedding. But soon thereafter the young mother died. In May 1775, at the age of twenty-five, Amand Broussard stood with Attakapas family and friends, including his young son Joseph, to celebrate his marriage to sixteen-year-old Anne Benoît. Anne had been born in exile in Maryland to Acadians. Like Hélène Landry's parents, they had made their way to Louisiana with their young daughter. By the time of his second marriage, Amand Broussard had faced death and disruption far beyond his years. But he was now a householder himself and owned one of the larger stocks of cattle in Attakapas. This time he was able to welcome his second bride into their own home, where she would care for his first son and their subsequent children, keep the house, work in the family garden, and weave cotton to make the family's clothes.[11]

Toward the Revolution?

Despite the circumstances of their arrival, the Acadians did well in Louisiana. They wrote to their fellow Acadians dispersed throughout the Atlantic world of the "goodness of the soil and climate of this colony" and the wealth to be made there.[12] The Louisiana Acadians grew both in population and in influence. Part of their prosperity came from selling their grain to the British in West Florida through the cross-empire trade of Oliver Pollock.[13]

Still, Louisiana's Acadians had not forgiven the British, whom they blamed for the years of war, imprisonment, and continuing exile. Living as a community in the place they called "New Acadia," they cast themselves as the heroes and the British as the villains in stories of the good life in French Canada, the breathtaking beauty of the rocky and fir-lined Acadian coastline, the bravery of their fathers and mothers, the Halifax prison, and the injustice of exile. When rebellion within some British colonies became war, they enjoyed Britain's troubles but little dreamed that this new war could be the opportunity to avenge their parents and prove themselves worthy Acadian heirs.

PART II

What to Do About This War?

NEW YORKERS CALLED 1777 the "year of the hangman." John Adams and the rebellion's other leaders would surely soon hang for treason, from real gallows shaped like the three sevens in "1777." In September, British General William Howe drove back George Washington's Continental Army at Brandywine Creek and then marched victoriously to the American capital at Philadelphia. John Adams, John Hancock, Richard Henry Lee, and the other members of Congress fled Philadelphia for western Pennsylvania as Howe's forces entered the city in triumph. Just over a year after the Continental Congress had boldly declared independence, the congressmen were on the run with a price on their heads. This was all-out war, and in 1777, betting against the British crown was a huge long shot. There were even rumors circulating among colonists and Indians in the south that George Washington had resigned his commission as the Continental Army's commander in chief and that the rebellion's end was imminent.

Still, that it was taking the British years rather than months to put down the rebellion revealed the truth in Thomas Paine's warning that the war would "try men's souls." Then in October, American generals Benedict Arnold and Horatio Gates won a surprise victory over British General John Burgoyne at Saratoga, New York. Over four hundred British soldiers died, and another several thousand surrendered. As the war dragged on, both the rebels and the British empire were busily recruiting allies. Each was trying to persuade undecided colonists and Indians that its side could best promote their political, economic, and personal independence and provide them imperial connections that would enhance their security and prosperity. Whichever side recruited the most powerful and active global allies would win the war. Colonists and Indians far from Philadelphia witnessed the recruitment efforts and discussed and debated the war, both to predict who would win and to determine how they could take advantage of the conflict.

CHAPTER EIGHT

Independence in Creek and Chickasaw Countries

AS DRUMS CALLED the council to session in the spring of 1777, Alexander McGillivray walked through Little Tallassee's public square and entered one of the council cabins. Wearing the standard Creek garb of a bright red turban, a white English-made linen shirt, blue leggings, and deerskin boots, he found a seat amid the growing crowd. Two older men in ceremonial dress entered slowly, singing softly and carrying conch shells and gourds. The vessels were filled with "black drink," a noxious liquid made by steeping a holly plant in water. Likely to induce nausea and perhaps vomiting, black drink symbolized renewal and ensured that participants had heads cleared from alcohol or heavy meals. The two men offered the drink to the town's two leading headmen. Each drank for as long as his server sustained a long fluctuating note. Then the assembled headmen, advisors, warriors, and visitors passed the shells. When McGillivray's turn came, the lukewarm liquid was bitter on his tongue, but it would not do to show any disgust. As the speeches began, he occasionally took a puff from a shared pipe and worked to follow what the men were saying.[1]

There was a lot to talk about in Creek councils in 1777. Indians between the Appalachian Mountains and the Mississippi River hoped that British soldiers would put the rebellious colonists back in their place, literally. The rebels should return to being loyal British subjects and obey their empire's Proclamation of 1763 ordering them to stick to the coasts and out of Indian country. Yet hoping for the empire's success and sending one's people to fight and die for it were quite different matters. As Alexander McGillivray was learning, Creeks did not necessarily agree that fighting for the British was their best path. McGillivray, like Payamataha among the Chickasaws, would find himself deep in debates over these questions as war spread far beyond Boston.

A Go-Between

At the start of the war, British officials urged Indians to stay out of what they believed would be a short conflict with some unruly colonists, but when the rebellion spread, Commander of British Forces Thomas Gage reversed policy and ordered Superintendent John Stuart to prepare southeastern Indians to "take arms against His Majesty's enemies."[2] By the time of McGillivray's arrival at Little Tallassee, Stuart and Deputy Indian Agent David Taitt were desperately trying to recruit Indians, sending them tens of thousands of pounds' worth of supplies. Rebels, too, began sending diplomats and gifts, hoping to gain their allegiance or at least their neutrality. At councils in the spring and summer of 1777, McGillivray heard both British and Choctaw emissaries discuss joining with the Creeks against Georgia.[3]

British officials hoped that McGillivray would help them recruit the Creeks. They had some reasons to be optimistic. Unlike Payamataha with his strategy of peace, McGillivray had no inclination to stay neutral in this war that had already taken his father's home and livelihood and threatened his mother's. On their return to Little Tallassee from his father's home in Georgia, he and his sister Sophia reintegrated themselves into his mother's household, which included their older sisters, Sehoy and Jeannette, and their children. McGillivray would have a particularly important relationship with his sisters' children because, as their maternal uncle in a matrilineal system, he was their closest male relative. With family and friends, McGillivray worked to refresh and improve his skills in the Coushatta Creek language he had spoken as a child and probably practiced occasionally when Upper Creeks visited Savannah. About a year after his arrival, McGillivray married Elise Moniac. By Creek and Chickasaw matrilineality, Elise Moniac was Chickasaw and could therefore help McGillivray establish Chickasaw connections.[4]

McGillivray also made an important patron, Creek headman Emistisiguo. Emistisiguo had met Lachlan McGillivray when he came as a young trader to live in Little Tallassee and had known Alexander since he was born. With Emistisiguo's help, Alexander McGillivray traveled around the sixty or so towns, getting to know Creeks and their country. He spent many an evening lounging in town plazas drinking with other men and betting on games of chunkey. As he traveled, he learned history from older Creeks, who used belts of beads to remind them of past events.[5]

McGillivray's town of Little Tallassee was growing in importance in the 1760s and 1770s. In Creek cosmology, white is the color of peace and diplomacy, and Little Tallassee was a "white town." When the British took over Mobile and Pensacola at the end of the Seven Years' War, Little Tallassee gained direct access to the British and became less dependent on the Creek towns that lay on the trading paths to the Atlantic coast. As the outbreak of the Revolutionary War made it harder for Creeks to get to Savannah and Augusta, trade and diplomacy at Pensacola and Mobile became more essential to the Creek Confederacy, and Little Tallassee's prominence grew further. As a member of the Wind clan with useful connections to British colonies, McGillivray was included in the councils of both Little Tallassee and the Creek Confederacy's periodic National Councils. Creeks gave him a title of respect, *Isti Atcagagi,* or "Beloved Man."[6]

Still, persuading the Creeks as a whole to fight for the British was far beyond McGillivray's power. No one could dictate foreign policy to even one Creek town or clan, much less the loose Creek Confederacy. And McGillivray had several strikes against him. Despite his lineage and connections, he was not a Creek headman or even a proven warrior, and the Creeks had plenty of both. He had lived outside the nation for most of his life. If he wanted an important role in Creek society and politics, he would need to brush up his skills in language and in the rough game of Creek stickball.[7]

Defending the Proclamation Line

Growing differences between the Creeks and the British added to the difficulties of serving as a go-between. Although allies, they disagreed about the war's purposes. The British sought to squash a rebellion by defeating armed rebels while persuading others to resume their loyalty to the crown. But to Creeks, land-hungry settlers were the problem. Arguments within the British empire over liberty, taxation, and representation were of no concern. British governance mattered only in its ability to prevent violations of the Proclamation of 1763.

Creeks figured that, as Little Tallassee headman Emistisiguo put it in 1776, "I have sat quietly a long time without joining either party, but the Virginians are now come very near my nation and I do not want them to come any nearer."[8] Creeks believed it was primarily Britain's job to crack down on its out-of-control colonies, but they were willing to join occasionally as long as they could fight in their own way. On his travels through Creek country, Alexander McGillivray could see small parties preparing for war against settlers and returning with tales of triumph or loss.[9]

Creek raids on the western settlements of Georgia and the Carolinas could advance Creek objectives and aid British military efforts by distracting rebel militia forces. As Superintendant John Stuart reported, Creeks were "willing to assist us but it must be in their own way . . . by excursions in small parties upon the settlements."[10] Surprise attacks, often at night, could be very effective. Frightening enemies with their wild cries and painted bodies, as much as their military might, was exactly the Creeks' idea of how to fight. A Creek warrior would fire one shot from his muzzle-loading musket on someone traveling or working in the fields and then rush forward with his hatchet for a short bout of hand-to-hand combat before retreating. Surprising isolated targets decreased the likelihood of Creek losses, served Creek warriors' desire for relatively easy victories and spoils, and could persuade the victims' surviving neighbors and relatives to cut their losses by moving back east. Equally important in the Creek Confederacy, small-scale raids required no unanimity. If an individual headman persuaded men of his own or other clans or towns to ride east to wreak havoc on illegal settlers, he needed no higher approval.[11]

Because they were punishing violators of the British Proclamation Line and assisting in Britain's own war, Creeks believed that the British should supply their raids. Creeks who went to British posts did not ask for supplies; they demanded them. European officials often viewed Indians as greedy and unreasonable, but their demands should be understood within the context of the region's diplomatic customs. Indians expected allies (whether European or Indian) to give them presents and host them lavishly when they visited to discuss possible joint warfare, just as they did when they hosted allies. For most American Indians, gifts and hospitality symbolized ties between peoples, and no time was more important for this kind of treatment than when one people asked another to go to war with them. The British repeatedly proved themselves stingy, and Indians learned to be wary.[12]

In contrast to Creek objectives, the British were fighting a war against rebel leaders and the Continental Army, not against settlers. British officials could never commit themselves fully to the prospect of Indian warriors scalping enemies or attacking settlers who were on Indian land but not rebelling against the crown. Attacks on settlements, especially if atrocities were committed, might convert non-partisans into rebels, the last thing the crown needed. The crown needed the same settlers the Creeks were targeting in order to rebuild the colonies after the war.[13]

As a diplomat, McGillivray knew that British officials were worried that Indians would create more rebels by committing atrocities, so he made a point of assuring John Stuart that they "did not massacre women and children, only attacking bodies of the rebels wherever they found them under arms."[14] But Stuart's superiors wanted more than assurances. They insisted that the Creeks were not to initiate conflict. British officers would order Creeks into battle when and where they needed them. However, like the colonial militiamen whom British officers were also trying to recruit and control, independent-minded Creek warriors did not want to fight where and how British officers chose.

Recent Cherokee history added to Creek reasons to avoid full-fledged war. Cherokees had attacked frontier settlements of Virginia and the Carolinas in the summer of 1776 and been badly defeated. As rebel forces destroyed towns, crops, livestock, and storehouses, hundreds of Cherokee refugees flooded into Little Tallassee and other Creek towns. Cherokee losses made many Creeks think twice about risking war. The refugees' tales of violence "damped the spirit of the Creeks," as John Stuart put it.[15] Also decreasing the appeal of war was refugees' pressure on food supplies, already short because of the previous year's poor corn harvest. In spring 1777, Stuart wrote that "the scarcity of provisions" among the Creeks "borders on famine."[16]

While Creeks weighed British requests, rebel leaders courted them without asking for much. Indeed, the rebels hoped that the Creeks would simply stay home. Georgia trader George Galphin was the rebels' best hope. He was a trader in Creek country who had married a Creek woman and participated in the Augusta Congress of 1763. In the summer of 1776, some two hundred Lower and Upper Creeks accepted Galphin's invitation to Augusta, where he read them an address by the president of the Continental Congress, John Hancock. Hancock informed them that the Revolution "is a family quarrel," not a concern to Indians whatsoever.[17]

The tour continued to Charleston, where the rebels put on a show, parading their garrison and militia for the visitors, showing off their batteries and forts, sailing around Sullivan's Island, walking Creeks through magazines of arms and ammunition and storehouses of goods, and welcoming them on board allied French ships in Charleston Harbor to demonstrate that Britain did not have a monopoly on sea power. Unfortunately for Galphin's efforts, a rogue rebel force from Georgia, mistaking the Creek delegation for a Coweta war party that had killed several Georgians, promptly marched them to prison in Augusta. Galphin rescued them and hoped that the Georgians had not destroyed his hard and expensive work.[18]

Despite Georgians' animosity, Creeks could see benefits in staying out of the quarrel. In October 1777, a group of Lower Creeks explained to John Stuart the rationale for neutrality. They agreed with John Hancock that the Revolution was a "quarrel among you and you are the same as one family." The Lower Creeks asserted that all Creeks had now agreed that "as you white people are at war with one another we are determined to sit neutral until you make the matter up with each other."[19]

Although they were exaggerating Creek unanimity, it was true that the Creeks were not putting all their eggs in the British basket. They could tell that Stuart was promising more than he could deliver. He claimed that the empire was organizing large forces of Indians and redcoats for a southern campaign, but the Creeks had seen no British soldiers. In the fall of 1778, Creeks accused Stuart of having deceived them. The failure of the British to end the rebellion, take back Georgia and the Carolinas, or protect the Cherokees caused plenty of discussion in Creek country. The Creeks naturally wondered whether their independence lay in continued alliance with the British. One Creek headman explained that, while he was "firmly attached to His Majesty's cause" and depended on Pensacola for supplies, he also knew that "the rebels though poor were numerous and powerful and had plenty of arms and ammunition." Because he "saw no force ready either to assist or protect" the Creeks, he worried that if he fought, he and his family might be driven from home, "as the Cherokees had been."[20]

After all, the empire could lose. The British had confidently assured Indians that they would mop up the little trouble in the north and then come south to reinstate order there too. Stuart rightly lamented that "until the Indians see the King's Troops get footing" in some of the southern provinces, "they will not be convinced that it is possible for His Majesty's arms to reduce them."[21] While his superiors might imagine that Indians served British interests, Stuart knew that they needed more than vague imperial assurances to inspire confidence. From 1776 through most of 1778, Creeks pursued a variety of options. Some Creeks raided while others stayed out of the fight, and some continued to meet with rebels.

Coordinating a War Effort

Because the British did not open a southern front, McGillivray was not under much pressure to align British and Creek action. Perhaps if the British had launched a full-scale attack on the southern colonies in 1776, they and their Indian allies could have persuaded the south to abandon the rebellion, thereby confining it to Pennsylvania and New England and perhaps ending it altogether. But that was a long shot, and the British never put it to the test. Instead, Stuart and his deputies kept assuring the Creeks that the king's troops were going to attack Georgia and the Carolinas "very soon."[22]

In the meantime, McGillivray found opportunities to show himself useful to both the British and Creeks. In September 1777, he was on the road from Little Tallassee to Okfuskee when he encountered a small group of Creek warriors. He asked them where they were bound, but they refused to answer, which was unusual and troubling. After several similar encounters with Creek riders, McGillivray stopped at a smaller Creek town for the night and sent a note to warn British Indian Agent David Taitt in Little Tallassee that something was going on. He was soon glad that he had. At sundown, an armed party of some 120 men, including, he believed, all of the headmen and warriors of Okfuskee as well as some from other towns, rode into town. They made no secret of their purpose: They were on their way to Little Tallassee to kill Taitt and Deputy Indian Superintendent Alexander Cameron.[23]

Drawing on all he had learned from Emistisiguo and other leaders about Creek speechmaking, McGillivray persuaded the party's leaders to come down from their horses to talk. After a prolonged discussion, they agreed to turn back and avoid the civil war that might result if they violently captured men protected by other Creek towns. In return, the party insisted that the British lay aside any plans to attack the rebels through Creek country with Creek help. They had promised the rebels not to help the British, and giving them free passage was help. McGillivray promised them that the British would consider their position, and he recommended to Stuart that he comply. When McGillivray got back to Little Tallassee, he was relieved to learn that Taitt and Cameron had gotten his message and fled to West Florida.[24]

By saving David Taitt and Alexander Cameron, McGillivray acted in accordance with Little Tallassee's mission as a "white" or "peace" town charged with keeping good relations both within and outside the confederacy. Emistisiguo and other Creeks certainly saw a useful ally in the young man with good British and Creek connections. When McGillivray wrote Stuart from his home in September 1777, Creeks literally surrounded him, pressing in such that "I can scarce turn about," talking and jostling, wanting to know what he was recording and how Stuart might reply.[25] And McGillivray's actions earned recognition from British officials. John Stuart wrote British Commander in Chief in North America William Howe, "I entertain great hopes and expectations from Mr. [Mc]Gillivray's alacrity and good sense. . . . His relations are powerful and will protect him."[26]

McGillivray was also able to take credit for Creeks riding to the rescue when rebels from Georgia threatened St. Augustine in August 1778. Confident from the victory at Saratoga and sure that the French would join their effort soon, Congress ordered the Continental Army and South Carolina and Georgia militia troops to invade East Florida. Unlike earlier alarms, to which the Creeks had not responded, the timing was good for the Creeks. They had just completed the Green Corn ceremony, a late summer celebration of thanksgiving honoring the ripening of the late corn, and they had reaped a good harvest. As Creek women picked, processed, and stored the corn, Creek men had the time and the provisions to head into battle.[27]

Several Upper and Lower Creek parties went to defend St. Augustine, while others raided settlements on the borders of Georgia and South Carolina, hoping to draw the rebel militia away from East Florida and back home to defend their farms and families. Later in August, another "war whoop was brought into the Nation," and at least two hundred Upper and Lower Creeks set out against Georgia.

McGillivray noted that the Creeks were "in high spirits," being "flushed with success" against the rebels, "accustomed to beat [them] at every skirmish." They told him to tell Stuart that they "have taken up the hatchet against the enemy and will never bury it until they have orders, from you."[28] Even Okfuskee seemed uninterested in the rebels' attentions, for now at least. Although the rebels had turned back before most of the Creeks reached East Florida, they had made a difference. Stuart grumbled that the Creeks "entertain very high ideas of their own consequence, thinking that we depend entirely upon their aid and assistance" but had to admit that the Creeks and Choctaws had "most certainly been very instrumentally conducive to the preservation of the two Floridas."[29]

The first big test of the Creek-British alliance and McGillivray's role in it came when British forces finally moved south at the end of 1778. Frustrated in the north, the crown decided to try to pick off its more valuable southern colonies one by one, starting with Georgia. British Lieutenant Colonel Archibald Campbell sailed with over three thousand troops from New York to Savannah. Guided by a local slave, Colonel Campbell attacked the Georgia militia from behind, and he and Admiral Peter Parker took possession of Savannah on December 29, 1778. Colonel Campbell combined his forces under General Augustine Prevost, who brought two thousand regular and loyalist militia forces north from St. Augustine. Officials hoped that once Georgia was secured, large numbers of loyalists from the Carolinas would flee there and form a base of fighters to retake South Carolina from the southeast while Creeks attacked from the southwest, Cherokees and Ohio Valley Indians struck from the northwest, and the navy blockaded the Atlantic ports.[30]

In the meantime, Chickamauga Cherokees and confederated Indians in the Ohio Valley sent wampum belts to the Creeks and other southeastern Indians to coordinate action against the Americans. Near the beginning of the war, when Cherokee leaders had made peace in exchange for land cessions, a young leader named Dragging Canoe continued the fight. He and around five hundred Cherokee families established new towns in the Tennessee Valley closer to the Upper Creeks, becoming known as the Chickamaugas. The belts they sent were stained red and black to indicate war plans against rebels. The emissaries called for all Indians "to forget former quarrels and to unite against the Virginians." A conference of Shawnees, Ottawas, Chickasaws, Cherokees, and Alabamas assembled at the Tennessee River to consider spring attacks on the rebels. Creeks sent a white wampum belt with Shawnee emissaries to Indians in the Illinois country proposing an alliance against the rebels.[31]

At last the long-promised British offensive had reached the south. British Secretary of State for the Colonies George Germain hoped that "seeing a body of victorious troops arrive in the southern provinces" would convince the Creeks "of the greatness of the King's power" and "the inability of the rebels to resist His Majesty's arms." In February 1779, David Taitt arrived at Little Tallassee from Pensacola and gave McGillivray and Emistisiguo the instructions for the Creeks to send large parties. Some were to raid rebel settlements on the Georgia and Carolina frontiers, while most should head for Augusta to cooperate with the king's troops arriving from Savannah and St. Augustine. Together they would reduce the rebels "to a state of obedience to their King."[32] He had already sent messengers to all of the Upper Creek towns to convene in Little Tallassee on February 20. McGillivray, Emistisiguo, and other Creeks listened to Taitt read Stuart's announcement that "what I have long and so frequently told you is at last come true—your great father is determined not to neglect you but has sent a considerable force in order to subdue the rebellious Southern Provinces."[33] At council, the Creeks decided to send out war parties. Within two weeks of the notice some five hundred Creek men set out, a surprisingly quick decision for such a major mobilization.

Communications, however, threatened to derail the British-Creek collaboration before it had really begun. Four hundred Creeks and loyalists started along the Upper Trading Path for Augusta on March 5, 1779, intending to meet Colonel Archibald Campbell. That very day, as Alexander McGillivray and David Taitt rode with the force, Taitt received a letter from Colonel Campbell accusing the Creeks of not coming when they were called. Not anticipating the months that letters took to travel from England to Pensacola and then the 250

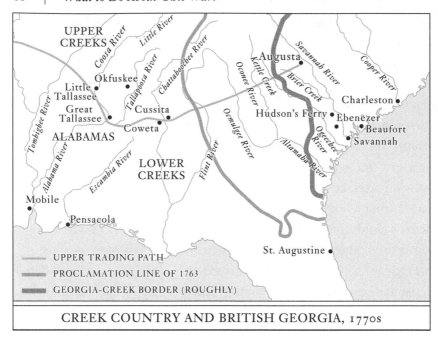

UPPER
CREEKS

Coosa River   *Little River*

Okfuskee
Little
Tallassee
Great
Tallassee
Tallapoosa River
Cussita

Chattahoochee River

ALABAMAS

Coweta

Tombigbee River

Alabama River

Escambia River

LOWER
CREEKS

Flint River

Ocmulgee River

Oconee River

Kettle Creek

Augusta

Brier Creek

Savannah River

Cooper River

Charleston

Hudson's Ferry   Ebenezer
Beaufort
Savannah

Ogeechee River

Altamaha River

Mobile

Pensacola

St. Augustine

——— UPPER TRADING PATH
▬▬▬ PROCLAMATION LINE OF 1763
▬▬▬ GEORGIA-CREEK BORDER (ROUGHLY)

CREEK COUNTRY AND BRITISH GEORGIA, 1770s

miles up to Creek country before Taitt and McGillivray could even begin to rally the Creeks, Colonel Campbell had set off with one thousand troops from Savannah to Augusta on January 24 intending to become the first officer "to take a stripe and star from the rebel flag of Congress" and proceed from there to invade South Carolina.[34] Yet when he reached Augusta on January 31, the original order for the Creeks had made it only as far as Pensacola. Knowing none of this, Colonel Campbell waited fourteen days at Augusta, dangerously far from the protection of his base at Savannah. Running low on provisions, he then received the news that American General John Ashe was on the march with over a thousand North Carolina troops.[35]

Hearing no word from his Creek and loyalist reinforcements, Colonel Campbell abandoned Augusta on February 13, 1779, and backtracked toward Savannah, taking a position at Hudson's Ferry. In anticipation of the British offensive, some 1,400 Georgians had sworn allegiance to the king and joined loyalist militia companies. But Colonel Campbell's retreat and South Carolina rebel militia Colonel Andrew Pickens's victory at Kettle Creek, on the other side of Augusta, prevented loyalists from coming south to join Campbell. Those setbacks, combined with violent intimidation by rebel militia, stopped new loyalist declarations. The most devoted loyalists had long since fled Georgia and the Carolinas for the Floridas, and the rest, having lived in rebel-controlled territory since 1776, saw the dangers.[36]

Knowing none of these developments, McGillivray and the other Creeks proceeded toward Georgia, and Taitt sent riders ahead to inform Colonel Campbell and General Prevost. Slowly, rumors began to spread among the Creeks that the British army had already been defeated or that this was all a rebel trick to attack Creek towns while the warriors were away. Some began to argue for returning home. On March 23, as Creek parties prepared to cross the Ogeechee River, Taitt finally got an answer from General Prevost ordering them to join him as soon as possible at his Ebenezer encampment, twenty miles from Savannah on the road to Augusta.[37]

These attempts to work together placed Creek and British objectives in stark contrast. The Creeks argued with Taitt over whether they could break into small raiding parties to plunder settlements on the Ogeechee River. Taitt knew that his superiors wanted not to anger loyalist or neutral settlers, but Creeks argued that these were all illegal settlements on their land.[38]

Disgruntled by Colonel Campbell's retreat and Taitt's attempts to command them, the Creeks split into smaller parties, and most turned northeast to attack frontier settlements between Augusta and South Carolina. McGillivray, the interpreter Jacob Moniac (McGillivray's father-in-law), and another fifty to eighty men continued on toward Savannah. On about April 2, a rebel force of about two hundred surrounded them near the Little River in Georgia. Under heavy fire, McGillivray rode to safety. When the smoke cleared, six Creeks and two of their white comrades lay dead. Two more white men were missing, presumably captured. McGillivray recovered and rode more somberly to Ebenezer. Taitt and a few others soon arrived in Ebenezer as well, but news had spread that General John Ashe's North Carolina troops had crossed the Savannah River and taken a position on Brier Creek to try to cut the Creeks off from the Army. The effort was beginning to seem like a fool's errand. When General Prevost's army was ready to march on South Carolina, a force of Upper and Lower Creeks joined, but all were driven back toward Savannah in May by

Continental Army General Benjamin Lincoln. Most of the Creeks went straight home, and those who stayed complained about the officers and demanded increased supplies for their extended service.[39]

The attempt to take Georgia had been the best chance for Creek and British war efforts to come together, but they failed. Although no one with any experience in the region believed that the Creeks would agree to be auxiliaries under the command of the British army, they might have coordinated their own large-scale raids with British army tactics. Similar combined efforts had worked for the French and their Indian allies in the early years of the Seven Years' War. But coordination proved frustrating for both the Creeks and the British. The Creeks were bewildered by Colonel Campbell's precipitous retreat from Augusta. British Secretary George Germain was furious that the Creeks had come late, and he charged Stuart with raising false expectations among the British "that parties were always in readiness to act with the King's Forces."[40] Most Creeks returned to supporting Creek-led raiding and diplomacy with both sides. Germain determined to cut funding for the Southern Indian Department, believing that it simply encouraged "a dissipation of the public treasure without obtaining any essential advantage from the service of the Indians."[41] This decision made future collaboration even less likely by severely limiting the supply of diplomatic presents to the Creeks.

While in Georgia, McGillivray had a chance to imagine a life outside Creek country. When Colonel Campbell occupied Savannah back in December 1778, Lachlan McGillivray returned from Britain to his nearby plantation, Vale Royal. Alexander McGillivray and his party stayed several months with him there. McGillivray might have made his home at Savannah, taking up his father's life as a planter and leader in the again-royal colony of Georgia. But the war was not over yet, even in Savannah. In September 1779, the British occupying the town were surprised to see a twenty-two-ship French armada under the feared French Admiral Charles Hector, Comte d'Estaing, appear off the coast. A few days later, Vale Royal found itself positioned between the French and American troops on one side and the earthen redoubts that hundreds of slaves were building to fortify the city. In early October, Admiral d'Estaing bombarded Savannah, while Continental Army generals Benjamin Lincoln and Casimir Pulaski attacked the redoubts. The city suffered heavy damage but held out. The French and American troops then launched a coordinated assault on Savannah but had to fall back after heavy losses, including the death of Pulaski. Worried by low supplies, sickness in the ranks, and the approaching hurricane season, French and Americans abandoned the siege on October 17.[42]

But McGillivray had left Savannah by then. The Creeks with him, discouraged by the long fight and homesickness, insisted on leaving during the siege. McGillivray chose to return with them to the place that was now his home too. Since his arrival in 1777, he had established himself as an important go-between for the Creeks and the British. He was exactly what both Creek and British leaders wanted: a man who understood both peoples and whose interests lay in helping them to get along. The British crown appointed him agent as well as commissary for the Upper Creeks.[43]

McGillivray knew that being a respected go-between could give him a life of prosperity and prestige in Creek country. A good leader provided for his people and made sure they knew it. McGillivray used his status to send notes with headmen or warriors bound for Pensacola or Mobile asking officials to give them supplies. When the British complied, McGillivray looked influential. When he distributed presents that the British sent for the Upper Creeks, he added to his prestige. Whenever Creek raiding parties went out against the rebels, McGillivray reported them to John Stuart, implicitly taking some credit, and he often met with various headmen among the Upper and Lower Creeks to ask for assurances of their alliance that he could pass on to the British. In one letter to Stuart, he called himself "the half-breed."[44] To a modern ear, "half-breed" sounds derogatory, but McGillivray was conveying to Stuart that being both Creek and British was a powerful combination. To Creeks, he also presented himself as both British and Creek. Being born to a mother of a matrilineal society and a father of a patrilineal one enabled him to have legitimacy in both societies. At the same time, McGillivray established his home and plantation on the Coosa River near Little Tallassee. Around his house was a "small village" of slave cabins and houses for family and friends. He prided himself on hosting both Indian and European visitors.[45]

As the war continued, McGillivray would keep trying to maintain the alliance between the disjoined Creeks and the overstretched and underfunded British. The task would become even more complicated as the Spanish entered the war. The Alabamas, part of the Creek Confederacy, were in charge of diplomacy with Spanish New Orleans and did not want to break with Spain. McGillivray's difficulties would increase with his ambitions in the coming years. In part because of his frustrations in trying to lead the Creeks to war, he eventually would seek to build a more unified Creek nation that could remain independent in a changing world, a mission that would prove at least as challenging as uniting thirteen colonies into an independent country.

Chickasaw Peace and British War

As McGillivray tried to coordinate Creek actions against colonists, the spreading war within the British empire would test Payamataha's policies of peace. Since the Seven Years' War, Chickasaw and British mutual desires for stability had reinforced each other, but now that the British were at war, they assumed that their longtime Chickasaw allies would send warriors to fight on their side. West Florida Governor George Johnstone expressed the common British view of the Chickasaws at Mobile in 1765, calling them "generous friends . . . whom neither dangers could startle nor promises seduce from our interest."[46] In the Revolutionary War, British officials hoped that the Chickasaws, the Choctaws, and the Quapaws would join "in a general confederacy with the Creeks and Cherokees to act as shall be judged best for His Majesty's Service."[47] General William Howe commended the Chickasaws and other southeastern nations on "receiving the Great War Belt"—the call to arms against the rebels—"with so much cheerfulness," which "alarms the rebels."[48]

Chickasaw protection of the Mississippi was a vital component of British strategy. As early as 1776, Deputy Indian Superintendent Charles Stuart—John Stuart's brother—had predicted that rebels could "with great facility come down the Ohio into the Mississippi and take possession of all the western parts of the colony" because of Britain's lack of troops and strong settlements.[49] Talking in the awkward style that high-ranking British officials often used for Indians, General Howe expressed his confidence in a letter to southeastern Indians that "the Red people will jointly have a watchful eye over the back parts of this country while the warriors of the great King . . . are employed to subdue and bring to reason the bad white people who in so unnatural a manner have raised the hatchet against the red brethren as well as against their father the great King."[50] British officials also urged the Chickasaws to keep an eye on Spanish shipping on the Mississippi in case New Orleans was supplying the rebels, as merchants like Oliver Pollock were indeed doing.

At Mobile in 1777, Payamataha pledged his nation's continuing allegiance to Britain; however, that he brought only forty Chickasaws was a troubling sign for the British, who knew that important diplomatic negotiations involved hundreds of representatives. Payamataha explained that most Chickasaws had stayed home because of rumors that the rebels were going to invade. A few months earlier, Chickasaws had hinted that they might not be able to guard the Mississippi River because they might need to be hunting. While of course Chickasaws did need to hunt and to protect their towns, the British were rightly worried at the wavering of their presumed best ally. The British representatives urged Payamataha not to let the Americans talk them out of their longstanding British alliance. John Stuart did his best to encourage the distinction between rebellious settlers who wanted "to possess themselves of your lands" and the king, who, he alleged, with the Proclamation of 1763 had summoned "all the force of the laws and the greatest vigilance on our parts to preserve your lands."[51]

Despite his assurances to the British, Payamataha used his time in Mobile to work on a wider peace. Although Stuart believed that the strategy "to sit still and remain inactive spectators of the rebellion" was the "insidious" advice of "rebel agents and some worthless traders," the man he thought was his strongest ally was one of this strategy's main proponents.[52] Indians knew Payamataha as the man who

could broker peace deals between Indian nations. In Mobile, Payamataha helped negotiate between the Creeks and the Choctaws. When
the Choctaws wanted help forging an alliance with the Cherokees
and the Creeks wanted the same kind of help with the Quapaws, they
all, as a British agent observed, "applied to the Chickasaws." This role
was not lost on the British, who worried that these efforts would
spread to Spanish alliances. And indeed, in 1777 Payamataha sent a
commission across the Mississippi River to discuss joint interests with
the Quapaws and the Spanish.[53]

Attack on the Mississippi

For the first few years of the war, Payamataha was able to assure the
British of Chickasaw loyalty while in fact not guarding the Mississippi or putting any warriors at risk at all. But in the spring of 1778, a
rebel force came down the Ohio and Mississippi, just as General
Howe had feared, and exposed Payamataha's strategy. In July 1777,
Congress's Indian Affairs Agent George Morgan proposed to Congress that the rebels plot with the Spanish governor of Louisiana, Bernardo de Gálvez, to take West Florida from the British. Morgan would
coordinate through Oliver Pollock, whom he knew as the New Orleans representative for his company, which had sent furs from the
Illinois country down the Mississippi before the war. After hearing
Morgan's proposal, John Adams, Samuel Adams, Benjamin Harrison,
and other members of the Board of War recommended that the Congress fund one thousand men, to be led by Continental Army General
Edward Hand and supported by Spanish artillery, supplies, and
ships.[54]

Congress had to decide whether attacking West Florida would
weaken the British and bring new assistance and benefits to the American side or drive undecided West Floridians into the arms of the
British, just as the British feared that attacking settlers would drive
them to rebel. In late July, representatives including Pennsylvania
Congressman Robert Morris spoke on the floor of Congress in favor
of invading West Florida. They extolled the benefits of destroying

British trade on the Mississippi, seizing British goods, deflecting British military action from the thirteen colonies, and damaging Britain's "connections with the Indians" by revealing British vulnerability. Benedict Arnold, with whom George Morgan had conferred before taking the plan to Congress, deemed it "an object of importance, not only as an acquisition of territory," but also to "open a door for a very considerable and lucrative trade, with the Spaniards and Indians." Arnold and Morgan hoped to make West Florida "the fourteenth state in the American union" by sending at least a thousand men from Fort Pitt and a naval force from the Gulf.[55]

Other Congressmen raised powerful counterarguments. The United States had no men and supplies to spare for a new front and could not hold it if victorious. West Florida's loyalists would defend against the attack. The opposition feared that fevers of the south would weaken the troops, that Britain had strong Indian allies there, and that they might trigger a British or Creek attack on the rebelling southern colonies. Delegate Henry Laurens, representing South Carolina, one of those vulnerable colonies, feared that Governor Gálvez would "entertain no high estimation of our political forecast" if American troops embarked with the assumption that the Spanish would supply an expedition "before treaty or even consultation."[56] The southern colonies of South Carolina and Georgia were only barely willing to risk revolt. If the fight came south and sparked rebellion or flight among the region's slaves, those colonies might flee back to the British.

There were not enough votes to approve Morgan's proposal to invade West Florida; however, a few Congressional supporters of the idea embarked on a strategy that belied their principles of representative government. Without approval from Congress as a whole, Congressmen Robert Morris of Pennsylvania and William Smith of Maryland approached James Willing, a man with connections in both Philadelphia and New Orleans. James Willing was from a prominent family that included mayors of Philadelphia. His older brother Thomas was a partner in Robert Morris's mercantile firm Willing and Morris, the firm with which Oliver Pollock had begun his career. In the early 1770s, Thomas Willing had helped his brother James establish a dry goods store north of Baton Rouge, in partnership with Pollock. Like Pollock, James Willing had urged his neighbors to join the rebellion against their empire and make West Florida the fourteenth colony represented at Philadelphia. However, Willing was not nearly as successful in business as Pollock, and his talk of revolution had mostly occurred when he was deep in drink, a not uncommon state. When he fled for Philadelphia in 1777, many assumed that he was escaping his debtors.[57]

Congressmen Robert Morris and William Smith commissioned James Willing as a captain in the navy and ordered him to pick off vulnerable British posts along the Mississippi, seize loyalist property in the name of the United States, and appeal to Governor Gálvez and Pollock at New Orleans for support. Not long after, at Fort Pitt at the forks of the Ohio River where the Allegheny and Monongahela rivers come together (where Pittsburgh now lies), Willing presented General Edward Hand with this supposed commission and orders to provide him with men, a gunboat, and a share of the gunpowder, musket balls, and provisions that Pollock had already sent there.[58]

Carried swiftly by the Mississippi's high late-winter waters, Willing's gunboat, the *Rattletrap*, floated down the Ohio River from Fort Pitt and then down the Mississippi right past where the Chickasaws were supposed to be guarding. At the very time that the *Rattletrap* was descending, John Stuart was assuring British Secretary of State for the Colonies George Germain that the Chickasaws and Choctaws were examining every boat that tried to descend the Mississippi. If there was any blockade at all, Willing and his men easily got past it. They surprised the British posts of Natchez and Manchac, pulled down each fort's Union Jack, and raised their own standard—a homemade combination of stars and stripes. Some of Willing's men overtook the crew of the sixteen-gun schooner *Rebecca*, anchored just off British Manchac and loading for London. Completely ignoring Congress's concerns that violence would increase the appeal of imperial protection, Willing and his men attacked private homes and farms on the British side of the river, surprising inhabitants, capturing slaves, and taking property.[59]

George Germain charged that it was the Chickasaws' fault that "so inconsiderable a body of the rebels" was able to get through. He could not "conceive it possible that, after so large an expense incurred in the Indian department," Indians could not have managed to guard the river.[60] Germain had paid a lot of money and gotten little in return. Stuart had to agree that "had the Chickasaws done what was required of them we might have had earlier intelligence of this invasion."[61] Maintaining a blockade on the Mississippi was not as easy as Secretary Germain assumed. The Mississippi is wide, with many islands to hide behind and great trees with overhanging branches to obscure the view. All kinds of boats and canoes passed all the time, and rebels out of uniform did not look noticeably different from normal river traffic. More important, Chickasaws aggressively patrolling for the British and Quapaws doing the same for the Spanish would threaten their newly forged peace with each other. The safest choice was for both to ignore European traffic on the river altogether.[62]

Smoothing over Differences

Still, Chickasaw inaction went far beyond letting James Willing slip past. Southeastern Indians had a well-established system of passing news from community to community. Yet no Chickasaws even sent word when Willing was raiding plantations and forts on the Mississippi River, and no Chickasaws came to the British when they called for help. As Willing forced people to show their hands, Payamataha found his strategy of peace exposed. It was easy enough to pledge support when no follow-up was necessary. It would take some skillful diplomacy to keep the strategy from backfiring and creating enemies out of disappointed allies.[63]

In staying out of the fighting, Payamataha and the Chickasaws also went against the Northern Indian Confederacy, which by 1778 was urging Nativist alliance against the American rebels. Nativists knew that a major point in their own favor in the eyes of the Chickasaws was Benjamin Franklin's tireless recruitment of a French alliance for the United States. A Shawnee visiting the Chickasaws spread the news, knowing that the Chickasaw history of wars against the French would

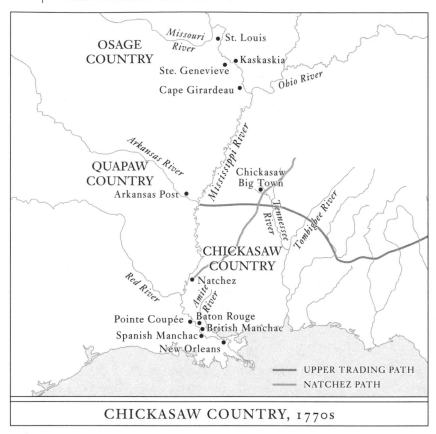

CHICKASAW COUNTRY, 1770s

increase the appeal of fighting against an alliance of France and the land-hungry rebels. Still, fighting against even the French would violate Payamataha's strategy. Chickasaws therefore continued to make vague promises while staying out of the fighting.[64]

Payamataha also faced pressures that had nothing to do with the war against the Americans. Deer and other game were declining on Chickasaw lands as Indians and Europeans ventured onto Chickasaw lands to pursue new populations. In turn, Chickasaw hunting bands began traveling west of the Mississippi, where their new alliance with their old Quapaw enemies was essential. The Quapaw population had declined dramatically from at least five thousand in the 1680s to fewer than a thousand, and Quapaw hunters were happy to have allies along on their hunts to fend off their greater enemy, the Osages.[65]

Payamataha traveled to Pensacola in the summer of 1778 to persuade the British that their alliance was still intact. For several days, he met with John Stuart to explain Chickasaw reasons for letting the British down. He claimed that Chickasaw country was dangerously close to Fort Pitt and other rebel strongholds on the upper Ohio. Returning to his language of self-deprecation, Payamataha explained that the Chickasaws were too "intimidated" to act very strongly in the king's interest, for fear that the rebels might attack their homes. He also claimed that the Chickasaws were such steadfast British allies that they would not fight against men who, although rebelling, were still British.

Stuart tried to assure Payamataha that the rebels "had forfeited their right to the protection of the Great King and the British nation by their apostasy and rebellion." But he could not claim that they were not British. After all, the whole point of the empire's war was to return the rebelling colonies to imperial control. Insisting on the common Britishness of the empire and its rebelling subjects, Payamataha agreed that rebellion might give the British reason to crack down with violence, but "he could not bring himself to imbrue his hands in the blood of white people without the greatest reluctance." Payamataha was speaking through an interpreter, so it is not clear what Chickasaw phrase he used. His term may have been less racialized than the interpreter's "white people," for certainly in the past he had not hesitated to kill Frenchmen. In any case, Payamataha turned his refusal to fight for the British into a virtue, claiming that he "shuddered at the apprehensions of committing some fatal blunder by killing the King's friends instead of his enemies."[66]

A flimsy excuse delivered humbly may win over someone who wants to be persuaded. Payamataha surely knew that Stuart was not completely convinced that rebels five hundred miles away could awe the Chickasaws or that Payamataha could not send news of armed vessels without bloodying his hands. But what choice did Stuart have? He entirely depended on Payamataha as his connection to the Chickasaws. Payamataha and Stuart finally agreed that in the future the British would not ask Chickasaws to attack rebels. Instead, Chickasaws would only stop armed parties from descending the river and Spanish supplies from ascending to aid the rebels. Payamataha "cheerfully acquiesced" and promised to try to persuade the rest of his nation.[67] Stuart resumed assuring George Germain that the Chickasaws were "out scouting upon the banks of the Ohio and Mississippi" to stop or at least give notice of rebels. According to Stuart, the Chickasaws and Choctaws were prepared "to act in defense of this province upon any orders for that purpose from me." He had to admit to Germain that he was telling the Chickasaws that reinforcements were imminent and was spending large amounts of funds because Indians had suffered from shortages and because they knew "that in fact we have not been able to do without them."[68] The Chickasaws understood their power.

While Payamataha's support for the British was tempered by his desire to avoid war, he was not tempted to ally with the rebels. He might tell Stuart that loyalists and rebels looked the same to him, but when real rebels came calling, Payamataha identified them as land-grabbers who showed no respect for Indian or British authority. When in May 1779 Virginians were sending militia troops west to fight the British in Illinois, they proposed alliance and threatened violence if the Chickasaws did not accept. Payamataha reacted strongly. He rejected the false claims of power that future Americans believed came with the Revolution and independence. In contrast to the show of self-deprecation toward the British, the Chickasaws responded in a letter that portrayed themselves as a dominant and well-connected nation and the rebels as unruly children. They countered an American avowal of fraternal friendship by writing, "I can't see how you can call us brothers when we are daily informed" by Indians from the Ohio Valley that they were "threatening to destroy us and take our land from us." Payamataha knew that mentioning Ohio Valley Indians would put fear into Virginian hearts, and he added his own explicit threats. "Take care that we don't serve [you] as we have served the French," the Chickasaws warned, and "send you back without your heads."[69]

The Chickasaws reminded Virginians of what the British empire had given all of them. "When we were distressed by our enemies and likely to be a lost Nation," the British crown had helped them both against the Choctaws, the French, and their other enemies. Since the Seven Years' War had ended, the Chickasaws said, "we increase and live in peace and plenty therefore you cannot expect we will throw such a faithful Father's hand away." Highlighting the hypocrisy and peril in the Virginians' request for French assistance, the Chickasaws declared themselves "very much surprised that you would cry for assistance to a people"—the French—"who some time ago would roast you and even eat you." When the French threatened the British colonies, the Chickasaws recalled, King George "rose up and assisted you and drove your enemies and made you live happy." Now, the Chickasaws warned, "if you are desirous of being brothers with us you must bury the hatchet you lifted against our Great Father and take it up against the French."[70] Payamataha, Mingo Houma, and other Chickasaw headmen wrote a similar letter to the Spanish to warn them to avoid allying with the French if they wanted to remain friends with the Chickasaws.[71]

Conclusion: *While the Sun Shines*

Although the British hoped for more active assistance, Payamataha was living up to his promise from more than twenty years earlier that "the day shall never come while sun shines and water runs that we will join any other nation but the English."[72] He was not tempted to ally with the rebels. But Payamataha's strategy of peace was not even-handed neutrality. He hoped that his people could be allies of the British and enemies of the French without having to risk their lives or their new alliances with Indians of the region. He struggled to prevent Chickasaw alliances with any Europeans or Indians that would draw them into war.

As the war came to the Mississippi Valley and Gulf Coast, the Creeks and the Chickasaws would continue to work on behalf of their own interests, which were precipitously diverging from fighting alongside the British.

CHAPTER NINE

To Fight for Britain?

IN MAY 1777, as Petit Jean drove cattle across the flatlands just north of Mobile, he saw the camps of thousands of Chickasaw, Creek, Choctaw, and other Indians, including Payamataha, who had come to town to conduct diplomacy with the British and one another. For a slave, the threat of war, like most things, meant work. While Petit Jean drove cattle into Mobile to provide feasts for the Indian delegations, other slaves in West Florida and Louisiana worked alongside colonial soldiers to fortify the coast's defenses.

Every place in the colonies that the war was fought saw neighbors pitted against neighbors as they were forced to take sides. Along the Gulf Coast, imperial and regional reasons to choose a side ranged from expanding or defending one's empire, to seeking the upper hand in changing regimes, to promoting trade, to individual glory or revenge. For those advocating involvement in the war on either side, recruiting people of diverse backgrounds and conflicting motivations would not be easy. Even persuading their own people to risk their lives could be tricky.

The American Revolution proved that British officials could not take the loyalty of colonists for granted. As war began to threaten the Gulf Coast's security and prosperity, imperial officials would have to persuade colonists that short-term sacrifices would advance their long-term interests. Just as Indians understood their importance to the British, the colonists, who in time of peace had little influence over their empires, could now perceive both opportunities and dangers.

Petit Jean and the Opportunities and Dangers of War

Both the British and their rebellious subjects were ambivalent about arming enslaved and free blacks. East Florida Governor Patrick Tonyn established black militia companies to defend against invasion by rebels from Georgia in 1776, but West Florida faced no such invasions early in the war. At the same time, the evidence of a planned slave insurrection at Natchez had increased white West Floridians' fear of slave violence. After the fall of Savannah in 1778, Congress declared that the states should enlist slaves and that Congress would compensate masters and give freedom and fifty dollars to any who survived the war, although recruiters in South Carolina and Georgia refused. On the British side, General Henry Clinton, who replaced William Howe as commander in chief of British forces in America in 1778, extended Lord Dunmore's Virginia promise that any slaves who ran away from rebelling masters to fight for the British would win their freedom.[1]

Some British officials saw these proclamations as a legitimate use of state power because the slaveholders were in open rebellion against their king, but even on this issue there was a debate in Britain. Arming slaves was not a new practice, but promising freedom for service was. The opposition claimed that undermining the state's obligation to protect property was a dangerous precedent. In contrast to Spain, where there was no such debate, British lawmakers saw protecting private property as the state's primary responsibility. Certainly there was no such proclamation for non-rebelling colonies. British officials feared that even temporarily requisitioning slaves from loyalist masters might nudge them into rebellion. Indeed, the war within the British empire in part resulted from differing opinions on the legitimate authority to govern and appropriate gentlemen's property.[2]

The Spanish did not hesitate to use enslaved and free black militias. Throughout the Spanish and French empires, militias included slaves. Some officials even thought they made better soldiers than free men, in part because they were accustomed to following orders or had fewer ties to home.[3]

In the spring of 1778, word spread through the region's slave communities of James Willing's attacks on Mississippi Valley plantations. The men burst into homes with their guns drawn, declaring they were acting in the name of the United States of America. The rebels seized all the valuables they could load onto their vessels, including enslaved people. They could have swelled their ranks by recruiting the slaves into their expedition, but Willing treated the slaves as property and sold them in New Orleans with the help of Oliver Pollock. Nearly a hundred men, women, and children were auctioned in New Orleans to new owners. The expedition's supporters in Congress had instructed Willing to sell enslaved people and goods to finance American independence.[4]

Families were torn apart as Willing treated them as the spoils of war. Many of the enslaved people had not been in West Florida long, having already fled from the Revolution with their masters. Enslaved men and women in Mobile and other parts of West Florida and Louisiana shuddered to think that these raiders could seize them from their homes and communities to sell them to unknown masters in unknown places. Some of those whom Willing's men had captured tried to escape, in some cases back to their West Florida masters. For example, a few slaves who found themselves in New Orleans saw their master, Anthony Hutchins, who had come to New Orleans looking for them. They escaped to join back up with Hutchins.[5]

Fleeing back to one's master is not the kind of escape we expect from slaves, but returning to home, friends, and family was often preferable to being enslaved among strangers. Often, freedom from enslavement could seem a considerably less pressing goal than security and community. A man named Seraba escaped from the man to whom Willing had sold him and found his West Florida master, a man named Watts. Knowing Watts was also in New Orleans, Seraba disguised himself and hid until his master could find a boat to take them back home. Other slaves took advantage of the chaos to escape their masters. One of Oliver and Margaret Pollock's own slaves, a young man named Wilks, escaped from New Orleans on a British boat heading for Manchac. Perhaps the captain promised him freedom, or possibly Wilks paid for his passage, posing as a free man. He gambled that an unknown future would be preferable to the slavery in New Orleans he knew well.[6]

The contrasting stories of Seraba and Wilks remind us that enslaved people were individuals with their own desires, priorities, and decisions. Upheavals among their masters offered opportunities for the enslaved, who were on the alert for chances to better their situations, however they defined that improvement and in whatever ways they could seek it. Petit Jean and his wife would keep their eyes open to see how the war developed.[7]

The Bruces and Family Independence

As absentee slaveholders, James and Isabella Bruce did not face the terror of refugees near the Mississippi when James Willing came through. Still, their plantation on the Amite River was "reduced to ashes." Thirty of their enslaved women and men either fled or were captured. The marauders destroyed the indigo works being prepared for the Bruces' first indigo harvest. The Bruces estimated that Willing's raid cost them over two thousand pounds, and it endangered their whole reason for being five thousand miles from home: to profit from plantations.[8]

James Bruce earned a small salary and a percentage of Pensacola's port revenues, but land was the route to wealth in the British colonies. As James later recalled, "having a family and finding the business of the port but inconsiderable," he had decided "to settle a plantation."[9] By 1777, the family had acquired several plantations, amassing over ten thousand acres along the Amite and Mobile rivers and Thompson's Creek. All of these areas were west of Pensacola, inland enough to escape the coast's sandy soil but not so far inland to anger Choctaws or Creeks.[10]

How the Bruces built their holdings reveals much about the British colonies' dependence on cheap land to create colonial prosperity. Some of the land was James's original four-thousand-acre grant, which had drawn him to West Florida in the first place. In addition, under the headright system, designed to encourage immigration and economic development, James claimed one hundred acres as a householder and an additional fifty acres of land for each of his dependents. As the West Florida land boom accelerated, the Bruces also gained another two thousand acres as a second royal grant, a thousand acres of which was in Isabella Bruce's name. She did not own these acres—under coverture, married women could not own land in the British empire. Rather, the Bruces doubled the maximum royal grant the governor could give them by asking under two separate names, a strategy employed by many other members of His Majesty's Council for West Florida and the governor himself, who registered land in the name of his live-in companion, Martha Ford. For landowners, continued prosperity depended on regional stability and, at least for Floridians, a strong British empire.[11]

James would take occasional months-long trips to his plantations over 250 miles from Pensacola, traveling by ship out to the Gulf, past Mobile, across Lake Pontchartrain and Lake Maurepas, and then by smaller boat up the Amite and Iberville rivers, knowing that Spaniards, Choctaws, or other Indians could appear on these contested rivers at any time. Because the family lived in Pensacola, James did not build a plantation house but instead stayed in the one-room house built for his overseer. From there, he could see imposing old oaks, corn fields, a flour mill, chicken houses, hog pens, and slave quarters. About thirty slaves, men and women of African and possibly American Indian descent, did the work that made the plantation profitable. While the Amite River plantation produced mostly cornmeal, neighbors' plantations raised indigo, tobacco, and rice. If James Bruce toured in the months before James Willing's raids in the spring of

1778, he would have seen the slaves clearing some land and setting up vats and drying sheds to process it into dye for England's textile mills. The pine logs they cleared were destined for the ships and buildings of a growing empire.[12]

For now these were outlying plantations, but the owners hoped someday to live there in a thriving town with its own fort, church, and school as well as access to the Gulf via the Amite and Iberville rivers. Peter Chester, who became West Florida's governor in 1770, hoped that settling that region would help West Florida "become one of the most flourishing colonies in America" and place it in a position to seize Louisiana from Spain with help from the Choctaws, Chickasaws, and smaller tribes along the Mississippi if war erupted. The Bruces hoped to have their own plantations and to speculate on the land as well. When a growing population increased the value of their Thompson's Creek lands, they sold a thousand acres of it.[13]

James Willing and the Ambitions of West Floridians

The congressmen who secretly supported James Willing's expedition down the Mississippi hoped that West Floridians like the Bruces would rally to their cause. They assumed that West Floridians had a natural desire to join the forces of liberty and that only Britain's iron fist held them back. West Floridians had protested against the Stamp Act and the Intolerable Acts. Plus, the region had been French only fifteen years earlier, and surely the French colonials had no loyalties to their British conquerors. Congress amended its Articles of Association in June 1775 to add West and East Florida, along with Canada, as provinces that "shall be admitted into, and entitled to all the advantages of this Union" should they choose to join.[14] Samuel Adams spoke for many when he declared that "nature designs we should have" the Floridas and Canada.[15] Congressional Indian Affairs Agent George Morgan believed that only the presence of British troops kept non-rebelling places "under the dominion of England."[16]

But Morgan was wrong. By the time of Willing's raid, much of

West Florida's population had fled the violence of the Revolution only a year or two before. The huge emigration from South Carolina and Georgia helped the rebels gain a popular edge in those colonies but nudged public opinion in the Floridas toward Britain. And Willing's violence and thieving prompted British and French West Floridians to join together in condemnation of Willing and, by extension, the rebels. Over the previous fifteen years, the French speakers whose lands became British after the Seven Years' War had grown accustomed to British governance. Sharing the same goals of profitable commerce and independent daily living as English-speaking colonists, they proved to be fairly amiable neighbors with each other and with colonists across the Mississippi in Spanish Louisiana. In contrast, this band of "Rebel Freebooters," as British Deputy Indian Superintendent Alexander Cameron called them, did not inspire rebellion among the already-nervous people of West Florida.[17] They soon wanted protection from these armed raiders more than from British taxation. Virginian George Rogers Clark believed that West Floridians might have joined the United States if Congress had sent more appealing emissaries, rather than men for whom "plunder is the prevailing passion."[18]

In a 1778 circular letter sent to the English- and French-speaking communities between the Appalachians and the Mississippi, British Lieutenant Governor and Superintendent of Indian Affairs at Detroit Henry Hamilton outlined what the British empire offered them that the rebellion did not. What did residents of "so remote an establishment" want? "Nothing more . . . than the enjoyment of a free trade, the secure possession of property, and the tranquility of private families." All of those interests were best served within "the dominion of the King of England." Any who turned against the king would not only lose those benefits, Hamilton threatened, but be invaded by the king's troops and his Indian allies.[19]

Willing's behavior was evidence to support Hamilton's letter. The crown's opponents in the thirteen colonies were pirates and perhaps traitors to the empire, not rebels with a cause. Pensacola had been on edge since the previous fall, when Indian Agents Alexander Cameron and David Taitt rode their winded horses into town with their tale of how Alexander McGillivray had narrowly saved their lives. Hundreds of Upper and Lower Creek men and women had followed Cameron and Taitt to Pensacola to assure the British that the threats were an anomaly and that the Creeks were committed to their British alliance. They came in peace, but for the Bruces and other Pensacola residents, the large numbers of Indians were also a palpable—and probably intentional—reminder of Creek power. In the winter and spring of 1778, Pensacola was full of Creeks, Cherokees, and Choctaws, with large parties arriving weekly, including one with Alexander McGillivray.[20]

Visiting Indian warriors were one of several signs that the war might reach Pensacola and endanger the life that the Bruces had built on this far edge of empire. News that the British had taken Philadelphia in September 1777 had prompted hopes that the war would end soon, but Willing's descent sent Pensacolans back to worrying over their inadequate defenses. As Isabella Bruce walked in the streets named for British kings and politicians, the town's fortified garrison in the middle of the square was a reminder that if Pensacola was attacked, she and her family would take refuge there. In the meantime, it was the center of the town's business and social life, where the large clock marked the passage of time and British soldiers and visiting Indians conducted business at the king's storehouse. From Pensacola, she could see the ships in the bay below and, on the heights above, the fort named for King George, where James Bruce went for the meetings of His Majesty's Council.[21]

Defending West Florida

Conversation at the Bruce dinner table surely included talk of the war and the possibility of invasion. Back in the fall of 1776, James Bruce had voted with the rest of His Majesty's Council for West Florida to recommend that the crown fortify Pensacola's and Mobile's defenses and send more ships to protect its waters. The council and the governor established a horse patrol above Pensacola to bring advance warning of any attack. Rumors of impending invasion circulated, made more frightening by the fact that it could come from any direction. The Bruces, like many of their neighbors, suspected that Spain's neutrality would not last.

Even before Willing's attack, Governor Peter Chester had asked British Secretary George Germain for more troops. Germain approved work on a barracks at Pensacola and the use of a frigate and an armed schooner to guard Lakes Pontchartrain and Maurepas from invasion. However, he refused Chester's request for troops and supplies, determining that the threat of rebel invasion was too slight to draw resources away from active fronts. If attacks came, so would Indian allies to defend West Florida. In denying Governor Chester's request, Germain exhibited the common bureaucratic view of Indians as at the empire's disposal. He assumed that the supplies Britain had provided its Indian allies in the past had bought their willingness to send warriors to defend any threatened posts. He would soon learn otherwise.[22]

Not only did Governor Chester and the Council not have substantial aid from the regular army or Indian allies, they could not even increase West Florida's tiny militia. The colony had hundreds of able-bodied men who might have formed a formidable militia. The trouble was the General Assembly, the lower house of West Florida's legislative branch. The twelve appointed members of His Majesty's Council, including James Bruce, served as the upper house. To provide balance, the colony's voters elected the fourteen members of the Assembly. Back in 1772, because of a dispute with the town of Mobile over its representation, Governor Chester refused to call the Assembly into session. With the Assembly never in session, the colony could not pass a law making militia service mandatory. After six years without a session, Governor Chester finally called the Assembly to Pensacola on October 1, 1778, but without Mobile representatives. On the first day, he addressed both houses, declaring that he had countered James Willing with "every measure" possible, and he called for a militia bill so that the colony would be prepared for the next attack, perhaps by France. Protesting that they lacked the authority to pass laws for the entire colony when Mobile was still not represented, the Assembly resolved that "this denial of the right of representation to the town of Mobile" was a "high breach of their privileges."[23] They refused to consider any legislation. The governor replied that his office gave him the prerogative to summon the Assembly whenever and however he thought proper.[24]

Despite the need for militias, James Bruce, John Stuart, and the other members of the Council could not make themselves participate in the erosion of representative government, and they did not support Chester. The Council deputized three of its members to try to persuade him to back down from such an "ill-timed" stance.[25] After all, 1778 was an awkward time for supporting royal governors against their people. James Bruce and the others were strong loyalists but were also certain that this was not the right time to be limiting representative rights in loyal colonies—what happened in Boston could happen in Mobile.

James Bruce reluctantly informed the delegates of the Assembly that the Council's mediation efforts had failed. Chester was too angry about the conflict over representation to back down. Chester decreed on November 5 that the Assembly would not meet again until the first Monday of September 1779, putting off the militia bill for at least ten more months. Although Mobile did not rise in armed rebellion as Boston had, the lack of a strong militia left West Florida vulnerable. Chester's detractors thought him a tyrant, yet he believed enough in representative government not to declare martial law, which would have allowed him to force locals into the militia. Caught between extremes of local control and monarchical absolutism, West Florida did not build its militia.[26]

If Chester was not willing to enlist slaves or declare martial law, he could not raise a sufficient fighting force to defend West Florida. To attract volunteers into the local provincial corps of the British regular army, he offered land to be given out once Britain put down the rebellion, just as British officers had offered to provincial volunteers in the east. Land bounties made recruiting somewhat easier, but they would cause postwar conflict with Indians if the British won.[27]

John Stuart had organized about two hundred men into four cavalry companies of loyalist refugees from families who had fled the rebelling colonies, but only a few other West Floridians volunteered for an expedition against Willing. Mobile resident Adam Chrystie led a force of fifteen or twenty men upriver in early March. They went first to the Amite River, where they found the plantations, including that of the Bruces, "plundered and ruined, all the buildings and a large quantity of corn reduced to ashes." Arriving at Manchac a little before daylight, they killed the rebels' sentinel. From there, they sneaked to the guardhouse, where they killed or badly wounded five rebels and took thirteen prisoner. Some two dozen rebels escaped into boats and desperately paddled across the Iberville River to refuge in the Spanish fort.[28]

Stuart's loyalist refugees combined with a force of about two hundred Choctaws to follow Choctaw Headman Franchimastabé to Natchez, on the Mississippi River. By their arrival on April 19, Natchez residents had forced out the men whom Willing had left behind and had raised the British flag again over the fort. The arrival of the Choctaw and loyalist military force confirmed the desires of civilian residents and secured British control of the town. As they left Natchez, Franchimastabé declared to the people of Natchez: "We are now obliged to go to leave you," but "in case you are threatened with an attack from the rebels remember we are behind you." His promise held not only security but also an implicit threat, which he made explicit for anyone who had missed the subtlety: "But on the other hand should you offer to take the rebels by the hand, or enter into any treaty with them . . . we will look on you as Virginians and treat you as our enemies."[29] Choctaws were a useful ally, but they reminded British settlers that their usefulness came from their military might, which it would do well for the settlers to remember.

The British could claim little credit for retaking Natchez. Beating back someone who created enemies everywhere he went was hardly a great victory, and Natchez residents and Choctaws did most of the work. Indian Agent David Taitt noted that, if it had not been for Stuart and the Choctaws, Manchac and Natchez "must unavoidably have been ruined" or even turned to rebellion.[30] The results did not bode well should someone more appealing or more adept invade.

Making matters worse, a hurricane in October 1778 crippled Pensacola's defenses by pounding the fort and sinking some of its cannons. Raising water levels an estimated twelve feet above normal high-water, the hurricane killed seven Pensacolans and carried away much of the wharf, including some newly mounted batteries. Ships in the harbor were dashed upon the shore by the crashing waves, some ending up so far inland that no one could get them back into the water. The hurricane had damaged many of the houses on the bay, possibly including the Bruces' home.[31]

British colonists on the Mississippi who were as shocked by their empire's failure to protect them as they were repelled by Willing's brutishness had a third option: becoming Spanish subjects. Some of the West Floridians who took refuge in Spanish Louisiana decided to stay. Manchac's most prominent merchant, John Fitzpatrick, blamed the British empire because, "for want of a small assistance in due time," he had lost a great deal, both of his own property and that of his debtors, who now could not repay him. Fitzpatrick explained to people in Pensacola that these reasons "obliged me as well as many others to accept of that generous offer made us by his Excellency Don Galvez of taking protection under his banner since unhappily for us we cannot enjoy it under" the British empire "that was formerly so dear to us." Fitzpatrick was one of many West Floridians who came to believe that the Spanish empire could best protect their prosperity without interfering with their independence. In the coming years, the Spanish would try to persuade many more British subjects to abandon the empire that "was formerly so dear" and take protection under the Spanish banner.[32]

World War

The governors of West Florida and Louisiana would garner significantly more attention from their empires once the war expanded. In the summer and fall of 1778, news reached West Florida and Louisiana that France had signed a treaty with the United States and that Britain had declared war on France. What had begun as a local rebellion could affect the Atlantic, the West Indies, Europe, India, Africa, the Mediterranean, and the Gulf Coast. Alliance with the revolutionaries could be a chance for France to make up for the humiliating loss of the Seven Years' War.[33]

Spain's alliance with France and desire to take the Floridas might pull Spain and its colonies into the war openly. Already British observers noted a "Spanish gentleman," Havana trader Juan de Miralles, hanging around Philadelphia with no official office but "particularly noticed by the Congress." He walked in the procession alongside French partisan Stephen Girard when John Jay was elected president of the Continental Congress in 1778. Loyalist William Franklin reported to British Secretary George Germain that "the healths of the Kings of France and Spain were drunk as two of their public toasts" at Jay's inaugural celebration.[34] For those who had stayed loyal to the British empire, former British subjects toasting Catholic European monarchs was a hideous sight.

With France and its powerful navy in the war, British troops in Philadelphia were suddenly in a vulnerable position. The United States had never had much of a navy, and most of what did exist had been captured on Lake Champlain in 1776. Before the French alliance, if Washington's army had attacked Philadelphia, the British troops would have had access to the sea for supplies and escape if necessary. Now that France had joined the Americans, all of those calculations changed. A dominant French navy could enforce a blockade. Not only was defending Philadelphia more dangerous, capturing it in the first place had proven fruitless. The whole purpose of seizing the American capital was to push the rebels into surrender, but they had not. The rebel Congress was not dependent on one locale for its organization to proceed. Now there seemed little point in trying to hold on to the vulnerable and tactically useless city. Therefore, in June 1778, British Commander in Chief Henry Clinton evacuated Philadelphia and moved north in hopes of cutting off New England and consolidating his troops at New York City in case the crown needed to send them to defend the Floridas, Jamaica, Ireland, or even England against the French.

James and Isabella Bruce had plenty to fear from the French declaration of war. West Florida, with its meager five hundred regulars and tiny militia, seemed vulnerable to French attack. It was also a likely location for conflict with Spain, should it join the war, although West Floridians still hoped that Britain and Spain would remain at peace. If they did not, the British navy might be outmatched by its enemies. King George III and Secretary George Germain recognized the importance of West Florida's proximity to both the Mississippi River and southeastern Indian nations, who were "essential to the security of His Majesty's possessions in West Florida, and to the protection of the King's faithful subjects, and their property."[35]

For the moment, Pensacola was dangerously vulnerable to attack from New Orleans or Havana, but, if secure, its location could be a key to expanding British power in the Gulf and Caribbean. The British empire could benefit greatly from a decisive victory over France and Spain. With Pensacola, the Bahamas, and some key island victories, Britain could block both routes of Spanish access through the Caribbean to its American mainland. If the British engaged Spain in Honduras and Nicaragua, they could establish a base in the Pacific. In the meantime, the Floridas could supply timber and provisions to the British fleet. Expanding in the Caribbean and perhaps into the Pacific and probably regaining Georgia and perhaps South Carolina—all that would more than compensate for losing the northern colonies.[36]

King George ordered General Henry Clinton to send three thousand more men plus supplies to the Floridas. When Clinton received the order, he did not want to lose his valued regulars, who were well-trained career soldiers sent from Britain whose current utility resided in defending New York and battling the French in the West Indies. Instead, he sent "foreign troops and provincials whose loss to this army will not be so much felt."[37] The foreign troops were about seven hundred soldiers from Waldeck, one of the principalities of the Holy Roman Empire that supplied soldiers to George III. The provincials were army recruits from the colonies (part of the regular army, therefore distinct from militia, but less professional than the British regulars): the 170-man Pennsylvania Loyalists Battalion and the 313 men of the Maryland Loyalists Battalion. On the last day of October 1778, the Maryland and Pennsylvania Loyalists in their redcoats and the Waldeckers in their blue uniforms boarded ships and left New York City. Spanish spies at the dock observed that even though winter was coming, the men removed the woolen linings from their coats. The Spanish deduced that the British troops must be bound for Jamaica or a similarly warm destination, perhaps to attack Louisiana or another Spanish colony. In fact, they were bound for Pensacola, under the command of General John Campbell (not to be confused with Colonel Archibald Campbell, who at the same time was gathering troops to take Savannah). Their orders were to build a new fort to protect the Mississippi and strengthen fortifications at existing posts.[38]

Conclusion: Calling for Reinforcements

Once in Pensacola and fearing attack from any direction, General John Campbell in February 1779 called for more help from General Clinton. Campbell's small force was shrinking from disease and desertion. In one night alone, seventeen men deserted from the Maryland Loyalists Battalion, along with their arms and about a hundred rounds of ammunition, reportedly intending to walk back to Maryland. Campbell proposed a solution to Clinton: Send the Rhode Island Negro Regiment to West Florida. Echoing a racist stereotype common to European thought of the time, Campbell believed whites were constitutionally incapable of working in the hot and humid West Florida summer. On the other hand, black troops might "be employed to more advantage in West Florida than anywhere else in North America."[39] Amazingly, Campbell believed that black New Englanders would be better suited to the climate than white Marylanders and Floridians. Clinton would refuse this request as well. His troops were stretched thin and were particularly focused on taking Georgia and South Carolina. Indeed, by the summer, the British officers defending Jamaica were actually asking Campbell for help from Pensacola. Clinton ultimately delayed his attack on the Carolinas to answer the cry for help from Jamaica, the colony Britain could not afford to lose.[40]

In March 1779, British Superintendent of Indian Affairs John Stuart died, leaving the Southern Indian Department in disarray. No one had Stuart's extensive knowledge and experience. After several months with no successor in place, word arrived in the fall of 1779 that the crown wanted the Southern District divided into two districts: the Mississippi District for the Chickasaws and Choctaws under Deputy Superintendent Alexander Cameron and the Atlantic District for the Creeks and Cherokees. Germain's decision moved Cameron away from the Cherokees and Creeks, whom he knew well, and assigned South Carolina loyalist Thomas Brown, who had no experience in the Indian Department, as their agent. The Creeks scoffed at Brown's instructions that they should now come only to St. Augustine and not Pensacola for diplomacy and trade. At the same time, because of the failed Creek coordination in Georgia and the failure of the Chickasaws to guard the Mississippi, Germain decided that Stuart had spent too much on Indians. Cameron lamented that his budget of £1,400 was barely enough for the salaries of the agents and interpreters, leaving nothing for presents and provisions for "Indians who have been necessarily accustomed to such large gratifications" even before "the present competition to gain their affections."[41] Germain had replaced John Stuart, Britain's most effective diplomat in the region, with a system that decreased stability, local knowledge, and funding. It was not good preparation for the next time the British called on Indians for serious military assistance.

At the same time, choosing their right to be left alone over their obligations to the empire that kept them secure, most of West Florida's men refused to join the militia, to work on the Mississippi forts, or to lend their slaves' labor. Alexander Dickson, commander of British forces on the Mississippi River, was so short on labor that he was hiring Spanish subjects for defense construction work, even though Spain was a major reason for reinforcing the forts. Although the Declaration of Independence accused King George of attempting "the establishment of an absolute Tyranny over these States," in fact the liberties of British subjects in West Florida were greatly impeding its defense. In a war in which persuading people to fight was vital, the British empire was not doing well anywhere. The question for the Gulf Coast would be whether Spain could do any better.

CHAPTER TEN

To Fight for Spain?

IN JANUARY 1777, Oliver Pollock stood in the hall of the New Orleans Cabildo, the main colonial government building, anxiously waiting to meet with the new governor, Bernardo de Gálvez. Good relations with Louisiana's Spanish governor were vital to Oliver and Margaret Pollock. In the 1760s, the patronage of Governor Alejandro O'Reilly had allowed Oliver Pollock to establish himself as a prominent merchant in Havana and New Orleans and to skirt the regulations that kept other traders at bay. Yet he sensed that the governor who succeeded O'Reilly in 1769, Luís de Unzaga y Amezaga, had come to dread his visits. A dedicated supporter of the American Revolution, Oliver Pollock had repeatedly asked Unzaga to assist the rebels far beyond what the governor felt he had the authority to do. But now Unzaga had been promoted to captain-general of Venezuela, and Pollock was hoping for a fresh start and a more fruitful relationship with the new governor, Bernardo de Gálvez. To Pollock's delight that January, Governor Gálvez greeted him enthusiastically, asked him questions about George Washington and his army, and, as Pollock later wrote, "gave me the delightful assurance that he would go every possible length for the interest of Congress."[1]

Louisiana was a colony on the fringes of the Spanish empire, but its position on the frontier with British West Florida made it and its loyalties strategically important as the American Revolution drew in the empires of Europe. During the Seven Years' War, the British had captured Havana, the Spanish empire's most important port and the third-largest American city after Mexico City and Lima. Spain got Havana back in the postwar negotiations, but the crown would not forget the lessons of the war—always be ready to defend against the British. Trying to guard a spread-out empire, many believed that Louisiana was the key to the defense of Mexico.[2]

As the Spanish looked toward the nineteenth century, they saw possibility for imperial growth in the rebellion Britain faced and the war losses that had pushed France out of mainland North America. Yet there were dangers too. Supporting a rebellion against an empire was not a natural choice for a monarch. The Spanish and French kings might have refused to aid an independence movement except that such movements had proved failures in Europe. The independent republic of Geneva had experienced so much internal strife that its leaders had appealed to the French king to intervene, which he did with an armed intervention in 1738. In the 1760s and 1770s, movements in Sweden, Hungary, Milan, and France had been put down easily. Misinformed about American culture, Spain's ambassador to France suggested that Americans, "many being Quakers," would be gentler neighbors than Britain.[3] For Spain, the trick would be to damage Britain while it was distracted by this rebellion.

Whether Spain entered the war militarily or not, the Revolution could hurt Britain and accelerate a renaissance of the Spanish empire, bringing advantages to Spain's subjects and friends. But to take advantage of Britain's vulnerability, its adversaries would have to appeal to both Spanish and British subjects' desire for security, prosperity, and some measure of independence.

Partners in New Orleans

In Bernardo de Gálvez, Oliver Pollock gained a patron committed to undermining the British. Governor Gálvez exemplified the new order of an old and vast empire, stretching from Tierra del Fuego to Alaska. Gone were the conquistadores of the fifteenth and sixteenth centuries. The men who rose to prominence now were Enlightenment-influenced administrators committed to running a well-organized and efficient bureaucracy. Chief among them was Bernardo de Gálvez's uncle, Minister of the Indies José de Gálvez. This new class of ministers and governors had the full support of their king, Bourbon King Carlos III, who in his rule from 1759 to 1788 concentrated power, sought to rule the colonies more directly, and expelled the Jesuits from the colonies in order to destroy a rival power base.[4]

The crown committed itself to contesting the idea that the torch of empire had passed to Britain. Britain was Spain's greatest threat but also was the model for encouraging commerce, easing state and company monopoly powers, strengthening the navy, introducing agricultural reforms, and increasing the colonial population. Minister José de Gálvez sought to emulate Britain in some ways but retain Spain's more hierarchical governance system. As he wrote with disdain, "We do not aspire to entirely adapt the liberty and other maxims of the English." No laws were passed in the Spanish colonies, but there was some measure of local governance. In Spain, the Council of Castile passed laws, and the crown issued royal orders. On the ground, crown-appointed officials enforced the law, while local *cabildos* (town councils, similar to His Majesty's Council for West Florida) and *audiencias* (courts), also appointed by the king, served as a check on local officials' power.[5]

Although Spain was not at war, Governor Gálvez revamped Louisiana's trade policy in opposition to Britain. Previously, official policy had held that only Spanish ships could do business on the lower Mississippi River. British ships were supposed to access the Gulf via Lake Pontchartrain and Lake Borgne, not the Mississippi and the port of New Orleans, but they had long done so without consequence. Now,

Louisiana Governor Bernardo de Gálvez (Reproduction of eighteenth-century portrait by José de Alfaro, ca. 1900, Louisiana State Museum)

Gálvez officially welcomed American and French traders to the port of New Orleans and began seizing British vessels found between the mouth of the Mississippi and Lake Pontchartrain. The British governor of West Florida expressed his "great surprise" at Gálvez's change of policy "in a time of profound peace."[6] British Admiral Clark Gayton sent an armed sloop christened the *West Florida* from Jamaica to patrol Lakes Pontchartrain and Maurepas. In the spring of 1777, the *West Florida* captured three Spanish ships on Lake Pontchartrain, claiming that they were carrying British timber. Gálvez was incensed. He increased patrols on the Mississippi. Eleven vessels were brought in on charges of smuggling. The British estimated losses at almost fifteen thousand pounds.[7]

Oliver Pollock delightedly informed Congress of Gálvez's edict that "the Port of New Orleans should be open and free to American commerce and to the admission and sale of prizes made by their cruisers." That is, if they captured enemy ships, not only would they be safe from prosecution in New Orleans, they could also sell the ships' booty. Fully casting off his position as a British merchant, Pollock also gathered information on the British forces in Pensacola and the likelihood of British attack on the thirteen colonies from the west and forwarded the information to Philadelphia. The crackdown on British shipping suited Pollock's pocketbook as well as his political beliefs. But at the same time, the Revolutionary War endangered everything the Pollocks had built. Because of his spying, Britain branded Oliver Pollock a traitor, a crime punishable by death. In May 1777, the British called on still-neutral Spain to surrender him to their custody, but Governor Gálvez refused.[8]

Gálvez sought to encourage Louisianans' loyalty to Spain in case war came. Unlike the British in West Florida, Gálvez recruited a strong militia and proved an able marketer of the war effort. When he discovered that the upper class of New Orleans did not serve in the militia "because they do not want to serve in formations next to their own shoemakers and hairdressers," he established an elite cavalry order called "Carabineros de la Luisiana," complete with fancy uniforms down to the gilt buttons, gold thread buttonholes, and matching sabers to lure them. He increased the size of the New Orleans free black militia. In West Florida, slaveholders resisted arming free blacks, but Gálvez made a particular effort to enlist locals of all kinds in the militias.[9]

Gálvez created ties of patronage and friendship within Louisiana's colonial population, including marrying the daughter of a prominent New Orleans family, Marie Felice de St. Maxent. This marriage brought Gálvez into Oliver and Margaret Pollock's circle of New Orleans elite. Like the Pollocks, the Maxents were a prominent merchant and planter family with connections in ports far beyond New Orleans. Marie Felice's mother's dowry and father's connections with the French colonial government and with Indians west of St. Louis had combined to create a lucrative fur trade. In 1752, Marie Felice's sister had married Governor Unzaga, a marriage that improved Unzaga's relationship with Louisiana's French population and expanded the Maxents' business connections into the Spanish empire. When Gálvez arrived in New Orleans, Marie Felice was the young widow of a wealthy French Louisianan. Their marriage improved his financial and social situation within New Orleans and sealed her family's position within the empire. They could all see a promising future in the growth of the Spanish empire.[10]

These family ties did not impress the Bruces, across the Mississippi River in West Florida. In October 1777 James Bruce wrote to an acquaintance in England, a retired undersecretary of state, of the new governor's arrival. "His name is Galvez," James Bruce wrote, "nephew to the Spanish minister for the Department of the Indies; he is young, gay and courteous," all the better for winning over the French inhabitants of the Mississippi Valley. The Bruces had heard that Gálvez "enters into all their parties of pleasure and amusements and professes what really seems to be very natural to him, an evident partiality for the French nation." James Bruce wrote, "the gay, volatile inhabitants of Louisiana ... have now got their every wish, their trade is opened, and even their very foibles countenanced by their new governor, in return for which they almost pay him adoration, in so much that in the event of a war between our Crown and theirs it's generally believed that it would take thousands where hundreds only would have been necessary before his arrival" to take New Orleans. The governor's recent seizure of British ships "in defiance of the public faith and recent treaties" and his "courting and tampering with the Indians" on both sides of the Mississippi only made clear his intent.[11]

Indeed, Gálvez dispatched Indian agents with presents to recruit Indian allies. He met in New Orleans with smaller Indian nations of the lower Mississippi Valley, including Attakapas, Biloxis, Chitimachas, Natchitoches, Opelousas, and Pascagoulas. Delegations from Creek and Choctaw towns whose traditional diplomatic purview was New Orleans came as well, including Alabamas of the Creek Confederacy and Choctaws from the Six Towns, which were closer to New Orleans than the other two divisions (Eastern and Western). Six Towns Choctaws went home with the message that Governor Gálvez and "Rebel Agent" Pollock wanted Choctaws "to take no part in the quarrel between the white people."[12] In New Orleans, Pascagoulas and Biloxis discussed how Gálvez might help them regain their lost lands in West Florida, and he smoothed over recent conflict between

Attakapas and Biloxis by providing goods and mediation. He also spent a good deal of money. As he explained, the "generosity distributed on behalf of His Majesty has caused a lot of admiration, and in recognition of that they have offered to stay loyal." To prove it, the Indians surrendered to Gálvez their British medals, even though he did not have any Spanish ones on hand to give to them. Gálvez requested his superiors that medals "be sent to me as soon as possible" for formalizing the alliances.[13]

With the secret support of the crown, Pollock and Gálvez sent some seventy thousand dollars' worth of munitions to the American commander of Fort Pitt, and they encouraged the expedition of Pollock's old business colleague James Willing. Oliver Pollock was glad to receive a letter from Congress's Commerce Committee in the spring of 1778 informing him that Willing was coming down the Mississippi. The letter also officially appointed Oliver Pollock Congress's "Agent in His Most Catholic Majesty's Province of Louisiana."[14]

But news soon filtered into New Orleans that was less promising. Because Willing's mission lacked official Congressional approval, there were only about forty men instead of the recommended thousand, and there would be no warships coming to attack from the sea. The West Floridians who streamed into New Orleans for safety brought tales of Willing's marauding that did not inspire confidence in Willing's ability to recruit West Florida settlers to the American cause. In March, Willing sailed the *Rebecca* across Lake Pontchartrain and made his triumphant entrance into New Orleans. If Pollock and Gálvez expected a shipshape officer with well-trained troops, they were disappointed. Willing and his men wore no uniforms. They were a scruffy lot but heavily armed and jealously guarding their plunder. The other men and women who disembarked were the enslaved people seized by Willing's men from plantations along the lower Mississippi. They unloaded cask after cask of blue indigo powder, countless logs ready for the lumber mill, bundles upon bundles of furs and hides, and blankets full of a motley assortment of items that had been West Floridians' personal property: silverware, clothes, bed and table linens, food, and wine.[15]

If Spain and Britain had been at war, James Willing might have been a hero of the Revolution, the "River Fox" of the western front. He might have used guerilla tactics to raid the British and then retreat behind Spanish lines, thereby diverting British troops from the eastern fronts. But Britain and Spain were not at war, and, lacking an army, Willing targeted plantation owners and their slaves instead of soldiers. The victims vividly saw that the British and especially the Spanish empires were better protection than the rebels. Willing could only sheepishly write his backers in Congress that "I have now run up a great expense to the States and have not as yet been able to fulfill my mission."[16] Oliver Pollock wrote to Congress on July 6 that "the small party you sent here under the command of Captain James Willing without any order or subordination, has only thrown the whole river into confusion and created a number of enemies and a heavy expense."[17]

As Willing lingered in New Orleans for months, all of the territory he had seized fell back into the hands of the British, including the Bruces' destroyed plantation. Oliver Pollock became so eager to see him go that he funded Willing's travel by ship from New Orleans to Philadelphia. As Willing boarded the ship, he handed Pollock another handful of bills. A British fleet caught up with the ship off the coast of Delaware and took Willing as a prisoner to New York, where he languished for a year or so before being exchanged for a British prisoner. Willing's plundering had alienated almost everyone, including his hosts in New Orleans.[18]

In addition to the money wasted on Willing, Oliver Pollock was providing financial backing for George Rogers Clark of the Virginia militia. Ohio Valley Indians had been raiding Virginia's western settlements in the Kentucky country (part of Virginia at the time). Unable to stop those raids directly, Governor Patrick Henry issued Clark a commission to lead Virginia militia against British posts that were presumably supplying the Indians with munitions. The ultimate goal would be British Detroit, but first Clark would try to take British posts just north of the Ohio River in the Illinois country (present-day Illinois and Indiana), across the Mississippi from Spanish St. Louis and Upper Louisiana. Spanish and French merchants in the colonial towns of St. Louis and Kaskaskia outfitted Clark with thousands of pounds of gunpowder and other goods for his men and the Indians they hoped to recruit. In Clark's pockets that late summer and fall were receipts for over six thousand Spanish dollars from merchants in Kaskaskia alone (worth at least one hundred thousand dollars today), all put on Pollock's credit in the name of the State of Virginia. Clark's total bills to Pollock would eventually climb well past forty thousand dollars. Virginia and Congress sent no reimbursements for Clark's or Willing's missions.[19]

Oliver and Margaret Pollock began to see the impact of their support for the Revolution on their family's finances. In early 1779, they had to sell some of their slaves and rent out others to the New Orleans public works to cover Clark's bills. Oliver Pollock borrowed money from other New Orleans merchants at steep interest rates. In May, he swallowed his pride and wrote Governor Gálvez that "it will be entirely impossible for me to complete what has already been begun, as well as to continue with the rest which is planned for the service of the States of America, if Your Excellency does not condescend to make me some advances of money on behalf of these States." In asking for the loan, Pollock assured Gálvez that they would be repaid through the credit Congress had established with the Spanish king and the "considerable quantity of flour" that the States would send down the Ohio and Mississippi to New Orleans.[20] Gálvez bailed out his friend and ally with government loans eventually totaling $74,000, a sum worth well over a million dollars today.[21]

But the war was still on, and the Pollocks believed that it would all be paid back in reimbursements and economic opportunities once Britain surrendered. Indeed, the action on the upper Mississippi inspired them to hope that it would soon be cut off from the British empire and therefore be eligible for American-Spanish trade. And Oliver Pollock would be best positioned to reap the profits.

Amand Broussard and Another Rebellion

Like Oliver and Margaret Pollock, Isabella and James Bruce, and countless others, Amand Broussard hoped to found his family's prosperity on land ownership and a thriving imperial economy. While Pollock imagined a postwar career as an American citizen with commercial ties to the Spanish empire, Broussard and the Acadians had grown to see Spain as their protector. In Spanish Louisiana, Amand Broussard's family was rebuilding a life, one that not only was more secure but promised greater opportunities for prosperity because the Broussards could buy slaves to raise cattle and crops for New Orleans city dwellers and grow indigo and perhaps rice for export.

The Acadians had only to cast their eyes across to West Florida to remember what they needed protection against: the British who had evicted them from their homeland. From the sidelines, the Broussards surely enjoyed news of the rebellion within the British empire, having lost their own rebellion in Acadia. Like most of his male neighbors, Broussard was a member of the local militia. But Acadians also knew the dangers of war; it would be safer if the war played itself out far from their new home. Actual war would threaten the life that Amand Broussard and Anne Benoît had struggled to build for themselves, five-year-old Joseph, and their newborn, Edouard.[22]

In theory, the alliance between Spanish King Carlos III and French King Louis XVI obligated Spain to join the war against Britain once France did. But King Carlos took some persuading. France promised that the war would return Gibraltar—a land mass on the southern tip of the Iberian peninsula—and the Floridas to Spain and that France would ensure that the United States did not try to expand into Spanish territories. With France and Spain united against Britain, it was clear which side the Broussards would support.

Spain Joins the War

In June 1779, Spanish King Carlos III declared war on Britain. As the rebellious colonies fought a war against empire, Spain devised a war *for* empire, a war to win as much of the British empire as possible. Sensing that the Revolution was another war that would shift colonial boundaries—but not fearing that the war would threaten European colonialism itself—Spanish officials hoped to use the conflict to make the Gulf of Mexico a Spanish lake again. The conflict held out several tantalizing prizes for Spain, in addition to the humiliation of a hated enemy. During the War of Spanish Succession early in the century, the British had taken Gibraltar and Minorca, an island in the Mediterranean off Spain's eastern coast. There were plenty of rich targets in the Caribbean as well, particularly Jamaica with its sugar plantations. Victories at sea could reestablish Spanish control of shipping routes between the Americas and Europe. And retaking East Florida, lost in the Seven Years' War, would be strong proof that the Spanish were back on top. West Florida was an appealing target too. It could expand Mexico's buffer zone, and the ports of Mobile and Pensacola could add to Spain's Gulf and Caribbean shipping. West Florida would be a key extension of a growing empire. Spain could build on Britain's economic development and reap the profits of its plantations.

Through the influence of Minister of the Indies José de Gálvez, King Carlos III had become entirely convinced that his empire could expand at Britain's expense. He nearly quadrupled spending in Louisiana for 1779 and kept it at that level for many years to come. The king wanted General Gálvez to take quick action, so he ordered Cuban Governor Diego Josef Navarro to assist him with "whatever land and sea forces it is possible to assemble in those dominions" for an attack on Mobile and Pensacola, "the keys to the Gulf of Mexico," as well as British posts on the Mississippi, "which should be considered as the bulwark of the vast empire of New Spain."[23]

Scores of Spanish and French ships headed for England. The Spanish and French hoped to end the war quickly by taking it to England itself, but coordination delays, smallpox, and bad weather prevented a swift attack. In the meantime, the British prepared their defenses, and by October the French and Spanish called off the attack on Britain because of the coming winter storm season. The Spanish ships instead sailed for Gibraltar, and over ten thousand infantry and cavalry headed there by land from Spain. The new plan was to take Gibraltar quickly, block Britain's access to the Mediterranean, and invade England the following spring.[24]

The Gulf Coast was an important part of Spain's new war to restore and extend its empire. British West Florida's illegal trade on the Mississippi and recruitment of Indians in Louisiana as well as British warships' insults near New Orleans formed part of King Carlos's public justification for war. José de Gálvez explained to officials in Havana that "the King has decided that the principal objective of his arms in America during the war with the English is to drive them from the Gulf of Mexico and the banks of the Mississippi, where their settlements are so prejudicial to our commerce, as well as to the security of our richest possessions." He was hopeful that this was the time to strike: Britain, "pressed by superior forces in both hemispheres, abandoned by other nations, who for a long time have been irritated by her odious dominance, and on the point of having her own island invaded by a French army of more than forty thousand men, will find herself unable to resist our efforts if we act with prudence and energy."[25]

Spain's declaration of war sparked a debate in Britain's House of Commons and among the king's advisors over whether to let the rebellious colonies go in order to concentrate on protecting the West Indies, the Floridas, and England itself against European enemies. But the king believed that granting the rebellious colonies their independence would only encourage other colonies to follow their example, from Florida and the West Indies to Canada and India. Best to nip it in the bud.[26]

Conclusion: A Rebellion Within an Imperial War

To the Broussards along with their neighbors on the Gulf Coast and decision-makers in France and Spain, the rebellion was simply a spark. The real war was the one now in place involving Europe and much of the Atlantic world. While the American rebels eagerly anticipated that Spain's powerful assistance would open an additional front in mainland North America and establish a combined fleet now bigger than that of Britain, most people saw the conflict as a rematch of the Seven Years' War. It would either restore the French and Spanish to their previous imperial prominence or solidify British dominance over the North Atlantic and most of North America. Imperial correspondence referred to the conflict as "the war between France and England," making no reference to the rebelling colonies.[27]

For Spain, the American rebellion was a mere catalyst to war for their own imperial goals. At the start of the war, the Spanish crown had worried about the precedent of supporting a colonial rebellion, but now there seemed little to fear. Willing's expedition confirmed most people's impressions of the fledgling United States as a pale shadow of a true government: too diffuse and too weak to control its own people, who seemed bent on lining their own pockets at anyone's expense. If Willing was the best Congress had to offer, the rebel movement would create at most a weak state, dependent on its Spanish and French allies. West Florida rebels did not come streaming out to join Willing. Much the opposite: he turned neutral parties into loyalists as they came to see his violence as the greatest threat to their liberty. Congress and the states were indebted tens of thousands of dollars to Oliver Pollock and the Spanish crown, and Congress was unable to make good on the debts. U.S. Indian Commissioner George Galphin gave impressive talks to any Creeks who would listen, but he had no goods with which to seal any deals. British possession of Savannah and blockade of Charleston guaranteed that these shortages would continue.[28]

Compared to the British, Spanish, French, Creeks, Choctaws, and Chickasaws, the Americans seemed minor players, unlikely to decide anyone's fate. The United States might promise independence to its citizens, but it lacked the financial or military power to back up such pledges. Indeed, its lack of power was inextricable from its independence, as George Washington knew well. He was trying to form an army out of people who distrusted things like armies: locally minded, independent men and a Congress unwilling to support anything that smacked of that symbol of despotic empire, a standing army. The rebels had started the fight, but the real war would be between Britain and its French and Spanish enemies, with Indians lining up on one side or the other or staying neutral to see who prevailed.[29]

Because there were very few actual Spaniards on the Gulf Coast and Mississippi Valley, Spain would need the help of the region's non-Spaniards now under its rule, including people like Amand

Broussard, Anne Benôit, and Oliver and Margaret Pollock. Just as valuable would be persuading Indians like Payamataha and Alexander McGillivray, slaves like Petit Jean, and loyalists like James and Isabella Bruce at least not to support Britain with much enthusiasm.

What none of them knew was that men like James Willing, such as George Rogers Clark, would help the United States to defeat the British and eventually to expand across the continent, at the expense of both the European and Indian powers of the 1770s. More or less self-appointed commanders who attracted a few men with big promises and inspiring leadership would keep the rebellion alive, terrorizing the British and anyone they identified as loyalists while George Washington kept the Continental Army intact. Willing himself, though, inspired too little confidence and loyalty and found himself on a British prison ship.

PART III

The Revolutionary War

AS THE REVOLUTIONARY WAR spread south and west on the continent and drew in other European kings, it was time for the people of the Gulf Coast to decide where their allegiances lay. As people chose whether to fight and for whom, they considered which side could best forward their own prosperity without impinging too much on their independence. British and Spanish leaders needed to persuade not only allies but also their own people to take up arms.

The empires' needs put power in the hands of the Gulf Coast's people. Those who were not firmly in either camp required those who wanted their help to persuade them that it was in their interest. And, of course, anyone who committed to one side or the other also risked becoming dependent on its fate.

CHAPTER ELEVEN

Inspiring Loyalty

THE SUN HAD NOT yet risen as Amand Broussard gathered with the other men of his camp just south of the Iberville River in Spanish Louisiana. The ten-foot-wide trunks and knobby knees of cypress trees rose out of the early morning mist. Although the air was muggy on that morning of September 7, 1779, the temperature was bearable if one stayed out of the sun. As he stood surrounded by his brothers and cousins, Broussard caught sight of Louisiana's governor, Brigadier General Bernardo de Gálvez, on his horse above the crowd.

It was a big crowd: more than 1,300 armed men. The over six hundred militiamen included French-speaking Louisianans, both Acadians like Broussard and those who had settled in earlier decades when Louisiana was French. Some of the militiamen were British refugees who had left West Florida after James Willing's raids on the lower Mississippi had revealed Britain's inability to protect them. Along with some Canary Islanders, they had founded Galveztown on the Spanish side of the Louisiana–West Florida border and named it for the governor who protected them. At least eighty members of the New Orleans free black militia were there, serving in segregated units and led by their own officers. There were about five hundred regular Spanish troops plus twenty light cavalry. They were joined by 160 Houmas, Six Towns Choctaws, Alabamas, and other Indians of the lower Mississippi. Seven Americans, including Oliver Pollock, marched under an American battle flag, probably the Stars and Stripes. Governor Gálvez had spent the previous weeks assembling them all with the news that Spain had recognized the United States as an independent country and that Britain might retaliate against Spanish Louisiana. Still, it seemed a strangely large gathering just to make a defensive tour of southern Louisiana.[1]

Once Gálvez began to speak to the troops, Broussard listened to a French translation of Gálvez's Spanish, as other interpreters hurried to keep up in English, Houma, Alabaman, and Choctaw. The news was startling. King Carlos III had not simply recognized the independence of the United States; he had declared war on Britain, and he expected the people of Louisiana to do their part. A roar of appreciation burst out, loudest among the Broussards and the other Acadians. They could remember the horrors that the British had put them through, imprisoning them and driving them from Acadia into exile in Louisiana, where they had built new lives with the permission of French and Spanish governors. Fifteen years earlier, as the last French governor of Louisiana handed half the colony to Spain and the other half to Britain, he had predicted that the Acadians would be a bulwark against further British expansion because it was "unlikely . . . that these people, who refused to submit to English rule . . . and who consequently were treated harshly by them, would now join the British." Now in 1779, when the Spanish asked Broussard and other Acadians to take up their weapons and make the rounds of southern Louisiana with the regular troops, they answered the general's call.[2]

Marching north from New Orleans, Gálvez recruited white and black subjects and Indians to join his ranks. By the time they reached British territory, nearly two-thirds of Gálvez's force was militia, thanks to his inspiring speeches. Militiamen could easily have refused. As Governor Gálvez explained to his uncle José de Gálvez, Spain's minister of the Indies, "due to the many variations of languages of the different nations," his appeals had to be astute.[3] Despite schools set up to teach young men the Spanish language, most Louisianans still spoke it poorly, if at all, and certainly did not identify themselves as Spanish. And, as George Washington understood, militias were poorly trained, inclined to scatter after firing a round or two, and considerably better fighters when defending their homes than when sent to fight in far-off battles. Gálvez wrote his uncle, "I am certain of their good will," but "Your Excellency knows very well that one cannot count much on them, because, as war is not their profession, they do not wage it with enthusiasm" and "always have in mind, in view of the danger, the consideration of their families."[4]

Gálvez managed to persuade Louisiana's French men and women, Canary Islanders, slaves, free blacks, and British refugees that their hopes for independence and prosperity lay in Spanish rule, not British. Like the minutemen of Concord, Massachusetts, 1,500 miles to the northeast, they fought not for abstract principles but to protect their local political and economic independence, which they now saw as threatened by the British.[5]

Neither the Spanish nor the British could count on their colonial subjects' loyalty when asked to risk their lives and commit their scarce resources. Now that war between Spain and Britain had brought fighting to the Gulf Coast, each side would have to work to recruit allies to come to its aid, to persuade its imperial hierarchy to devote military resources to this new front, and to convince its own colonists that "the consideration of their families" lay in an empire that protected and provided for them. Which side would persuade the peoples of the lower Mississippi and Gulf Coast that it could best protect both their local independence and the prosperity brought by global economic connections? Whoever could do that would stand a good chance of winning the war on the Gulf Coast.

Hurricane

Three weeks earlier it had seemed that the Spanish offensive would not happen soon. On August 18, 1779, Margaret and Oliver Pollock were watching from New Orleans as heavy storm clouds gathered over the Gulf and the winds grew stronger. In this era before radar, people had to judge a storm by sight, sound, and feel. The hurricane had been circulating in the Gulf for days as it grew to hundreds of miles across with winds of over 100 miles per hour. Knowing that storms move fast, Oliver collected his books and papers including receipts proving that Congress owed him tens of thousands of dollars while Margaret gathered their children and a few personal belongings. They headed north, making "a narrow escape for our lives."[6] The family survived, but the hurricane destroyed a large part of New Orleans. Storm surges crashed several ships in the lower Mississippi. The armed schooner *Rebecca,* which Oliver Pollock had rechristened the *Morris* for his business associate Congressman Robert Morris, was on the lower Mississippi as the hurricane hit. The crew could only try to stay above water as the waves and high winds smashed the ship to pieces. Eleven men drowned while the rest clung to what was left of the ship until rescue boats picked them up, frightened and waterlogged. In less than three hours, the hurricane demolished houses in New Orleans and the surrounding countryside, destroyed the harvest, killed cattle on which the city depended, and left the city the "most pitiful spectacle imaginable."[7]

A hurricane was devastating under any circumstances, but this one also threatened to destroy Oliver Pollock's and Spain's ambitions. Just a few days earlier, Governor Gálvez had called him to his office and told him that King Carlos III had declared war on Britain and ordered Gálvez to take the Mississippi Valley and West Florida as soon as possible. Gálvez was keeping the news a secret. While Pollock obviously supported the effort, the loyalties of Louisiana's majority-French colonial population were less clear. After all, some of them had rebelled against Spanish rule only eleven years before. Plus, once the news was public, British partisans in New Orleans would immediately inform West Florida, which might not yet have received the news. Before announcing war, Gálvez sent orders to his commandants to prepare lists of their male inhabitants who would be eligible to fight in the militia in an emergency and began, as secretly as he could, to improve the city's defenses and acquire vessels for transporting troops. He invited Choctaws, Chickasaws, and other Indians to New Orleans to urge them not to support the British. Gálvez invited Pollock to come along on the mission, which Pollock "most cheerfully agreed to."[8] Then the hurricane came, and New Orleans lost the ships that were supposed to protect it. New Orleanians focused on repairing their city instead of war, and the reinforcements expected from Havana, which had also been damaged, were delayed. British West Florida, meanwhile, was spared any damage. It was not clear that Gálvez would be able to inspire New Orleanians to abandon their clean-up efforts to work and fight for the glory of Spain.[9]

Two days after the hurricane, Pollock listened as Gálvez spoke to the discouraged inhabitants of New Orleans in the Place d'Armes (now the French Quarter's Jackson Square) in front of the Cabildo building. Even before the hurricane, Louisianans had seemed as likely to rebel against Spanish officials as to follow them to war. Just a few months earlier, Gálvez had reported to his uncle that his own lieutenant governor, a Frenchman named Francisco Bouligny, was claiming "imaginary rights" in the governance of Louisiana, "which the court has never granted him." He complained that Bouligny and members of the New Orleans *cabildo* (town council) were conniving against him and that it was "composed of French individuals," some of whom had risen up against Spanish governance in 1768 and still maintained "a spirit of rebellion and hatred for the Spanish nation, which they cannot hide, even in their most reserved conversations." They still considered themselves French and assumed that the Spanish occupation was temporary. Gálvez despaired that he had been working to convert them for more than two years "but without success."[10] How would he lead these people to battle?

Part of the answer would be recruiting French and Acadian support by emphasizing what they shared with the Spanish: economic interests, religion, hatred of Britain. In the Place d'Armes, Gálvez announced that Spain had recognized the independence of the United States but that "there was still peace and Spain wanted to keep the peace as long as England did not break it." New Orleans was in danger, he claimed, only because "with no other motive" the British might "start hostilities with us just as they had with the French." Gálvez announced that the king had appointed him brigadier general and made his previously temporary appointment as governor of Louisiana permanent. To accept the appointments, he told the crowd, he needed to take an oath "to defend the province." However, he informed them, he was not sure that this was a promise he could make in good faith.[11]

Pollock listened to the murmurings of the crowd, who wondered how their brave young governor could hesitate when the king called him to service. It was not for lack of faith to the king, he assured them; he would "shed the last drop of my blood in sacrifice for my Sovereign." He turned the oath into a contract of his own with the people. To swear to defend Louisiana given "the unfortunate state of the colony" with "the few troops that I had" would surely be a hollow oath, he told the crowd, unless the people of Louisiana "promised me to fulfill it." They took the bait. Showering him with effusive compliments and assurances of their fidelity, "they almost carried me in their arms to the Cabildo, forcing open the doors without waiting for the keys." Inside, they hailed him with "the greatest acclamations of joy" and "promised me they would sacrifice their lives in service to the King and do the same with their property."[12]

Therefore, a mere eight days after the hurricane, Margaret Pollock and Marie Felice de St. Maxent bade adieu to their husbands as they rode out of the city to recruit more followers in Amand Broussard and Anne Benôit's Attakapas and other communities north and west of New Orleans. More accustomed to sea travel, Pollock struggled to ride "through dense forests and impassable roads" with insufficient stores and few campaign tents. Still, Pollock had "no doubt [that Gálvez] will soon reduce the British troops, Tories, and savages in this part of the world."[13]

Meditating Conquests

Like Oliver Pollock, leaders of the Revolution greeted Spain's declaration of war with delight, welcoming a strong ally and the prospect of Britain's loss of the Floridas. Congress appointed a committee to negotiate its own treaty of alliance with Spain. Thomas Jefferson, newly elected governor of Virginia, wrote Gálvez that Spain's declaration "has given us all the certainty of a happy issue to the present contest of which human events will admit."[14]

The initial goodwill could not hide the fact that Spanish and American expectations of their alliance did not line up. While Spain needed the rebels only as a distraction to Britain, Congress needed its French and Spanish support for its very survival. The states and Congress were desperate for funds to continue the war. In his letter to Gálvez, Jefferson asked him to advance Pollock over $65,000 to buy supplies to send to Virginia's war effort. Jefferson had to explain that he could not send the flour promised to Pollock for repayment because Virginia had experienced "the most unfavorable harvest ever known since the settlement of this country," nor could he send cured beef and pork because of "the want of salt."[15] Congress resolved that given the "distressed state of our finances and the great depreciation of our paper money," it hoped the Spanish king "will be induced to lend" five million dollars, an enormous sum in 1779.[16]

The Spanish knew that the United States needed loans. In return Spain expected military assistance in taking the Floridas from Britain. Representatives of Congress promised to send troops against St. Augustine and perhaps Pensacola using Spanish funds. But when Congress sent a delegation to confer with George Washington on the matter at his winter quarters at Morristown, New Jersey, in December 1779, Washington declared that it would be "highly imprudent" to send precious troops to the far side of British-occupied Georgia when he was barely holding the army together in the north and was surely going to have to devote troops to defending the Carolinas. Washington proposed just the opposite. Spain and France should send troops and ships to Charleston to help *him*. If they could together secure the Carolinas and Georgia, then "the combined force should proceed to the reduction of the British garrisons in East or West Florida."[17] As Washington put it in a letter to General Benjamin Lincoln, the commander of his Southern Department, "we shall find ample employment in defending ourselves without meditating conquests." The last conquest the Americans had meditated was the disastrous 1775 attempted invasion of Canada. Washington had learned his lesson. The Continental Army had more than enough on its hands in winning independence for its own states. Trying to conquer new territory might doom the whole endeavor.[18]

The Spanish crown, for its part, had no desire to join the venture proposed by Washington and would send no more money without some recompense. Gálvez replied to Jefferson's request for funds by reminding him that Spain was "engaged in a costly war" and that Louisiana "is one of the most exposed" provinces, "having the enemy at its doors." He concluded that "the immense and innumerable expenses occasioned to the crown in this country" as he tried to take West Florida "do not permit me to make the slightest advance of money."[19]

Spain and the United States could not even agree on a treaty. Late in 1779, Congress appointed John Jay minister to the Spanish court. He sailed across the Atlantic to negotiate a treaty of alliance between his country and Spain. His high hopes soon faltered. Disinclined to respect the unsophisticated emissaries of rebellions, the Spanish crown did not officially recognize Jay or receive him at court. When he finally opened negotiations with Spanish Prime Minister José Moñino y Redondo, the Count of Floridablanca, Jay quickly learned that Spain would not consider granting the United States free navigation of the Mississippi, a requirement Congress had included in Jay's instructions. In September, Floridablanca responded sharply to Jay's request. The war was to consolidate Spanish control over the Mississippi, not share it. Floridablanca persuaded Jay that "the King would never relinquish" navigation of the Mississippi and that the crown regarded uncontested control of the Mississippi to be "the principal object to be obtained by the war" and "far more important than the acquisition of Gibraltar."[20] Jay was stuck between the two sides. James Madison wrote Jay on behalf of Congress's Committee for Foreign Affairs assuring him that "Congress entertain too high an opinion of the equity, moderation and wisdom of his Catholic Majesty" to believe that reasonable arguments would not persuade him.[21]

Unbeknownst to John Jay, an unofficial British emissary was also in Spain negotiating to end the war between Spain and Britain. Former West Florida governor George Johnstone was involved in sending the emissary in hopes of removing Spain from the conflict. The British proposal reveals how little Europeans believed the Americans might win this war: Britain would keep South Carolina and Georgia; Spain would get Gibraltar and West Florida; East Florida might go to either. The proposal went nowhere because Spain could make no agreements without participation by its French ally, and soon Spanish victories on the Gulf would make the offer less appealing to Spain.[22]

On the Gulf Coast, Pollock and Gálvez had to cooperate, even if their countries did not, and they needed to portray the Spanish-American alliance as amiable and cooperative to those who might join it. Pollock and Gálvez sent nagging letters to Congress and Virginia on the same ships, Pollock often translating for Gálvez. Pollock had plenty to complain about. He supported an independent United States in part for economic opportunities, but so far, the United States was letting him down. The complete failure of Congress and Virginia to fund even the measly missions of James Willing and George Rogers Clark left Pollock's finances in a shambles. Gálvez had run out of funds to lend him, particularly because he needed to reserve cash to supply his own militia if he sent them into battle in West Florida. Because Spain and Britain were still at peace until June 1779, Pollock had trouble selling the goods that James Willing had given him. Spanish officials in Havana denied Pollock's request to sell the goods there, deeming them illegally seized, while Gálvez ordered him to return goods taken from any victims who were Spanish subjects. Seized peltries Pollock shipped for France were taken at Saint Domingue by someone to whom Congress also owed money.[23]

Another order for ten thousand dollars in goods from Virginia Governor Patrick Henry and Pollock's desire to help the American cause pushed him even further into debt. Gálvez and various New Orleans merchants, who all knew that Pollock's credit was shaky and that Virginia's was even worse, said no. So Pollock mortgaged part of his property. With good reason, he grumbled to Governor Henry that he had been providing goods to Virginia since 1776 and had often written, "but am sorry to be obliged to inform you I've never been honored even with a single line from the Executive Power of your State." Pollock suggested many ways Virginia could repay him, such as flour, pork, tobacco, tallow, or oil he could sell or trade in New Orleans.[24]

Why did Oliver Pollock gamble his family's fortune and reputation for the risky cause of the United States? Oliver and Margaret imagined a postwar future in which the British empire had lost its hold over North America. Catholics and Protestants alike could be part of the region's "flourishing commerce." Connected to the Spanish and French empires, backcountry settlements would grow crops that could be sold through the posts of Manchac and Pensacola, where "we can import our supplies of goods immediately from Europe and dispatch them up to the back settlements."[25] As in the thirteen colonies, part of American patriotism was the sense that it would be easier to get rich under the Americans than under the British. Pollock's fantasies of Gulf Coast development would eventually come true, although perhaps not soon enough for him and his family.

When Pollock finally received a response, the Commerce Committee explained that Congress's flight from Philadelphia had caused the delay. The Committee sympathized with his plight, writing that "it gives us real pain when we reflect on the many difficulties you have labored under by your exertions for the public cause." In response to his letters, Congress had finally passed a resolution that the Committee was "fully empowered to exert every possible means of making you remittances." But the rest of the letter was bad news. All Congress could offer in payment was useless Continental dollars. None of the vessels loaded with goods that he had sent to them had arrived. At least three had been captured in the Atlantic, including the one carrying James Willing, and nothing had been heard of the others. The previous year's wheat crop had been nearly destroyed in Maryland and Virginia by the Hessian fly (called that because Americans blamed Britain's Hessian mercenaries for bringing it). Further, there was an embargo on exporting produce because the Continental Army and the French fleet at Boston needed it. The Congressmen hoped that the coming season's wheat crop would improve and that the currency crisis "has at length opened the eyes of the people" to "consent to large taxations in order to sink a part of the circulating paper, so as to appreciate gradually the remainder and thereby bring it back near to its original standard." Of course, hatred of taxation was what bound Americans together, and there was no way they would accept

Continental three-dollar bill, designed by Benjamin Franklin. An eagle fights a crane, with the motto "Exitus in dubio est," "The outcome is in doubt." (Museum of the American Revolution, Philadelphia)

this plan. At that moment, printing millions of dollars in currency and letting its value deflate was the only politically viable way of financing the war.[26]

Pollock wrote the Continental Congress that Gálvez, with "his noble spirit," had generously harbored Willing and, when the British threatened, had "laughed at their haughtiness and despised their attempts." Pollock asked Congress to show its "gratitude to this Governor" by "sending a sufficient number of Troops to guard this River above, and if possible to spare a sufficient number to take Pensacola."[27] Congress demurred. The Board of War decided on October 31, 1778, that "from the variety of operations in which we are at this time engaged it is impracticable for these states now to undertake an enterprise of the magnitude necessary to take possession of and secure as well the country on the Mississippi."[28]

For the moment, Margaret Pollock was in danger of losing her house. In 1780, Pollock received a credit backed by France from the State of Virginia for $65,814, which he used "to pay off my most pressing debts," but other bills remained. He sold land and slaves to pay these and feared that "in all probability my dwelling house will come next upon the carpet."[29]

Spain, meanwhile, had lost interest in the prospect of coordinating with American troops. The United States seemed weak and disorganized, a fairly useless ally and a neighbor who would be easy to push around after the war. Although Gálvez had initially been excited about the rebellion, Congress's decision to send Willing "before treaty or even consultation" with him had exactly the effect that South Carolina Congressman Henry Laurens had feared during the Congressional debates over sending a mission down the Mississippi, alienating potential allies. Congress added a hint of intellectual incompetence to Gálvez's growing impression of American economic and military incompetence when Gálvez learned in the spring of 1778 that no Americans had been able to read the letter he had sent to Congress the previous August because not a single member of Congress or person they trusted in Philadelphia could read Spanish.[30]

Gálvez and Pollock continued to send some support to the rebels, but Gálvez's enthusiasm had waned. When the Americans proved incompetent militarily and a drain financially, there was really nothing left. Spain's support for them had nothing to do with their cause. Just as Chickasaws, Creeks, and Choctaws allied with the British for their own purposes in countering American expansion, Spain's reasons were all about defeating the British and expanding the Spanish empire. American political structures seemed designed for failure.[31]

Accustomed to the centralized Spanish empire, Gálvez was not impressed with a nation composed of sovereign states with "unconnected interests," as one Virginian explained to him.[32] Spanish and American interests diverged even further over plans for the future of Florida. Patrick Henry proposed "annexing West Florida to the American Confederacy," but Gálvez had other ideas.[33] He wanted West Florida for Spain. Spanish and British officials alike believed that it was only a matter of time before the rebellion surrendered, noting that the rebels still did not have any money and that Washington had only just over ten thousand troops, many of whom were, as William Franklin put it, militia conscripts, "boys, Negroes and Indians."[34] To

Spain, the American war for independence was a risky opportunity to gain back a piece of the British empire. The rebellion had thrown the British colonies up for grabs, and it was time to act.

Marching on British Manchac and Baton Rouge

After Amand Broussard heard the news that war was on, he received his orders to assault British Fort Bute at Manchac. It was an easy conquest because Commander Alexander Dickson had evacuated most of his forces and artillery fifty miles northwest to Baton Rouge, whose defenses he had built up for this purpose. The Spanish forces took Manchac's fort after light resistance from the two dozen British soldiers who had stayed behind. Fifteen years after being expelled from Acadia, Amand Broussard helped to take territory back from the British. And he had the Spanish empire to thank.[35]

Knowing Manchac would be immediately vulnerable to counterattack by water from West Florida, General Gálvez put his limited naval forces to work. During the Willing crisis of 1778, the British armed sloop *West Florida* had stepped up its raids on Spanish ships in Lake Pontchartrain and Lake Maurepas. For the nearly two years since, the sloop had controlled the lakes. Its dominance there meant little to the normal business of Louisiana, which had the port of New Orleans, but Gálvez and Pollock knew that if they could control the lakes, the British posts on the Mississippi would be cut off from Mobile and Pensacola. After the hurricane, Gálvez's men had raised a schooner from the river bottom, which Gálvez gave to Pollock to replace the *Morris* (the old *Rebecca*).[36]

On September 10, 1779, the former captain of the *Morris*, William Pickles, and his crew sailed the new schooner into Lake Pontchartrain and drew up alongside the *West Florida* so that his men could board it. In the ensuing twenty minutes of close combat with guns and swords, the captain of the *West Florida* was killed, and his men surrendered. When the smoke cleared, Pickles had actually lost more men, but he had taken the *West Florida* and soon took possession of settlements on Lake Pontchartrain and established control over the lakes. Around

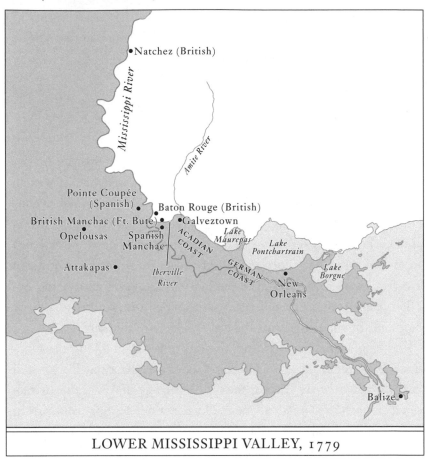

Natchez (British)

Mississippi River

Amite River

Pointe Coupée
(Spanish)
Baton Rouge (British)
British Manchac (Ft. Bute)
Galveztown
Opelousas
Spanish
Manchac
ACADIAN COAST
Lake Maurepas
Lake
Pontchartrain
Attakapas
*Iberville
River*
GERMAN COAST
New
Orleans
Lake
Borgne

Balize

LOWER MISSISSIPPI VALLEY, 1779

Galveztown and on the river, the Spanish seized several vessels coming from Pensacola with provisions and soldiers, as well as other ships heading back to Pensacola after dropping off provisions and ammunition at Manchac, all without alerting the British at Mobile or Pensacola. The first steps toward taking West Florida had worked.[37]

On September 13, 1779, Oliver Pollock, Amand Broussard, and most of the Spanish troops left Manchac. When they were about a mile and a half from Baton Rouge, they set up camp. British Commander Dickson had made a good choice to take his stand there. Spanish scouts reported that the tall earthen fort was protected by a ditch eighteen feet wide and nine feet deep and a stockade of sharpened vertical stakes. The Spanish did not have enough provisions for a long siege, and Gálvez did not want to risk losing a large number of

Bernard Romans, *A General Map of the Southern British Colonies in America*, detail. (North Carolina Collection, Louis Round Wilson Special Collections Library, University of North Carolina, Chapel Hill)

men in an assault considering "that most of my small army was composed of inhabitants; and that any setback would cover the colony with mourning."[38] While Amand Broussard and the militia supported him now, they could change their mind with little warning. Regulars served far from homes that did not necessarily expect them to return, but the militia required more care. Spain could easily lose their support in this action and for the future, and these men's satisfaction would be essential to maintaining Spanish rule in the region. Gálvez wrote that "I do all that is possible to conserve the lives of Militia men who are fathers of families which comprise half of the colony. In these we have the hope of an enlarged, future force."[39]

Considering his constraints, General Gálvez chose deception. Eighteenth-century siege tactics required building a series of trenches. First, a zigzag trench would connect the base camp to a trench dug parallel to and facing one of the British redoubts. As the men dug that parallel trench, they would throw the dirt from it in front of the trench to form an earthen parapet behind which they would mount a battery of heavy artillery. From there, the men would dig new zigzag trenches to new parallel trenches until the artillery and troops could come close enough to take out the opposing redoubt without being overly vulnerable to British artillery fire. The ideal place outside Baton Rouge to establish batteries was where the forest drew closest to the fort. After nightfall on September 20, Gálvez sent a detachment of Alabamas, other Indians, and white and black militia to this spot. He told them to look busy. Some chopped, others dug holes, and a few occasionally fired on the fort from the safety of the trees. While the British focused on these decoys, on the other side of the fort in a place less obviously advantageous but hidden behind a small orchard fence, enslaved laborers were digging real trenches. They built up dirt to form a protective parapet and mounted cannons. Mounting cannons was hard work. The soldiers carried in wooden platforms on which to position the cannons. Because these large siege artillery pieces re-coiled up to twelve feet each time they fired, the platforms had to be deep and well anchored.[40]

During the night, the British in Baton Rouge's fort heard the hammering of nails into platforms, realized their mistake, and changed the direction of their firing. But the completed earthworks sheltered the Spanish. Once the sky began to lighten on the morning of September 21, Gálvez ordered his artillery to open fire. After three and a half hours, the Baton Rouge fort was in such bad shape that Dickson surrendered. The residents of Baton Rouge agreed that to continue to fight "would have had no other effect than the sacrifice of brave men in a garrison no longer tenable."[41]

The Briton Dickson surrendered to the Spaniard Gálvez in their only common language, French. Dickson agreed to evacuate Natchez's Fort Panmure as well, because, now completely cut off from the ports of Mobile and Pensacola, it could receive no supplies or reinforcements. After a day to bury their dead, four hundred regulars and about a hundred militia paraded out of the fort. The regular troops surrendered their arms and became prisoners of war, while the militia returned home on the promise to fight no more for the British. About this time, good news arrived in the Spanish camp that three war sloops and four transports had arrived from Havana. Not yet the thousands promised by the king, the 650 men of the second battalion of the Infantry Regiment of Spain with provisions and supplies were nonetheless very welcome.[42]

The militia had been essential in the capture of the lower Mississippi Valley. General Gálvez wrote his superiors that "the militias have done the most." Broussard and the "Acadians particularly" remembered "the past war and the damages and cruelties that the English inflicted upon them and for which reason they abandoned their land," and they had fought with all their strength. Gálvez also praised New Orleans's free black militia for taking part in "every advance, sham attack, and scout mission; always shooting at the enemy and bearing themselves with as much valor, humanity, and selflessness as the Whites." Indians had pleased him in their restrained warfare, "superior to that shown many times by some of the Civilized Nations of Europe." It had particularly touched him that they had brought their women and children to meet him after the battle. He rewarded his militia with two months' pay, although the mission had taken only a month, for "their spirit, their valor, their loyalty and good will which they have shown in defense of their monarch." All this he used as evidence to the crown that "this same province that formerly gave doubts about its loyalty to the Spanish nation has given the clearest, most solid, and truest proof of its unceasing love and loyalty to its Monarch."[43] King Carlos III commended Gálvez in turn for "the happy success of the expedition carried out with such spirit and speed" and "the great valor and courage shown by their scanty forces."[44]

Pollock worked to assure British settlers in the occupied territory that Spain and the United States were on the side of liberty. There were only around a hundred people living in West Florida's Mississippi Valley settlements, but they could make a great deal of trouble for Spain if they resisted occupation. Gálvez and Pollock hoped that they would instead agree with the West Floridians who had moved to the Spanish side of the Mississippi in the wake of James Willing's expedition. Pollock wrote open letters to West Floridians asserting that Spain would protect their property and their liberty. He sent news to the people of Natchez that, "well knowing your favorable sentiments respecting the glorious cause of the United States, I cannot express the joy and happiness I feel when I come to acquaint you that his Catholic Majesty the King of Spain has declared their independency, and also war against our tyrannical enemy, Great Britain." Spain and the United States were united, Pollock wrote, and "the cause is now become common. Freedom and liberty are now secured." Spain protected its subjects, respected their property rights, and gave them access to a profitable market in Louisiana. Spain's "powerful and good monarch" would grant them "the full enjoyment of your religion" and good prices for their produce.[45]

The cause was not quite as "common" as Pollock alleged. The ambiguity surrounding who had taken Natchez—"the glorious cause of the United States" or the "powerful and good monarch"—revealed a fissure between Pollock's ambitions and those of Spain. Pollock wrote more bluntly to Congress's Commerce Committee in January 1780 that "I am still at a loss respecting who is to possess the Province of West Florida." Behind Gálvez's back, he urged Congress to use Willing's brief 1778 seizures of Natchez and Manchac and Captain Pickles's success on the lakes to claim ownership of what Spanish troops had just taken, and Congress's Commerce Committee concurred.[46]

In surrendering to Pickles as the representative of the United States, the British settlement on Lake Pontchartrain declared itself won by the Americans, not by Spain. The settlers called themselves, in somewhat confused language, "true and faithful subjects to the United Independent States of North America" (which of course had citizens, not subjects).[47] From Lake Pontchartrain to Natchez, the vast majority of West Floridians chose not to fight for the British empire. Unlike most of their neighbors, these people on Lake Pontchartrain believed that the United States, rather than the Spanish empire, could best allow them to "enjoy property and privileges." Although Pollock and Gálvez celebrated together in 1779, their shared victories portended border difficulties between Spain and whoever won the war between Britain and its rebelling colonies.

Pollock and Gálvez had given signs that the United States and Spain would protect the property rights of West Floridians, whereas the British had showed a shocking inability to protect them against either armed pirates or the Spanish army. Only a few determined loyalists fled the occupied towns, formed armed bands in Chickasaw country, and sought to build an underground resistance to the Spanish takeover. Had Spain alone been the conqueror, more might have joined, but the dual promise of Spanish protection and American liberty seemed a better bet than the British.[48]

The seizure of Baton Rouge and Natchez carried tremendous strategic and symbolic significance. The victories propelled the Spanish army onto the path to take all of West and East Florida. Britain had to defend its colonies on yet another military front. The progress showed that the Spanish were fully involved in the war on the continent and could win important victories. The effort increased the loyalty of French Louisianans while paving the way for future efforts to make loyal Spanish colonists out of French- and English-speaking West Floridians. Also, taking territory that the British had gained at the end of the Seven Years' War showed that those gains were reversible. Given these losses to the Spanish and the British failure to subdue the rebels, perhaps Britain was not destined to rule the continent after all.

Defending West Florida

In Pensacola, Isabella Bruce could hear the noise of building Fort George and two redoubts on the hill above Pensacola as well as the constant sound of drumming from the troop drills. Workers were mounting a new battery of artillery on a manmade hill near the storehouse and a floating battery in the bay. Troops drilled every day. Creeks, Choctaws, and other Indians crowded into town to get news and supplies. In hopes of getting more British gifts, they repeatedly mentioned that the Spanish were trying to recruit them. High prices in the shops were another reminder of the war. James kept coming home with bad news. French Admiral Charles Hector, comte d'Estaing had taken St. Vincent and Granada in the West Indies and was now besieging British-held Savannah (the siege in which McGillivray found himself). In early September 1779, Pensacola learned of the Spanish declaration of war. Just a few days later came the worst: Col-

onel Dickson had surrendered Baton Rouge, Natchez, and the surrounding lands, including Thompson's Creek and the Amite River.
The Bruces' plantations were now within the Spanish realm.[49]

At first Pensacolans did not believe the news, thinking the Spanish
must be spreading false rumors to draw the troops away from Pensacola and leave it vulnerable to attack. Once it was confirmed, the
people of Pensacola waited to see if their general, John Campbell,
would order troops and ships to advance on New Orleans or if the
Spanish would attack them first. "As soon as a person awakens," one
soldier wrote, "he looks out to sea to check if a Spanish fleet has arrived."[50] If ever there was a moment to rally West Floridians to defend
their empire, this was it.

British officials strategizing in Whitehall had high hopes for the
war on the Gulf. Former governor of West Florida George Johnstone
was now an admiral and member of Parliament. Back in 1770, after
returning home from West Florida, he had insulted George Germain
seriously enough to cause a duel between them in Hyde Park, which
they both survived. Johnstone had at first objected to the empire's war
against the rebellion, but when Spain joined the war, he renewed his
dreams of a glorious Gulf Coast empire. Together, the former duel-
ists drafted a plan to take Spanish Louisiana. Drawing on his experience in the region, Johnstone assured Germain that the French
residents of Louisiana were unhappy with Spanish rule and would
join the British to overthrow the Spanish. Johnstone knew that local
residents' concerns for their families' independence would drive their
loyalty, but he did not know that Gálvez had already gone a long way
to win it.[51]

As soon as Germain learned of the declaration of war, he sent orders to General John Campbell at Pensacola to attack New Orleans
with help from Indian allies and militia. He ordered Admiral Peter
Parker and Governor John Dalling in Jamaica as well as General
Frederick Haldimand in Quebec to offer Campbell their support. On
September 9, Campbell received Germain's letter and had orders
sent to Dickson at Manchac to put himself "upon your guard against
any sudden attack or surprise from the enemy."[52] Alas, Campbell's letter arrived too late.

When war broke out, Spanish General Bernardo de Gálvez and British General John Campbell found themselves with parallel orders to take the neighboring province with few troops, ships, or supplies and with uncertain support from their own people or Indian allies. Like General Gálvez, General Campbell was an experienced soldier charged with centralizing administration and regularizing the army, navy, and local militias, all with an eye toward economizing for his overextended empire. Both men served in money-losing colonies, which their empires funded for strategic purposes. These colonies received so much imperial funding that the cry of "no taxation without representation" had little resonance. Both Campbell and Gálvez considered themselves men of reason, well suited to their posts, trained in the spirit of the Enlightenment. As a young soldier in the Earl of Loudon's Highlander Regiment, Campbell had fought at the Battle of Culloden in 1746 for the British against fellow Scots, including Alexander McGillivray's namesake. He had stayed in the British army, coming to the Americas during the Seven Years' War, when he was wounded at Ticonderoga and helped to seize Havana, briefly, from the Spanish.[53]

But while Gálvez was determined to make the most of his assignment, Campbell was disappointed to be sent to the distant and vulnerable post of Pensacola. Campbell's letters to his superiors were full of complaints. Provisions were hard to find; even if he could find them, he had little money and poor credit; barracks were incomplete; there was no transportation for troops to the Mississippi posts; defenses were inadequate and he had no proper tools for reinforcing them; high water was threatening the levees; he had only one engineer, no ship carpenters, little artillery, and not enough ships to protect the coast. The soldiers worried Campbell as well. He wrote that many of the regulars were convicts, and though the German Waldeckers were well disciplined and well led, they were not fit "for the woods and wilds of America." Campbell deemed the Maryland and Pennsylvania Loyalists Battalions terrible soldiers in "tatters and rags instead of uniforms."[54]

Rather than compete with Gálvez for the hearts and minds of West Floridians and Louisianans by reminding them of the benefits of belonging to the strongest and most commercially successful empire in the world, Campbell accused Gálvez of cheating. Campbell grumbled that Gálvez's "enterprising spirit" had long been implicitly recruiting settlers on the British side of the Mississippi by allowing them to sell their rice and buy cattle from the Spanish side and not enforcing the Spanish imperial requirement that Protestants convert to Catholicism. He believed that Gálvez offered land and money to any British soldiers who would desert and settle in Spanish Louisiana. Campbell's report to his superiors more than doubled Gálvez's thousand-man expedition against Baton Rouge into over 2,500 men, including "negroes (of whom two hundred were armed)."[55] Campbell believed that in Spanish Louisiana every military-aged man had to fight when the governor ordered it because Spanish iron-fisted governance meant they were permanently "subject to martial law." He imagined that Gálvez commanded with absolute authority, whereas West Florida's inhabitants "seem averse and backward to military duty [unless] compelled by law."[56] While it was true that male Louisianans of military age were required to serve in the militia if called, in reality Gálvez had spent considerable effort to persuade Louisianans to act.

While he complained about Gálvez, Campbell ignored West Floridians' increasing disgruntlement with royal governance. Early in the summer of 1779, Adam Chrystie, the speaker of the House of Assembly, along with over a hundred other men of Pensacola and Mobile, signed a petition to King George asking that "weak-minded" and "avaricious" West Florida Governor Peter Chester be removed. The signatories explicitly denied affiliation with the rebels but decried Chester's "mismanagement" as "subversive of our liberties." They accused him of illegally adjourning the assembly, allowing James Willing to wreak havoc, and granting land to himself and his favorites.[57]

When Germain received the petition and all the bad news from West Florida, he agreed that the colony's military and civilian leadership were letting the empire and its subjects down. Germain upbraided Campbell for his lack of initiative and reminded him of the importance of Indians and the necessity of entertaining and providing for them at Pensacola. He thought that West Florida could have countered Gálvez earlier and even taken New Orleans if Campbell had built up defenses on the Mississippi, which was part of his mandate. Germain also criticized Governor Chester for not calling the Assembly and ordered British Indian Department Agent Alexander Cameron to live with the Choctaws or Chickasaws rather than in Pensacola.[58]

Following the bad news from Manchac and Baton Rouge, Pensacola was in a constant uproar. Occasionally, the lighthouse would send up smoke, signaling that unidentified ships were approaching. People would shade their eyes, squinting out into the Gulf to see if doom or hope approached. Troops loaded onto ships, ships lifted anchor to sail out toward the mouth of the harbor, and artillerymen ran to the batteries. As James and Isabella Bruce rushed to the fort with their children and a few belongings, questions must have crowded their minds. Would they be safe? Where would they sleep? Would they see the children's bodies destroyed by Spanish mortars? Or watch them slowly starve as a blockade held up the precious food that could keep them alive? Would Archibald and Charlotte survive only as orphans to face a future of British decline and Spanish ascendancy, perhaps forcing them into servitude or Catholicism?

Campbell might have led his troops, ships, and Indian allies to retake the lakes and Manchac (which Gálvez would have had as much trouble defending as Dickson) and marched from there to Galveztown and New Orleans. Or he could have taken advantage of Gálvez's absence and attacked New Orleans by sea. At first, he had the troops' baggage and provisions loaded onto ships in anticipation of sailing. But on October 24, he waffled and ordered that the baggage and provisions be unloaded. Hamlet-like, he changed his mind again that evening and ordered that the ships be reloaded "as quickly as possible" because the troops would embark the next day. Frustrated with his indecision and revisions, Governor Chester and the Council, including James Bruce, convened a meeting with him the next morning where they read all the reports Campbell had received. The governor and Council recommended that it was too late to send troops against the Spanish assault on the Mississippi and that the best course of action was to secure Pensacola. Campbell ordered the ships unloaded once again. One can only imagine the wearied reaction of the men doing the loading and unloading.[59]

His wavering notwithstanding, Campbell did have reason to complain. Despite George Germain's orders, no reinforcements came from Jamaica or Quebec, whose governors both found their own security concerns too urgent to be sacrificed to West Florida. Indeed, nothing seemed to be going Britain's way. French and Spanish ships continued to besiege Gibraltar and Minorca. They had already taken St. Vincent and Grenada and threatened the Leeward Islands, Jamaica, and England itself.[60] Compared to Gálvez's access to black troops from both Cuba and Louisiana, white West Floridians were much less willing to enlist and arm large numbers of nonwhites in their ranks. When Campbell asked Governor Chester to call the Assembly to try again for a militia bill, Chester replied that he saw no reason to think that the Assembly would be more inclined to do so than a year earlier, even though war against Spain had broken out since then. The council debated the wisdom of declaring martial law, but Chester decided against it because he worried that inhabitants would flee if he tried to force them to fight. Campbell must have wondered where exactly Chester thought they could run with battlefronts on all sides. Although some men did form militia companies, Campbell deemed most West Floridians as "self-interested and without public spirit, whose minds are only attached to gain and their private concerns."[61]

But it was exactly their "private concerns" to which Campbell should have appealed. According to a German chaplain at Pensacola, the city's carpenters refused to work on defenses, arguing that "neither the governor nor the general can force them to work as it is against English independence." The chaplain marveled that "these carpenters consider themselves to be gentlemen equal to the governor and general."[62] Campbell should have known, as Gálvez did, that colonists needed inspiration. People like the Bruces and their neighbors needed to believe that their personal and family independence depended on remaining in the British empire. Unpersuaded, most of them refused to contribute to a defense they saw as futile. Instead they were working, according to Campbell, "to secure their property under whose dominion soever they may be." The French-speaking inhabitants were equally unwilling to help. While Johnstone had predicted that French Louisianans would fight on the British side because Spanish rule was "hateful to their French subjects," Campbell concluded that had been true "sometime ago," but in recent years "cajoling and lenient methods of managing them have been adopted, in which their present governor [Gálvez] in particular has been very successful."[63]

Conclusion: Future Expeditions

General Campbell might have used the war to bring West Floridians together under the common cause of defending their land and empire against the Americans, represented by the roguish James Willing, and against Catholic, monarchical France and Spain. Perhaps he could even have fulfilled George Germain's and George Johnstone's ambitions to seize Louisiana and spread the British empire west. Perhaps he could have rallied Choctaws, Creeks, and even Chickasaws to forge a stronger alliance that would work toward a new vision of a centralized empire that protected Indian independence and promoted mutually beneficial trade. Perhaps he could have led his forces to make a bold and unexpected attack on the Spanish, inspiring Indians, West Floridians, and his superiors to have confidence in his ability and in the possibility of expanding the British empire at Spain's expense. He tried none of these. He just sat in Pensacola, where he worried and complained.

At the same time, General Gálvez decided to go on the offensive under similar conditions. He hoped his successes thus far would inspire more support from his superiors in Havana and Spain, from Spanish subjects in both Louisiana and the conquered part of West Florida, and even among the captured regulars, especially the German Waldeckers, many of whom exchanged their captivity for service in the Spanish army. Excited at the prospects, Oliver Pollock wrote Gálvez to offer "your Excellency my services on any future expedition you may see proper to undertake." He believed that Mobile and Pensacola would be next, with Jamaica not far behind.[64]

CHAPTER TWELVE

A Wartime Borderland

IN SEPTEMBER 1779, Payamataha received word from British General John Campbell that because Spain had declared war, the Chickasaws and Choctaws should prepare "to march where ordered."[1] Payamataha and other Indians throughout the Mississippi Valley had already heard the news. The decisions that they made in the coming months would help to determine the victor, and both Europeans and Indians knew it. As Campbell's order indicated, he wanted Indians to be available to assist British defensive or offensive needs in spite of having no budget to increase supplies for military or diplomatic purposes. Spanish General Bernardo de Gálvez understood his weaker position with fewer Indian allies than the British. He promised Indians goods and trade in return for merely their neutrality.

As war heated up, Indians argued over how to respond to Campbell's and Gálvez's requests. Indians willing to fight alongside the British against the rebel settlers were much less eager to join the British against the Spanish empire. Like the British empire, Spain promised to balance the interests of allied Indians with those of its subjects. At the same time Britain was looking less and less like an ally who could actually protect Indian independence from settlers. Neutrality and collecting goods without having to fight were real and appealing possibilities. At the same time, local residents, free and enslaved, would have to decide how to respond as Spanish victories and British weakness opened opportunities.

Staying Out of War

The Chickasaws' failure to report enemy actions or show up for battles was increasingly obvious to the British. As British Deputy Indian Superintendent Alexander Cameron put it, the Chickasaws still "did not seem to approve of taking any active part in the war."[2] Loyalists fleeing Natchez and Baton Rouge and seeking refuge among the Chickasaws would also complicate Chickasaw neutrality. However, the British could neither force the Chickasaws to fight nor afford to punish them for not fighting. Indeed, Payamataha would use Spanish overtures to increase his access to goods and his leverage over the British.

In December 1779, Payamataha traveled to New Orleans. The Spanish received him and his delegation with "all possible display and pomp."[3] Payamataha accepted gifts, a Spanish medal, and a commission signed by Bernardo de Gálvez. Gálvez asked that the Chickasaws help persuade their neighbors that "all of the Nations should live together in good accord under the orders and law of the Great King of Spain." While Spanish successes created some pressure on Indians in the vicinity of the Gulf Coast, for the most part they created opportunities. Having two empires actively seeking their assistance or, even better, their neutrality could fit perfectly with Payamataha's peaceful plans while fostering Indians' independence and prosperity.[4]

Both Bernardo de Gálvez and John Campbell felt the squeeze of increasing Indian expectations. In the wake of military victory, Native diplomacy overwhelmed Gálvez in New Orleans. He wrote his uncle that "the multitude of Indians who come to this city . . . take up my time which is needed in the various affairs of the government."[5] He ordered an astounding and quite specific 4,000 rifles, 40,000 pounds

D. BERNARDO DE GALVEZ

439 220

CORONEL DEL BATALLON FIXO DE LA PROVINCIA DE LA LUY‑
SIANA, GOBERNADOR INTERINO DE LA CIUDAD EL NUEVO
ORLEANS, COMANDANTE GENERAL DE DICHA PROVINCIA, è
INSPECTOR GENERAL DE TODA LA TROPA REGLADA, Y MILI‑
CIAS DE ELLA.

Chicachas Opayé Mathaas Grand Chef des Chis, Il Saura par L'envoyé du Général Espagnol qui Lui tend la main et qui Veut que Son Pavillon Soit Respecté Dans toutes Les Nations Sauvages Comme Chicachas, Abenaquis, Talapouches, Casuita, Alibamons, Charaquis, et toutes

Bernardo de Gálvez's commission for "Opayé Mathaas" (Payamataha), 1779. (CO 5/81, British National Archives)

Les autres Nations
Voisines, á Cette fin que toutes
Les Nations ensemble
Vivent d'un bon accord Sous
Les Ordres et Loix du
Srand Roy D'Espagne.

Nouvelle Orleans
le 17 Decembre 1779

Bdo de Galvez

of shot, 1,800 hatchets and axes, 800 copper kettles, 6,000 blankets, 500 pounds of vermillion dye, 596 medals and gorgets, 2,760 shirts, and 2,000 hoes. The hoes had to be seven inches wide, he insisted, because Indian women had rejected the previous ones as too narrow. Gálvez soon found that the stock of presents that seemed generous to him was insufficient for Indian demands. He worried that "the English by force of presents and gifts will upset their good disposition." Gálvez could only "hope to keep them content with promises" until more goods arrived.[6]

Knowing that the British would make the same calculations as Gálvez, Indians collected presents at British Mobile and Pensacola as well. Less diplomatic than Payamataha, Choctaw Red Topknot declared to the British that "now the Spaniards give us presents, two people love us." He alleged that "whoever gives the most, will be the most regarded so I would advise you to give presents superior to the Spaniards."[7] To counter Spanish efforts among the Chickasaws and Choctaws, British officials planned a congress at Mobile for March at which they would give presents that Secretary of State for the Colonies George Germain had promised were being sent on the ship *Earl Bathurst*. Deputy Indian Superintendent Charles Stuart advised Alexander Cameron that "great attention be paid" at the congress to Payamataha, "whose importance is not only great in his own nation but extends over the whole Choctaw nation." Charles Stuart credited the Chickasaws with a "free and independent spirit," yet he failed to see the Chickasaws as truly independent, writing that "by proper management [they] may be made serviceable." Payamataha had no intention of making his people "serviceable."[8]

While General Campbell's calls were going out for Chickasaws and Choctaws to come to the congress at Mobile, the *Earl Bathurst* had arrived. When the ship was unloaded, however, General Campbell could see that the goods intended for Pensacola were missing, leaving him both in dire need of supplies for his own troops and without sufficient presents for Indians. He concluded that, out of incompetence or insubordination, someone must have unloaded the supplies in Jamaica. The few presents for Indians were "in a very bad condition."

Many of the blankets and cloth were "entirely damaged," as was most of the gunpowder. Germain had written that the five hundred barrels of pork on board were to go to John Stuart at the head of the Indian Department, but Stuart was dead, and one of his executors in Pensacola seized the pork as personal property to be distributed to Stuart's heirs. The losses were disastrous.[9]

The shortages did not help Alexander McGillivray's efforts to inspire Creeks to fight alongside the British. After the 1779 failures to coordinate a large effort against Georgia, members of the Upper Creek Council argued that small raiding parties were safer and more effective. The Council declared at the end of April 1779, while some Creeks were still fighting in Georgia, that they would send only small raiding parties from now on, a decision many Indians were making.[10]

In the summer and fall of 1779, an even more devastating development kept Creek minds off war and limited their ability to contribute. The troops for New York that had reinforced Pensacola had brought the smallpox virus, which killed 40 percent of the Maryland Loyalists. When it arrived in Creek country, healers there recognized the symptoms. First came the fever and then the headache and backache. Proof that it was something worse than usual came with the first rash in a sick person's mouth and throat, along with a spike in fever. Over the next two days, the first victim's skin began to blister. There was no cure, and the only way to avoid smallpox was to get away from the breath, scabs, and clothing of the infected. The Creeks had suffered from smallpox before, but not in recent years. The latest attack of smallpox had been in 1760, so some people had acquired immunity, but by 1779 no one under eighteen had been exposed, so the effects on them were especially dramatic. By the fall, the epidemic was raging. Across the continent, this outbreak, which began in 1775 and continued in different parts of North America until 1782, would eventually kill over one hundred thousand people, far more than the Revolution's battles.[11]

Creeks practiced quarantine, cutting off communication with any Indian towns that were infected as well as all British towns, which they assumed were the most likely source of smallpox. By October, people in Creek towns that were not affected had fled with their families into the woods, camping in smaller groups until they were confident that it was safe to return home. Quarantine was the best solution before the adoption of inoculation, which was widely practiced in much of Asia and some of Africa and Europe by the late eighteenth century but was only slowly taking hold in the Americas, where it remained controversial—George Washington imposed it in 1777 on the Continental Army against stiff resistance. The process required being infected with the smallpox virus, which carried a risk of death (somewhere between a half a percent and two percent), although a much lower risk than the disease itself. The Creeks had no access to inoculation, so those in infected towns hoped to recover or stay uninfected, while the rest of the Creeks lived and hunted in the woods. For the Creeks and their neighbors, the smallpox epidemic carried more weight than the news of Spanish victories at Manchac and Baton Rouge. It was a good time to stay away from battles, war councils, and other large gatherings and instead concentrate on feeding their families and keeping them safe.[12]

By the fall of 1779, Alexander Cameron had to conclude that the Creeks were "tired of the war, and would much rather hunt the bear who are very numerous about them at present than the rebels."[13] The spring's offensive had brought casualties but no benefits, and the distances and conflicting expectations had left everyone dissatisfied. The news that came to Creek country in October that Spain had declared war against Britain only made matters worse. Creeks continued to demand supplies for the small raiding parties that continued to venture out, perhaps spreading smallpox to South Carolina and Georgia, where it broke out soon thereafter. But they were not in the mood to consider another joint offensive with the British.[14]

The Siege of Mobile

Fort Charlotte sat on a gently sloping bank at the top of Mobile Bay with most of its thirty cannons pointed seaward. It was a large bastioned fortress, faced in brick, which the French residents still called by

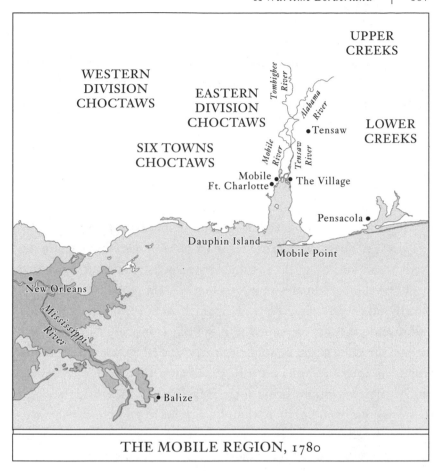

THE MOBILE REGION, 1780

its pre–Seven Years' War name of Fort Condé. Founded by the French at the beginning of the century, the town of Mobile circled the fort to the west, north, and east. The wealthier French residents lived in large one-story brick houses built around courtyards (naturalist William Bartram believed they were imitating the layout of Creek buildings). Poorer residents, probably including Petit Jean, lived in standard French colonial cypress-framed houses that were filled in with brick, plastered, and white-washed. Much of the fort had fallen into ruin since the Seven Years' War, but General Campbell had appointed as commanding officer Captain Elias Durnford, an army engineer and lieutenant governor of West Florida. He did his best to restore it and coordinate his three hundred regulars plus Royal Artillery, engineers, loyalists, and militia. The Spanish would soon test them.[15]

In General Bernardo de Gálvez's calculations, taking Mobile would rob the rest of West Florida of the meat that Mobile provided, putting it instead in the mouths of Spain's troops. Gálvez's supply request to Havana included not only two thousand troops, provisions, bombs, mortars, siege guns, and grenades but also large quantities of salt to make salt meat from the cattle they would commandeer around Mobile. Plus the Spanish could use the post of Mobile to recruit Chickasaws, Choctaws, and West Florida's French colonists, whom Gálvez promised he would "release from slavery." By "slavery," Gálvez meant unwanted British rule, but he would also need the help of Mobile's literally enslaved people, including Petit Jean.[16]

Petit Jean's work with cattle was part of Mobile's value to both the British and the Spanish. Petit Jean grasped early that his home might be the next Spanish target. Death could come for him or his family and friends at the end of a Spanish gun or from the starvation and disease that accompanied war. If Petit Jean were captured by a foreign force, he might be sold, probably away from his wife and into worse circumstances than his life as a cattle ranger. But one never knew what war might bring for a slave: the chance to defend his master's empire and perhaps thereby win his freedom, the chance to earn his freedom by assisting the enemy, or simply the opportunity to escape in the chaos. In the meantime, Petit Jean worked, as usual. He contributed cattle to the 3,353 pounds of fresh beef and 1,860 pounds of salt beef provided to visiting Choctaws at Mobile in late November and December 1779 and the stores being set aside in case of siege.[17]

At his home in Attakapas in early January 1780, Amand Broussard received word that his militia company was to report to New Orleans for another expedition. Some of the militia "protested that they were not obligated to serve the King on the seas, but only on land, and in the bayous."[18] Manchac and Baton Rouge were just up the river, but Mobile and Pensacola were a journey, and militiamen often balked at serving so far from home. However, Gálvez's officers managed to persuade most of them that conquering all of West Florida would benefit them. Because there were not enough ships to transport all of the troops, Amand Broussard's company waited in New Orleans. Nearly three hundred regulars, over three hundred white militia, one hundred free black militia, two dozen slaves, and two dozen American volunteers sailed from New Orleans on January 11 to rendezvous with the troops heading for Mobile from Havana.[19]

Pollock did not come this time. He had asked Congress for an American military commission, explaining that "I had the honor to serve with his Excellency General Galvez as his voluntary aid on his campaign at the reduction of the British posts on the Mississippi."[20] In war he would be safer with a military commission, which meant that if captured he would be treated as a prisoner of war rather than as a traitor. But Congress had refused, leaving him vulnerable to the noose. Yet Pollock was too much of an American patriot to accept Gálvez's offer of the rank of colonel in the Spanish army to reward him for being "at my side for all of the campaign."[21] He chose to remain an American in New Orleans with Margaret.

In both Mobile and Pensacola, Petit Jean and the Bruces could see smoke rising from their lighthouses—ships had been spotted. The bad news soon followed that they were Spanish, a fleet coming to attack either Mobile or Pensacola. Reflecting on the fate of West Florida, General Campbell wrote to his commanding general, Henry Clinton, that it would soon "be decided whether it is to belong to Great Britain or Spain." Like Gálvez, he did not consider the United States as a possibility. For the next few days, Pensacolans and Mobilians nervously waited.[22]

Pensacola's lookouts had spotted the ships because the Gulf winds had pushed part of the Spanish fleet east past its destination. For weeks, stormy weather had frustrated the fleet's attempts to get close enough to Mobile Bay to enter. When yet another tremendous thunderstorm arose, the remaining ships each tried to sail through the pass between Dauphin Island and Mobile Point into Mobile Bay to escape the churning seas. Six ships were beached on sand banks near the entrance to the bay. From noon until one the next morning, the crews tried to drag the heavy ships back toward the water. The men succeeded with three of them, but the other three, including the king's frigate *El Volante*, would not budge. Two days later, when the weather settled, the crews of the other ships sent launches to save the stranded men and some of the supplies and artillery. As they were working, they were pleased to see most of the ships that had dispersed in the storm return to Mobile Bay.[23]

Durnford called all of Mobile's people to its defense, including enslaved and free blacks, while the Spanish forces reconvened. On the afternoon of February 19, the Spanish salvaged what they could and set up camp. They were soon joined by a small fleet from Havana with about six hundred troops of the two thousand that Gálvez had requested. Together with Gálvez's roughly 750 men, they made their way up the eastern side of the bay, hauling the artillery. Twenty-two Indians, whom Gálvez recorded only as "of the English party," so probably Eastern or Western Division Choctaws or possibly Creeks, met with him to promise neutrality and friendship.[24]

The Bruces and their Pensacola neighbors were relieved to learn that the smoke was a false alarm and that Mobile was the Spanish target, but they remained focused on defending their homes. When General Campbell called for the men of Pensacola to march to Mobile's aid, James Bruce and most of his neighbors refused. To Campbell's disgust, he rallied "the whole number of four volunteers."[25] James Bruce chose to stay home with Isabella, Archibald, and Charlotte in case the war came home. On March 5, Campbell left with two infantry divisions and over a hundred Indians (probably Choctaws). The Bruces watched the majority of Pensacola's forces march away from their defense.

It was an uncharacteristically bold move for Campbell to lead nearly all his force to Mobile. Because they needed to avoid the Spanish ships in Mobile Bay, they walked a less developed path for seventy miles toward Tensaw, thirty miles north of Mobile. Marching in the rain, they waded through bayous up to their knees, walked through grass higher than their heads, and crossed fallen trees on a path that was seldom obvious. At night, they sat around fires and cooked meat the Indians had hunted during the day. Four men drowned crossing the Perdido River (the present-day border between Alabama and

Florida). As one participant recorded, "How difficult the journey through such a wilderness, where one could not find his way, nor still less, encounter a human habitation, I can not describe it accurately."[26] They assembled at Tensaw on March 10 and built rafts to place atop canoes to ride down the Tensaw River to the Mobile River to Fort Charlotte. On the night of March 12 at Tensaw, Campbell noticed that the sound of cannons that he had been hearing for some time had stopped. He delayed the advance until he could get news, which turned out to be bad. A scout reported that the Spanish flag was flying over Fort Charlotte. He was too late.[27]

It had taken only a day of heavy fire for the Spanish artillery to open two breaches in the fort. The British in Fort Charlotte had returned fire vigorously but then ran out of ammunition in the proper caliber. At sunset on the 12th, Durnford raised the white flag, and the next day he proposed articles of capitulation. Amand Broussard's ship from New Orleans arrived on March 14, the day that three hundred British regulars and militia marched down to the breach in Fort Charlotte and surrendered their arms. As soon as Gálvez occupied the fort, he repaired its breach and mounted artillery to defend against Campbell.[28]

Campbell turned his men back toward Pensacola as soon as he heard of the Spanish victory. He might have had a good chance to retake Fort Charlotte, but he chose to reestablish Pensacola's defenses. During Campbell's retreat, a Spanish party attacked his rear guard and took several men prisoner, only adding to the mission's futility. At some point on the dreary march back, Campbell realized that he had missed his best chance to take New Orleans. As he admitted to British Commanding General Henry Clinton, "to furnish a force wherewith to attack Mobile, the entire Province of Louisiana was drained of every man fit to bear arms whether white, Negro, or mullato, and would have fallen an easy conquest to a handful of men." Without ships, he could not have gotten his full force to New Orleans, but he could have transported "a handful of men," which might have been enough.[29] Rather than gaining ground, he had lost most of West Florida.

Petit Jean in Spanish Service

Petit Jean may have been among the Mobilians cheering Gálvez and his army as they marched into town. Celebrating as a foreign army marches in is not necessarily a sign of anything but quick wits. Still, West Florida's second city had fallen so quickly in part because French residents of Mobile felt little reason to fight for British rule. If the British had acted sooner, they might have converted French West Floridians by appealing to their political and economic liberties. After all, most of them were longtime residents of the Gulf Coast, not Acadians with recent reasons for despising the British. But the British had not managed to advertise the benefits of their rule. Given French West Floridians' (illegal) economic ties to Spanish Louisiana, the Spanish alliance with France, and the lack of British military protection or political representation, the British empire had little claim on their loyalty.[30]

The enslaved population of Mobile may have cheered—and sincerely so. The Spanish had a reputation, not always deserved, for granting more rights to slaves and free blacks and more opportunities for slaves to gain freedom than the British. When Mobile was under siege, Petit Jean may have fled into Fort Charlotte with his wife and other Mobilians to wait out the siege to the sound of cannon fire. Or if he was with his cattle, he probably stayed clear of the fort and Campbell's force until the siege was over. In either case, he could have seen that the Spanish soldiers marching into Mobile included at least four hundred armed men of African descent. The New Orleans free black militia wore striking white jackets with gold buttons and round hats topped with crimson cockades. Free men of mixed ancestry formed a different company within the free black militia: the New Orleans "pardo" militia. They wore green jackets with eye-catching white buttons and lapels. At least fifty slaves and free blacks, possibly including Petit Jean himself, had defended Mobile, but there were fewer of them, they were not a permanent force, and they did not have uniforms. If not freedom in absolute terms, would Spanish rule convey more liberty, economic independence, and outward signs of respect for enslaved peoples relative to British rule?[31]

Petit Jean took the chance and became a courier and spy for Spain. It is not clear whether Petit Jean offered his services to a Spanish officer or if a Spaniard learned of his knowledge of Mobile's surroundings after the siege and requested him from his master. He may even have run from Mobile to the Spanish during the siege. On February 23, a slave escaped from Mobile and brought the Spanish the news that only three hundred men guarded the fort, news that helped Gálvez plan his attack. In any case, Petit Jean knew that his skills and knowledge of the region and its peoples, including the land and waters between Mobile and Pensacola, would be valuable to the Spanish and might benefit him as well.[32]

The Spanish made full use of the region's enslaved workforce. In charge of the occupying force at Mobile, Colonel José de Ezpeleta requisitioned slaves from their owners and employed them mostly in the daily work of rebuilding, maintaining, and supplying the fort. Enslaved women and men grew crops, drove cattle, cooked food, and processed timber as they had before, but now they worked to supply the Spanish king's troops. The cattle that Petit Jean had tended supplied the large quantity of meat needed for some two hundred soldiers. Other slaves baked loaves of bread by the hundreds in the fort's ovens. Slaves began building the roads the army would travel to Pensacola, built carts and barrels to carry their supplies, and forged horseshoes and gun parts in the blacksmith shop.[33]

By mid-April, Petit Jean was serving as a courier for the Spanish. He delivered messages and horses to the Spanish forces building roads to Pensacola. As Petit Jean proved himself, his responsibilities grew. He carried messages to and from Gálvez's ship in the Mobile River. In late April he reported to Gálvez the news he had collected at Mobile: A party of Chickasaw and British loyalist men were raiding the French and Spanish settlements to the north, and those inhabitants requested Spanish soldiers to protect them. His communications delivered, Petit Jean received Gálvez's replies for the Mobile commander, probably was fed and put up for the night, and then returned to shore the next morning to carry Gálvez's reply back to Mobile. Through the summer and beyond, Mobile Commandant Henrique Grimarest and Colonel Ezpeleta conferred with Petit Jean when they wanted a local's opinion.[34]

Petit Jean's missions also afforded him authority over other slaves. When he asked Grimarest for four men to take a canoe to the other bank to lead the horses, Grimarest agreed. By then, Gálvez was familiar enough with Petit Jean that Grimarest did not have to explain who he was in his letter informing him of Petit Jean's actions. Gálvez replied that Petit Jean could choose the slaves he wanted for his mission. In British Mobile, slaves had needed passes if traveling more than two miles, and they were forbidden from bearing arms, trading goods, and owning cattle. Wartime and Spanish rule had changed all of that.[35]

Some slaves used their increased access to officials and importance to Spanish goals to gain leverage over their masters and enforce Spanish law regarding the treatment of slaves. When the slaves of one master came to complain that he mistreated them and owed them money, Gálvez ordered an inquiry into the matter and warned that the master must "understand that in these circumstances he must agree to deal gently with his slaves and pay them what is legitimately due."[36] In May 1780, several slaves from New Orleans fled to Mobile, hiding in the bayous along the way. They presented themselves to Ezpeleta, telling him that their masters had "punished them much" and that one had even taken a shot at one of them. They asked to remain together at Mobile in Ezpeleta's service. Ezpeleta wrote Gálvez to ask if they could stay, stressing the abuse and the fact that he had "very few blacks here for the many jobs for which they can be used."[37] Wartime gave slaves greater influence over commandants desperate for their labor. Even if they were unlikely to be freed, small differences in influence and autonomy meant a great deal.

From the empire's perspective, however, empowering a skilled slave did nothing to challenge slavery, directly or theoretically. It was the king's authority over all his subjects, free and enslaved, that enabled Spanish officials to appropriate slaves' labor away from their masters. When Petit Jean requested slaves to assist his missions, he was in effect mustering masters' property in the name of the king. The system that allowed opportunities for slaves also ensured that these opportunities never changed Spanish officials' position at the top of the local hierarchy and Petit Jean's position well below them. The Spanish knew that giving enslaved people responsibility did not lead to slavery's end. On the contrary, it seemed to strengthen the system. And Petit Jean was an exceptional case. The slave trade continued as ever, both to and within the Gulf Coast. At least one woman from Mobile found herself advertised by the Spanish in New Orleans for sale for five hundred pesos: "young and a good worker, and she cooks and irons."[38] While Petit Jean enhanced his own independence, this woman was simply sold. Both served the Spanish empire in America. Wartime created opportunities for individual liberties or even freedom from slavery, but no side promised to abolish slavery.

The News from Mobile in Philadelphia

In June 1780, Continental Congress President Samuel Huntington was getting bad news. George Washington reported that soldiers in the Continental Army's winter camp at Morristown, New Jersey, on short rations and having received no pay for months, were on the verge of mutiny. British General Henry Clinton had sailed south from New York with a large force in December 1779. He hoped to extend British victories in Georgia by taking Charleston. Indians and closet loyalists would surely then increase their support for the British, who could split the south from the rebelling middle colonies and New England. Huntington knew that if the British won back the profitable southern colonies, the remaining United States would find nationhood much more difficult economically and diplomatically. On May 12, 1780, the Americans surrendered Charleston to Clinton, losing their entire southern army plus four of their precious few warships. Clinton returned to New York but left General Lord Charles Cornwallis in a good position to march out of Charleston and reconquer Georgia and the Carolinas. As Huntington contemplated American losses, the hero of Saratoga, Benedict Arnold, was feeling increasingly unappreciated and resentful. Always seeking parity among the states, Congress had not promoted him to major general because his state of Connecticut already had two major generals. In addition, Arnold was increasingly pessimistic about American chances to defeat Britain. In September, Huntington and other Americans would learn that Arnold had begun spying for the enemy. In the meantime, John Adams reported from Europe that the latest British peace proposal still insisted that New York, New Jersey, South Carolina, and Georgia remain under British rule. The war was not going to end soon.[39]

In this dreary context, Bernardo de Gálvez's letter to Congress announcing victory over the British at Mobile was a cause for compensatory joy. Huntington immediately wrote General Washington, "I have at this moment received authentic information that the Spaniards have taken Mobile."[40] The next day, he had Gálvez's letter read on the floor of Congress. The letters that soon followed from Oliver Pollock reminding Huntington how much Congress owed him did not diminish Americans' joy at Britain's loss. Keeping a close eye on British newspapers, John Adams believed that losing Mobile deflated British hopes, which had risen after Clinton's conquest of Charleston. "The affair of Mobile," Adams wrote Huntington, plus uncertainty in the naval war against France and Spain, "begin now to sink their spirits again."[41]

The British southern strategy depended on loyalists and Indians, but both groups had waited three years for a major British effort and then were disappointed with the failure of Archibald Campbell and Augustine Prevost to take all of Georgia in 1779. The capture of Charleston had accelerated the effort, but now the Spanish and French were involved. Their presence made some Indians less willing to fight with the British than when the enemy had been merely rebellious and land-hungry colonists, and Britain now seemed less certain to prevail than it had at the start of the war. Perhaps the British had missed their chance.[42]

The News from Mobile in Little Tallassee

The first news that Alexander McGillivray received about Mobile was a message from General Campbell in early March 1780 that Pensacolans had spotted a Spanish fleet. McGillivray was returning from the Lower Creek towns intending to raise another party to raid the Georgia frontier. Within a short distance of Little Tallassee, he received the call from General Campbell for, as McGillivray put it, "all the assistance in my power to afford him against the enemy."[43] Like Campbell in Pensacola and Gálvez in New Orleans, McGillivray needed to persuade people to fight who did not have to. In Gálvez's case, as both governor and commanding general, he was Louisiana's legitimate ruler, but French Louisianans were not really his people. For General Campbell, Pensacolans were mostly Britons, but they did not consider themselves under the command of a military rather than civilian leader. For McGillivray, the Upper Creeks were his people, but he was not their leader.

For the past three years, McGillivray had worked to increase his influence among the Creeks. He had been meeting headmen and influential warriors, giving speeches before groups of Creeks, and answering women's concerns about the reasons for fighting and the security of the nation if its men went to war. He reminded Upper Creek women and men of their alliance obligations to Britain and the goods and provisions the British would provide to the warriors and their families. He had to answer concerns that Governor Chester was making land grants beyond the Creek border with West Florida. It was a harder sell getting Creeks to fight Spaniards than to fight Americans, so he stressed Creek interests in the overall war as well as the opportunities for glory on the Gulf Coast.[44]

Now that General Campbell's call to protect the coast had come, McGillivray accelerated his efforts. Summoning the warriors to council was always a tricky decision. Calling men in from the hunt for no reason could have disastrous effects on the Creek economy and his own influence. General Campbell's message was urgent, so McGillivray and Emistisiguo spoke to Little Tallassee's warriors and sent messengers to other Upper Creek towns asking anyone home from the hunt to gather at Little Tallassee. Their efforts paid off. On March 20, about six hundred Upper Creeks set off with McGillivray, and Emistisiguo was to send more hunters to follow as they returned home. Not knowing where the fighting would be by the time they reached the coast, they headed for Pensacola, with McGillivray charging their expenses along the way to the Indian Department.[45]

When the Upper Creeks arrived in Pensacola in late March 1780, they expected General Campbell to receive them with gratitude as loyal allies and to host them with a feast and formal ceremony. But Campbell had just returned from his futile march to Mobile. He was despondent about the fall of Mobile and now had no immediate use for McGillivray's forces. Making matters worse, no ship had arrived with new Indian supplies to replace the damaged and missing ones, and the shipload that he and Cameron had scrambled to assemble in Pensacola and sent to Mobile for the planned congress had been captured by the Spanish as they sailed into Mobile Bay. Campbell sent word to McGillivray that he was "sick" and could not attend the ceremony to welcome the Creeks and about three hundred Choctaws who had also come to Pensacola's rescue. For two weeks the Creeks and Choctaws waited at Pensacola. In the meantime, another 1,100 Upper Creeks and nearly two hundred Lower Creeks arrived.[46]

After the expected supply ships did arrive, Campbell met with the Creeks and Choctaws on April 12. His first words were to assure them that there would be presents for them as soon as the ships were unpacked. A Creek spokesman responded that he was "pleased to have the opportunity to see and shake hands with the greatest warrior of the big-brother-across-the-big-water," perhaps implying that Campbell had better be the king's "greatest warrior" to keep them waiting two weeks. The speaker bristled at Campbell's assumption that the Creeks' first interest was goods, saying that he "did not come here to get presents, but had heard rumors . . . of a war with their common enemy, Spain."[47] Of course Creeks did expect supplies to compensate for their trouble, but they did not like being treated as mercenaries. Deputy Indian Superintendent Alexander Cameron despaired that Campbell "does not understand anything of Indians or their affairs.

He thinks they are to be used like slaves or a people void of natural sense."[48] McGillivray must have cringed with embarrassment and soon found himself hounded by Creeks demanding to know why their reception was so different from what he had promised.

Still, McGillivray could be proud as he surveyed the wide expanse of deerhide tents outside Pensacola. He knew that Spanish scouts could easily see that the Creeks were defending the town. As he put it, "I have the vanity to think such a respectable Indian force appearing so timely here had a very good effect ... on Don Galvez."[49] Indeed, Gálvez expected to attack Pensacola immediately after securing Mobile, but when a sufficient sea force did not arrive from Havana, he decided not to attempt it. Deputy Indian Superintendent Alexander Cameron agreed with McGillivray's interpretation that the Spanish had held back only because of "the great number of Indians that speedily repaired here to our assistance."[50]

McGillivray was particularly pleased to learn that Gálvez, intimidated by the Indian force, wrote Campbell on April 9 proposing that they agree "not to employ Indians in our national quarrels." Gálvez's justification was that Indians were apt "to pillage and destroy all the inhabitants which are of another nation," while the European commanders desired that "a war which we carry on through duty and not hatred, might not be rendered still more bloody."[51] Gálvez knew better. He had noted after taking Baton Rouge that Indians had plundered, killed noncombatants, and raped less than sometimes was the case among "the Civilized Nations of Europe."[52] Doing a similar calculation of their relative numbers, Campbell rejected the suggestion.[53]

Despite knowing he depended on his Indian allies, Campbell continued to frustrate them. Hearing that Spanish parties from Mobile were foraging for food and water along the Perdido River between Mobile and Pensacola, the Creek men were, as McGillivray noted, "very desirous ... to harass them."[54] However, Campbell told them not to, "for fear of indiscriminant murders."[55] As a result, the Creeks waited around idly, drinking rum and wondering why they were there. McGillivray tried to persuade the Creeks to stay in case of attack, but their reluctance grew as many of their number became ill on salt provisions, bad water, and the increasingly muggy heat as spring turned into early summer. Supplies ran low as merchant ships avoided Pensacola, fearing the Spanish. Creek grumbling increased as they knew that the women at home had prepared to plant without their help and that the Green Corn harvest festival would come before long. By mid-May, Creeks in Pensacola had persuaded McGillivray that "it is unnecessary to keep them much longer." As he explained to the Indian Department, out of "a desire of being serviceable they have acted much contrary to their usual customs," but they could not be expected to continue to do so.[56]

Creek bands began to leave Pensacola. McGillivray held out the longest, but he finally headed home on June 17 after more than two months spending his political capital on a frustrating and fruitless effort. On their departure from Pensacola, Cameron gave them provisions and other goods for their service, but he could still hear "great murmuring and complaints" because of the shortage of rum. McGillivray also had to gloss over Cameron's repeated "preaching" that the king wanted them to conduct their diplomacy not at Pensacola but at Savannah, which the British had taken in 1778. Cameron told them that Savannah "is the place where they are to repair to, and be supplied in their wants . . . except when we want their service here." Cameron had no budget for the Creeks, because they were supposed to be under a different administrative district, but this explanation seemed ridiculous to the Creeks. Pensacola was much closer to the Upper Creek towns and safe from dangerous Georgia militia. They had just demonstrated their important ties to Pensacola by coming to its defense and expected to be compensated directly. Some Creeks told Cameron that if the English did not supply them, "the Spaniards will do it with pleasure."[57] On their way out of West Florida, Creeks compensated themselves by stealing cattle and horses from inhabitants and even from the army.[58]

McGillivray was learning lessons on how allies should and should not act. The lack of British organization was shocking. As agent for the Upper Creeks, McGillivray was supposed to receive a small salary but had yet to be paid, even as he put himself "considerably in debt for the King's Service." To lead Creeks, he needed to spend like a

Creek headman. As he explained to the British, he needed "to keep my usual consequence among my people." To McGillivray, being a leader of "my people" and "promoting the King's interest" were still compatible, for now at least, but both required money.[59]

Creeks and Choctaws flexed their muscles with the Spanish as well as the British. As they left Pensacola, many of them went the sixty miles west to now-Spanish Mobile to conduct diplomacy. Huge parties of Creeks and Choctaws demonstrated their power to Mobile Commanders José de Ezpeleta and Henrique Grimarest. After they quickly blew through the goods seized from the British ship, Creeks complained to Grimarest about his paltry gifts. In July, a large Upper Creek party "hissed" during the distribution of what they considered insufficient food and brandy. Ezpeleta bought all the brandy he could from Mobile residents to give to the Creeks. When a group of Choctaws was departing in July, Ezpeleta noted that they had required "much expense" while performing "little service."[60] Some Creek and Alabama headmen traveled to New Orleans that summer, where they "pledged their devotion" to the Spanish king. They accepted flags, medals, collars, and gifts from Gálvez and recalled Spanish history in the southeast stretching back to the original founding of Pensacola by Spanish explorers.[61]

In Mobile alone that summer, the Spanish gave Creeks 160 barrels of rum, 50 pounds of gunpowder, 100 pounds of musket balls, 100 gun flints, 55 barrels of cornmeal, 132 pounds of sugar, 235 pounds of tobacco, 34 pounds of fresh meat (some perhaps brought in by Petit Jean), and 276 pounds of bread, plus assorted knives, salt, shirts, and vermilion paint. And still Ezpeleta had to promise the Indians to complete their provisions and goods when the Spanish took Pensacola. Alabamas who had served with Gálvez complained that they had not received the rewards he promised them for the Baton Rouge campaign.[62]

Threats and rumors dominated all discourse. The Creeks said they should be treated as steady Spanish allies, as opposed to the Choctaws, who were "going to give their hands to the English"; then the Creeks immediately revealed themselves to be less steady than they claimed, threatening to "go to Pensacola."[63] Alabamas threatened to persuade the Choctaws to attack Amand Broussard's town of Attakapas. Indians spread rumors that other Indians planned to attack posts the Spanish had taken. There were some Choctaws who actually did attack the Spanish. By late summer 1780, they had hemmed the Spanish into Mobile. Choctaw attacks around Mobile were so successful, an officer recorded, "that no one dares to go a half mile into the woods."[64]

With little reason to stay at Pensacola, nearly all the Chickasaws, Creeks, and Choctaws left, but then Campbell heard that a Spanish brig had sailed from Havana for Pensacola with six thousand troops. He ordered Cameron to send runners to collect Indian allies, including Choctaws who had left a few days before. After they returned, the Choctaws persuaded Campbell to attack the Spanish at their weak spot, a place near Mobile called the French Village or simply the Village (today's Spanish Fort, Alabama). Because the mouth of the Mobile River was brackish, Spanish troops had to travel from the Mobile fort to this Village at the northeastern edge of the bay to get fresh water. If the British could take the Village, it could be the stepping stone to retaking Mobile.

Just before daybreak on January 8, 1781, several hundred British regulars and Maryland and Pennsylvania Loyalists and over four hundred Choctaws and Lower Creeks attacked the Spanish post at the Village in what would be Britain's best chance to retake Mobile and reverse the course of the war on the Gulf Coast. The British troops shot their weapons and then crossed bayonets with the Spanish troops who came out of the fort. Someone managed to set the Spanish magazine on fire. Even so, the 150 Spaniards won a decisive victory, killing or wounding thirty-eight, mostly Maryland and Pennsylvania Loyalists.[65]

The News from Mobile in Chickasaw Country

Unlike the Choctaws and Creeks, Chickasaws noticeably failed to respond to British cries for help. Payamataha heard the news of the

Spanish fleet as it approached Mobile but did nothing. The highest-ranking member of a small Chickasaw party that arrived in early April to defend Pensacola was a young warrior, clearly not accustomed to representing the Chickasaws. As he gave his formal speech to the British, his fellow young Chickasaws catcalled, teasing him for what was clearly his first important speech outside the nation. The young man explained that the experienced chiefs were all in the Ohio Valley because they had heard there was going to be an attack on the British there. Those who had come to Pensacola were young men who "still had to earn their good names in war."[66]

It was true that there was a Chickasaw force in the Ohio Valley in the spring of 1780, a response to a direct American assault on Chickasaw land and independence. In January 1780, Virginia Militia General George Rogers Clark established a base south of the juncture of the Ohio with the Mississippi. The fort was on Chickasaw land and a clear violation of Chickasaw sovereignty. The Virginians finished "Fort Jefferson," named for their governor, in April 1780. When a Chickasaw delegation informed Clark that he was trespassing, he asked to buy the land. The Chickasaw council considered the request and decided against it, but the Virginians refused to leave. Over the next several months, Chickasaw forces besieged the fort, picking off any people and livestock that ventured outside. Only a boat of goods shipped by Oliver Pollock allowed Clark's followers to hold out as long as they did. Giving up, Clark ordered his men to abandon the fort in June 1781.[67]

The Chickasaws fought against unauthorized settlement on their land and sent a few young warriors to Pensacola, but they otherwise generally followed Payamataha's strategy of peace. Starting in 1780 or 1781, some Chickasaw headmen and warriors formed part of a delegation of Chickasaws, Shawnees, Delawares, and Cherokees traveling to visit large and small tribes east of the Mississippi and south of the Ohio. They discussed a broader alliance among themselves, no matter what happened in the war among Europeans. At the same time, Payamataha made the most of the opportunities that Spanish victories provided. He sent the commission signed by Gálvez in December

1779 to Cameron, using it to convey to the British both Spanish recruitment and his own loyalty to the British in handing it over. It seemed that he could still have it both ways.[68]

Payamataha repeatedly employed his best rhetoric to persuade the British that he was still on their side, despite his absence. That spring, he admitted to Cameron that "we received several inviting talks from the Spaniards." He insisted, though, that they were talks of peace, advising "us to take the Choctaws Cherokees Delawares and Creeks by the hand, to sit and drink together but to do no mischief." He also admitted that Americans tried to persuade the Chickasaws "that the English were not our friends" but instead planned "to throw us all in the fire and get us all killed." Payamataha assured Cameron that "we never intended to accept them." He reminded the British of their shared history, recalling that "ever since I was a young man, I was taken notice of in Charlestown and elsewhere." He recalled meeting with the king's "great warriors" in the past and accepting their flag, "which I have by me still." Now that "I am grown old," he claimed that nothing "should induce me to leave or forsake the English." Noting the Spanish alliance with the Chickasaws' old French enemies, Payamataha pledged, "as for the French or Spaniards, I never intended to take them by the hand nor never will so long as I live."[69] Despite his promise, Payamataha continued to conduct diplomacy with the Spanish because it supported his policy of universal peace. In the fall of 1780, Quapaws, Chickasaws, and Spaniards were negotiating another treaty.[70]

The small party of young Chickasaw warriors at Pensacola suited Payamataha's strategy. There was no way that Payamataha could prevent all violence on the part of young Chickasaw men, assuming he even wanted to, but he used his skills within and outside the nation to keep it as small scale and diplomatically advantageous as possible. Payamataha claimed to Cameron that "our people are daily going to war" on the British side, but in fact little violence occurred.[71] In June, for example, a Chickasaw raiding party returned to the nation with nine scalps and one French woman and her daughter. Attacking French residents surely appealed to most Chickasaws and could appease the British without attracting too much anger from the Spanish.[72]

Payamataha colluded with Choctaws to shape Spanish impressions. Disagreements over foreign policy were stronger among Choctaws than among the Chickasaws or Creeks. Some Six Towns Choctaws had joined the Spanish side in the engagements on the Gulf Coast, while Choctaw parties from the Eastern and Western divisions attacked Spanish forces that ventured outside the fort at Mobile. It would take skillful diplomacy to keep the Choctaws from having to fight one another. Payamataha told the British that he had lectured the Choctaws to stop meeting with the Spanish and "return immediately to the English, hold them fast by the hand." Choctaws sent excuses that the rapid Spanish conquest of Manchac, Natchez, and Mobile had surprised them, after which "General Gálvez flattered them out of several medals and commissions and in return gave them Spanish ones."[73] They now surrendered these to Cameron, who credited Payamataha for inspiring this new Choctaw show of allegiance. As the increasing amounts of goods given at British Pensacola and Spanish New Orleans and Mobile attest, Indians near the Gulf Coast saw opportunities for fruitful diplomacy that could attract gifts and trade without endangering their lives or their alliances with other Indian or European nations.

Conclusion: *The Spanish Press On*

Spanish victories on the Gulf Coast encouraged Spanish expansion elsewhere on the continent. In November 1780, inspired by the victories at Mobile and along the Mississippi, Balthazár de Villiers, commandant of Spain's Arkansas Post, rowed across the Mississippi River to an empty stretch of woods and there declared Spanish possession of the eastern bank of the Mississippi from Gálvez's victories in the south to north of the Arkansas River. To stake his claim, he buried a tin box with documents stating Spanish sovereignty and sealed with the king's coat of arms. Then he rowed back to his post on the west side of the Mississippi. To the north, sixty Ottawas, Potawatomis, and Illinois Indians proposed to Spanish Commandant of St. Louis Fernando de Leyba a joint attack on British Fort St. Joseph on

Lake Michigan. With sixty-five St. Louis militiamen, they traveled through the snow and took Fort St. Joseph on February 12, 1781, without a shot. The militiamen planted the Spanish flag in the town square and declared the region the possession of Spain. King Carlos III sent word that he greeted the "conquest of the post" with "the utmost satisfaction and gratification."[74]

While the British cared little for these supposed losses (and soon reoccupied Fort St. Joseph), the victories inspired Louisiana's Spanish and French residents and buoyed Spanish claims of an expanding empire. The Spanish victory at Mobile accomplished both of these goals and also sank British spirits, as John Adams noted. Britain's southern strategy against the rebels had seemed promising, but now the Spanish had opened another front in the southwest, and it all was going Spain's way there. General Campbell, whose spirits had never been high, seemed incapable of profiting from his assets, including his Choctaw and Creek allies. Perhaps it was time to start thinking about what they would all do if Britain lost this war.

At the same time, General Gálvez was making his case to the crown. Now was the time to strike Pensacola, before British reinforcements could arrive, Campbell could build further fortifications, or British General Frederick Haldimand's raids from Quebec into the Mohawk River Valley extended southward and threatened the Spanish. In contrast, if Spain could conquer Pensacola, Indians would see Spanish power and completely desert the British. The French, British, and Indian residents of the region were warming to the idea that Spain was both more powerful than Britain and not a threat to their autonomy. Gálvez could see a new era dawning for the Spanish empire, as long as it gave him a few resources. King Carlos III agreed, ordering Gálvez to "expel the English from the Gulf of Mexico" and make Pensacola Spanish again.[75]

In early January 1781, Mobile Garrison Commandant José de Ezpeleta called Petit Jean to his headquarters. In confidence, Ezpeleta told Petit Jean he had just received news that General Gálvez was sailing to Pensacola from Havana. Ezpeleta was to ready his forces to march to Pensacola. Petit Jean was to carry orders to Pedro Piernas, the acting governor of Louisiana in Gálvez's absence, to load troops and provisions onto ships to meet them all at Pensacola. After packing food and water for the journey, Petit Jean left Mobile and headed west. As he trudged through the marshes, the bayou's placid surface was so reflective that he could make out tiny details from the cypress branches a hundred feet above him, their wide, dark branches covered in gray beards of Spanish moss.[76]

Out of context, one might reasonably assume that a slave moving quickly through a North American swamp, looking over his shoulder for men with guns, was running away from slavery. But Petit Jean was carrying news vital to two empires and beyond. He crossed the mouth of Lake Pontchartrain and headed into New Orleans. As soon as Acting Governor Piernas heard Petit Jean's message, the slave headed for the governor's kitchen to get a hot meal and dry out in front of the fire. Piernas called his officers to tell them the long-awaited attack on West Florida's capital was about to begin.

CHAPTER THIRTEEN

The Spanish
Siege of Pensacola

BY FEBRUARY 1781, Pensacola had been effectively blockaded
for months, as Pensacola merchants feared to send their ships into the
Gulf and ships from outside avoided it for fear that the Spanish navy
would arrive. Inflation and shortages caused Isabella and James Bruce
"disagreeable uncertainty," as he put it, in feeding and clothing their
family. For now, there was enough flour to keep them from starving,
but without sugar, tea, coffee, wine, or rum, life would be reduced to
the bare necessities. It had been a year since the fall of Mobile, and
Pensacolans had started to hope that the Spanish were not coming.
They even imagined that, as James Bruce wrote, a recent hurricane
had killed "our most inveterate foe, Don G—z." Bruce rejoiced in the
hope that he "will no longer persecute us" but perhaps "may be forgiven, where we suppose he now is, for the evils he hath brought on
us."

As the town seemed safer, an announcement came that a ship was
finally daring to try to leave port, so Isabella Bruce began compiling a
list of clothes and other articles for herself and the children. James
would send it to one of his London business partners, whose wife

could shop for the items and send them on a return ship to Pensacola. Both children needed a variety of clothes. Charlotte May needed six pairs of cotton gloves or mittens, and Archibald needed two pairs. James added an order for some port and British national lottery tickets for himself and the children, noting that "I hope a fortunate number may turn up for them in order to compensate for these misfortunes of their father for these last two years." It had not been good times for commerce in West Florida, but if Bernardo de Gálvez was dead, prospects would surely improve, even if the Bruces did not win the lottery.[1]

But on March 9, cannons rang out and smoke rose again from the Pensacola lighthouse. The ships stationed at the mouth of Pensacola Bay—the *Mentor* and the *Port Royal*—had spotted a large Spanish fleet. General Gálvez was not dead. The siege of Pensacola had begun. Leaders among the British, Spanish, Creeks, Choctaws, and Chickasaws had to decide how important Pensacola was to them and how much they should sacrifice to defend or take it. Gálvez hoped that Petit Jean's message would get through to reinforcements in New Orleans. From Pensacola, General John Campbell sent calls for help to Indian country and to Jamaica, carried by a ship that managed to slip out of Pensacola Bay soon after the Spanish ships came into view. He pleaded that "we must undoubtedly fall unless we are relieved."[2]

The problem for both sides at Pensacola was that none of these decision-makers, whether Indians within a few hundred miles or imperial officials in the Caribbean and Europe, saw Pensacola as the chief point of conflict in the spring of 1781. Although the Spanish crown enthusiastically supported Gálvez's attempt to expand Spain's empire, both Spanish and British forces were occupied with other fronts of the American Revolution on land and on sea. British officials were receiving other urgent cries for help, from St. Augustine and Charleston and from General Charles Cornwallis for his crucial advance in the Carolinas. Some members of Parliament bemoaned the cost of fighting "so many enemies" at once and claimed that the large sums already spent on defending Pensacola had already reached more than it was worth. British Colonial Secretary George Germain argued against this position, but it was true that trying to tax the American colonies to pay off debts from the Seven Years' War had sparked another costly war, which had now spread even to colonies not in rebellion.[3]

For their part, the Spanish and French were pouring resources into a siege they had begun almost two years earlier against the British at Gibraltar. Spain was sending troops to fight its own rebellions: a tax-inspired revolt in New Granada with similarities to the American Revolution and an indigenous uprising in Peru led by Tupac Amaru. Southeastern Indians had problems unrelated to the fate of Pensacola, including smallpox, a succession of bad harvests, and wartime trade stoppages. As the Revolution dragged on, these problems grew more severe, and talk of pan-Indian alliances continued. The advice of Payamataha and others to stay out of European wars had persuaded many men and women across the southeast. Isabella and James Bruce could only hope that someone would heed General Campbell's call.[4]

Pensacola Bay

While Pensacola Bay is deep and wide, the only way into it by ship is through a narrow channel between the eastern finger of Perdido Key to the west and Santa Rosa barrier island to the east. On Santa Rosa's tip, overlooking the channel, was a hill for mounting artillery that the Spanish themselves had built before the Seven Years' War. The town of Pensacola sat on the northern shore, far inside the bay. In peacetime, Pensacola was a thriving port city of several thousand people, where Creeks and other Indians traded skins, furs, and tallow for goods from Europe, Africa, Asia, and the Caribbean. But during the war, as Isabella Bruce and her family could attest, few traders came from inland, and there were few ships docked at the wharves.

Parts of Pensacola lay within a five-sided stockade that the Spanish had built and British slaves had reinforced and expanded. Campbell had added a new fort less than a mile up the hill above the town. He named it Fort George for King George III and named the hill Gage Hill for Thomas Gage, then the commander of British forces in North America. From its height, the cannons of Fort George could bombard

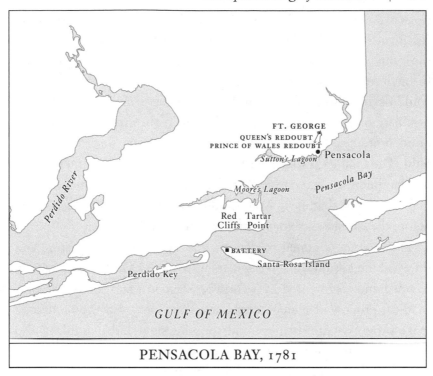

FT. GEORGE
QUEEN'S REDOUBT
PRINCE OF WALES REDOUBT
Sutton's Lagoon Pensacola

Moore's Lagoon Pensacola Bay

Red Tartar
Cliffs Point

■ BATTERY
Santa-Rosa Island

Perdido River

Perdido Key

GULF OF MEXICO

PENSACOLA BAY, 1781

anyone who tried to take Pensacola. Fort George itself was a double stockade: two circles of tall, upright, sharpened pine logs with a barrier of sand in between. Another 350 yards above Fort George was a supporting battery, the Prince of Wales Redoubt, and about the same distance farther north was the larger, crescent-shaped Queen's Redoubt. Mounted artillery protected the fort and both redoubts, although not as many as Campbell had asked for. Taking Pensacola would not be easy.[5]

Eighteenth-century tactics for seizing a defended location were clear, methodical, and not to be rushed. If all went well for Gálvez, there would probably be four steps. First, his ships would take control of the bay. Second, he would establish a base on the mainland where he could combine his forces and artillery with reinforcements from Mobile and New Orleans. From the bay, the ships could supply this camp with provisions and ammunition. Unless the British either drove off the Spanish or surrendered during the first two steps, a classic siege would then commence. The Spanish troops would gradually move their camp and artillery close enough to the British fortifications to bombard them but, Gálvez hoped, remain out of range of the British artillery. This third step would be the most arduous, requiring the army to haul artillery, tents, food, and ammunition for miles through rough terrain without the help of oxen or even many horses, while risking being shot by muskets or, as the army got closer to its destination, artillery fire. With each advance, the army would have to build protective trenches and batteries and hope that they would hold. The final step would be to force a British surrender, either by bombardment or starvation. The four steps could take months, but Gálvez figured that early May would leave enough time to succeed before the worst heat, storms, and disease of late summer.

The defenders aimed to counter the Spanish at every step, and they had the advantage. On the marshy, irregular Gulf Coast, heavily wooded and fragmented by waterways, lagoons, and inlets, the methodical process of a siege could stall. Not only did the landscape make progress with artillery and supplies slow and painful, it also made the army an easier target for the far less methodical and far more mobile Indian forces. Eighteenth-century Indian military tactics were perfectly suited to slicing off bits of an invading army as it trudged inland. Indians would not have to kill all of the invaders. If they could do enough damage and slow the Spanish down, then disease, hunger, and attrition would end the campaign. As General Campbell explained, Indian forces could, "by continually harassing and hanging on the enemy's rear," at least "impede the operations, if not totally defeat and disconcert the designs of any force they can send against us." On March 9, the Spanish ships anchored in the Gulf off the south side of Santa Rosa Island, and the troops began to disembark.[6]

Persuading Empires and Indians

The British commanders of Manchac, Baton Rouge, and Mobile had surrendered fairly quickly, knowing they did not have the forces to counter Gálvez. But Pensacola was West Florida's capital and had reserved most of the army for its own defense. Whoever could muster the most resources to last through the siege would have the upper hand.

Spanish General Bernardo de Gálvez had been more successful than General Campbell or Alexander McGillivray in persuading constituencies that there was much to gain in the war. And at last officials in Havana had provided the ships, troops, and supplies to West Florida that the king had ordered when he declared war. Gálvez had reminded them that, with few resources, he had taken Baton Rouge, Natchez, and Mobile. With a little more support, he could win all of West Florida and advance the Spanish empire far into North America. His arguments carried the day. On February 13, Gálvez left Havana on the sixty-one-gun flagship *San Ramon*. Accompanying him was a fleet of twenty brigantines, frigates, and convoy ships bearing over 1,300 sailors and soldiers from Havana's permanent regiment and companies sent from Spain as well as the provisions and armaments for war. Once the winds were favorable, the convoy set sail.[7]

Isabella Bruce and her neighbors were frustrated that the British empire seemed less determined to defend West Florida than Spain was to take it. She must have shuddered when her husband came home to report that Campbell had suggested to His Majesty's Council for West Florida that if the Spanish attacked, the best way to protect Pensacola's women and children would be to ask Gálvez to take them on a ship or somewhere else away from combat. Outraged, the Council wrote Campbell that giving the enemy their women and children was "unprecedented in any society." In their view, protecting dependents should be Campbell's main concern, not something to entrust to the enemy.[8]

The Bruces hoped that Campbell's lackluster defense of West Florida did not represent British intentions. Certainly West Florida was not yet a profitable colony. But James Bruce spoke for himself and his family and neighbors when he wrote that "we are still in hopes" that the crown would defend West Florida. After all, the crown had spent heavily on the colony, expenditures that would be justified if British forces could take New Orleans and Louisiana, giving them access to the Mississippi and the Gulf. Then the Bruces could reclaim their property on the Mississippi, and West Floridians could continue to develop plantations and export their produce through a more convenient port. But the administration would have to become more aggressive. James Bruce worried that "if the war is carried on even another spring without the proposed reinforcement, we must fall, for even our Indian allies begin to think that we scarcely belong to the Great King, or he would not suffer us to be so long in being able to drive out the Spaniards from the places they have taken from us."[9]

When the Spanish ships approached, General John Campbell had some 1,700 soldiers under his command in Pensacola and its supporting fortifications. Despite repeated requests, he had only three armed ships, all much smaller than the *San Ramon*. Because Campbell did not record militia numbers, it is hard to know how many people ultimately defended Pensacola. With few white Pensacolans eager to serve, many of the militiamen were of African descent. One account mentions a detachment of "50 negroes" that went out on one sortie. The regular troops included German Waldeckers in British service and the Pennsylvania and Maryland Loyalists Battalions.[10]

These soldiers would be essential in Pensacola's defense, but the lack of reinforcements from Jamaica meant that Campbell depended even more on Chickasaw, Creek, and Choctaw warriors. He assumed that Indians would compose well over half of his forces, and they could also hunt venison for the troops at all of the posts. Yet whether they would come was uncertain. Three times between the spring of 1780 and early 1781, Campbell had sent word to Alexander McGillivray to come to Pensacola's defense against the Spanish, and each time another messenger soon followed saying it was a false alarm and that the Creeks should not come.[11]

The British at Pensacola had insufficient supplies for rewarding Indian allies, especially for multiple trips. General John Burgoyne, organizing in Canada, estimated that the muskets, gunpowder, and other supplies Indians required beyond what they actually used in battle meant that one thousand Indian fighters cost more than twenty thousand British regulars. Burgoyne was exaggerating, but still, Indians were expensive. As Alexander Cameron explained to George Germain, "the Indians in general have been long accustomed to receive lavish gratuities, even when their services were not immediately called for, and they now consider as their due, what they formerly received as great favors." Now, "when we are daily desiring" their help, was a bad time to economize.[12]

Nonetheless, Germain sent no more goods but only the hope that the British victory at Charleston two months earlier would "serve to confirm the Indians in their attachment to His Majesty, and encourage them to exert themselves in His Cause."[13] Cameron warned General Campbell that "refusing presents to the Indians at so critical a conjuncture may be very hurtful to his Majesty's interest." As "at present our principal dependence is on the Indians for the protection of this place," Indian allies should be retained and supplied nearby so they could come in case of attack on Pensacola and in the meantime scout for Pensacola and raid around Mobile to keep the Spaniards entrapped.[14] Campbell refused to supply such a plan and could not even promise that there would be provisions and presents for visiting Creeks. He told Cameron that he wanted to see Creeks only when their aid was "absolutely required."[15] The defenders of Pensacola could only hope that Alexander McGillivray would bring large forces and that British ships would soon appear on the horizon.

Several hundred Choctaws, forty Creek men and their families, and a few Chickasaws were already in Pensacola when the Spanish arrived. When Campbell issued and then rescinded his latest cry for help in January 1781, they had come anyway, seeking food and ammunition for hunting. After this disappointment, the visiting Indians had considered their next steps. Should they head home—some two hundred miles for the Creeks and Choctaws and nearly four hundred for the Chickasaws—or stay to see if anything developed in Pensacola? While the others lingered, Choctaw Headman Franchimastabé and about half of the Choctaws left for home on March 6. On the trail the next morning, about eighteen miles northwest of Pensacola, they were receiving rations of rum from one of the British Indian agents when Deputy Indian Superintendent Alexander Cameron caught up with them. He descended from his horse and told the Choctaws that at last the Spanish were coming.[16]

Franchimastabé agreed to return immediately to defend Pensacola but declared, "I will not answer for my people returning, for we received but little provisions[,] and the presents the great warrior [Campbell] made us were for nothing." He told Cameron, "You may speak to them as they are here and will answer for themselves." Like other southeastern Indian leaders, Franchimastabé did not command warriors. Chiefs of the Southeast could only persuade with words, with goods, or by example, and Franchimastabé was already known among the Choctaws as supportive of the British. He was a war leader who was in the process of becoming an important Choctaw chief in part because he had been able to acquire British goods for his military services and funnel them to supporters within the Choctaw nation. This connection put Franchimastabé in a tight spot. He needed more goods than the British were currently giving, but if he turned his back on them, he would have no goods at all. Franchimastabé simply told his fellow Choctaws that they could choose: Make the long day's walk back to Pensacola, turn in the other direction toward Spanish Mobile and try their luck there, or resume the journey home, hoping to kill enough deer and other game along the way to keep their trip from being a complete waste of time. About half decided to return with Franchimastabé to join the few hundred Choctaws who had not yet left Pensacola; the other half continued along the path toward home.[17]

Lining Up the Forces

Choctaws, Creeks, and Chickasaws looking down from the British fortifications at Red Cliffs saw the Spanish making progress. On March 10, troops crossed Santa Rosa Island and discovered no artillery there to fire on incoming ships. General Campbell had hoped to rebuild and staff the battery on Santa Rosa, but he spent his limited resources on the fortifications on the mainland and in any case was short on cannons. The Indians on Red Cliffs saw the flagship *San Ramon* approach the channel but not enter the bay. The captain worried that the ships would run aground in the bay's shallow entrance without a local pilot boat to lead them. For a week, the Spanish ships floated outside the bay as Pensacolans wondered what would happen next. On March 18, an audience at Red Cliffs assembled again as a corsair brigantine, a two-masted sailing ship designed for maneuverability, hoisted a flag signaling that it was now the flagship of the fleet. It maneuvered past the *San Ramon* and the frigates and into the bay. The ship was the *Galveztown,* named for the general. Captaining it was Bernardo de Gálvez himself, frustrated with his captains' timidity. Seeing the brigantine make it, the lighter frigates followed him into the bay.[18]

The British fired their cannons madly at the lead ship. As an observer later wrote, the artillery fire "passed through sails and riggings," but the *Galveztown* "entered the port without the least damage." The other warships and convoy ships followed the next day, none running aground. The artillery at Red Cliffs rained down hundreds of shells without causing serious damage. Campbell had had high hopes for the "exceedingly well executed" fortification he had built, but his engineers had positioned it so high in an effort to avoid cannon fire from ships in the bay that its artillery could not accurately target the ships below.[19] The Indians saw the British *Mentor* and *Port Royal* give up guarding the mouth of the bay and sail up toward Pensacola. British soldiers began to torch log blockhouses and storage buildings on the shore of the mainland to prevent the Spanish from taking them. These were not good signs. Some Indians went to Campbell's headquarters and threatened him, saying that if he did not provide more supplies, they would not stay. Others packed up and left Pensacola to its fate.[20]

Each night, around campfires and in the makeshift wooden huts the Indians had built north of Red Cliffs, there was a lot to discuss. Indian opinion had swung over the previous few years toward viewing British alliance as useless, and what Indians could see from Red Cliffs lent credence to this opinion. Wartime trade stoppages made British alliances unprofitable, and the recent Spanish victories could not be ignored. The counterargument to all of this was that the Spanish were fighting on the side of the American colonists, the very people whose westward expansion most Creeks wanted to oppose.[21]

The Indians who stayed accused Campbell of robbing them of

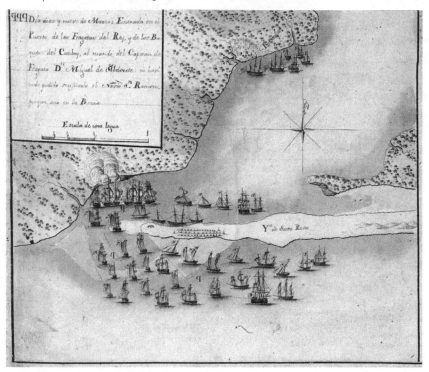

Siege of Pensacola, 1781, as the Spanish ships sailed past Red Cliffs. (*Toma de la plaza de Panzacola y rendición de la Florida Occidental a las armas de Carlos III*, Ministerio de Defensa, Archivo del Museo Naval, Spain)

pledged goods, especially ammunition. Because the British had failed to send supplies to their towns, they said, their people would be unable to defend their homes if the Spanish came inland. Even the additional goods they were earning by defending Pensacola were in danger because the British kept the goods in the fort, which they believed would soon fall. And they feared for their wives, sisters, and children who were nervously sequestered in the town of Pensacola with the British civilians.[22]

Despite their grumbling, the Indians who were at Pensacola did their best to defend it. Each day, bands spread out along the coast and inland between Red Cliffs and the Perdido River, about five miles away. The Indians suspected that troops coming from Mobile would walk the nearly fifty miles and would have to cross Perdido Bay, where the Perdido River widens before it reaches the Gulf. Crossing the Perdido in launches, the soldiers would be vulnerable to gunfire from the eastern shore. That would be the time to strike. Indian bands plus nearly one hundred troops from Fort George patrolled the eastern side of the Perdido, but it was a difficult task. The shore of the Perdido is extremely curvy, forming some thirty miles of coastline.

Several times over these few days, Indian parties saw ships approaching from the Gulf and fired on them, preventing them from sending men ashore to look for Spanish Colonel José de Ezpeleta and his troops from Mobile. At one point, an Indian party discovered a group of Spanish sailors who had anchored in Perdido Bay and had ventured away from the boat to cut some grass in the marshlands to feed the cattle they had on board. One of the troubles with transporting provisions in the eighteenth century was the lack of refrigeration. Drying and salting meat kept it safe for later consumption, but Cuba could not cure enough meat to feed an army for months, and soldiers preferred fresh meat anyway. Bringing live animals solved these problems but created others, such as feeding the animals and disposing of their waste. Leaving the ship to collect feed and stretch their legs seemed a useful diversion to the sailors, afflicted with the combination of edginess and boredom particular to combat missions. But it was not a good idea. The Indians who found them were also eager for action. When they came upon the eleven Spaniards cutting away at the long grasses, they killed ten of them and marched the eleventh to Fort George at the end of a rope. There, they presented the ten scalps and the prisoner for payment. Indian fighters in the region treated war captives harshly. They would have killed him had Campbell not ransomed him for his information.[23]

Although only a small percentage of the Indians Campbell hoped for had arrived, they still did most of the killing. Their mission was to pick off Spanish troops and little by little make the siege impossible. The British troops mostly stayed within the fortifications except for occasional forays once the Spanish drew closer. For their part, the Spanish troops coming with Colonel Ezpeleta from Mobile feared Indian attack. These troops were marching on narrow paths through dense, thorny woods. An armed Creek could be a few yards away behind a bushy young pine tree. The Spanish would not know he was there until he had fired a shot.[24]

Ezpeleta managed to sneak past them. Realizing from scouts' reports that Indians were patrolling east of the Perdido, Ezpeleta changed the route. Rather than going directly by land from Mobile to Perdido Bay, he and the troops took boats to the southeastern edge of Mobile Bay, right on the Gulf. From there, they walked along the beach and in the early morning of March 21 crossed the three-hundred-yard strait to Perdido Key on armed launches provided by the *San Ramon* as it lingered outside the bay. (The keys that hid the bay gave it its name, Perdido or Lost Bay.) The Choctaws had forced Ezpeleta's men to march without rest and killed several of them, but they failed to stop their progress.[25]

On the morning of March 22, Amand Broussard was sailing from New Orleans toward the fight. When Acting Louisiana Governor Piernas had received the news from Petit Jean of Gálvez's impending attack on Pensacola, he sent out the call for militia units to assemble in New Orleans. Broussard and his Acadian neighbors in the Attakapas settlement wasted no time in checking their muskets, bidding adieu to their families, and rowing themselves downriver to New Orleans. In the afternoon of March 23, sixteen vessels bearing Broussard and some 1,600 other militiamen and regulars from New Orleans with arms, ammunition, and a three-month supply of provisions approached Pensacola Bay. They were delighted to see Gálvez's ships floating in the bay already. Like the others, they marveled as they sailed past Red Cliffs under fire that did no serious damage.[26]

The hearts of Pensacola's defenders sank as they saw the approaching fleet from New Orleans. Here were additional Spanish reinforcements, while the forces expected by land from the Chickasaws, Creeks, and Choctaws and by sea from Jamaica still had not appeared. With every day that passed, their arrival seemed less likely. Frustrated, General Campbell evacuated his troops from the town of Pensacola and stationed them in Fort George and the two redoubts above it. The battle for Pensacola would be decided there.[27]

When most of the troops moved to Fort George, Pensacola's civilians and the families of Creek and Choctaw warriors stayed behind. A few days earlier, on March 21, Governor Peter Chester and General

Campbell had written to General Gálvez asking that the town of Pensacola be exempt from the fighting so that noncombatants could be protected. It was not unusual to shell besieged cities, but Gálvez agreed, as long as Campbell removed all British troops from the town. Therefore, as the troops left, James and Isabella Bruce found themselves between the British fort on the hill above the town and the Spanish warships in the bay below, each firing on the other. The place that was supposed to be safe for civilians ended up between the warring parties.[28]

James Bruce wrote of "the distresses of the inhabitants" as they were "between the guns of both."[29] Cannons from both sides boomed day and night. When stray cannonballs landed within the town walls, Pensacolans rushed to put out fires. Isabella Bruce could too well imagine the death and destruction that would result if one hit her house by the water or the shelter in which she and her family now took refuge. Her neighbor Mrs. Morison died during the siege, leaving John Morison a widower with five small children to take care of under these siege conditions.[30]

Beyond the immediate fear of the bombardment lay the terror of every person under siege—running out of food and water. For now, there were enough supplies in the town, but no one knew how long the siege would last. The bay was blocked, and there was little possibility of goods coming by land past the Spanish forces. And in any case, the nearest British posts were in Georgia, 450 miles away. The longer the siege lasted, the more danger the Bruces and their neighbors faced.

Making matters worse, the Indian and European civilians did not get along well in tight quarters under tense circumstances. Pensacolans accused Indians of theft and lawlessness, while the Indian women complained of inadequate food and vulnerability to Spanish capture. Campbell returned a few soldiers to Pensacola to help deal with the conflicts and fires, prompting charges from Gálvez that he was violating the sanctuary of Pensacola, a complaint that served to make the people in town even more nervous. Isabella Bruce could only hope that her empire would send reinforcements, and soon.[31]

Converging on Fort George

After sailing into Pensacola Bay, Amand Broussard's ship rounded Tartar Point and anchored on the northeastern side of Moore's Lagoon. As he disembarked, Broussard could see why the ships from New Orleans had stopped here, safely between the cannons of Red Cliffs and those of Fort George and the redoubts. Having completed the first step of taking the bay, here they would begin the second step of establishing a camp on the mainland and slowly advancing toward Fort George. To the northeast lay Sutton's Lagoon, which the troops would have to get around.[32]

Broussard's militia company was assigned a spot on the side of the camp nearest Fort George, where they settled in to guard the camp and prepare for their advance. On March 27, José de Ezpeleta and his bedraggled soldiers from Mobile arrived with tales of terror from their journey. It was hard enough to travel during the day through the dense woods and over the undulating hills. Night brought total darkness. At one point in the dark, several Spanish soldiers heard a rustling on their flank and began to fire. From the direction of the sound came musket fire in return. Several men lay dead and wounded before their comrades realized that both sides were part of Ezpeleta's army.[33]

The Spanish camp was a frightening place to sleep. Amand Broussard and his thousands of comrades tried to drift off in the ominous silence between Indian attacks. One participant recalled the camp being "in the middle of the forest and surrounded by savages, who insult us at all hours, hiding themselves for that purpose."[34] The soldiers expected musket fire but never knew when it would break out or from which side of the camp it would come. It seemed that every night musket balls pierced the fabric of tents and wounded or killed soldiers within. Even if Indians only once in a while killed a soldier bathing incautiously or serving guard duty, it made the Spanish very nervous. They also worried about disease, which could slowly eat its way through the attacking army as the defending army simply waited them out.

On the evening of March 28, Broussard heard gunfire close by.

Several hundred Indians and about a hundred British had opened fire on the camp's guards. Broussard heard his orders—a Spanish officer sent white and black militia out against the attackers. Broussard charged out of camp as the artillery fired overhead. The militia pushed back the attacking parties into the woods. Hoping that they had retreated to Fort George, Broussard and his comrades returned to camp, ate their dinner, and settled into an uneasy sleep. Near midnight, Broussard woke with a start. The sound of gunfire came from all directions. He pulled on his shoes, grabbed his musket, and headed for action. Rather than retreating, the Indians who had attacked earlier had spread out in smaller parties and, after nightfall, crept toward the camp from several sides. They killed and wounded several on the Spanish side before drawing back into the woods again. The Spanish forces knew that if the British and their Indian allies kept up this kind of attack, the Spanish effort was doomed. The attackers barely put themselves at risk, and if they could inflict several casualties every night, they would halt Spanish progress and eventually weaken the besiegers so much that they would have to give up.[35]

Therefore, just over twenty-four hours later, before dawn on the morning of March 30, Amand Broussard was with one thousand advance light troops following General Gálvez himself in a march around Sutton's Lagoon. They nervously walked through unknown terrain, imagining Indian fighters behind any tree or bush. Even if the human enemies did nothing, the panthers, bears, alligators, and poisonous snakes could kill just as easily. At one point, scouts reported an Indian ambush up ahead, but Gálvez ordered cannons fired into the woods, and the ambushers scattered, perhaps simply having been deer. At 10:30 Broussard and the others emerged with Gálvez onto the beach on the northeastern side of Sutton's Lagoon a little over a mile from Fort George. There they met the ships that landed artillery and the troops from Havana. They sent a message that they had secured the spot and that Ezpeleta could begin sending the rest of the army in launches across the mouth of the lagoon. Soon after they began, an Indian force fired at the launches and at the outposts of the new camp. Broussard advanced from the camp with the light troops, firing his musket.[36]

The Maryland Loyalists and fifty black slaves sallied out of Fort George. They brought two howitzers, a highly mobile piece of artillery. One shell from the howitzer fell among thirteen boats crossing Sutton's Lagoon and frightened Ezpeleta's forces into rowing quickly back to the far side. The lagoon battle raged, as the Indian troops shot from behind the trees and brush that surrounded the beach. After four hours of heavy fighting and a few casualties on each side, the Maryland Loyalists and enslaved troops retreated back into Fort George. Seeing the retreat, the Indians fell back into the woods. Broussard and the other Spanish troops and laborers returned to the work of setting up camp, including building the earthworks for the sides not protected by the bay or the lagoon.[37]

As the rainy morning of March 31 dawned, Amand Broussard enjoyed a celebratory round of aguardiente, a hard alcohol made from sugar cane. Since moving their camp, the Spanish troops had completed the second step and were ready to advance together toward Fort George. In contrast, the British were depressed, and the Indians were angry. Choctaw Headman Franchimastabé was "in a passion," Alexander Cameron later wrote. The Choctaw side had inflicted major casualties on the Spanish and might have been on the verge of a decisive victory, but the British troops had retreated, and Gálvez had achieved his objective. Franchimastabé charged that the Choctaws "have done everything in our power," whereas the British effort had been half-hearted. Campbell pledged more support next time, so Franchimastabé promised he would not "leave Pensacola before its fate was determined."[38]

Franchimastabé may have begun to think that its fate had been written already. The Spanish were slowly gaining ground, just as they aimed to do, and the way to stop them was to do what Franchimastabé's men had done, attack aggressively at vulnerable places and times. But if the British gave up so easily, why should Franchimastabé's men risk their lives and expend their precious gunpowder, especially when most Choctaws already thought they were wasting their time?

But the Spanish did not move immediately. The ship bearing six battering cannons from Mobile had run aground in Mobile Bay and been captured by the British. Without that artillery, taking down the batteries would be impossible. While the Spanish waited in hopes of more artillery from Havana, the Choctaws, Creeks, and Chickasaws were steadily picking off the troops. Ezpeleta informed Gálvez that the constant Indian attacks meant that he would need at least eight hundred more soldiers to maintain a siege for more than a few days. If artillery and troops arrived for the Spanish, they would regain the advantage. But if British or Indian reinforcements came instead, they might push Gálvez's men back onto their ships and away from Pensacola.[39]

Alexander McGillivray finally rode into Pensacola on April 8 or 9 with about forty Creeks, a far cry from the six hundred who had ridden with him to Pensacola a year earlier. When Campbell's call came in March, McGillivray had spread the news to Okfuskee, Tuckabatchee, Great Tallassee, his own Little Tallassee, and other Upper Creek towns. He again urged Creeks to put on their war paint, conduct their ceremonies, strap on their muskets and hatchets, and defend their British allies. But most Creeks were tired of being treated poorly. If they could be sure that they would return from Pensacola with food, musket balls, and gunpowder, it might be worth the trip, but those who had made the most recent journey of nearly two hundred miles to Pensacola had received barely enough supplies for the return home. Trade stoppages, smallpox, and crop failures had left the Creeks needing outside aid, but they were learning not to rely on the British. Creek women may have reminded the men that they were needed at home to help with the planting and to hunt for small game. Other divisions of the Creek Confederacy—Alabamas and maybe even some Upper Creeks—might show up on the Spanish side, and the Creeks did not want to risk facing other Creeks in battle. Some young men wanted to fight but not against the Spanish. They had joined the raids of Cherokee leader Dragging Canoe against Virginia's frontier settlements. Many Creeks doubted whether the Spanish actually would come this time, and some wondered about McGillivray's motives, given that he was receiving a salary as a British agent.

McGillivray did his best to counter these arguments. He reminded the Creeks that cultivating interdependence with the British would facilitate Creek protection of their eastern border, where the British were fighting the Creeks' most hated enemies, Georgians and Virginians. However, it was an impossible task even for a man of McGillivray's rhetorical skills. The British were clumsy allies, and killing Spaniards seemed a circuitous defense against Georgia and Virginia. Some of McGillivray's clan members and a few others packed up to go with him to Pensacola, but this time most Creeks stayed home.[40]

In addition to the forty Creeks who arrived with McGillivray, another forty followed a few days later, and on April 15, a new party of about ninety Choctaws showed up. Some fifty Chickasaws arrived with James Colbert, a Scottish trader, interpreter, and British Indian agent who had lived with the Chickasaws since at least 1740. His force was mostly composed of his Chickasaw sons and other relations. These two-hundred-odd Indians bolstered and invigorated those already there. Still, Pensacolans remembered that 1,500 had come the first time Campbell called.[41]

Even worse, some Creeks were indeed in the Spanish camp, believing the British loss likely. While McGillivray was recruiting for the British in the Upper Creek Towns, some Alabamas were already with Gálvez, and on April 5, several Upper Creek headmen arrived at the Spanish camp. They were not there to join the fight; they would not have fought against McGillivray and the Creeks who were with the British. However, they offered non-combat assistance as part of their responsibility to sustain diplomatic relations with the Spanish in hopes of paving the way for good postwar Spanish relations.

There was some Nativist thinking within the Creeks' reluctance to participate in any bloodshed. An Upper Creek man explained to a Spanish officer that the Creeks were "frugal with the blood of their compatriots, for the reason that the nations consist of a small number of individuals." He explained that "in the world there were three races of men: white, black, and red; that the first and the second were innumerable, and therefore the loss of some of them was not a cause for grief; but that there were very few of the third, and therefore it was necessary to preserve them with great care." The Spanish officer observed that "during the siege, they were quick to harass the English every time they were ordered to do so, but never could they be persuaded to attack those Indians who were allies of the English."[42]

Indeed, there is no evidence that Indians killed one another at all in the Pensacola conflict. Ultimately, despite Campbell's hopes, this was not their fight. The ways in which they served one side or the other gave them access to payment and glory without exposing them to much physical risk or using much of their valuable and scarce ammunition and gunpowder. Although a headman from "a small nation" (probably near the Mississippi) came with ten warriors and declared, "We come to aid the Spaniards" and "We know how to shed our blood for our friends," he and his warriors did not actually fight.[43] When General Campbell tried to persuade the Choctaws to encamp near Fort George, they insisted instead on a spot four or five miles from the fort, on the road that led to their towns. From there, they could make a quick getaway if necessary. As the Spanish advanced, Campbell had trouble persuading Indians to put up much opposition. When they did attack, on March 30, Campbell believed they had done so "with more noise than advantage."[44] On April 9, he managed to get Choctaws to agree to stay another four days only by giving them extra presents. Occasionally, they did make an easy raid. For example, on April 30, some parties of Indians approached under the cover of thickets to within half a musket shot of the Spanish camp and opened fire on the advance post, then retreated back into the forest and emerged near the Spanish launches to kill four unsuspecting sailors bathing in a creek.[45]

Although Indians were highly selective with the risks they took, to the Spanish, the Indians on the British side seemed great in number and frightening in their ability to strike at will from the cover of the woods. The Spanish knew nothing of Indian reticence about joining this battle. They imagined that thousands were on their way or were already entrenched in Pensacola's defenses. In what was surely an intentional deception, a British deserter told Gálvez that three hundred Creeks came in early April, when the real number was only eighty. Another deserter reported the ninety Choctaws as five hundred. Many of Gálvez's tactical decisions reflected the threat—both real or imagined—that Indians posed. Spanish troops spent much of their time chopping down trees and clearing brush surrounding the camp to reduce the number of hiding places from which Indians could shoot. They built entrenchments and redoubts to provide cover from Indians attacking the camp and the supply launches. And Gálvez posted soldiers and cannons to guard the front of the camp against Indian attacks.[46]

Waiting for Help

Over the next two weeks, Amand Broussard joined in the exhausting work of the third step: relocating the camp again and again as the Spanish advanced northward toward Fort George, always keeping their back to Sutton's Lagoon. Each time they nervously built new defenses and dreaded the night. In one move, they left the tents up in the old camp until they could transfer nearly everyone to the new one in hopes of fooling the Indians. When they settled on a final spot, with its back to the lagoon, the Spanish protected the other three sides of this camp with a tall log wall; earthworks as high as a man, several feet thick, and topped with artillery; and a moat. They hoped "to ensure against the sudden violent attacks of the Indians." When Indian parties approached, the New Orleans free black militia, known by Louisianans as "famous marksmen," would sally out to drive them away. But even here Choctaws, Creeks, and Chickasaws killed men in the tents by climbing into the dense foliage of the trees overhanging the camp wall. And the defenses did nothing to keep out the Gulf Coast's rain, which dampened both clothes and spirits. Fort George and the Indians' temporary huts suffered some damage, but they were built for the elements, and they could take heart that rain would be a worse enemy for an invading force. In the less-prepared Spanish camp, rain soaked the ammunition, brought most of the tents to the ground, and left soldiers vulnerable to disease.[47]

As expected, the third step of the Spanish plan was turning out to be the most difficult. The Spanish had four thousand troops to advance on Fort George, but Choctaws, Creeks, and Chickasaws combined forces to slow their progress through the dense woods that led uphill from the base camp to the fort. As one of the officers later remembered, "Many Indian nations, warlike, cruel, excellent marksmen skillful in the handling of muskets," continually impeded his army's progress "in the march it had had to make in a country full of dense forests and with many obstructions, the most appropriate land in the world for ambushes." As Gálvez recorded, "Each step was a peril and a clash with the Indians." Now that the Spanish were closer to Fort George, the British troops could easily come out to attack them together with Indian parties, bringing their relatively light and extremely damaging field artillery.[48]

Altogether, the Indian and British military forces totaled almost two thousand, and they inflicted casualties on the Spanish forces every day. Each time Gálvez gained a little ground, he lost men and morale. The miserable conditions and loss of life made many consider "all their work to be useless," and they "despaired of the whole undertaking." On April 12, Gálvez was out with the light infantry when an Indian spotted the general and fired a musket ball straight at him. It hit a finger on Gálvez's left hand and continued on to graze his abdomen. With help, he made his way back to camp and let the surgeon bind his wounds. While he was recovering in the hospital tent, a torrential rainstorm blew in. The surgeons feared that the weather would kill off their commander and many more of their patients, but the skies cleared the next day, and Gálvez survived.[49]

Both sides watched the sea. The British sent a pilot to wait at Red Cliffs in case a fleet arrived to relieve them. On April 18, Amand Broussard rejoiced when two Spanish ships brought supplies and the news that Gálvez's father, Guatemalan President Matias de Gálvez, had recaptured Fort Inmaculada in Nicaragua from the British. The next afternoon, a large number of ships approached through a thick fog over the Gulf. Rumors began to fly: fourteen ships . . . twenty . . . two hundred. As the ships approached, lookouts could see that they flew no flags. Many shared Gálvez's "intense fright" and Campbell's "hopes and fears" as they waited to learn the nationality of the ships.[50]

Only once the incoming captains saw the Spanish ships in the bay did they unfurl their Spanish and French flags and fire their cannons into the air. Gálvez's pleas had been answered: fifteen warships, three frigates, and over a hundred transport vessels under the command of Vice Admiral José Solano bore Field Marshal Juan Manuel de Cagigal and 1,600 infantry from the regiments stationed at Havana, a naval force of over 1,400 sailors, and the ammunition, provisions, and artillery that would make taking Fort George possible. With them were about seven hundred French troops to support their ally's effort. Hasty preparations in Havana had left no time to send word to Gálvez that the fleet was coming, but it was a very welcome surprise.[51]

Why did Spanish officials decide to reinforce Gálvez's effort? First, his success thus far had persuaded the king himself of the feasibility of taking West Florida, which would atone for the humiliations of the Seven Years' War and advance Spanish imperialism in North America. Second, although Spain was deeply involved in battles for the Caribbean and Gibraltar, it could spare, at least for a few weeks, ships and troops for the opportunity at Pensacola. Finally, what tipped the scale was that a few weeks earlier a fisherman off the west coast of Cuba had spotted eight British warships and a frigate. The news made Havana's governing council nervous. The council inferred that the British in Jamaica had gotten the news of Gálvez's attack and were sending help to Pensacola. Fearing the king's wrath if they let West Florida slip away, the councilmembers dispatched a fleet to Gálvez, which included French ships that had been anchored in Cuba.[52]

Jamaica Governor John Dalling had sent only two ships to aid Pensacola, both with crews so undependable that they attacked and looted rival ships rather than going to Pensacola. Britain's more reliable forces were stretched thin. The previous fall's hurricane had damaged the British fleet and killed over twenty thousand people in the Leeward Islands alone. British troops at Jamaica were suffering from disease. As British Colonial Secretary George Germain explained to Campbell, "Mortality among the troops in Jamaica had been so considerable" that Governor Dalling "judged it unsafe to lessen his force." Governor Dalling and Admiral Peter Parker were focused on fighting the French and Spanish in the Caribbean, Honduras, and Nicaragua (against Gálvez's father) and protecting Jamaica itself from attack. And now the Dutch had joined their enemies.[53]

The British ships that the Cuban fisherman spotted may have been headed for the Dutch Caribbean island of St. Eustace. The Dutch, with their strong merchant class, had hoped to make profits from the war by remaining officially neutral while taking over trade routes that had been dominated by the British. St. Eustace had been sending supplies to the American rebels by the shipload, and British officials felt that closing it was essential to the war effort. Britain declared war on the Dutch in October 1780 and attacked St. Eustace the following February. British reports returned saying that even the beach "was covered with hogsheads of sugar and tobacco" worth more than three million pounds and destined for the rebels. For his part, Campbell doubted his superiors' motives and believed that the fleet failed to come to his aid because British leaders coveted the valuable Dutch cargoes.[54]

As for the British army in North America, Cornwallis was trying to conquer Virginia, and General Henry Clinton was defending New York against the combined forces of George Washington's Continental Army, French General Rochambeau's troops, and the French navy. In late April, a mounted messenger arrived at Fort George with news of a Cornwallis victory in the Carolinas. The Fort George artillery and soldiers fired volleys to celebrate, and a rumor circulated that the messenger had also brought news of "an intended reinforcement for this garrison," but in reality the news only affirmed that Pensacola was on its own. Letters from Germain indicating that he could not spare assistance for Pensacola were in transit but had not yet arrived. His letters optimistically assured Campbell that Indian assistance and Pensacola's seaside fortifications should suffice for its defense.[55]

The seaside fortification at Red Cliffs fired, ineffectually, on the new Spanish and French fleet as it entered the bay. Choctaws and Creeks reported to Fort George that thousands of men were disembarking and joining the Spanish camp with boatloads of supplies. Company by company, army and navy troops were assigned spots to set up camp. Amand Broussard and the rest of the camp greeted them with "infinite rejoicing." The Spanish troops now totaled well over seven thousand, while fewer than two thousand men were defending Pensacola. No one in the Spanish camp complained as they set to work enlarging the camp and building new defenses.[56]

Taking Pensacola

When the sun rose on April 29, Alexander McGillivray could see, only about half a mile west of Queen's Redoubt, a parallel trench with substantial earthworks protecting it. Spanish soldiers were fast at work building up the battery and mounting their cannons. Behind the parallel trench, men were widening the zigzag trench that connected to the Spanish camp.

In Pensacola, prospects for victory appeared ever slimmer. By the end of April, Isabella and James Bruce had been trapped inside the walls of Pensacola's fort for seven weeks. They had a disheartening view of Gálvez's growing fleet and the thousands of troops and artillery sufficient "to attempt at least the island of Jamaica," as James put it. Unable to leave the town walls, the Bruces had plenty of time to rail against those who had not come to their rescue. James called Admiral Peter Parker one of the "unworthy sons of Neptune who have disgraced their country." He still hoped that Admiral Rodney would take the opportunity of "saving this colony and destroying the force collected against it," which "would be a stroke of more national consequence than perhaps in this or any other war ever offered." Caught between the Spanish navy and Fort George, James Bruce lamented that he and the other men could "either trust our women and children etc. to the power of the merciless savages in the woods, or accept the generosity of Don Gálvez who has offered a sanctuary to our women and children and property until the capitulation of Fort George."[57]

The Bruces did not know what would happen to their family if Pensacola fell. In early May, Isabella Bruce could still see the British flag flying over Fort George although it had sustained "a very heavy cannonade for these six days past." She knew that the enemy was "working hard night and day to get nearer our batteries with his heavy artillery." James wrote his business partners in London that unless Pensacolans had "another miraculous escape there is little doubt but that so superior an army, fleet and artillery must at last carry their point." James was "determined" to leave quickly if the siege went against Britain. The Bruces would not attempt a life in a Spanish colony.[58]

In the dark early morning hours of May 4, over a hundred provincial troops and eighty German Waldeckers crept out of their forts and quietly made their way around the newest Spanish parallel trench, which was not yet protected by cannons. They waited at the edge of the woods closest to the trench. In the early afternoon, a "lively mortar, cannon, and howitzer fire" began to issue from the British redoubts. What the Spanish did not realize was that the artillery was firing without shells so that the small parties could advance without being hit by friendly fire. The Spanish officers in the trench, knowing that the earthworks would protect them from the artillery fire and not knowing about the 180 men sneaking up on them, continued to eat their lunch. One Spaniard later ruefully remarked that the officers ate as if they were "as safe and beyond risk as if they were in Madrid's Plaza Mayor."[59]

While the Spaniards ate, the British troops emerged from the woods wielding their bayonets. The first group they attacked tried to flee backward into the zigzag trench behind them, and, according to one observer, panicked cries rang out of *"Somos perdidos, que nos pasan a cuchillo!"*—"We are lost, we are put to the knife!" The British killed and wounded more than forty Spanish soldiers, including most of the officers in the advanced trench, which added an extra panic to the Spanish retreat. The British troops spiked the five cannons within the advanced trench to prevent the Spanish from using them again and set fire to the fascines and cotton bales supporting the earthworks and the wooden cannon mounts that the Spanish had laboriously constructed and hauled. As the victorious parties returned to the woods, they heard the whoops of the British soldiers who had stayed back to guard from the woods "shouting joyfully and throwing their hats into the air." By the time Spanish light infantry arrived to retake the advanced trench, the British soldiers were long gone, their pockets full of the silver utensils, buckles, and coins they had stripped from the fallen Spaniards.[60]

However, the small triumph did nothing to change Pensacola's prospects. By that time, the Spanish had men and cannons to spare. The Spanish rebuilt the cannon mounts and earthworks and advanced to a final parallel trench within two hundred yards of Queen's Re-

The Taking of Pensacola, engraved by H. G. Berteaux and Nicolas Ponce, Paris, 1784. (*Recueil d'estampes représentant les différents événemens de la Guerre qui a procuré l'indépendance aux Etats Unis de l'Amérique*, Rare Book Collection, Louis Round Wilson Special Collections Library, University of North Carolina, Chapel Hill)

doubt. As General Campbell wrote Germain on May 7, "Our fate appears inevitable. We are attacked by an armament that shows the importance of the conquest in the estimation of Spain." In contrast, he noted, British Pensacola had "been neglected." He was going to hold out as long as he deemed reasonable, but he suspected that his next letter "will be the unpleasing and disagreeable task of reporting the triumph of Spain and their acquisition of a province under their dominion."[61]

In the morning of Tuesday, May 8, "a terrifying noise" rang out from Queen's Redoubt, and "a great column of smoke" rose into the air. As both sides soon learned, a Spanish shell had burst by the door of the British powder magazine, the small building where the gunpowder was stored, and blew it up. The blast killed nearly a hundred men, mostly soldiers from the Maryland and Pennsylvania Loyalists Battalions and sailors working on shore. Some were blown up by the explosion, others were buried under the rubble, and many died later from painful injuries. When a soldier of the Maryland Battalion named William Augustus Bowles entered Queen's Redoubt just as the shell hit, he saw "the melancholy spectacle of near a hundred men blown into the air." Observers from all sides saw the flames cover the redoubt. Those British troops who were able to walk picked their way across the fallen bodies and the holes in the ground made by the shells to the Prince of Wales Redoubt about two hundred yards away, carrying as many of the wounded as they could. From there, the British exchanged fire with the Spanish troops who rushed to occupy what was left of Queen's Redoubt. But with the Spanish commanding the heights, British defense was futile. General Campbell raised the white flag over Fort George.[62]

After negotiating the exact terms, Campbell on May 10 officially surrendered all of West Florida to the Spanish. As evening fell, the British troops marched out of Fort George following Campbell and the other officers to the sound of the drums. James Bruce processed out of Pensacola with Governor Peter Chester and the other civilian leaders. The Spanish and French officers and troops, including Amand Broussard, marched to meet them. No Indians surrendered. After the magazine exploded, Alexander McGillivray and the Creek and Choctaw warriors quickly gathered the women and children out of Pensacola, grabbed what they could carry out of Pensacola's warehouses, and headed home. Seeing the Indian women she had been living among depart, Isabella Bruce must have wished she too were headed home with her husband and children rather than to an unknown fate. When all were assembled outside the town, Generals Gálvez and Campbell advanced and solemnly greeted each other. Gálvez accepted the flags that the British guards surrendered. The British troops then set down their arms, and Spanish troops entered the fort and raised the colors of Spain. French officers took command of the Prince of Wales Redoubt.[63]

That night, Amand Broussard celebrated the victory. His "Hourra!" mixed with the Spanish regulars' "Viva Gálvez!" and the Irish regiment's "Hurrah!" Cheers rose from the several hundred men who looked more like Petit Jean but who were themselves diverse: enslaved and free; black and mixed-race; born in Louisiana, Cuba, or West Africa. Among them were the New Orleans free black militia, who had just won their third victory under Gálvez, and slaves from New Orleans who were seeing their very first action. Perhaps mixed in but probably in their own separate camp, Upper Creeks and Alabamas hailed their victory in their languages and looked forward to claiming the spoils of Pensacola's stores.[64]

The next day, a priest led the Spanish forces in a *Te Deum* to thank their god for the victory. More than seventy men on their side had died of battle wounds and several dozen more of illness. They had been lucky to be spared a more serious outbreak of disease. Over a hundred more had been wounded, many so seriously that they would soon die. Seven of the wounded on the Spanish side were slaves, and if Gálvez kept his promise, the survivors would have a chance for freedom. On the British side, nearly a hundred soldiers had died, and around fifty more had been wounded. Indian losses were far fewer, with perhaps only one death.[65]

The following day, James, Isabella, Archibald, and Charlotte Bruce boarded one of the ships for Havana that the Spanish and French had loaded with artillery, troops, and more than a thousand prisoners. Gálvez was already planning his next siege—St. Augustine? the Bahamas? Jamaica? In New Orleans, Oliver and Margaret Pollock cheered the news, and Oliver forwarded it to Congress, jubilantly declaring that the Spanish victory meant that U.S. merchants could now trade freely all along the Mississippi and Gulf Coast. Oliver Pollock wrote Gálvez congratulating him for winning West Florida and thanking him "for all your past favors and protection." Pollock hoped that the funding he had provided to the Spanish effort and his friendship with Gálvez would prove profitable investments.[66]

On the way home, Indians and their British agents discussed what this change in West Florida might mean for them. As the Chickasaws and Choctaws took their paths for home, they promised Alexander Cameron that they would help the British if they tried to retake West Florida. When the rest of the party arrived at the Upper Creek towns on the Tallapoosa River, McGillivray and the other Creeks demanded that Cameron write down their version of events to forward to Germain. Creeks surrounded Cameron as he wrote, instructing him to describe their commitment and bravery. He did so faithfully, recording the details of Creek and Choctaw participation, particularly mentioning McGillivray and Choctaw Chief Franchimastabé and praising the Indians' "great spirit and attachment," bravery, and honor. The Creeks demanded that he ask Germain to send goods overland from Georgia, as hard as that would be, because they should be rewarded for their service. Different Indians shouted to Cameron that they would go to the Spaniards for rum and ammunition or to Augusta to make their case personally before the British there. After Cameron left for Georgia with the letter, discussions continued about what to do next. When the Alabamas and Upper Creeks who had been with Gálvez returned, they too must have given their version of the siege and their opinions about the Creeks' future.[67]

Conclusion: *The Resurgence of Europe's Oldest Empire in the War for Independence*

The siege of Pensacola decided the fate of an important part of the British empire, for the next few decades at least. The victory was a startling reversal from British dominance in 1763. As a result of the surrender, Spanish imperial claims now stretched from Tierra del Fuego at the tip of South America to Alaska and included both sides of the Mississippi up to the Great Lakes. The Seven Years' War had driven Spain out of its lands in eastern North America, but that now seemed like a temporary reversal. The thirteen colonies' war for independence had strengthened Europe's oldest and largest empire. The victory was proof that the Spanish empire was on the rise again and that the Bourbon reforms enacted in North America after 1763 were working. Enlightened leaders, cutting-edge military tactics, careful Indian diplomacy, and an inclusive military force had been wildly successful.

If Indians had come in the numbers that the British expected, they would have made a difference, quite likely allowing the British to preserve Pensacola. Alexander Cameron asserted that "had my advice been regarded by General Campbell in time, instead of having 500, I should have had 2,000 Indians to oppose the Spaniards at the siege of

Pensacola."[68] Historians have tended to agree with Cameron and to judge Campbell harshly for failing to support his Indian allies. It is true that some well-timed supplies and, even more important, demonstrations of respect might have helped. After all, as Cameron told Germain, although Governor Gálvez "has very little to give them besides tafia [rum], commissions, and medals," he had the right spirit. "He will even humble himself so low as to kiss their warriors from ear to ear and pay them every respect that is due to great chiefs."[69]

Yet Campbell was in a difficult situation. Southeastern Indian allies not only cost a great deal of money, they were also too independent to come when called. Their failure to come showed that they did not think British control over Pensacola mattered much—the Spanish in Louisiana seemed to be as useful as trading partners and diplomatic allies and asked less in return. General Campbell's bumbling had simply added to their growing belief that British alliance was not worth the cost. At the same time that the Spanish crown increasingly identified an opportunity on the Gulf Coast worth risking lives and resources, Indians had decided the Spanish-British battle was not worth joining.

The surrender's repercussions were already apparent from Creek country to the Caribbean. The British had lost a colony that had not rebelled. The loss would help push them toward the decision after Yorktown to cut their losses and recognize American independence before things got any worse.

Yet the siege of Pensacola has not taken its place alongside Yorktown in the written histories of the American Revolution's weighty events. Historical significance is seldom set in acts of battle but in the words that come after. Whose independence would be won and whose would be lost? The answers would be hashed out by diplomats in Paris and by countless men and women on the ground across the eastern half of North America. Far from settled in 1781, the lives of people in and around the Gulf Coast would continue to change with the fortunes of empires and nations.

PART IV

The Paradox of Independence

AS THE BRITISH evacuated Pensacola and other port cities, people of the Gulf Coast wondered what the new order would bring. The most likely configuration seemed a continuation of multiple sovereignties, as Chickasaws, Creeks, Choctaws, and other Indian nations continued to rule their own territory, trading with one another and with colonies populated by combinations of French, Spanish, English, Scottish, Irish, German, and African people. Spanish imperial ambitions for North America were growing but might be compatible with or even assisted by strong allied Indian nations.

In contrast, this geography would sit uneasily beside an American republic that had rebelled against Great Britain in part for access to new land. The Treaty of Paris would end the American Revolution, but it would answer few questions about the future of the continent. Could the United States become one of many connected sovereign nations on the continent, securing its independence from Britain through interdependence with its neighbors? Or would its territorial ambition—the quest for new property by both American states and individual families—preclude the kinds of connections that would allow for sharing a continent?

CHAPTER FOURTEEN

Nations, Colonies, Towns, and States

AS JAMES AND ISABELLA BRUCE sailed out of Pensacola Bay in defeat, they could only hope that, as General John Campbell put it, the defense of Pensacola had caused the "diversion of such a powerful armament of France and Spain" for long enough that British fleets and armies elsewhere had "acquired conquests and victories that will more than compensate and counterbalance the loss of Pensacola."[1] It was a reasonable hope in May 1781. Still, the loss of West Florida was important. Britain had, for the first time in the war, lost a colony that had not rebelled. The stakes were higher than ever. With the victory at Pensacola, Spanish and French forces were now free to take on St. Augustine, the plantation islands of the West Indies, British-occupied posts in New York or the south, Gibraltar, Minorca, India, or England itself. British officials now planned defenses based on what the empire could afford to lose and what it could not.[2]

Despite Campbell's hopes, other fronts did not go well for the British. Augusta fell to Colonel Henry "Light Horse Harry" Lee a month after Pensacola, when Creek forces did not get there in time. In the meantime, Continental Army General Nathanael Greene's forces harassed British General Charles Cornwallis into marching north from the Carolinas and unwisely positioning his eight thousand men at Yorktown, Virginia. While Cornwallis might have taken Virginia and consolidated his hold over much of the south if he had been able to recruit large numbers of Indian allies, he chose dependence on regulars. He backed himself into Yorktown in hopes that its peninsula, easily reached by the British navy, would prove an effective position. If General Campbell's "diversion" at Pensacola had held out longer, Cornwallis might have been right. Instead, fresh from the victory in West Florida, Spanish ships rushed to protect French shipping throughout the Gulf of Mexico and Caribbean, freeing French Admiral François Joseph Paul, the Comte de Grasse, to head for Yorktown to join with General George Washington's Continental Army and French land forces. After they besieged Yorktown for several weeks, General Cornwallis surrendered to the French and the Americans on October 19, 1781.[3]

The American rebellion had resulted in much more damage than anyone in the British empire had imagined in 1770. The French, Spanish, and Dutch took advantage of the conflict to take over British trade and colonies. Indian allies who had seemed secure at the start of the war had not put British aims and tactics above their own. Britain, having lost West Florida and some of its Caribbean islands, stood to lose even more. By 1782, the English public had lost its patience with a long and expensive war that risked further defeats. On February 27, 1782, Parliament voted to stop attempts to suppress the rebellion. Two weeks later, Prime Minister Lord Frederick North resigned, and the new administration embarked on a commitment to peace, including granting independence to the rebellious thirteen colonies if absolutely necessary.[4]

Britain was on the defensive, but the continent's future was far from certain. The rebellion's leaders in Georgia feared that the British withdrawal was just a temporary measure to focus on the West Indies "and then return with redoubled fury" to reclaim its rebellious colonies.[5] The Continental Army's victory was fragile, and it had depended on massive assistance from European allies. The new nation was still deeply in debt, to individuals like Oliver Pollock and his friend Robert Morris as well as to the Dutch, French, and Spanish. Under the Articles of Confederation, the Congress had limited power to raise revenue because it could not tax income or property or levy duties on imports and exports. Like the United Nations today, Congress could only ask its member states for money, of which they had little to give. No one even knew how large the national debt was because so much of it took the form of receipts in the pockets of individual investors like Pollock for goods and services provided during the war.[6]

While war against the British might end soon, powerful Indian nations still posed a formidable threat to the new United States. Indians of the Northern Confederacy in the Ohio Valley had joined with Mohawk Joseph Brant's force to raid the western parts of the colonies from Tennessee to Pennsylvania. Despite Britain's failures with Creeks, Chickasaws, and Choctaws in West Florida, the Northern Confederacy was coordinating with the British better than at any time earlier in the war. With the exception of the Cherokees, southeastern Indians had fought very little during the war. Under Payamataha's guidance, they had built new alliances with one another and with the Northern Confederacy to ward off future problems. Spain was poised to have colonial possession over most of the continent, if it cooperated with Indians. Any worries that the Spanish monarchy had at the start of the war about the American Revolution being a threat to empires seemed disproven. Gálvez's military victories and success in inspiring loyalty among colonists promised a strong and growing Spanish presence in North America. Spanish troops had put down the Tupac Amaru and other rebellions in its empire, while in Europe, independent republics seemed to be a dying breed. The independent states of Geneva, Sweden, and Poland and the Dutch and Venetian republics all seemed too unstable to remain independent, much less republican, while parliamentary reform had failed in England and Ireland.[7]

The map of the continental United States today so neatly spreads from east to west that it would be easy to imagine that it was the country's "manifest destiny" to stretch "from sea to shining sea."[8] But this concept developed much later, in the nineteenth century. A patchwork of European colonies and sovereign nations was the most likely outcome of the war. It might include Spanish colonies, British Canada, the thirteen states (separately or together), multiple Indian nations, a pan-Indian confederacy in the Ohio Valley, other newly independent colonies, and free black colonies under the Spanish or British realm. Whatever the configuration, in 1781 it appeared that, despite the changes of war, multiple sovereignties would continue across North America, as different kinds of people continued to ally and fight for what they saw as their independence and opportunity.[9]

Making Spanish Subjects

Once the Spanish won West Florida, Gálvez had to decide how to prevent future rebellions and keep West Florida under peaceful Spanish rule. The Spanish could reference a common religion and system of law when dealing with French-speaking colonists on both sides of the Mississippi, but British West Floridians had strong prejudices against Spanish Catholic rule. Should he use the iron fist to impress upon his new subjects that the Spanish did not tolerate treason? Or should he continue his velvet-gloved strategy of persuading West Floridians that their best chance of peace, independence, and prosperity lay within the Spanish empire? Gálvez did both. After a small group of Natchez loyalists and Choctaws attacked Spanish-held Natchez in April 1781, his officers arrested a few leaders for violating the oath they had sworn to the Spanish king when they surrendered Natchez in 1779 but otherwise promised that anyone who renewed the oath of allegiance to Spain would receive amnesty. He circulated an order that anyone who raised the Spanish flag outside their houses would be recognized as loyal and would not be bothered. By distinguishing a few "traitors" from the rest of West Floridians, Gálvez demonstrated that Spain punished treason but welcomed peaceful subjects.[10]

Gálvez knew that Spanish triumph, his promises of prosperity and respect, and his decision after all of his victories to let the opposing militia return home without punishment had convinced some West Florida families that they had been wrong about Spanish tyranny and that they could happily live and work their lands under Spanish protection. Even some American families from the Carolinas immigrated to Spanish West Florida, finding peace and opportunity that they did not have in their war-torn home. Gálvez urged the crown to promote loyalty and prosperity by helping West Florida and Louisiana grow.[11]

With every reason to agree to whatever Gálvez suggested, the king assured Louisianans and West Floridians that the Spanish empire would promote prosperity. In a royal proclamation of January 1782, King Carlos promised colonists that "their welfare should suffer no impairment." The king granted New Orleans and Pensacola the right to trade freely with not only other posts in the Spanish empire but also France and its colonies, a rare privilege in this era when legal trade was usually restricted to one empire. While he lowered duties for all smaller ports in the empire, he completely exempted Louisiana and the Floridas. To encourage plantation agriculture, the king exempted slaves imported into Louisiana and the Floridas from import duties for ten years. The proclamations demonstrated the crown's confidence that Gálvez could build a strong Spanish colony where Spanish, French, and English people could live in peace and prosperity alongside allied Indian nations, if at the expense of enslaved Africans.[12]

The words and actions of Gálvez and the king persuaded many French- and English-speaking landowners to remain Spanish subjects. Although many of the English speakers hoped that Britain would win the Revolutionary War, they gradually adapted to rule by their enemy. The end of the conflict on the Gulf Coast and Spain's encouragement of commerce allowed many to buy slaves and export the tobacco and indigo they grew from New Orleans and Pensacola. The Spanish crown required its subjects to be Catholic, but as long as they did not publicly practice Protestant Christianity, the Louisiana and West Florida governments did not enforce the requirement to convert.[13]

War Continues

Although Britain had lost key battles and Spain had won West Florida, the British had not yet completely given up, and neither had Alexander McGillivray. While few Creeks had followed him to Pensacola, in the aftermath of British defeats at Pensacola and Yorktown, Creeks and their allies fought with much more persistence against the Americans. Creek bands, along with loyalist refugees, Choctaws, and Cherokees, raided the western edge of the southern states. Hearing rumors that the French and Americans were besieging British Savannah, Little Tallassee Headman Emistisiguo led a party of around 150 warriors there to see if they could help the British and also collect ammunition for their war on the Americans. In the early morning hours of June 24, Emistisiguo's forces routed one of the American camps, destroying ammunition and supplies. The Creeks estimated that they killed or wounded at least a hundred Continentals and lost only seventeen of their own men in General Anthony Wayne's countercharge. However, one of the fallen seventeen was "the brave, gallant Emistisiguo," the respected Upper Creek headman and mentor of Alexander McGillivray.[14] As the Creeks continued toward Savannah, they saw a small force, which seemed to be British. They sent twelve Creeks to parlay, but it turned out to be a contingent of Wayne's army, commanded by Continental Army General Thomas Posey. General Posey captured the twelve emissaries and reported the incident to General Wayne, who was so angry at his losses to the Creeks that he ordered the men executed, despite Posey's protests that killing a parlay party was murder. The Creeks had learned why his own men called him "Mad" Anthony Wayne.

When the surviving Creeks reached Savannah, they learned much worse news. The British were preparing to evacuate there too. Not only was their ally pulling out of another key port, but now, in order to ride home, the Creek party would have to cross territory that General Wayne controlled. Instead, the Creeks boarded British ships and sailed to St. Augustine in East Florida, the last remaining British post on the southern mainland.[15]

When the Creeks finally arrived home from St. Augustine, Alexander McGillivray learned the terrible news of Emistisiguo's death and the British withdrawal. Would St. Augustine "have the same fate," Creeks wondered, leaving their nation "at the mercy of its enemies"? Some headmen charged the British with violating treaties and "abandon[ing] them in their necessity contrary to the talks of the Great King."[16] With or without the British, they determined to continue their fight against American immigration.

As the mainland remained contested, the war for the West Indies continued as well. Leaving New Orleans in the summer of 1781, Bernardo de Gálvez, his wife, Marie Felice de St. Maxent, and two daughters sailed to Havana, where Gálvez contemplated where to strike next: Jamaica, the crown jewel of the British sugar islands? The Bahamas, an annoying base for privateering against Spanish and French ships? St. Augustine, whose capture would solidify Gálvez's gains in West Florida? The port of Halifax, from which Spain might conquer Canada? The general knew that he had to act quickly if he wanted to press his advantage. Negotiators had agreed to meet in Paris, and if they agreed on a treaty, military strikes would have to cease. In the meantime, Spanish forces seized the Bahamas and the island of Minorca, in the Mediterranean Sea off the coast of Spain, and readied for their next attack. Jamaica seemed likely to be next. Foreseeing an attack on their most valuable colony without forces to fortify it, the British cut their losses.

The Treaty of Paris, 1783

Late in 1782, American, British, French, and Spanish representatives gathered to negotiate an end to the war and hash out what it meant for the territories they claimed. Although Indians had fought in most regions where the American Revolution was waged, none were invited to the negotiating table. The negotiations in Paris would establish American independence, but British desire to put the war behind them as quickly as possible created a shaky treaty. It set up conflicts over borders and sovereignty that would continue into the next century.

Spanish officials believed that they had succeeded in their war for empire. Spanish forces held the formerly British posts along the Gulf of Mexico and on the eastern bank of the Mississippi. Spain's claims stretched from the Pacific Ocean to the Flint River in Georgia (well within today's state of Georgia) and from the Gulf to the Great Lakes, plus their progress in other parts of the globe. Spain had helped the rebellion by defeating Britain in the south, preventing the British navy from cutting off American supplies, and providing financial assistance, including through Oliver Pollock. King Carlos III knew his diplomats in Paris would have to defend his expansive claims against those of the British. The new republic on the eastern seaboard seemed much less likely to be a threat.[17]

In the uncertain days of the war, Americans had desperately needed Spanish assistance and had imagined sharing the trans-Appalachian west with their ally. In 1778, Virginia Governor Patrick Henry assured Gálvez that the United States had "more land than can be settled for many ages to come."[18] The same year, John Jay, the American diplomat in Spain, wrote that a mutually beneficial agreement with Spain was worth giving up any claim on the Floridas, "to which we had no title," or navigation rights to the Mississippi River, "which we should not want this age."[19] Upon receiving a letter from Oliver Pollock about Gálvez's victory at Pensacola in 1781, Massachusetts Governor John Hancock wrote to congratulate Gálvez and anticipate commercial intercourse "between the two countries to reciprocal advantage."[20] Initially Congress had hoped that Jay could persuade Spain that sharing the Mississippi was in Spain's interest. But in the middle of the war, when the British looked poised to take the south and Congress was desperate for a Spanish loan, Congress sent instructions to Jay in Spain to give up the demand for navigation of the Mississippi in order to get a treaty.[21]

Even then there were signs of emerging conflict between Spain and the United States. During the war, Oliver Pollock had, behind Gálvez's back, tried to persuade Congress that the Floridas, the Mississippi Valley, and navigation of the Mississippi River were essential to the future prosperity of the United States. In 1779, he warned Congress, "I make no doubt you know the value of West Florida too well to give it up either by treaty or otherwise to any power upon Earth." Pollock described for Virginia Governor Patrick Henry a postwar era in which Manchac and Pensacola belonged to the United States: "We can import our supplies of goods immediately from Europe and dispatch them up to the back settlements." Under those circumstances, Pollock was certain, "the country would get completely settled and a flourishing commerce immediately take place after the war."[22] He pointedly sent a copy of the surrender of the Lake Pontchartrain settlers to Congress. Because they had worded their surrender as capitulation to the United States rather than to Spain, Congress might be able to use it to stake a claim to the Gulf region. Congress forwarded the document to Jay in Madrid, where they hoped it would add leverage.[23]

By 1782, Jay was so frustrated with his inability to reach an agreement with Spain that he hoped the British—his enemy—would retake West Florida, believing that they would be more likely than the Spanish to allow Americans access to the Mississippi. Clashing ambitions veiled during the war were exposed in Paris. In September 1782, Jay joined Benjamin Franklin and John Adams in Paris, where he railed against the "extravagance" of Spanish claims extending to the Great Lakes and Appalachians. Instead, Jay said, the United States should possess all land east of the Mississippi and north of Pensacola and Mobile, leaving Spain the same sliver of coast the Choctaws had granted Britain after the Seven Years' War. Of course, the Choctaws would have reminded him that it was their land, not his country's or Spain's.[24]

Following Pollock's lead, the American delegates in Paris used the victories of Virginia Militia General George Rogers Clark in the Illinois country and Continental Navy Captain William Pickles on Lake Pontchartrain to support their claims, even though the United States held nothing in between. Franklin belittled Spain's northern claims, noting that "the Spaniards having taken a little post called St. Joseph, pretend to have made a conquest of the Illinois country." Franklin asked rhetorically, "While they decline our offered friendship, are they to be suffered to encroach on our bounds, and shut us up within the Appalachian mountains?"[25] U.S. representatives shuddered at the thought that most of the Americas' land mass, including rich farmlands west of the Appalachians, could be in the hands of the Catholic, monarchical Spanish, who had been until the 1770s a hated enemy and since then an imperious and lukewarm ally.

Trying to appease their American and Spanish allies, the French proposed a compromise. The Spanish would get the Floridas and everything between the Gulf and the Tennessee River (the present-day states of Alabama, Mississippi, and most of Tennessee), the United States would get the lands between the Tennessee and Ohio rivers (Kentucky and eastern Tennessee), and Britain would keep everything north of the Ohio River (Illinois, Indiana, Ohio, and the Great Lakes region). The proposal made sense. Each party would get a large swath of trans-Appalachian land, and there was a lot to go around. Each could deal with the Indians who claimed and lived on the land by allying with them or trying to conquer or buy their lands.[26]

The Mississippi Valley had always been split into multiple sovereignties, even when the chiefdom of Cahokia ruled over much of it five centuries before. Since the late 1600s, European imperial and Indian national sovereignties had overlapped. The region's riverine geography suggested many ways of dividing ownership. The people of the United States might desire some western land, but their country did not have the resources or stability to go far west of the Appalachians or overturn the sovereignty of the Indians who controlled the land.

Nonetheless, Americans were unlikely to recognize Spain's or Britain's claims to the very trans-Appalachian lands that had sparked conflict in the Seven Years' War, Pontiac's War of 1763, and the American Revolution itself. At the same time, if Iroquois leader Joseph Brant won his war, the Ohio River would be the northern border of the United States, which combined with Spain's claims might leave the United States with none of these lands. Knowing the tensions between the United States and its French and Spanish allies, the British proposed a separate peace between themselves and their newly independent colonies. Wishing to defend the rest of its empire from Spain and France more than punish the rebels, the British negotiators secretly offered the American delegation everything between the At-

SPANISH PROPOSAL

FRENCH PROPOSAL

U.S. PROPOSAL

TREATY OF PARIS, PROPOSALS

lantic and the Mississippi from the Great Lakes to the Floridas. In a secret provision of the treaty that attempted to thwart Spain's claims, British negotiators wrote that if Britain regained West Florida from Spain, Congress would assent to a West Florida border at N 32° 28', but if Spain retained West Florida, Britain would support the Americans' position that the West Florida border was farther south, at the 31st parallel (the northern border of today's state of Florida). This article, if enforced, would give the United States an extra band of land five hundred miles horizontally by ninety miles vertically, including most of the lands of the Choctaws, Creeks, and Chickasaws.[27]

Because John Jay had never managed to complete a treaty of alliance with Spain, Congress was free to make a British treaty without the Spanish, but signing a peace treaty without the support of its French ally should have been unthinkable. During the war, Congress had passed a resolution denouncing "wicked" rumors, "derogatory to the honor of Congress and of these United States," that Congress would consider a separate peace without France. But now the British negotiators were offering more than the United States could refuse. In addition, according to John Adams, the British threatened that if the Americans did not agree, Britain would send troops to take West Florida from Spain and create a strong British presence to threaten the southern United States.[28]

In November 1782, the American delegates agreed to the preliminary separate treaty with Britain and informed France and Spain of its provisions. They secretly wrote to Congress to ask for guidance on the matter of the West Florida border. Congress debated the question in March 1783. American Foreign Affairs Secretary Robert Livingston proposed honesty with the French minister and delaying a final agreement with Britain "until peace shall be actually signed between the Kings of France and Great Britain." Congressman Eliphalet Dyer of Connecticut rose to oppose Livingston's proposal and say that the border question "did not concern the interests of France." Several other congressmen agreed. However, John Francis Mercer of Virginia worried that "it was unwise to prefer Great Britain to Spain as our neighbors in West Florida." Indeed, some congressmen thought it

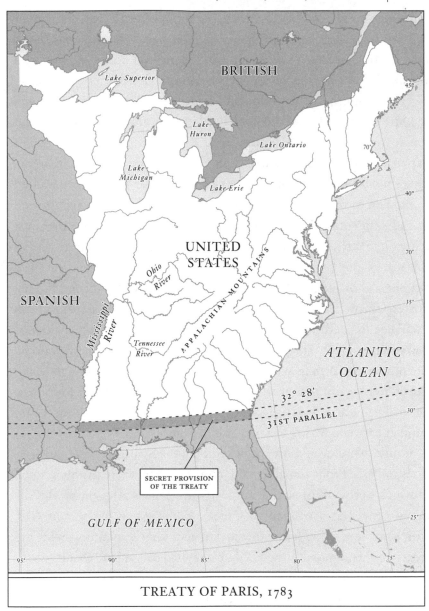

TREATY OF PARIS, 1783

"very reprehensible" of John Adams to withhold information from a country that had been an ally, if an unofficial one, in the war.[29]

Congress was thousands of miles away, so the delegates in Paris proceeded. On September 3, 1783, John Adams, Benjamin Franklin, and John Jay hurried through the narrow streets of Paris's left bank into a fine hotel and up the stairs to the room where a British member of Parliament was waiting. There, the men signed their names to the final version of the treaty ending the American colonies' war with Britain and acknowledging American independence.

France and Spain had reluctantly assented to the treaty, although the Spanish probably would not have done so if they had known about the secret West Florida border. Like Britain, France wanted to cut expenses, which were growing into such a large war debt that the king's ministers were considering new taxes. The French also wanted to hold on to their gains in the West Indies and feared losing ground in India. In contrast, the Spanish crown hoped to do more than just hang on to current possessions but rather to take Gibraltar as well as the rest of the Gulf, from East Florida to Jamaica. To end the war, Britain acknowledged Spanish possession of West Florida and French possession of the island of Tobago and gave Spain East Florida in exchange for getting back the Bahamas and Grenada, which France had taken in 1779. Thus Britain lost sixteen American colonies in the Revolutionary War, as well as Senegal in West Africa. Though Spain hoped to get Gibraltar, it would not give up Pensacola and Mobile to get it. The failure to agree on a border for West Florida set up future conflict between Spain and the United States.[30]

Indians were even more disgusted than the Spanish by the negotiations in Paris. From Canada to the Floridas, they wrote protests, some of which were published in European newspapers. Alexander McGillivray convened a council of Creeks, Chickasaws, and Cherokees, which wrote a joint letter to the Spanish king explaining why the treaty could not possibly be valid: Britain had ceded land that it "never possessed . . . either by cession, purchase, or by right of conquest." The letter explained that "we the Nations of Creeks, Chickasaws and Cherokees" did not "do any act to forfeit our independence and natural rights to the said King of Great Britain."[31] They were independent nations, and to them Britain's surrender did not change anything about their territory or their sovereignty.

The United States denied that Indians between the Appalachians and the Mississippi were sovereign nations, insisting that they were subordinate allies or even subjects of Britain and therefore had lost the war. A Congressional Committee on Indian Affairs claimed in 1784 that Indians "were themselves aggressors in the war, without even a pretense of provocation." They "determined to join their arms to those of Great Britain and to share her fortunes" despite "the friendly temper and designs of the United States." In treaty negotiations, Congress even asserted that Indians' British "friends" had failed them, "having made no stipulation in their favor." Their land was simply "reasonable compensation for the expenses and alarms to which they have exposed their unoffending neighbors," the United States.[32]

In this radical rewriting of history, Indians had no independent sovereignty—they had ceded their independence to Britain during the colonial period and must "share her fortunes." As early as 1777, in an effort to recruit Indian allies, British Superintendent of Indian Affairs John Stuart had warned Indians that "if the rebels should prove victorious you may be certainly assured that they would immediately endeavor to possess themselves of all your lands and extirpate you" and "would not leave a red man on the east side of the Mississippi."[33] It seemed laughable in 1777 that the rebels would prevail over anyone, but now, Indians wanted to persuade Britain not to back down. A variety of rumors circulated among Indians and colonists: "the Spaniards have given Mobile and Pensacola to the English"; "the Americans have made peace with the English"; the Creeks have been "massacred with swords by American cavalry"; "the Shawnees are also conquered"; the Americans were coming down the Mississippi "to take Natchez, Manchac, and New Orleans"; the British were amassing an army at St. Augustine.[34]

In late 1782 and early 1783, thousands of Creeks, Chickasaws, Choctaws, Mohawks, Senecas, Delawares, Shawnees, Tuscaroras, and Cherokees, including the Chickamauga leader Dragging Canoe, crowded into St. Augustine, the last British outpost in the south, to express their opposition to the Americans. They asked if the king really had ordered British troops to return home and had offered Indian lands to the United States and Spain. Surely "this talk is a Virginia lie," they insisted.[35] Another Creek headman declared, "We have heard that the Great King intends to throw away this land." In the war, he said, "we took up the hatchet for the English, at a time we could scarce distinguish our friends from our foes" and "lost in the service a number of our people." What could make the king go back on his promises? the man asked. "Is the Great King conquered or does he mean to abandon us. . . . Does he intend to sell his friends as slaves, or only give our lands to his and our enemies?" When British Deputy Indian Superintendent Thomas Brown advised them to make peace with the Americans and ally with the Spanish, Creeks replied, "we cannot take a Virginian or Spaniard by the hand[;] we cannot look them in the face."[36]

Indians discussed "confederating the whole body of Indians on the continent." In St. Augustine, they joined loyalist refugees and their slaves, some twelve thousand in all, who had come by land from other parts of East Florida and by ship from Savannah and New York City as the British evacuated those cities. Surrounded by people urging him to continue the fight, Brown was still writing hopefully to British Commander in Chief of North America Guy Carleton in February 1783 that the British and their Indian allies could retake Pensacola and then take New Orleans. However, orders from King George III to prepare to evacuate East Florida because Britain and Spain had signed a preliminary treaty ceding it to Spain were already on the way. When McGillivray received the news, he could not believe it. As he put it, Britain "has no right to give up a country she never could call her own."[37] The Creeks suspended their fighting to see what the peace would bring, but they knew that the Treaty of Paris would create more problems than it would solve.

The Chickasaws and the Dangers of Peace

Theoretically, the end of the war should have brought peace between the Chickasaws and all of their neighbors. Payamataha had long worked for peace, and now British pressure to fight would end. The British had advised Indians to make peace with the Spanish and the Americans, and that was exactly what Payamataha intended to do. Yet the fact that actual land possession and sovereignty were still undetermined made keeping the peace as tricky as ever. Whereas in

1763 Chickasaws had cheered as their French imperial enemies left, the withdrawal of their British ally meant that the Chickasaws lost supplies, protection from settler encroachment, and the security of a border that they had defined. Scottish trader and loyalist James Colbert would bring the Chickasaws and Spain to the brink of war, which would take all of Payamataha's diplomatic skill to prevent. To continue Payamataha's policy of peace, the Chickasaws would need to manage all of these neighbors with care.

Southeastern Indians had already identified the Spanish as the obvious new ally who could deliver European goods and military support. Throughout 1782 and 1783, Chickasaws and other Indians visited Spanish New Orleans, Mobile, Pensacola, Galveztown, Baton Rouge, Natchez, and St. Louis in huge numbers. The crown nearly tripled spending on Indian gifts from the previous year, ten times what they had spent in some prewar years, and still Indians pressed for more. Esteban Miró, who became the acting governor of Louisiana in Gálvez's absence, wrote from New Orleans that he was going through Indian presents at an astonishing rate and was "on the verge of exhausting the innumerable gifts" they required.[38] At all the posts, Indians "daily present themselves" asking for muskets, powder, musket balls, linen, calicos, ginghams, blankets, hats, needles, thread, pins, scissors, knives, paint, mirrors, hoes, hatchets, saddles, and bridles.[39]

Chickasaw alliances with other Indians and with the Spanish needed ongoing attention. Chickasaw diplomats met with individual Indian nations, and the delegation of Chickasaws, Shawnees, Delawares, and Cherokees that had been traveling south of the Ohio River since 1780 or 1781 arrived in St. Louis in March 1782 to meet with Spanish Commandant Francisco Cruzat. They carried wampum belts of peace and asked for "the protection of our Catholic sovereign" and "a firm and sincere peace with the Spaniards." Cruzat agreed, eager to have these valuable multiple alliances. For the Spanish and for most Indian peoples of the region, the end of the war could bring stability and security.[40]

But a small group of resolute British loyalists threatened that peace, including the Scottish trader and loyalist James Colbert and his Chickasaw sons. Whereas Lachlan and Alexander McGillivray were able to align their diplomatic and economic goals with both Creek Headman Emistisiguo and British representatives, Colbert worked against Payamataha while trying to advance a British-Chickasaw military alliance. During the James Willing crisis, Colbert had tried unsuccessfully to persuade individual warriors to fight for the British. For his efforts, the British made Colbert assistant commissary to the Chickasaws and military leader of any volunteers he could recruit, hoping that he would be more aggressive than Payamataha. Colbert neglected Chickasaw ways of making foreign policy, and most Chickasaws rejected his interference. In the past, Chickasaws made it clear that they saw Colbert as a Briton, not a Chickasaw, by complaining to British officials that Colbert's hunting party was intruding on Chickasaw lands and that he was illegally trying to establish a plantation.[41]

Colbert had fled Chickasaw country after the Spanish took Mobile and Pensacola, but by 1782 he was back and had attracted a small band of hardcore loyalist refugees from Natchez and other formerly British communities, his own sons from within the Chickasaw nation, and a few other young Chickasaw men. While the Spanish saw him as a rebel against their legitimate authority on the Mississippi, Colbert saw himself and his loyalist followers as "English subjects" and himself as a "Captain in his Majesty's Service."[42] Like small bands in many places and times who seek to force the hand of a powerful empire, Colbert's men employed tactics of terrorism and kidnapping.

Upon his return to Chickasaw country, Colbert began leading raids on the Mississippi River. Barges carried products from Indian hunting and French farming downriver with the current to New Orleans, then free and enslaved riverboat men poled the barges with imported goods more slowly back upriver. In early May 1782, an opportunity for Colbert came up the river with both significant booty and the potential for leverage over the Spanish. Nicanora Ramos, the wife of St. Louis Commandant Francisco Cruzat, was on a barge heading up the Mississippi to St. Louis with their four children and four of their slaves, along with two merchants, the crew, and a barge-load of goods for colonists and Indians around St. Louis. Knowing the St. Louis commandant's wife was on board, Colbert and his men captured the barge at gunpoint, informing Ramos and the others that they were "prisoners of the King of Great Britain."[43] Ramos was on her way back to St. Louis with her toddler Josephe, Marie Gertrude (who would turn four during the ordeal), six-year-old Antoine, and the oldest, Joseph, who was around twelve. The slaves included a young black woman probably named Marie Andrée, who served as the children's nanny.[44]

Colbert's plan was to take the booty, ransom Ramos in return for loyalist prisoners, and, if all went perfectly, spark a war that would kick the Spanish out of the eastern Mississippi Valley. The word spread that Colbert's men were awaiting British, Choctaw, and Chickasaw reinforcements to attack American posts in the Illinois country. Could Payamataha's two decades of diplomacy with Spaniards, Quapaws, Choctaws, and others all be in vain? Would his nation be drawn into war by a man many Chickasaws did not even like?[45]

Kidnapping the wife of a colonial official and stealing goods belonging to the king's army was an act of war, and Acting Spanish Governor of Louisiana Esteban Miró reacted accordingly. He prepared two hundred troops to march from New Orleans to Natchez "for the destruction of these evildoers" and called for military assistance from the Quapaws.[46] In the meantime, Cruzat learned of his wife's capture from some Delaware Indians. He made plans to lead troops from St. Louis, and he encouraged Kickapoo Indians from Illinois to join as well.[47]

If fighting broke out, the Chickasaws were likely to be caught up in it. Knowing that the Chickasaws were the real power on that part of the Mississippi, Miró demanded that if the Chickasaws did not intend war against Spain, they should expel Colbert and the other British men and prevent them from raiding on the Mississippi. A Quapaw delegation soon arrived in Payamataha's town carrying a message from Governor Miró. He demanded to know if the Chickasaws intended "to wage war on us, or to live peacefully." If the Chickasaws wanted war, Miró said, then they should be following the rules of war and engaging in real battles, not allowing Colbert to attack women and others "that do not have arms to defend themselves."[48]

Both Spaniards and Chickasaws were relieved when Nicanora Ramos managed to persuade James Colbert to free her by needling him with reminders of what a dangerous and unvalorous act he had committed. The safe arrival of Ramos and her children in New Orleans calmed the escalating preparations for war. "With the arrival of Madame Cruzat," rejoiced Miró, "things have changed their appearances." He continued to prepare a force to lead to Natchez, but now its purpose would be to reinforce it against an attack by Colbert and Georgians, not war in Chickasaw country. Instead, Miró sent a Spanish emissary to meet with the Chickasaws "to reconcile, to calm, and to appease them" and to discuss Colbert as a mutual irritant.[49] Miró sent Payamataha a white flag and invited him to New Orleans to "give me his hand." We can almost hear Miró's sigh of relief as he wrote to Gálvez, "Your Excellency knows the small gain and the great loss" that the French suffered in their two unsuccessful attempts to defeat the Chickasaws. Fighting the Chickasaws would require a huge operation of thousands of men, lasting many months, with no guarantee of success in the end.[50]

Payamataha quickly took advantage of Ramos's freedom to mend fences. The episode had shown just how fragile his peace was. Now the Chickasaws and Spanish could agree that the problem was a handful of "fugitives from Natchez and . . . roving traders," who did not represent most Chickasaws or even most loyalists. Ramos's testimony helped. She declared that while Chickasaws knew of and received proceeds from the raiding, they had not participated in the actual capture and had "not done anything bad to her or the other prisoners."[51]

Payamataha and the Chickasaws conducted conciliatory diplomacy with Miró as well as with the Quapaws, Kickapoos, Kaskaskias, Cherokees, and Creeks. Quapaws and their Great Chief Angaska helped the Chickasaws mend fences with the Spanish, including Cruzat in St. Louis. The efforts paid off when Colbert and his followers attacked the Spanish Arkansas Post on April 17, 1783. The Quapaws declined to defend the post for fear of fighting any Chickasaws with Colbert, although they were close by and were supposed to be Spain's closest allies in the region. In August 1783, with Quapaw help, a Chickasaw party ratified the peace again with the Spanish at Arkansas Post. The emissaries assured the Spanish that, "except for Colbert's family, all are very contented" with Spanish friendship.[52] To keep lines of communication open with the Spanish, Payamataha sent Chickasaws to live near Arkansas Post and the Quapaw towns and arranged for the Arkansas Post Commandant to send a trader to live among the Chickasaws. In southeastern Indian tradition, Payamataha was exchanging *fanemingos,* or "squirrel kings," diplomats whose role was to keep good relations between allies.[53]

Following Payamataha's strategy of peace with all, the Chickasaws began to treat the United States as a legitimate country and to try to incorporate it into their policy of peace with all. For most of the war, the Chickasaws had treated the Americans as an internal problem for the British empire, not a potential Chickasaw ally; however, in July 1782 Payamataha dictated a message to all American leaders offering, in Payamataha's tradition, "to be at peace with you that our corn may grow and our stores increased for the benefit of our children." In his speech, Payamataha represented the Revolutionary War as a bump in the road of generally good relations and the future as a return to a prewar alliance with English-speaking neighbors, even those who had thrown off their empire. Payamataha claimed that they were "formerly very good friends and I thought we should be always so." There had only been "some small differences" when George Rogers Clark "settled a fort in our hunting ground without our leave." Now, Payamataha sent them a flag of peace and hoped "to see it as it used to be."[54] A delegation carried Payamataha's message to every settlement west of the Appalachians. In turn, the Chickasaws advertised to the Cherokees and others that being "at perfect peace with the French, Spaniards, and Americans" gave them "goods in plenty" and made them "contented and in a flourishing way."[55]

Payamataha would soon discover that it was difficult to negotiate with thirteen mostly independent sovereignties. As the plural "States" implied, figuring out who represented the "United States" was difficult. In July 1783, Payamataha and other headmen dictated a letter to the president of Congress. They had heard "that the Americans have thirteen councils composed of chiefs and warriors," adding, "We are told that you are the head chief of a grand council which is above these thirteen councils," yet people claiming to represent Georgia,

Illinois, Virginia, and assorted groups of settlers had approached the Chickasaws claiming the right to negotiate for themselves.[56] As a new nation, it was especially important for the United States to demonstrate its sovereign voice, yet representatives of Congress, state governments, and private individuals all claimed to be "Americans" with the power to make treaties, leaving Indians in doubt of American seriousness.[57]

Chickasaws proposed peace to any Americans they could find. In direct negotiations with a Virginia representative in October 1782, the Chickasaws blamed the British for past conflicts between themselves and Virginia. Payamataha, Mingo Houma, and a rising young leader named Piomingo (or Mountain King) declared that they had fought George Rogers Clark at Fort Jefferson only because "the English put the bloody tomahawk into our hands, telling us that we should have no goods if we did not exert ourselves to the greatest point of resentment against you." But now the British had "left us in our adversity," and Chickasaw "women and children are crying out for peace." The Chickasaws agreed to "bury the bones of our slain on both sides and forget all." In fact the Chickasaws had been defending their territory, and the British had no power to force the Chickasaws to wield "the bloody tomahawk" in any case.[58] Nevertheless, the British had been the Chickasaws' ally and provider of European goods for eighty years. If they were truly gone, it was safe to blame them.

The Chickasaws made their opposition to land cessions so clear to the Virginia negotiator at that October 1782 meeting that he did not even bother proposing any; still, Americans too often turned the conversation toward acquiring Chickasaw land. In January 1783, Virginia Governor Benjamin Harrison (whose son and great-grandson would be presidents of the United States) sent commissioners to the Chickasaws with orders to buy Chickasaw land while at the same time asserting that the United States already owned the land by conquest from the British and therefore could take it without paying for it. At the same time, George Rogers Clark sent one of his men to try to buy Chickasaw land south of the Ohio River in what he hoped to make part of Kentucky. Shawnees and Cherokees had been telling the

Chickasaws since at least the 1760s that Virginians were land grabbers. Perhaps they were right.[59]

Payamataha hoped that Congress would control these people who seemed to act independently with no regard for either proper diplomacy or the actions of other states. In July 1783, Payamataha and Mingo Houma appealed to Congress as the Americans' supposed supreme political body to control the various states and independent groups that were making offers and demands or even just "marking lines through our hunting ground." Payamataha expected to deal with the highest level of American government because "we are head men and chiefs and warriors also, and I have always been accustomed to speak with great chiefs and warriors." If American governmental structure was as Chickasaws understood it, Congress should "put a stop to any encroachment on our lands without our consent and silence all those people who send us such talks as inflame and exasperate our young men."[60]

Independent negotiators, unauthorized surveyors, and Congressional fecklessness were annoying, but they did not overturn Chickasaw control over their lands. The Chickasaws allowed loyalist refugees to live in Chickasaw country under Chickasaw rule, but independent settlements were not allowed. For example, in 1784, a group of speculators including North Carolina Governor Richard Caswell, Virginia Governor Patrick Henry, and future U.S. senator William Blount claimed lands south of the Tennessee River based on a Cherokee grant and Georgia permission, but opposition from Chickasaws and other Indians in the region kept it from happening. Although sovereignty and land possession might be contested, Chickasaws still controlled Chickasaw country. Their population continued to grow, and they spread their farms further across the landscape, continuing a process of decentralization that they had begun in the first years of peace after the Seven Years' War. Still, Americans' land ambitions obscured the path forward. Not everyone agreed that peace with everyone was best. Some Chickasaws tried to prevent negotiations with Americans as too risky, while others sought to minimize relations with Spain. Many wished that the British would return.[61]

The Ambitions of Alexander McGillivray

As with the Chickasaws, Creek sovereignty and control over the land endured in the midst of change. After Emistisiguo's death outside Savannah in 1782, Alexander McGillivray's prominence grew in both Little Tallassee and the Creek Confederacy. He had established valuable connections in many Creek towns and had shown the potential to become a prominent headman and diplomat. However, as the British withdrew from the southeast, he lost his European connections. McGillivray and the Creeks had to decide what they would do in a world without the British.[62]

At first, McGillivray explored the possibility of continuing the fight. In the spring of 1782, he traveled to Chickasaw country to discuss Creeks and Chickasaws fighting together against the Spanish and the Americans. As their official policy was peace, however, the Chickasaws said no. McGillivray also considered linking his efforts with James Colbert. He visited Colbert's camp while Nicanora Ramos was held captive there. In McGillivray's presence, probably trying to impress him, Colbert boasted of the many ways he was going to damage the Spanish "with fire and blood."[63] McGillivray chided him: "You talk very freely, and are making our projects known" to the captives, who "will not forget to publish our intention."[64] This encounter seems to have persuaded McGillivray that Colbert was too much like the irresponsible and unconnected James Willing.

McGillivray again had the chance to leave Creek country for good. According to McGillivray, Georgians repeatedly proposed "restoring to me all my property and that of my father." But he declined the offers.[65] Similarly, when McGillivray was in St. Augustine in the fall of 1783, British General Archibald MacArthur offered to evacuate him along with the other loyalists. He could have sailed to Jamaica or Britain or even joined his father in Scotland.[66]

But Alexander McGillivray chose to return to his mother's town and his growing family. By 1783, he and Elise Moniac had their own children, Alexander (Aleck), Margaret (Peggy), and Elizabeth (Lizzie), all of whom, in Scottish patrilineal tradition, he considered his own and taught to speak English. Because their mother was Chickasaw, they belonged to a matrilineal Chickasaw clan as well as being part of a Creek household in Little Tallassee. Even more important, McGillivray was the mentor of the children of his sisters, Sophia, Jeannette, and Sehoy. McGillivray envisioned a prosperous life in Little Tallassee with his family, slaves, plantations, and cattle as well as a future as a Creek leader. McGillivray would live the rest of his life in Creek country—"my country."[67]

But McGillivray's previously most useful connection—the British—was now largely irrelevant. Indians in the north had persuaded Britain to retain its Great Lakes posts, in defiance of the Treaty of Paris; however, once the British turned St. Augustine over to the Spanish, there were no British on Creek borders. Headmen Hoboithle Miko of the Upper Creek town of Great Tallassee (also known as Tallassee King or Tame King) and Neha Miko of the Lower Creek town of Cussita (also known as Fat King) were in charge of negotiations with the formerly British colonies of Georgia and the Carolinas. If McGillivray wanted to continue his career as a Creek diplomat, it would have to be with the Spanish and with other Indian nations. Having been one of the loudest Creek voices urging war against Spain, his new role would require a sharp reversal.[68]

Straight from his disappointment in St. Augustine, McGillivray traveled to Spanish Pensacola in early 1784 for his first negotiation with his old enemies, who, he hoped, would become the Creeks' new supplier of weapons and ammunition. If the Creeks could build interdependent economic and diplomatic relations with Spain, Creek warriors could defend their political and territorial independence, and McGillivray would have markets for the products of his plantations around Little Tallassee. In order to persuade Spanish officials of his value to them, McGillivray advertised himself as their greatest asset in Creek country, a man to whom they could relate and who in turn could relate to the Creeks. He explained to Spanish West Florida Governor Arturo O'Neill (another "wild goose" Irish Catholic, just like General Alejandro O'Reilly and Margaret O'Brien's father) that he was "a Native of this Nation and of rank in it." McGillivray assured O'Neill that the Creeks preferred to ally with Spain because "the protection of a great Monarch is preferred to that of a distracted Republic." The Creeks were also turning to Spain because, as McGillivray put it, "we have been most shamefully deserted" by the British.[69]

McGillivray's efforts with the Spanish succeeded. The Creeks approved establishing alliance and trade with Spain, and Spanish officials began writing about him with admiration and hope. José de Ezpeleta called McGillivray "an Indian of talent and education and a great deal of influence with those of his nation."[70] Miró called McGillivray a "mestizo by birth," meaning mixed Indian and European, who had become the best of both worlds. There were plenty of men of European descent living in Indian communities, but Miró drew the conclusion that McGillivray's talents and Creek lineage made him different. "As his mother was the daughter of one of the principal chiefs," Creeks "have adopted him as such in the entire Nation," and he held "a kind of authority" in all the Creek towns. Yet also, Miró wrote, his father had educated him "as a son of Europe."[71] As they got to know him in the mid-1780s, Spanish officials idealized McGillivray as someone who thought and acted European but whom the Creeks saw as an especially wise Creek.

This was exactly the reputation McGillivray wanted to have among Europeans, but in fact he gained prominence among the Creeks by old-fashioned Creek methods. As Miró recognized, McGillivray's family line made him eligible for leadership. He did not have the war experience of Payamataha or Emistisiguo, but he had proved himself brave enough during the Revolutionary War. Now he traveled throughout Creek country to build connections in every town of Upper Creeks, Lower Creeks, and even Seminoles. Part of the Creek Confederacy, the Seminole towns were composed of Creeks who had moved south into East Florida earlier in the eighteenth century and combined with Florida Indians and former slaves, some of whom had escaped during and immediately after the Revolution. Seeking to maintain intra-Creek relations and dissuade Seminoles from seceding from the Confederacy, McGillivray encouraged Spanish officials to establish a convenient trading house for them in East Florida. The Spanish eventually did so at San Marcos de Apalache (St. Marks) on

Apalachee Bay in 1787, and McGillivray traveled there to introduce the Spaniards to the Seminoles.[72]

As war ended and trade reopened, economic opportunities arose, and McGillivray took full advantage. Like his successful neighbors in the Floridas and Louisiana, he built his prosperity on the backs of slaves. Although he lost his father's Georgia plantations, McGillivray owned black slaves who grew cash crops and livestock on his father's old plantation at Little Tallassee and another half a mile up the Coosa River. He established a new plantation on the Tombigbee River north of Mobile as well. McGillivray sold his agricultural products in Spanish Pensacola and Mobile and bought slaves, who in turn expanded his production.[73]

Creeks had long owned and sold slaves, but plantation slavery had come to Creek country just in the past few decades. While most Creek men hunted and Creek women farmed as in the past, McGillivray and some other Creek men and women lived more like their wealthy white neighbors. They owned livestock and relied on enslaved men and women to farm. McGillivray lived in a log house with windows and a stone chimney, while most of his Creek neighbors lived in houses, built by Creek women, made of plastered vertical slats with horizontal woven cane. Although other Creeks practiced slavery and produced for the market, this new planter class increased economic disparities among Creeks, removed their families from the kinds of labor most Creeks did, and accumulated wealth at unprecedented rates. However, Creeks had long been diverse, and they had strong common interests in protecting Creek land and sovereignty and gaining access to European markets, whether for the fur trade or for plantation products. McGillivray understood that conducting Spanish diplomacy and distributing Spanish supplies would be central to his authority among the Creeks, and most Creeks seemed to see McGillivray as useful in their economic and diplomatic negotiations with Europeans.[74]

McGillivray encouraged both Creeks and Spaniards to allow British loyalists to live under their sovereignty. There was some extra land in Creek country and in Spanish West Florida and Louisiana. In return for protection and a little land on which they could build farms and businesses, these settlers would respect Creek or Spanish authority and help them withstand illegal incursions. If the settlers in Creek country had children with Creek women, their children would follow the matrilineal line and be Creeks themselves. For those who chose to settle in the Spanish Gulf Coast colonies, McGillivray advised West Florida Governor O'Neill, "If liberty of conscience would be allowed to them they could be contented and happy under the king of Spain's government." These offers should be only for loyalists, though, people whom the Americans had deprived of peace and prosperity and who would be willing to submit to Creek or Spanish authority. In contrast, Americans, "disposed to leave their own government and their taxes," should not be welcome. People who wanted to leave responsibility and authority behind would be a "rebellious crew," not useful subjects for either Creeks or Spain.[75]

Indeed, Americans were already trying to take Creek land, with or without Congress's approval. Hoping to persuade Creeks to cede some of their hunting lands, the Georgia legislature invited them to a congress in 1783. Creeks were busy preparing for the fall hunt and, in any case, felt that diplomacy with the Spanish, British, and other Indians was more urgent. Creeks knew that the Georgians would make similar requests and threats to those of Governor John Martin the previous year, who had said that Georgians wanted "to live in peace and friendship" and "provide plenty of goods of all kinds" but were not afraid "to send our warriors up to your towns . . . and lay them in ashes and make your women widows, and children fatherless."[76] Martin was clearly trying to hide weakness under bluster. Indeed, at nearly the same time he was writing General Nathanael Greene that Georgia "is much distressed at present for want of ammunition."[77] To the Creeks, the Americans seemed too obnoxious and divided to be promising allies. Therefore, when the Augusta meeting convened, only the two headmen responsible for maintaining good relations with the United States attended: Hoboithle Miko and Neha Miko.

Contemporary observers and historians have sometimes misunderstood divisions of diplomatic responsibility within southeastern Indian nations and confederacies as "factions." Rather than divisive political factions, these were really assigned roles given to regional leaders. Hoboithle Miko and Neha Miko were peace chiefs whose role was to promote peace with Georgia and the Carolinas, much as the "white town" of Little Tallassee was to keep the peace with Mobile and Pensacola. Even if other Creeks went to war, they were supposed to try to keep channels of communication open and to be ready to be the first negotiators if the Creeks wanted to make peace. Among the Choctaws, the Eastern, Western, and Six Towns divisions had different negotiating responsibilities, which is how Six Towns Choctaws ended up on the opposite side of the Siege of Pensacola from other Choctaws. The Chickasaws assigned specific diplomats to specific places as well. Although well-functioning roles could develop into real divides or even civil war, as they did among the Choctaws in the 1740s, these assignments did not necessarily indicate differences of opinion. In recognition of this role, Hoboithle Miko was sometimes called the Halfway-House King, a man who could negotiate for people on both sides. During the Revolutionary War, Hoboithle Miko and Neha Miko had regularly gone to Georgia to meet with U.S. Indian Commissioner George Galphin and others to collect goods and to maintain lines of communication, and they hoped to reestablish trade now that the war was over.[78]

At the 1783 meeting in Augusta, though, to the astonishment of both headmen, the Georgians presented them with a treaty to sign. This pre-drafted "Treaty of Augusta" stated that the Creeks would cede thousands of acres between the Ogeechee and Oconee rivers. This was not how treaties worked. The treaty with the British at Augusta twenty years earlier, for example, included not only headmen from every Creek town but also crowds of Creek men and women to witness and ratify the agreement. Treaties were days-long engagements in which each party dramatically demonstrated its ability to rule and speak for its side before they settled into the business of negotiations. The Creeks in attendance in 1783 represented only four of the at least sixty Creek towns. The two headmen told the Georgians that they had no standing to agree to a treaty on behalf of the Creek Confederacy. The Georgians' failure to perform their part left much doubt that they represented their country either. Through some com-

"Hopothle Mico, or, The Talassee King of the Creeks," engraving by John Trumbull, 1790. (Special Collections, Fordham University)

bination of promises and armed threats, the Georgia negotiators persuaded Hoboithle Miko and Neha Miko to sign, although they continued to insist that their signatures meant nothing unless the entire Confederacy ratified the treaty. When they returned home and explained what had happened, the Creeks held a National Council at which headmen representing all of the towns agreed to send a message to Georgia that land cessions, in McGillivray's words, "could only be valid by the unanimous voice of the whole, as joint proprietors."[79] Creeks began to call Georgians *ecunnaunuxulgee,* "people greedily grasping after the lands of the red people."[80]

The Creeks were annoyed, but they did not think that Georgia's outrageous claims were much to worry about. Although the Georgia Assembly named the land between the Ogeechee and Oconee rivers "Washington County" for their victorious general and offered land grants there to veterans, in reality it was still Creek country, and any Americans who tried to settle there were risking their lives. Indeed, Georgians feared a Creek war, especially if supplied by Spain, and hoped that their own aggressiveness would persuade Congress and surrounding states to come to their rescue. To outside observers, including the Creeks, unruly settlers pushing the boundaries of their states or seeking to escape them entirely were a sign of the weakness, not the power, of the United States. Such people had overthrown their empire for free land and no taxes. They could not be trusted to be loyal to their own new government. Now some of them wanted, as McGillivray put it, "to erect and establish what they call a western independence out of the reach of the authority of Congress."[81] Surely a country founded on disobedience could not last long.

Undermined by independent citizens and states, Congress itself was also dangerously independent in international affairs. In 1784, privateers captured an American ship off the coast of Morocco. While Americans believed that they could transcend the rivalries of the old world and could have free trading rights as neutral vessels, to the Barbary States (Algiers, Morocco, Tripoli, and Tunis) this freedom meant only that Americans were no longer protected by treaties with Britain. At home reading newspapers from London and Charleston, McGillivray reflected that the Americans and Barbary pirates were "well matched" in their penchant for theft.[82] The latest conflict was only another sign of American weakness. McGillivray noted that "the whole continent is in confusion. Before long I expect to hear that the three kings"—that is, of Spain, Britain, and France—"must settle the matter by dividing America between them."[83]

As Alexander McGillivray observed the difficulties of the thirteen states in establishing their legitimacy and of the Creeks in protecting themselves against the states, he determined to transform the Creek Confederacy into a nation. Nationalizing would have implications for both internal Creek affairs and their relations with others. Within the Creek Nation, towns and clans would continue to rule themselves, but in diplomacy and trade policy, they should act as one, much as Congress was trying to do for the states. As he gained prominence, he strengthened the National Council, which had been mostly an Upper Creek meeting called in times of crisis but became a more regular body representing all Creek and Seminole towns. McGillivray increasingly spoke for the Creeks in negotiations with outsiders. As McGillivray looked toward the nineteenth century, he believed that a more centralized Creek Nation could operate on the same level as other modern nations. In letters to Spanish officials, he began to refer to the Creeks as "a free nation," one that determined its own land use and foreign policy like any other nation.[84]

Americans, too, recognized that McGillivray sought Creek nationhood. One Virginian who knew him even speculated that he wanted the United States to "acknowledge the independence and sovereignty of the Creek nation, and admit them as a member of the federal Union."[85] Admitting an Indian nation as a U.S. state was not an outlandish idea in the 1780s, but it was not what McGillivray had in mind.

Of course Creek sovereignty was not a new idea—Europeans had never exercised sovereignty over the Creek Confederacy—but McGillivray developed a language of independent nationhood that carried particular weight with late-eighteenth-century Europeans and Americans. In the past, Creek governance was mostly an issue for Creeks to debate among themselves, not something they needed to assert to outsiders. Now McGillivray was explicit that the Creeks governed their own independent nation. As he put it in a letter to West Florida Governor O'Neill, the Creeks "consider themselves brothers and allies of Spain only," not Spain's subjects.[86]

Although Creeks continued to argue over foreign policy, there was little serious opposition to his beginning to represent a united Creek national foreign policy to the Spanish. He was not what some Spanish officials called him, the "supposed Principal Chief of the Creek Nation." He was too young to be a headman at all yet, so he was not even a member of the National Council. Even as he grew older, his Wind clan status would allow him to be only second headman of Little Tallassee, not first. Instead, McGillivray became the Creeks' chief diplomat to the Spanish. Later, Creeks added to his title of *Isti Atcagagi* ("Beloved Man") and called him *Isti Atcagagi Thlucco* or "Great Beloved Man," thereby singling him out as the Creeks' greatest advisor on foreign policy.[87]

McGillivray in turn used his advisory and diplomatic status to work for his nationalizing project. The lack of uniformity in Creek foreign policy during the Revolutionary War had frustrated him. Becoming a centralized nation, at least in foreign policy matters, would prevent such frustrations and allow him to act as a more powerful leader at home and with representatives of other nations and empires. Being recognized by European powers as a nation would increase Creek stature in the world and McGillivray's influence at home. Like Creek diplomats before him, McGillivray at times projected a greater power over Creeks than he had in order to influence outsiders and in turn increase influence at home.

Still, McGillivray answered to his fellow Creeks, much like Payamataha among the Chickasaws. Creek and Seminole towns continued to govern themselves, and McGillivray never set foreign policy alone. As he explained, "all my proceedings" were "directed by the general voice of the Whole Nation."[88] As the Creeks had confederated, they had transitioned from having individual towns or clusters of towns make foreign policy to having leaders of different towns be responsible for diplomacy with different peoples, as Hoboithle Miko and Neha Miko were with Georgia and the Carolinas and McGillivray was with West Florida and Louisiana. Similar to Congress's difficulties with individual state diplomacy under the Articles of Confederation, McGillivray grew frustrated with this multi-node style of diplomacy, which still allowed for contradiction. His desire to centralize Creek foreign policy to prevent U.S. expansion would bring him into conflict with Creeks who wanted to continue spreading diplomatic power across towns and matrilineal clans.[89]

The Congresses of Pensacola and Mobile, 1784

The lesson that most white Americans and Indians who lived within the boundaries of the United States and in the contested Ohio Valley took from the brutal fighting of the Seven Years' War and the Revolutionary War was that people of Indian and European descent were not meant to live together. In contrast, mutual hatred was not the lesson of the Revolutionary War on the Gulf Coast, where faith in interdependence was stronger than ever. Native and Spanish leaders believed that they could work together to forward mutual independence and prosperity.[90]

Although historians usually portray the years following the American Revolution as a decline in Indians' sources of European alliance and weapons, at least for a while the Spanish and many Indians living nearby saw potential for a new and better alliance. They all saw the Americans as people who did not share their values. Europeans and Indians in the Gulf Coast and the Mississippi Valley agreed on territorial integrity and political sovereignty. Indians could rule their lands while colonial powers had coastal towns and interior trading posts. Europeans could claim colonial dominion over allied Indian lands vis-à-vis other colonial powers without actually ruling on the ground. Europeans and Indians could and did disagree and even went to war over access to land and resources. Yet when compared to the belief expressed by Congress and the states that Indians were under their direct rule, late-eighteenth-century Spaniards and southeastern Indians were in much closer agreement about the reality of their relationship.

Bernardo de Gálvez was determined to use Indians' disgust at both the rebels and the British to expand Spanish North America. He wrote the crown that his experience north of Mexico had "demonstrated that the conservation and prosperity" of Louisiana and West Florida "depend primarily on the friendship of the Indian nations who inhabit them, and this can only be done by means of gifts and a well established trade."[91] Minister of the Indies José de Gálvez supported his nephew's desire to protect Spain's expanding northern empire however he thought best. Before leaving New Orleans, Bernardo de Gálvez sent his father-in-law, Colonel Gilbert Antoine de St. Maxent, commandant of Louisiana's white militia, to Spain to requisition goods for Indian gifts and trade. Maxent presented himself at court as Gálvez's representative to argue for $80,000 in one-time alliance-building gifts, $200,000 to set up merchants for permanent trade, and another $100,000 of goods to be available at New Orleans, Pensacola, and other posts to host visiting Indians. The king "at once agreed" and sent Maxent to the principal factories of Spain and its ally France to gather the merchandise.[92] In 1784, Governor Miró invited the Creeks to Pensacola and the Chickasaws and Choctaws to Mobile to discuss a grand alliance "on which the permanent tranquility of these Provinces depends."[93] As long as southeastern Indian and Spanish goals aligned, they could ignore the charged question of whether Indians were truly independent allies or subject vassals.

Over the previous year and a half, McGillivray had established himself as the primary Creek ambassador to the Spanish, so he would be the main Creek negotiator at the Pensacola congress. In preparation, representatives from throughout the Creek Confederacy met at Little Tallassee in April. They agreed to ally with Spain, and they commissioned McGillivray to write the governor of Georgia "a positive refusal to every thing they desired of us." A few weeks later, McGillivray and the rest of the delegation representing the Creeks set off for Pensacola.[94]

On June 1, 1784, the Creeks and the Spanish concluded an alliance of mutual recognition of sovereignty and mutually beneficial trade. McGillivray signed on behalf of the Creeks, and Acting Louisiana Governor Esteban Miró, West Florida Governor Arturo O'Neill, and Intendant Martín Navarro—Louisiana's chief financial official—signed for Spain. A casual reader of this treaty and the previous year's Treaty of Augusta with Georgia might assume that the Treaty of Pensacola was less legitimate. While fourteen Creeks signed in Augusta, only McGillivray did at Pensacola, and his Scottish name is less Indian-sounding than Hoboithle Miko and Neha Miko. But speaking and listening mattered infinitely more to Creeks than signatures, and the two assemblies could not have been more different. At Pensacola,

Creek headmen from every town participated in the negotiations, and interpreters worked to make sure everyone understood everyone else. Large numbers of Creek men and women witnessed both the speeches and the signing. McGillivray signed as their legitimate representative.[95]

The compatibility of Spanish imperial dominion and Creek political and territorial independence was central to the agreement. McGillivray and the other Creeks stressed that the Treaty of Paris was invalid because Britain had no right to cede Indian land to the United States. In accepting Spanish imperial dominion over the region, the "free nation" of Creeks, as they put it, "expect His Majesty to protect them against the intentions of those who believe they have a sovereign right in the villages." The Spanish negotiators agreed. They pledged that "the generous mind of his Most Catholic Majesty is far from exacting lands from the Indians." The Creek Nation was "the proprietor," and the king simply sought "to secure and guarantee to them, those [lands] which they actually hold, according to the right by which they possess them."[96]

Of course, Spain was not operating an empire for the benefit of indigenous peoples; still, it was possible that the Gulf Coast and its interior could be both Spanish and Indian. Indians could rule on the ground, while Spain could delineate the region as Spanish vis-à-vis its imperial competitors. Spanish explicitly placed their king in contrast to his competitors. "To prove how different his way of thinking is far from that of his Britannick Majesty," the Spanish negotiators pledged that if the Creeks ever lost their lands to any "enemies of his crown," the Spanish king would grant them lands elsewhere in his empire.[97] It was not a new position for Spain. Since at least 1532, the Spanish crown had explicitly recognized (although not always guaranteed) that "the Indians shall continue to possess their lands."[98]

McGillivray and the Creeks wanted more; they believed that the Spanish had a responsibility to defend the Creek border from the Americans. However, Miró and O'Neill did not have permission to make a pledge that would be so likely to bring about a war with the United States. Miró did promise to take the Creeks' argument to the king and "see if there was a way to remedy the marking of the boundaries."[99]

Spanish alliance was important to the Creeks not as much for Spain's military might as for its access to European markets and manufactured goods. Spain pledged to provide regular payments to the Creeks as well as "a permanent and unalterable commerce."[100] To support the pledge and seal the alliance, the Spanish handed out a huge amount of goods, much of it from the shipment that Gilbert de St. Maxent had recently sent from Spain. The Creeks received 300 guns, more than 8,000 knives, 200 pounds of beads, 6,000 gunflints, 12 large medals, 12 small medals, 30 gorgets (ceremonial collars), and large volumes of gunpowder and musket balls. The list went on for three pages. The Spanish assured the Creeks that the bounty would continue. The crown substantially increased its budget for Indian presents, including guns, powder, and ball. To ensure Creeks a world market for their furs and other products, the Spanish contracted with Scottish merchants, particularly Lachlan McGillivray's old friend William Panton and his partner John Leslie. While this situation was not ideal for Spain, southeastern Indians were accustomed to England's cheap goods and particular kinds of silver ornaments to which these Scottish merchants had access. And the important objective was, as Miró put it, that "the Americans do not introduce themselves into this trade."[101] In turn, the Creeks agreed not to trade with any other Europeans or Americans.[102]

The Spanish appointed McGillivray their commissary in the Creek nation, the same office he had held for Britain. His job was to enforce the Spanish and Creek trade agreement and to facilitate communication between the Creeks and Spanish officials in West Florida and Louisiana. At the Congress, the Spanish granted McGillivray "certain trading privileges," including the right to import goods from the Floridas into Creek country, which he made good on by partnering with Panton and Leslie.[103] Like Oliver Pollock, McGillivray hoped to work international trade on the Gulf Coast to his advantage.

McGillivray hoped that the Spanish alliance would demonstrate Creek power and persuade Americans to "drop the pretended right of sovereignty they claim over our country" and to see that "the right they found on the cession of Great Britain is unjust, the Creek Nation being allies and not subjects to that crown."[104] The Creeks made Hoboithle Miko return to Augusta to insist that the Augusta treaty was invalid. While doing so, he also instructed Americans in Creek diplomacy. If Georgia wanted land, it needed to convene a real treaty.[105]

Hoboithle Miko returned to Creek country in November with what McGillivray termed "a very satisfactory answer." The governor and assembly of Georgia had, according to Hoboithle Miko, forbidden settlement on the contested lands "in the strongest manner." McGillivray believed that the Creek-Spanish alliance had scared Georgians, who did not want to fight Spanish soldiers or Creeks armed with Spanish weapons. He told O'Neill that "the true reasons" that the Americans "pretend to be so moderate to us" was "their jealousy to Spain."[106] He was confused, then, at the later Georgian insistence on land west of the Ogeechee River. He wrote Georgia that the Creeks "protested in the strongest manner against your people settling over the old boundary of Ogeechee." He explained that the lands "between Oconee and Ogeechee form a principal part" of their hunting lands, "on which they generally take three thousand deer skins yearly."[107] Georgians' refusal to listen would plague the Creeks for years to come and make them more determined on a strong alliance with Spain.

While McGillivray and the Creeks sought a European ally and European munitions with which to threaten the United States, Payamataha and the Chickasaws were pursuing their strategy of peace when they met with the Spanish in Mobile a few weeks after the Pensacola congress. In contrast to the farcical Georgia-Creek Treaty of Augusta, the Chickasaws had signed a real treaty with Virginia the previous November, the Treaty of French Lick. Virginians had begun to move to Kentucky and to the Cumberland River around a town they would soon call Nashville for North Carolina Continental Army General Francis Nash. These places were borderland hunting grounds, far from the main parts of the Chickasaw, Choctaw, Cherokee, or Creek nations.[108]

The Chickasaws wanted to keep Americans from moving any

closer to their real hunting lands, including those on the Tennessee River (which they called the Cherokee River) west of Cumberland. In the negotiations, the Chickasaw headman Piomingo charged that "the White people have got a very bad trick that when they go a hunting." They "find a good piece of ground" and "make a station camp at it, and the next thing they go to building houses." The treaty pledged that Virginians would respect Chickasaw hunting rights along the Tennessee River, and it included no land cession. For their part, the Virginians asked the Chickasaws to drive out the Delawares living on the south side of the Tennessee River, because they had been attacking Americans on the Kentucky and Cumberland rivers. The Chickasaws agreed but did nothing; starting a war against the Delawares would defeat the whole purpose of Payamataha's policy.[109]

With these agreements in hand, the Chickasaws did not intend to work against Americans when they came to Mobile in June 1784 to confirm peace with Spain. Representatives of all the Chickasaw towns promised the Spanish "to maintain an inviolable peace and friendship" with Spain but also to "remain quiet in our land, without mixing in any war with the whites." Given Payamataha's past efforts, they somewhat redundantly pledged "peace and friendship" with the Creeks, Choctaws, Quapaws, and "all the other Nations of the Continent, especially those of the Mississippi River, excepting only the Kickapoo Nation," with whom all was not yet settled.[110] Remembering the trouble James Colbert had caused, the Chickasaws pledged to deliver to the Spanish any outsiders who proposed war between them and Spain, and they promised to try to keep their young men from raiding horses and cattle around Spanish posts and prevent any piracies on the Mississippi. The Spanish in turn promised "to provide to the Chickasaw Nation permanent and unalterable Commerce under the most equitable prices."[111] The Chickasaws returned home with tangible proof of their successful diplomacy. Counting what they consumed in Mobile, the Spanish had given them over 5,700 pounds of bread, 9,400 pounds of rice, and 2,400 pounds of beans, plus enough meat and cornmeal for their stay and medals for Chickasaw headmen.[112]

The month after the Mobile congress, Chickasaws attended a pan-

Indian conference in the Ohio Valley to discuss uniting the Northern Confederacy with southern Indians to form "a General Confederacy" of Indian nations. As in the past, the Chickasaws did not align perfectly with the confederationists' aims. The Chickasaws and Kickapoos at the conference had trouble getting along, and Chickasaws resisted other delegations' efforts to draw them into war against the Americans.[113]

Helping other Indians make peace with the Spanish was more the Chickasaw style. In the summer of 1784, Chickasaws and Choctaws led a delegation of over a hundred Iroquois, Shawnees, and Cherokees to meet Commandant Francisco Cruzat at St. Louis, where they declared that they had "wanted to get to know the Spanish ever since we heard they replaced the French." The Iroquois, Shawnees, and Cherokees claimed that the British "dominat[e] us tyrannically," preventing good relations with Spain. Now that the British and Americans had "formed two distinct nations," the situation was far worse. As the Indians explained, "The Americans, a great deal more ambitious and numerous than the English, put us out of our lands, ... extending themselves like a plague of locusts in the territories of the Ohio River." They baited Cruzat by saying that the Americans had asked them, "Why do you want to go to see the chiefs of a poor nation that will never give you anything?" But surely the Spanish would prove the Americans wrong. Cruzat pledged Spanish friendship and provided presents to prove that the Spanish were not poor. In meetings such as this one at St. Louis and the congresses at Pensacola and Mobile, Indians and Spaniards persuaded one another that they could share the continent and together contain the United States.[114]

Spanish and American Ambitions

In 1783, Congress gave Bernardo de Gálvez's portrait, presented by Oliver Pollock, a place of honor in the room where Congress met. Soon, though, Congress moved the portrait to a less public wall in the house of the president of Congress. Perhaps the Spaniard's eye upon their deliberations was more than they could take. By then, Congress was more worried about Spanish ambitions on the continent than grateful for Spain's help.[115]

Prospects looked good for an expansion of Spanish North America. Louisiana Intendant Martín Navarro figured that British trade on the Mississippi had totaled hundreds of thousands of dollars. With "free trade for all" and "a numerous population," Louisiana and West Florida could be more profitable than ever before and could protect Mexico from "new enemies who look at our situation and happiness with too much envy," meaning the Americans. He looked back to the model of Acadian settlement in Louisiana before the war and imagined similar success with new French, German, Irish, and West Indian settlers. After all, the Broussards and other Acadians had become loyal and valuable subjects of the Spanish crown. Prosperity would attract and foster loyal subjects, who in turn would be useful against "new enemies."[116]

The American states were already starting to look like potential foes. Their claims in the Illinois country, Kentucky, and west of Georgia were disturbing. After the Treaty of Paris, the Spanish crown continued to assert its most expansive claims. Spain declared in March 1783 that its possessions included the Illinois country, those lands north of the Ohio River that later became the states of Illinois and Indiana. Virginia was claiming the region on the basis of George Rogers Clark's seizures of the colonial Illinois posts of Vincennes, Kaskaskia, and Cahokia (with the financial help of Pollock and the Spanish), but the Spanish pointed out that the mostly French colonists did not actively support the United States, that Clark had failed in his attempts to take Detroit, that the Chickasaws had driven him out of their lands, and that the Spanish had taken Fort St. Joseph on Lake Michigan. The American states were obnoxious but also weak and poor, as their continuing debts to Pollock and Spain showed. Surely Spain could keep them in their place as dependent neighbors.

American officials knew the border with Spain would be a problem. U.S. Secretary of Foreign Affairs Robert Livingston was not alone in suspecting that the Spanish court's wartime "delays and slights" to John Jay were intended to preserve whatever territory Spain wanted after the war.[117] During the war, American officials prepared their arguments for having the Ohio Valley and Illinois country as part of the United States. In 1780, James Madison wrote Jay that Spain's only possible objection was that it took this territory from Britain and therefore "has a right to regard them as lawful objects of conquest." Certainly Gálvez would see this conquest as evidence enough for possession, but Madison reasoned that George Rogers Clark had won more posts and therefore that the United States had a greater right to the region. Madison concluded that, except for Natchez on the Mississippi River, "Spain has a claim by conquest to no post above the northern bounds of West Florida," which he defined as the 31st parallel.[118]

Madison imagined a prosperous future for the western United States: "In a very few years after peace shall take place," the Ohio Valley and Illinois country "will certainly be overspread with inhabitants." They could grow "wheat, corn, beef, pork, tobacco, hemp, flax, and in the southern parts, perhaps, rice and indigo, in great quantities," which they could send down the Ohio and Mississippi to Spanish and French islands in the West Indies. On the other hand, if Spain impeded American trade on the lower Mississippi, the goods would instead travel upriver through British Canada, and "France and Spain, and the other maritime powers will not only lose the immediate benefit of it themselves, but they will also suffer by the advantage it will give to Great Britain."[119] Congress could use the west for land grants to veterans and land sales to raise revenue "for discharging the debts incurred during the war."[120] Without the power to tax, selling public land was the most appealing source of revenue, which, as Oliver Pollock knew only too well, Congress desperately needed.

This uncontested future of global trade and profitable new lands resided only in American imaginations. Spain had controlled the mouth of the Mississippi for two decades, and its victories over the British only made that right more secure. Despite the Treaty of Paris, for now, Congress could only grumble over imperial ambitions and the "mutilation of our country."[121] Impatient with Americans' repeated insistence that the 31st parallel was West Florida's northern border, King Carlos III in 1784 closed the port of New Orleans to American and British traffic and forbade both from navigating the

Mississippi. He explicitly declared that the Treaty of Paris between the British and the Americans could not dictate the limits of territory that Spain had conquered during the war. In New Orleans, Governor Miró stationed soldiers at the mouth of the Mississippi to prevent American and British ships from entering. He ordered Francisco de Cruzat at St. Louis to treat American merchants "as smugglers, guilty of the crime of illegal trade."[122] Similarly, Bernardo de Gálvez decreed that no non-Catholic families could settle in Louisiana or the Floridas. French Catholic families living in now-American Illinois were invited to Spanish territory.[123]

Following a suggestion by Oliver Pollock, Georgia attempted to extend its claim as far south and west as Natchez, falsely claiming that, before the war, Natchez had belonged to British Georgia rather than British West Florida. In 1785, the Georgia legislature created "Bourbon County" along the Mississippi between the 31st parallel (south of Natchez) and the Yazoo River (north of Natchez). Commissioners from Georgia proceeded to Natchez, where, to the great shock of the Spanish commandant, they ordered him in the name of Georgia to surrender the fort to them. He of course refused, reiterating that the Spanish claim "is as far as the Tennessee if not further."[124]

In response to this assault on Spanish sovereignty, Acting Governor Miró prepared gunboats with five hundred veteran regulars from New Orleans, the ship *Galveztown* with troops from Pensacola, plus six hundred militia from throughout Louisiana and West Florida. Meanwhile Gálvez promised to send the nearly four hundred New Orleans troops that were still with him at Havana. West Florida Governor Arturo O'Neill was to work with Creeks and other Indians "to spread terror on the frontiers of Georgia and Carolina."[125] Spanish mobilization slowed when Chickasaws and Cherokees informed O'Neill in July that reports of an American force marching on Natchez were "imaginary."[126]

Rather than proceed with force, Georgia's commissioners had hoped that the colonial population of Natchez would again rise up against Spain, but Gálvez had persuaded them that Spain was the best protector of their independent livelihoods. Most residents of Natchez were English speakers. Some had been loyalists during the war, but most had come more recently for the economic opportunities, which were substantial. In August 1785, Natchez's 275 white families owned a total of 900 slaves, who produced an astounding $150,000 annually in tobacco, cotton, corn, lumber, and other products, mostly sold down the Mississippi through New Orleans. It was no wonder that Americans wanted the Mississippi for its route to market and its productive lands. But the Spanish empire was serving Natchez well, and its people had no desire to rock the boat.[127]

Not only did English-speaking locals not support Georgia's action; neither did Congress. Fearing war with Spain and international outrage, Congress in October 1785 resolved that "although Congress conceive they have an undoubted right to all the territory within the limits specified in the definitive Articles of peace and friendship between the Crown of Great Britain and these United States, yet they view with real concern the unwarrantable attempts of any Individual of these States to disturb the good understanding which so happily subsists between the two Nations."[128] For now at least, border-settling would be a matter of diplomacy, not war.

The Spanish crown sent a special envoy, Diego de Gardoqui, to negotiate the border with Congress. Gardoqui's company, based in Bilbao, had shipped goods to the rebels during the war, and he had an interest in forging postwar economic connections in North America. Gálvez instructed Gardoqui to insist on the broadest interpretation of Spanish possession and to ignore American threats. Spain had the right and the might. Congress should know that, as Gálvez put it, "we have in the province sufficient veteran troops, a war-wise militia, the friendship of many Indian nations who dislike the Americans, and more than enough experience in forest warfare."[129] It would be Gardoqui's job to secure Gálvez's victories.

In New York City, the nation's capital from 1785 to 1790, Diego de Gardoqui sat down with John Jay, now the American Secretary for Foreign Affairs, to resolve their countries' differences and to try to build a beneficial alliance. Jay weighed the importance of western lands against other financial considerations for his new country. While land grants and sales would help westerners and speculators, trade with Spain and Spanish colonies through eastern ports would provide a much-needed economic boost for merchants and farmers closer to the coast, who struggled to compensate for the British markets they had lost by revolution. Congress instructed Jay to get both, but Jay knew from his years of futile negotiating in Madrid during the war that Spain could not be pushed around. And, as Jay learned second-hand from Oliver Pollock, Spain was firm on keeping Americans out of Natchez and the lower Mississippi.[130]

Once they set the issue of Mississippi navigation aside, Jay and Gardoqui forged an agreement that could benefit both countries. The draft treaty opened free trade between the Spanish empire and the United States. Americans would have access to Spain's markets around the world, which paid in gold and silver, and Spanish products would flow freely into the United States. An agreement with King Carlos III would continue his tolerance of Congress's failure to repay its debt (or even make its interest payments). Jay presented the treaty to Congress, arguing "that a proper Commercial treaty with Spain would be of more importance to the United States than any they have formed, or can form, with any other Nation." If the United States broke with Spain, France would likely side with the Spanish, leaving the United States without either of its powerful European allies. Spain had already been helpful to the United States in establishing trade and diplomacy in North Africa and could help open markets in the Mediterranean. As for Florida's border, Jay believed that "it would be better even to yield a few acres, than to part in ill humor" with Spain, which could be either "a very convenient neighbor, or a very troublesome one." Navigation of the Mississippi was not worth fighting a war over, at least not yet.[131]

Congressmen in New England and the mid-Atlantic tended to agree with Jay that good commercial relations, including the right to sell fish in the Spanish empire, were worth compromising West Florida and the Mississippi. They supported changing Jay's instructions to allow him to back off on his demand for navigation of the Mississippi. In the summer of 1786, seven of the thirteen states voted to give up the demand. They had enough votes to change Jay's instructions, but James Monroe, leading the minority of mostly southern states with land interests in the west, introduced a motion stating that the decision needed nine aye votes under the Articles of Confederation because it was a matter of treaty ratification. It became clear that, even if Congress changed Jay's instructions, the final treaty would not be ratified. The stalemate would continue. To the Spanish, the failure of Congressional delegates to agree on a treaty was simply more evidence that the United States might not last to see the new century.[132]

Conclusion: Unsettled Borders

In the 1780s, a single country that stretched from the Atlantic to the Pacific and from the Great Lakes to the Rio Grande would have seemed an unlikely future. Surely the land would continue to be ruled by multiple sovereignties. Kentucky or another western settlement might become its own independent nation bordering the United States, the Chickasaw Nation, the Cherokee Nation, Spanish West Florida, the Creek Confederacy, and even perhaps a free black colony under Spanish protection. Different states and colonies might fight, ally, overlap, and change over time, but surely none of them could overrun all of the others.

Across North America, Indians still controlled most of the land. For two centuries, the Spanish, French, and British empires had tried to colonize the continent. They had built permanent posts, beginning with St. Augustine and Santa Fe, and established alliances, traded, and fought wars against and alongside neighboring Indians. Particularly in the British colonies, settlers had farmed previously Indian land and pushed hard against the Indians who opposed them. But by the American Revolution, Europeans still truly controlled less than 20 percent of the lands north of Mexico. Of course kings and imperial officials wanted to control their colonial claims, but their empires were large and spread out, and they had to adapt to a variety of local power arrangements.

By the 1780s, the French and Spanish empires were accustomed to ruling colonies of diverse peoples on the edges of powerful Indian nations. Colonial hierarchies gave subjects, from slaves to royal officials, a variety of rights and levels of social and political prestige.

People who could not be incorporated, such as independent Indian nations, could be allies and, ideally, strengthen the colony's security. As the British empire took more direct control over its colonies in the eighteenth century, it moved toward this model as well, one that the British would apply in India in the nineteenth century.[133]

Ultimately the United States would also be an empire, but of a different sort. In Thomas Jefferson's vision, it would be an "empire of liberty." But liberty for whom? As U.S. settlers moved west, they would establish new independent farms and take with them the ideals of agrarianism and republicanism. As part of the United States or as new countries allied with the United States or with Spain or Britain, these western settlements would not layer authority as European empires had. They would be places where white men and their families would prosper and rule. But in the 1780s, thousands of Indians and Europeans were determined not to let this vision come to pass. The decisions made in the coming years regarding how best to advance independence and prosperity would determine the shape of the world to come.

CHAPTER FIFTEEN

Independence Gained or Lost?

AS EUROPEAN, Indian, and American diplomats debated the future of the continent, people with less influence over world events found themselves caught in the flux of sovereignty. The founding of the American republic did not grant independence to everyone caught up in the Revolutionary War. The uncertainty following the Revolution left some with new opportunities and others with reduced autonomy.

James and Isabella Bruce had lost the war and would see their home ruled by their enemies. They hoped that the peace would provide them with a triumphant return to West Florida but would settle for a new start with land in a still-British colony. Petit Jean, Amand Broussard, and Oliver and Margaret Pollock were on the winning side, but it remained to be seen if victory would indeed improve their lives. War often provided slaves with some opportunities for freedom, especially for men of military age. Like many others, Petit Jean hoped that his wartime service would earn freedom for himself and his family. The Pollocks' hopes were high for prosperity and prominence in a country they had helped create, while Amand Broussard's wartime experiences left him eager to become a Louisiana planter within the Spanish empire.

Most people who had lived through the war on the Gulf Coast found the prospects for their economic well-being as uncertain as the borders remained in the 1780s. Many individuals wondered if they had gained independence or lost it.

Freedom and Slavery in a New Order

In statehouses, public meetings, and private conversations across the United States, as black and white Americans imagined the postwar continent, many wondered about the future of slavery. Would enslaved people remain so in the United States, or was slavery incompatible with American ideals of freedom? Would enslaved men and women who served any of the sides in the war earn their permanent freedom? If large numbers who served the Spanish cause became free, might Spain allow them to establish their own communities like Fort Mose in Florida before the Seven Years' War? Or could they create their own independent states between and allied with neighboring colonies or states?

These ideas seem unlikely in retrospect, but in fact some Georgia slaves headed south on the assumption that Florida, Spanish once again, would welcome runaways, as when Spanish officials had welcomed runaway slaves from South Carolina to undermine British security. Like his predecessors, East Florida Governor Vicente Zéspedes would have to decide whether to honor their requests. And Thomas Jefferson supported a Virginia state bill for gradual emancipation with the provision that young freed men and women should, upon coming of age, "be colonized to such place as the circumstances of the time should render most proper, sending them out with arms, implements of household and of the handicraft arts, seeds, pairs of the useful domestic animals, etc. to declare them a free and independent people, and extend to them our alliance and protection, till they shall have acquired strength."[1]

The Treaty of Paris between Britain and the United States said that King George III would withdraw his armies without "carrying away any Negroes or other Property of the American inhabitants." This short clause endangered thousands of men, women, and children who had sought freedom by fleeing to British lines during the war, including at least seventeen of George Washington's own slaves. British Commander-in-Chief of North America Guy Carleton thought the treaty's concession an outrage both because it was unjust to people who had trusted British promises and because it rewarded the rebels by returning their slaves. In violation of the treaty, General Carleton evacuated three thousand black loyalists along with one thousand white loyalists from New York City in the spring and summer of 1783.[2]

In the meantime, the abolitionist efforts of enslaved and free blacks in the United States began to bear some fruit. As Massachusetts's 1780 state constitution, drafted by John Adams, Samuel Adams, and James Bowdoin, stated, "All men are born free and equal, and have certain natural, essential, and unalienable rights."[3] Although this language did not necessarily abolish slavery, slaves filed freedom suits that eventually persuaded the Massachusetts courts to end slavery in their state. Vermont's 1777 state constitution also effectively outlawed slavery, and Pennsylvania passed a law to emancipate its slaves gradually as they came of age. Even Virginia, with considerably more slaves than New England or the mid-Atlantic, passed a law encouraging slaveholders to free their slaves. George Washington and some other Virginians freed slaves in their wills. In the years immediately following the Revolution, it was possible that the ideals of the Revolution and the intellectual arguments of black Americans would gradually abolish slavery. Writing his *Notes on the State of Virginia* in 1781, Thomas Jefferson expressed the hope that total emancipation was coming. The fact that Jefferson did not follow up his hopes with action for his own slaves illustrates how living up to one's ideals is less likely when the personal costs are high. Like many wealthy southerners, Jefferson depended on enslaved people for his and his daughters' financial independence.[4]

Slavery came under attack on the Gulf Coast as well, but only on an individual level. The war had not sparked the rhetoric of liberty that it did in the thirteen colonies. With no rhetoric of independence with which to charge Spanish policymakers of hypocrisy, individual enslaved men and women prepared their own way for freedom. Seizing opportunities opened by the war, they worked, saved, and served the Spanish crown to emancipate themselves and their loved ones. With claims over a vast land mass north of Mexico and almost no Spaniards both willing and able to come to this far edge of empire, a large population of loyal freedmen and freedwomen might be of great use to Spain.

Enslaved men and women had helped Spain to take the Gulf Coast. At New Orleans after the war, General Bernardo de Gálvez formally acknowledged slaves for their "zeal and rectitude" and "dedication to the Royal service." He gave medals to free and enslaved blacks who had distinguished themselves.[5] To slaves who had been wounded, Gálvez gave eighty dollars; others who fought received a few dollars each. Neither employing slaves in warfare nor rewarding them was unusual. For at least five hundred years, the Spanish had awarded wages, bounties, and—for extraordinary service—freedom to slaves who performed military service for the crown.[6]

Because slaves in the Spanish empire had the right to buy themselves, a financial reward could be the road to freedom. Under Spanish law, if a slave's master refused to sell or tried to set an unreasonable price, the slave had a right to go before a tribunal to determine a reasonable price. Indeed, in one of their petitions, Massachusetts slaves shamed their white neighbors by pointing out that "even the *Spaniards,* who have not those sublime ideas of freedom that English men have," grant certain rights to slaves, including the right of self-purchase and of having one day per week to work for themselves, in which they could earn money toward freedom.[7]

A loyal and ambitious black population was useful to the stability of Louisiana and the Floridas, but Spanish officials put a higher value on keeping French- and English-speaking white inhabitants happy. Demonstrating to slaveholders and ambitious would-be slaveholders that slavery could grow under Spanish rule was essential to winning their allegiance—or at least their quiescence. If they believed that the Spanish threatened an expanding plantation economy, they might seek British or American assistance or independence. Spain needed to keep its promises. During the war, Spain had pledged to surrendering Britons that, while no free blacks would lose their free status, "the negroes who have been hired out to work on the fortifications will not be taken from their owners, but these will be entitled to keep them along with the rest of their property." Slaves who had "fled from Pensacola during the siege" would be returned as well. Not only were slaves returned to their owners, but their owners also could rest assured that Spain agreed with Britain that they were "property."[8] The king's exemption of slave importations from import duties also helped persuade colonists that Spain supported their economic development. As a result of colonists' ambitions and imperial encouragement, thousands of enslaved Africans came to Spanish Louisiana and West Florida between 1784 and 1800, mostly from the Bight of Benin, as in the French period, and from farther south in West Africa, around Angola.[9]

Protection and promotion of the system of slavery, combined with opportunities for free blacks and the possibility of individual emancipation, seemed best for stability and economic growth. Spanish dependence on both slavery and a free black population struck a fine balance. In the context of postwar recovery and local misgivings about Spanish rule, promises of stability and growth, plus alliances with powerful Indian nations, seemed likely to expand and strengthen the empire.[10]

Amand Broussard would benefit from Spanish promotion of plantations. Broussard's prosperity in Louisiana depended on land worked by bound labor, much as Alexander McGillivray's did. In 1781, Broussard already owned land and cattle in Attakapas. As the economy of New Orleans improved, Broussard's cattle and land holdings increased, and he began to buy slaves to work in his growing operation. Their labor in turn would fund more purchases. By 1785, Broussard had bought four slaves to work in the fields and to tend the cattle, and he had his eye on more.[11]

Amand Broussard and Anne Benoît were building their family independence on enslaved labor, land, and the markets of the Spanish empire. They would eventually have at least eleven children together plus Broussard's son from his first marriage. Most of their children would marry other Acadians, strengthening their close community with bonds of family and inheritance. For example, three of their daughters would marry grandsons of Amand's uncle Alexandre.[12]

At the same time that slavery was growing through the importation of captured Africans, an astounding number of the Gulf Coast's black men and women were freeing themselves and their loved ones from slavery. They took advantage of numerous and varied opportunities, all with their own risks. Running away was the quickest but also one of the riskiest means of acquiring freedom. As an area of contested sovereignty, the Gulf region and the Mississippi Valley had long provided borders over which many slaves could flee to British, Spanish, Creek, Choctaw, or Chickasaw land, depending on whom they were trying to escape. As borders shifted during the war, this opportunity increased. Hundreds of men and women took advantage of war disruptions to run away and to live on the edges of plantations and in the bayous outside New Orleans. The Spanish called them "cimarrones," meaning *wild* or *runaway* (shortened by the English to "maroons"). These refugee settlements had existed since the 1720s, but their numbers grew during the war. Cimarrones obtained supplies from plantations, by either pillaging or relying on slaves to provide them, often in return for doing some of the slaves' work in the woods, such as gathering firewood.[13]

After the war, New Orleans planters demanded that Governor Esteban Miró do something about the problem of the cimarrones, as the responsibility of the empire to its law-abiding subjects. They were frightened of cimarrones' "robberies and insults" and knew that their success would encourage still more runaways.[14] Spanish officials faced a dilemma. If allowed to exist, cimarrón communities could actually protect a colony. In Jamaica, established cimarrón communities at times fought for their colonizers and returned new runaway slaves. Perhaps if Spanish officials had known what a threat the United States would eventually become, they might have developed alliances with cimarrones.

Instead, slaveholders persuaded Governor Miró to crack down. While Bernardo de Gálvez and Miró had occasionally sent Louisiana's free black militias to keep the cimarrones in check, French slaveholders demanded tougher action—and from white troops. Until the cimarrones were destroyed, slaves would have to carry passes from their masters if traveling, and free blacks would need to show papers proving their status. Any who disobeyed would receive twenty-five lashes. Miró also reiterated existing regulations requiring masters' written permission to conduct trade or to assemble and forbidding slaves from buying liquor, selling clothing, traveling by horse, and bearing arms (with exceptions for hunting or military service). In the spring of 1783, Miró sent out regular soldiers and militia, including "colored" troops, into the bayous below New Orleans.[15]

Miró also sent an enslaved man named Bastien to infiltrate the ci-marrón camp, and he eventually led the militia to the cimarrón hide-out. The cimarrones dispersed into the bayou, but the soldiers and militia used canoes to track them down in the waist-deep water. Bastien's master wounded the man rumored to be the main leader, Jean St. Malo. The militia recaptured over a hundred others. As they canoed back to New Orleans with their captives, inhabitants of the plantations along the bayou rushed out to thank the soldiers and to give them food and drink. The Spanish hanged St. Malo and three other men in the Place d'Armes, New Orleans's main square. Others were eventually either executed, branded, whipped, or sold to another colony. St. Malo's wife, Cecilia Canoy (or Conway), got her death sentence postponed due to pregnancy, and Gálvez eventually suspended her sentence, perhaps not wanting the spectacle of a woman dangling in the public square, even if she was a black runaway. Although Spanish officials might have preferred to ignore the problem, New Orleans slaveholders had brought the power of the colonial state down on their side.[16]

Running away was too risky a choice for most slaves, including Petit Jean and his wife. Even before the hangings in the Place d'Armes, they had chosen to stay put and work for their masters and for the Spanish crown. Slaves' beliefs about rights and liberties were as complicated as everyone else's in the age of revolution. Freedom without security was usually not worth the risk.[17]

Nonetheless, Petit Jean preferred freedom to enslavement. When he and his wife could do so safely and legally, they seized their freedom. Petit Jean earned his freedom through service to the crown. As Petit Jean had worked for his master and for the Spanish military and his wife had sold goods or services in her small amount of free time, they had been saving their earnings in hopes of freedom. At the end of the war, in 1782, Spanish officials freed him by paying four hundred dollars to his master and helped Petit Jean negotiate with his wife's master to buy her freedom with money they had saved. It was an important day when Petit Jean and his wife held their "cartas de libertad."[18]

They joined many others in exercising their right to self-purchase using wages and bounties earned during the war. In the war years and the two decades following, between one thousand and two thousand slaves in Spanish Louisiana and the Gulf Coast were freed by purchase. In Louisiana alone (not counting the Floridas), enslaved people and their families and friends spent at least $250,000 on freedom (five to ten million dollars today). Louisiana's free black population rose from under 200 in 1770 to about 1,500 in 1795 and was still rising. The Revolutionary War did not start self-emancipation, which had always been possible in Spanish colonies. Still, the opportunities provided by wartime service brought self-purchase within the grasp of more people. The astounding numbers attest to the devotion slaves put to the task. Gálvez's bounty of eighty dollars could be a significant down payment on freedom, but a slave's price would be at least twice that, and often much more, as the $400 price of the skilled slave Petit Jean attests. The influx of African slaves after the war actually helped self-emancipation by keeping the price of slaves from rising.[19]

When there was no clear path to freedom, measures of independence and autonomy within slavery had made Petit Jean's life better than it might have been. But when the possibility of freedom came, Petit Jean and his wife seized it as quickly as they could, making sure that they had their emancipation papers approved by the court in New Orleans. If she was still of child-bearing age, it was especially important to secure her freedom so that any subsequent children would be born free. As Broussard and McGillivray built their fortunes on enslaved labor, Petit Jean and his wife simply looked forward to a life of freedom.[20]

The Loyalists' Predicament

After Pensacola fell, James and Isabella Bruce sailed with their children and their furniture and papers on a Spanish ship. While most loyalists quietly stayed on in the rest of West Florida, Pensacola was different. The town's long months of waiting for attack before the siege had made its fall more bitter, and all but a handful of British settlers decided to leave. General Gálvez returned slaves to West Florida slaveholders who pledged loyalty to the Spanish crown, but those colonists who fled Spanish rule could not take their "property" with them. The Bruces' slaves became the property of the Spanish crown, who either sold them to locals or used them in public works.[21]

As on her journey twelve years earlier, Isabella's ship stopped at a southern port before turning north. This time it was Spanish Havana rather than British Jamaica. In Havana, the Bruces and the other refugees had to listen to the celebrations emanating from the city as Spanish subjects hailed the conquest of West Florida. From there, the ships took them to New York City, which in July 1781 was still occupied by the British. There, the Bruces found space among more than thirty thousand other refugees and tried to imagine a future without the land, slaves, and position that had promised a good life. For now, the Bruces were among their friends, people who had helped to make Pensacola a home.[22]

The Bruces hoped that they would return to West Florida once it returned to British rule. James had sworn in Pensacola that he would not live under Spanish rule, so they would not seek their future in the Spanish Floridas. Instead, he, Isabella, Archibald, and Charlotte, along with many other West Florida refugees, left New York for England, arriving in June 1782. They viewed London not as their new home but as a temporary haven for a temporary exile. That summer, the Bruces heard that high-level imperial officials had laid a plan before the crown to retake West Florida and take Spanish New Orleans. James Bruce added his voice to the call. The plan emanated from Lord Dunmore, the former governor of New York and Virginia. After General Cornwallis surrendered at Yorktown, Dunmore sailed to Charleston, which British forces still occupied. There, in conversation with West Florida refugees, Dunmore created a vision of a continuing British empire in mainland North America that accepted the loss of some of the northern colonies. He proposed leading a large force from Charleston, plus ten thousand slaves, who would contribute their assistance simply in return for their freedom.[23]

Writing on his authority as an eighteen-year resident and officeholder in West Florida, James Bruce promised the Earl of Shelburne, the British secretary of state, that retaking West Florida would be easy. Its defenses were "ruinous." Ignoring what had actually happened in the Revolutionary War on the Gulf Coast, he asserted that loyalists and Indians would eagerly fight alongside His Majesty's troops. West Florida, with its healthy climate and fertile lands, would more than make up for the loss of the rebellious colonies.[24]

Although James Bruce exaggerated the ease of taking West Florida, he was on firmer ground in describing how it could take the place of the thirteen colonies in the British imperial economy. With its ports and navigable rivers, West Florida was poised to provide the West Indies with lumber, rice, corn, and naval products: pitch, tar, turpentine, masts, timbers, and planks. James Bruce believed that it could dominate the fur trade, taking advantage of the fact that Indians were "unanimous in their aversion to the American revolters" (somewhat true) and "so implacable in their hatred to the Spaniards" (not true at all). Bruce doubted that Oliver Pollock's and Bernardo de Gálvez's promises of prosperity and security for West Floridians and Louisianans had persuaded the region's colonists. Spain surely would not encourage the development of indigo and tobacco plantations because they would create too much competition with its other colonies, and in any case Indian opposition to Spain meant they "will never permit settlers under that Government to enjoy security either for their property or lives." In contrast, if Britain took West Florida, it would thrive under Britain's "mild and equitable laws." Britain would regain the loyalty of its own colonists, attract loyalists "who have been ruined by the War," woo French and Spanish colonists with British liberty and markets, and demonstrate to "the deluded colonists" in rebellion "the difference between the happiness and prosperity of His Majesty's subjects settled in that colony, and those of their own divided and distracted States." Missing "that envied state which they once enjoyed," they might even "return to their natural connection with Great Britain."[25]

If the British regained West Florida, the Bruces and other West Florida loyalists could reclaim their property and begin rebuilding their family independence based on land, slaves, and access to British markets. Of course, James Bruce and Lord Dunmore proposed uniting people with contradictory visions of the future. Slaves would be fighting for their freedom, but white loyalists expected to restore and improve on the lives the Revolution had taken from them, which included plantations worked by slaves on the lands of Britain's Indian allies.

In any case, the 1783 Treaty of Paris ended talk of invasion, and the Bruces never regained their wealth and prominence. While in London, James filed a petition to the crown, asking for payment for losses caused by the Revolutionary War. Like many other loyalists, the Bruces believed that the empire owed them compensation for the havoc that the Revolution had wreaked on their lives. In establishing political independence, the United States had destroyed the lives that the Bruces and others had built playing by the rules and being enterprising imperial subjects. The suffering of wives and the diminished prospects for children were an important part of the claims. There were so many loyalist petitions that Parliament established the Commission for Enquiring into the Losses, Services, and Claims of the American Loyalists. James Bruce requested payment for his lost plantations on the Amite and Mobile rivers and Thompson's Creek as well as for the family's home in Pensacola and a cattle pen on the town's outskirts. He also filed for eight thousand pounds in lost revenue that he figured he would have netted from the Amite River plantation between James Willing's 1778 raid and the Bruces' departure from West Florida in 1781. He also hoped to recoup salary and commissions from customs he would have collected had the colony remained British.[26]

Many petitioners received recompense for losses due to the rebellion; however, West Florida was not covered because it was not "in the revolted provinces."[27] Its losses mostly resulted from the war with Spain, not the rebels. Impressed with a letter that former West Florida governor George Johnstone wrote commending James Bruce's character, property, and service, the Commission awarded him £135 salary covering 1781 for being Britain's commissioner of customs at Pensacola and recommended that he receive an allowance of one hundred pounds per year for the damage that the "rebel" James Willing had caused to the Amite property, valued by James Bruce at £2,134. But the Bruces could claim nothing for their other losses. The Commission ruled that, while James Bruce had "certainly lost by the war," it could not consider most of his losses, which were "not within the limits of the United States of America" and had been "destroyed by a Foreign Enemy."[28] When he went to collect the salary that the Commission had awarded, he learned that the Pensacola officers were not on the list to be paid. He appealed again, both to justice and to the fact that he had "a family totally unprovided for after serving His Majesty for upwards of twenty-two years," first in the Seven Years' War and then in Pensacola as collector of customs and a member of His Majesty's Council.[29]

The West Floridians found themselves with losses that, somehow, did not count. James Bruce, Adam Chrystie, and thirty-six other heads of household petitioned British Prime Minister Lord North that West Floridians were "equally entitled to a compensation for their losses, as their other fellow sufferers on the same continent." In 1787, they petitioned the House of Commons and published their petition as a pamphlet. They emphasized that their loyalty had caused their losses, reminding Britons that West Florida was "solicited by Congress to join in their confederacy, and declare the province of West Florida an independent state," but they had stayed true to the empire instead. With an exaggeration that General John Campbell would have vehemently disputed, they claimed to have "raised a considerable sum of money, by voluntary subscriptions, for erecting redoubts, and formed themselves into volunteer companies for their defense," some joining the militia and others the provincial army.[30] The crown instead offered them lands in Canada or the Bahamas, which the Treaty of Paris had returned to Britain. In 1790, Adam and Charlotte Chrystie took lands in the Bahamas for themselves and their daughters. The crown appointed Adam Chrystie colonial secretary of the Bahamas and West Florida's attorney general.[31] Chrystie rebuilt his family's life in the Bahamas, but there is no evidence that the Bruces ever moved there. If they did, they must have had so little success that they do not appear in the land or government records. They may have gone to Canada with similar results or stayed in Britain, perhaps harboring hopes of returning to the Floridas to reclaim their lost property and position when imperial boundaries shifted again.[32]

Whether Isabella Bruce lamented her family's loss of property and position or rejoiced to return home to Britain—the sources do not tell. What is clear is that for women, the Revolution could bring dramatic and often devastating change in individual circumstances but did nothing to change the institution of patriarchy under which they lived. Again, it was her husband's status and men's decisions that sent her back across the Atlantic and his success or failure in petitioning and in other economic pursuits that would determine her possibilities. What was increasingly becoming clear was that the sacrifices she had made to raise her children in a place of better opportunities had failed.[33]

The Debts of Victory

It is not surprising that James and Isabella Bruce found themselves adrift after their side lost the war. But Oliver and Margaret Pollock, who had backed the American cause and Spanish alliance from the beginning, should have had much brighter postwar fortunes. In reality the United States found itself ill equipped to repay debts. As tensions rose between Spain and the United States, the Pollocks' association with Spain began to shift in American minds from patriotic to suspicious. The years after the war would not bring the rewards and opportunities the Pollocks had imagined.

The Pollocks needed Congress and the state of Virginia to pay what they owed. With the war over, Oliver Pollock's New Orleans creditors expected to be paid for what they had provided the rebels on Pollock's account. One of Bernardo de Gálvez's parting actions as he left New Orleans in the summer of 1781 was to loan Pollock another five thousand dollars "on account of not having received the funds which should have been remitted by Congress."[34] That same summer, Congress was considering Pollock's receipts, on the insistence of Pollock's old business partner Robert Morris, now the superintendent of finance. Letters from Pollock and Gálvez were read on the floor of Congress, and the Commercial Committee resolved that the U.S. Treasury should pay Pollock more than twenty thousand dollars as well as repay Gálvez the money he had lent Pollock. Staying in Gálvez's good graces was part of Congress's motive. Morris drafted a letter from Congress to Gálvez in November 1781 to convey its gratitude, its respect for "your character and that of your nation," and its "wish for an intimate connection with your country." Unfortunately for all concerned, Congress had no funds to pay the bill.[35]

Without Gálvez in New Orleans to protect him, Pollock faced financial ruin. By January 1782, Pollock had run through Gálvez's line of credit, while a bill from Fort Jefferson for an astounding $237,320 arrived, an amount that exceeded all of Pollock's assets. The intendant in New Orleans demanded that Pollock immediately pay all of his debts or face imprisonment. Pollock shut down his store and sold his stocks of goods as well as his plantations, indigo works, house, furniture, and most of his slaves. As other slaveholders were taking advantage of peacetime to buy more slaves, the Pollocks were losing theirs. In May, Margaret said farewell to Oliver as he boarded a ship to go to the United States to argue his case in person. He carried notarized copies of his correspondence with Congress and the governors of Virginia, plus a letter from Governor Miró attesting to his service to American independence and describing "the sad situation" in which Pollock and his creditors found themselves. As he sailed away, Oliver lamented with "the anguish of my tortured soul" over leaving his wife and children "reduced to extreme misery and distress" for his choice "to serve a country whose gratitude and justice I had too much confidence in."[36]

Whether an ardent American partisan herself or not, Margaret Pollock's fortunes were, like those of Isabella Bruce, tied to those of her husband. If she had had wealth in her own name, Spanish law would have protected it from his creditors, but Oliver had made their fortune, and he had borrowed on it to aid the Americans. Now she did not even have a home. When Oliver Pollock sold the house, he arranged for the buyer to let Margaret and their four children stay in an upper part of the house and have use of the kitchen. That situation was humiliating enough, but when that buyer sold the house, the new owner, a Mr. McCarty, did not honor the agreement as dutifully. According to a letter that Margaret Pollock wrote Governor Esteban Miró, McCarty began sending his slaves to harass her in the streets of New Orleans with demands that she vacate his property. When complaints to McCarty went nowhere, she called on Miró, her husband's friend and comrade during the conquests of Manchac and Baton Rouge, hoping that "the cause will be a sufficient apology for the liberty I take" in addressing the governor directly. She asked Miró to give her "that justice . . . which is due a woman."[37]

Margaret Pollock might have no economic power, but she trusted that the combination of her class, her sex, and her husband's connections would protect her from the ultimate affront in her world—public insults from black slaves. But things got worse. McCarty established a cooper (barrel-making) shop on the ground floor of the house and staffed it with, in Margaret Pollock's words, "a band of Negroes" and "a banditti of whites," who have "insulted me and beat my servants." Pregnant and confined to bed, she was tormented by noises from downstairs "which no human creature can bear." From her room she sent McCarty "message after message begging" that he do something about the noise, "but it appears that he is destitute of all human feeling." Through the birth of her daughter Lucetta and a frightening two weeks with a sick child, the noise continued. We have only Margaret Pollock's version of the events, and she was not blameless in the conflict. She admitted that "I did strike a Negro boy of his, though it was not half the punishment he merited," but otherwise she was "much at a loss how to account for this treatment to me."[38] Her abuse of McCarty's slave could explain his workers' rudeness to her. Perhaps she had long been tyrannical and now, with her husband's ruin and departure, they could strike back. Or perhaps she lashed out from frustration at her decline. What is clear is that Margaret Pollock found herself without the financial means or protection that her class, race, and sex had led her to expect, all due to the support her husband had given to the American cause.[39]

Unfortunately, in the fall of 1783, Margaret Pollock offended the very man she had hoped would protect her. Their conflict exposes how both men and women could muster gender roles to make their case. The Pollocks' cook, an enslaved woman, was accused of a crime and imprisoned awaiting trial. Margaret Pollock confronted Governor Miró in person and by letter to request that "my cook that I certainly do miss" be released, and charging that "you have no right to detain her on any pretense whatever."[40] Miró responded that her comments were "very insulting to the authority of the government." If you continue, Miró threatened, "I shall let you know that the government has authority over women." He warned Margaret Pollock that she could submit petitions to the governor like any other subject but that their personal relationship had ended. He concluded, "I shall accept no other letter from you."[41] She did write again, and this time she abandoned all pretense of propriety. "So you threaten me," she began. She agreed that Miró did have authority "against ladies" but reminded him that wise leaders (whether governors or husbands) ruled not by "making one feel their influence" but by governing fairly. For her part, she believed she was enacting her proper role by promoting the cause of "the feeble and the innocent," her falsely accused slave. If he would not help the women for their own sake, he should remember her husband's importance to Spain and that the king was "indebted to render him justice."[42] Miró did not reply.

Meanwhile, Oliver Pollock was on his way to seek justice from the people who owed him money. After landing in Wilmington, North Carolina, he rode the 250 miles to Richmond, where he discovered that the Virginia Assembly was not in session. His attorney, Daniel Clark, had already written to Virginia Governor Benjamin Harrison that Pollock was in debt more than eighty thousand dollars "for the purpose of supporting your army to the Westward, which could not possibly subsist, or continue in that service, had not Mr. Pollock generously exerted himself on their behalf." His family, who once "lived in affluence and ease," were faced with "misery and distress." As Clark put it, "Ruin, from a victorious British enemy, Pollock might reasonably expect, but from a victorious friend, from Virginia, to whose service his life and fortune have been devoted, he had reason to expect a just, if not a general acquittal."[43] But Governor Harrison was powerless to act without the legislature's approval.

Unsuccessful in Virginia, Pollock next went to Philadelphia, where in September he outlined to Congress all of his dealings and debts. He concluded, "I have labored without ceasing, I have neglected the road to affluence, I have exhausted my all, and plunged myself deeply in debt, to support the cause of America, in the hours of her distress, and when those who called themselves friends, were daily deserting her."[44] Again Superintendent of Finance Robert Morris recommended that Congress make good on the debts, as did a special Congressional committee, which agreed that "public faith, justice and humanity require that the sundry accounts should be liquidated and the balances paid." The devil was in the detail at the end of the sentence: "whenever the state of our public funds shall render it practicable."[45] The entire debt was in the tens of millions of dollars, and many others were coming to Congress for payment, while speculators were scooping up the scrip held by soldiers and other small investors at a fraction of its face value. President of Congress John Hanson wrote Miró, assuring him that it was Congress's "firm determination to do justice to Mr. Pollock" but explaining that Congress had no money and no power to tax.[46] In the meantime, the Virginia legislature came back into session and resolved that Virginia indeed owed Pollock $136,466, to be paid in annual installments of ten thousand dollars, starting immediately. But it too had no funds to start paying.[47]

Back in New Orleans, Miró was no longer in the mood to accept assurance of future payments. He did not mention his altercations with Margaret Pollock, but they surely were on his mind when he responded icily to Oliver Pollock in October 1783 that he could no longer expect Virginia to come through. Miró reminded him that "one of your principal and most sacred obligations" was to repay Louisiana's "generous citizens," who "have suffered enough by bearing with you the long time of four years." He enclosed a list of debts totaling over seventy-four thousand dollars to the Spanish crown and over eighty-nine thousand dollars to individuals, details Pollock surely already knew by heart.[48] By the time Oliver Pollock received Miró's letter, he had heard from his wife. Unfortunately, their private correspondence does not survive, but we can see in Pollock's next letter to Miró how he tried to protect and excuse her. He charged Miró that "I little expected such treatment from a person I so highly esteemed, and always looked upon as a friend and a distinguished gentleman." Clearly Miró was not acting properly, but in case Margaret Pollock was also at fault, Oliver Pollock hedged a bit, asking the governor that "in case the person I hold most dear does not merit the former friendship and politeness your Excellency once pleased to honor us with, I hope your Excellency will not forget what is due to her sex" as well as to his old friend and "very obedient and humble servant, Oliver Pollock."[49]

In the meantime, unable to pay Oliver Pollock, Congress in June 1783 gave him an appointment as a commercial agent for the United States at Havana. Perhaps Pollock could start again, as he had in the 1760s, importing and exporting goods through Havana to the Atlantic and Gulf coasts. He sailed to Havana with new hope and two shiploads of goods, calling for his family to join him from New Orleans. Margaret Pollock must have been mightily relieved as she and the children boarded a Havana-bound ship and scraped the mud of Miró's New Orleans from their boots.[50]

However, Oliver Pollock found 1783 quite unlike the 1760s. Back then, he was one of very few merchants who could legally trade in both the Spanish and British empires, and he took advantage of his privileged position and the demand for his products. Now he represented the United States, a nation which Spanish officials were beginning to see as an international bully with no funds or military to back up its demands. When Pollock arrived in Havana in the fall of 1783, the governor of Cuba was none other than Luís de Unzaga y Amezaga, Bernardo de Gálvez's predecessor as Louisiana governor, the man whom Pollock had worn out with his requests to aid the American rebellion back in 1776 and 1777. Pollock was shocked to discover that Governor Unzaga had just issued a proclamation that no American vessels would be admitted in the port of Havana.

Angry about American and British dealings in Paris, the Spanish crown had determined to use its economic power to show the young upstart nation its true place in the world order. Governor Unzaga allowed Pollock to enter but required that his goods stay on board ship floating in Havana's harbor. In February 1784, Unzaga went further, ordering all American merchants to leave Cuba or face arrest. To Spain, the new nation could not sign whatever treaty it liked with their common enemy and then expect to retain the economic and military benefits of connections with the wartime allies it had just slighted.[51]

U.S. officials in the early years after the Revolution tended to think that they could operate as neutrals, free from the entanglements of empire, with good diplomatic relations and open ports to all of Europe. Their ambitions were similar to Payamataha's for the Chickasaws, but their diplomacy was less consistent and their claims more audacious. The failure of Americans' self-perception to line up with European (and Indian) views of the United States as presumptuous and transient led to many surprises like Pollock's, in which U.S. representatives were insulted and demeaned by imperial powers.[52]

Pollock's creditors in New Orleans received the news that his trips to Philadelphia and Richmond had not improved his financial situation. They sent a petition to Cuban Governor Unzaga, whom some of them knew from Louisiana, to imprison Pollock for debt. In May 1784, Unzaga did just that. An officer and two soldiers approached Pollock's house in Havana with bayonets fixed to the ends of their muskets. They took custody of his carriage, mules, and black coachman. While other American merchants and their families could leave Havana if they could liquidate enough assets to pay for passage, Pollock could not even do that, as the governor would not grant him a passport until he paid his "rebel debts."[53] One ship's captain seemed willing to take Margaret and the children but then left harbor with the family's baggage on board, deserting them "without a second change of clothes."[54] Having believed she would be safe from insults in Havana, Margaret Pollock must have been utterly devastated. Late in August, Unzaga finally agreed that she and the children could leave for Philadelphia, but Pollock would have to remain until he could provide "satisfaction to the many creditors who have presented themselves."[55] The ship that carried away Margaret and the children also bore more letters from Oliver Pollock to Philadelphia and Virginia begging for his money.[56]

With the British empire gone, trade should have flowed freely among the allied ports of New Orleans, Pensacola, Havana, Veracruz, Charleston, Philadelphia, New York, and Boston. Instead, Spain and the United States clashed over their visions of the future, especially in the North American interior, and the Pollocks found themselves caught in the middle. Like Isabella Bruce, Margaret Pollock would have to make a new home for her children when her husband's ambitions faltered. Women's relationships of dependence—with husbands and other important men—were supposed to protect and provide for them. When those same men could not or would not fulfill their part in a system of patriarchy, everything fell apart.

A few months later, Oliver Pollock finally received some good news. On February 4, 1785, Bernardo de Gálvez stepped off a ship in Havana. Rewarding Gálvez's victories, the king had made him captain general of Cuba in addition to governor of Louisiana and the Floridas. Importantly for Pollock, Gálvez was now Governor Unzaga's superior. Pollock wrote a letter detailing his travails since they last met, including the fact that he was under arrest right nearby. To Gálvez, Pollock's plight was an unwelcome reminder of the contrast between American ambitions and American irresponsibility. Gálvez informed Pollock that he had no power to overturn Unzaga's local decisions but that he would see what he could do in the courts.[57]

Before Gálvez had time to help Pollock, word came from Spain that the king had named Gálvez to succeed his father as viceroy of New Spain. Now bound for Mexico, Gálvez had no time to address

Pollock's problems through the legal process. However, he personally pledged security for Pollock's debts and granted him passage on the king's frigate to New York. Pollock gratefully boarded the ship along with other imprisoned American merchants and Spanish envoy Diego de Gardoqui, on his way from Gálvez's briefing to his negotiations with John Jay.[58]

Back in the United States, Pollock contrasted Gálvez's literal grant of freedom with what Congress was inflicting on him. True independence would come only when Congress paid its debts, for now Pollock's family, which "had formerly enjoyed affluence," was in "a state of dependency." In either a rented house or the home of a friend, Margaret Pollock gave birth again in June 1785, adding a newborn son to her other seven children, including the two-year-old who had been born over the cooper's shop in New Orleans. In St. Joseph's Catholic Church in Philadelphia, they christened him Bernard Galvez Pollock. Coming of age in a well-to-do New Orleans family, Margaret had looked forward to a life in which she and her children would be comfortable dependents of a responsible husband and father, not outcasts dependent on charity for their food and shelter. What a difference a revolution had made—and being on the winning side no less. For Pollock and his family, winning the war for independence produced nothing of the sort.[59]

At last, in late 1785, Virginia made the first installment on Pollock's reimbursements, giving him enough capital to begin his business again. He outfitted a ship and loaded it with flour from Philadelphia and slaves from the West Indies. The shipment made a good profit at New Orleans, where aspiring planters like Amand Broussard were clamoring for slaves. Pollock was able to fund another voyage and make a down payment on a house in the countryside between Philadelphia and Carlisle, Pennsylvania, where he already had a farm he had inherited from his father. His sister Mary lived on the farm, but, as the son, Oliver inherited. Small-town Pennsylvania was a long way from New Orleans, but Margaret surely was relieved to have a house again, and they also at some point acquired a home in Philadelphia, two blocks from Independence Hall. Still, her husband was merely "on parole," and his profits were far from enough to satisfy his creditors. Pollock wrote Congress again that he did not "know the moment the injured creditors may once more force me to part, and leave [my family] to the bounty of strangers for support."[60]

Conclusion: Individuals and Their States

Individual men and women found themselves caught up in the uncertainty of who was in charge after the war. Although the Gulf Coast had not experienced a political revolution that turned governance upside down, shifting imperial borders changed people's lives. Some, like the Broussards and Petit Jean and his wife, made the most of opportunities unavailable before the war. Others, such as the Bruces and the Pollocks, found their circumstances changed for the worse by the victories of the American republic and the Spanish empire.

At the same time, many U.S. citizens believed that the lands between the Appalachians and the Mississippi were key to the independence the Revolution had promised them. As these speculators and settlers pushed west, they would both clash with Spaniards and Indians and imagine ways of combining with them that might be more advantageous than remaining in the United States. From Natchez to Little Tallassee to Nashville to Augusta, people imagined futures of independence and prosperity and wondered what polities, if any, could promote them.

CHAPTER SIXTEEN

Confederacies

PAYAMATAHA LAY DYING. At the time of his birth, the Chickasaws could count the French, Choctaws, and Quapaws among their many enemies. Six decades later, in 1785, Payamataha could look back on a remarkable transformation. Once a formidable warrior whose hatred for the French was renowned, Payamataha had led his people to peace. For two decades, he had worked with other Chickasaw leaders to change his people's place in the world, and he had succeeded. Once called "the most military people of any about the great river," the Chickasaws were now known as peacemakers.[1] Only the Kickapoos remained to be fully folded into the Chickasaw peace. Payamataha could look back on his work with pride and hope that his successors would continue to protect Chickasaw independence through a commitment to peace.

However, in the coming years, Payamataha's small nation would have to contend with a changing landscape, as neighboring political entities sought to combine to increase their power. The next Chickasaw leaders would find it increasingly difficult to remain independent while confederacies grew around them. The fate of Payamataha's

THE SOUTHEAST AND TRANS-APPALACHIA, 1780s

people would illustrate the paradox of independence. He had worked to protect Chickasaw independence through unilateral peacemaking, but when coalitions insisted that the Chickasaws prove themselves by breaking peace with others, his strategy broke down. As in the past, independence depended on others.

Beginning in the mid-1780s, American immigrants by the thousands poured over the Appalachians, and many prominent Americans sought to speculate on large landholdings to divide and sell to settlers. While Chickasaw leaders continued to employ peaceful methods of diplomacy to protect their independence, other southeastern Indians, including Alexander McGillivray, advocated that Indians should surrender some local and national independence in favor of a Southern Confederacy that would join the Northern Confederacy being led by Mohawk Joseph Brant. Together they should form a "Grand Indian Confederacy of the Northern and Southern Nations" to fend off what we today would call illegal immigration, although the immigrants saw it as taking land that should belong to them. Alliance with the Spanish and British would keep Indians supplied with European weapons and trans-Atlantic legitimacy. Yet for the Chickasaws, McGillivray's plan for a Southern Confederacy threatened Chickasaw independent foreign policy-making and could potentially draw the Chickasaws back into war.[2]

As Indians debated which interdependencies would be useful and which were too dangerous, the westward migrants themselves raised new questions about sovereignty in the Gulf South. They opposed Indian control of the land and Spanish control of the Mississippi, yet they were equally disgusted with their new nation's failures to live up to the lofty ideals of the Revolution. Immigrants and speculators wanted independence from regulation and taxation but also access to economic connections and the economic security provided by American surveyors, diplomats, and soldiers. They wanted all of the benefits of a strong government with no intrusions on their independence. Congress struggled to honor their expectations while building a nation under the excruciating constraints of the optimistically named "Articles of Confederation and Perpetual Union." Some Americans wondered if Spain, Britain, or even Indians might better protect their independence and prosperity than this weak new government. Like Alexander McGillivray, George Washington and other national leaders found it difficult to persuade people to give up some independence to secure their country's permanent independence.[3]

The failings of the Articles of Confederation are well known, yet it is important to remember that they were in operation for over a decade during what John Quincy Adams, in his commencement address at Harvard in 1787, termed "this critical period." According to young Adams, "the prospect of public affairs is dark and gloomy," and "the bonds of union which connected us with our sister States, have been shamefully relaxed."[4] Both among and within the States, Americans found that their interests often seemed incompatible. In the 1780s, they would need to decide what sort of a confederation they wanted to be, if any at all. It might turn out not to be a "Perpetual Union."

Meanwhile, Spanish officials began to hope that the very immigrants who were causing the problems might cease being Americans and become independent Spanish allies or even dependent Spanish subjects. As multiple sovereignties tried to band together to defend against the others, land increasingly became the primary point of contention. The most powerful confederations and alliances would be those that could protect and advance their people's right to land and international markets for their products. The most successful path to sustained political and economic independence paradoxically involved ceding more power and authority to confederacies, as both McGillivray's Southern Confederacy and the federalist plan that would come out of the Constitutional Convention ultimately illustrated.

The Southern Confederacy

As Alexander McGillivray worked to centralize Creek foreign policy, he realized that it would be even more effective if implemented in conjunction with other southeastern nations and even Indians to the north. However, trying to make diverse polities contribute to united military action would be at least as difficult for southern Indians as it was for the British empire or the Continental Congress.

In 1785, knowing that Diego de Gardoqui and John Jay were negotiating borders in New York City and having promised the Northern Confederacy to convene a council to discuss coordinated action, McGillivray invited the Creeks, Chickasaws, and Cherokees to meet in a "general convention" at Little Tallassee in July 1785 to discuss what to do. The delegates crafted a joint resolution for the Spanish king. Because Congress would try to persuade Gardoqui that Creek, Cherokee, and Chickasaw lands belonged to the United States, the nations "in the most solemn manner protest against any title[,] claim[,] or demand the American Congress may set up for or against our lands, settlements, and hunting grounds." Because "we were not parties" to the Treaty of Paris, the Indians declared, they would "pay no attention to the manner in which the British negotiators ha[ve] drawn out the lines of the land in question." Indians had not been in Paris, and the British could not speak for them. The Americans well knew that "from the first settlement of the English colonies of Carolina and Georgia, . . . no title has ever been or pretended to be made by his Britannic Majesty to our lands except what was obtained by free gift or by purchase." Despite understanding the illegality of Britain's cession, Americans had, on the Cumberland and Oconee rivers, "divided our territories into counties and sat themselves down on our land, as if they were their own." The Indians called on Spain to use its power to challenge these baseless claims. They reminded the king that they did not "forfeit our independence and natural rights" to anyone.[5]

At the council, McGillivray proposed going much further than a joint resolution. He proposed that to defend their "independence and natural rights" against non-Indians, the Creeks, Cherokees, Chickasaws, and Choctaws surrender some of their national independence to a Southern Confederacy, to which they would also invite the Shawnees who had settled in Creek country. As "Nations in Confederacy against the Americans," with the Creeks as "the head and principal" in the south, they would fight the Americans together. Spain would fulfill its promises made at the end of the war to provide weapons and to negotiate for its Indian allies in the capitals of Europe and the United States.[6] The previous year's attempt by Northern Confederacy Indians to pull southeastern Indians into a "General Confederacy" had failed when the Kickapoos and Chickasaws could not get along, but a separate and allied Southern Confederacy might work.[7] Southern Indians had been at peace with one another since Payamataha's mediation of the 1760s, and the new Southern Confederacy could coordinate with the Northern one whenever possible. McGillivray figured he could be the glue holding the Southern Confederacy together, as he was already coordinating the Creeks' diplomacy with Spain. Indeed, by 1788 he would describe himself to Europeans as "head of a Numerous brave Nation, and of a Confederacy of the other Nations."[8]

McGillivray saw parallels between his efforts and the founding of the United States. Like George Washington and John Adams, McGillivray hoped to make a loosely affiliated people into a lasting nation. He held what he called "the honest ambition of meriting the appellation of the preserver of my country." Americans ought to recognize a little of themselves in the Creeks if their dispute in fact turned to war. After all, McGillivray pointed out to Congressional Superintendent of Indian Affairs in the Southern District James White, the thirteen colonies had come to a point in 1775 when, "after every peaceable mode of obtaining a redress of grievances having proved fruitless," they resorted "to arms to obtain it."[9]

There were internal parallels as well. Although McGillivray directed most of his centralizing efforts toward foreign policy, like the American revolutionaries he needed to persuade his fellow citizens to comply. Rather than the Revolution's tarring and feathering, McGillivray had a group of men from his clan who tried to intimidate people who opposed his policies. At one point in a disagreement with the headman Hoboithle Miko, McGillivray ordered his house and goods destroyed.[10]

If McGillivray could consolidate the Creek Confederacy into a Creek Nation, welcome additional towns such as the Chickamauga Cherokees and Shawnees who had moved to Creek Country during and after the Revolution, lead a Southern Confederacy in league with the Northern Confederacy, and secure supplies from Spain and Britain, he could create a network of interdependencies that could help them all stay independent of the United States. To continue his plans into future generations, he sent his nephew Davy Taitt, the son of his sister Sehoy and British Indian Agent David Taitt, and his son Aleck to be educated in Scotland. In 1782, when the British evacuated Savannah, Lachlan McGillivray had returned to Dunmaglass, where he grew up. While at Dunmaglass he managed the estates of his extended clan. Scotland had surrendered some political independence to England and in return received the commercial benefits of being in its union and local rule in most matters. This was not a relationship McGillivray would want for his Creek Nation, but it was a dependent role that he hoped others such as the Chickasaws would accept when joining the Southern Confederacy. He might have remembered, though, that Scotland did not join willingly.[11]

McGillivray was prepared to fight for Creek independence and, like the thirteen colonies, would need regional confederation and European alliance to succeed. By the 1770s, after decades of warfare, the Creeks, Chickasaws, Choctaws, and Cherokees were working as allies with one another and with the Spanish, in part because Payamataha had made them allies. Becoming the kind of Southern Confederacy that McGillivray had in mind would prove much more controversial. In the future, he would chastise and threaten southeastern Indians who violated the Confederacy he believed he had created.

War Against Georgia

Small-scale Creek raids against Georgia began again in the fall of 1785, and after the Congress at Pensacola with the Spanish and the meeting to create the Southern Confederacy, McGillivray was ready to urge the Creeks toward a more comprehensive war. Yet when the Creeks received notice from Congress that it had finally appointed commissioners Benjamin Hawkins, Andrew Pickens, and Joseph Martin, McGillivray agreed to meet with them, hoping that the appointments were a sign that Congress could discipline its states. Still, he chided Congress for taking so long. He wrote Pickens that "when we found that the American independency was confirmed by the peace, we expected that the new government would soon have taken some steps to make up the differences that subsisted between them and the Indians during the war, and to have taken them into protection, and confirm to them their hunting grounds." This kind of diplomacy would have been the right way to end a war. Instead, Congress had been silent, while Georgia was "entirely possessed with the idea that we were wholly at their mercy." Having heard nothing from Congress, McGillivray wrote, "we sought the protection of Spain, and treaties of friendship and alliance were mutually entered into: they to guaranty our hunting grounds and territory, and to grant us a free trade in the ports of the Floridas." Whatever border Spain and Congress eventually settled on, "we know our own limits, and the extent of our hunting grounds" and "as a free nation" would "pay no regard to any limits that may prejudice our claims, that were drawn by an American, and confirmed by a British negotiator."[12]

The Creeks decided not to send a delegation large enough to make an agreement. They knew the shenanigans that could take place in treaty negotiations with Americans. The Congressional commissioners' chosen meeting place was "Galphinton," a new town west of the Ogeechee River (and therefore on lands the Creeks claimed), named for George Galphin, the trader who had served as Congress's agent during the Revolution. In their role as negotiators with the United States, Hoboithle Miko and Neha Miko went to Galphinton with about sixty Creeks to "protest in the warmest manner against the encroachments" by American immigrants. They declared that their instructions were not to sign anything or even to discuss a treaty until Georgians evacuated the contested lands. The Creeks who went to Galphinton returned with tales of American incompetence. In the presence of the Indian delegates, the Congressional commissioners quarreled with Georgia's commissioners, who wanted to force a treaty even though most of the Creek towns were not represented. The Indians watching saw them as "completely ridiculous."[13]

After the Congressional representatives and most of the Creeks left in disgust, the Georgians again somehow persuaded Hoboithle Miko and Neha Miko to sign a treaty. McGillivray would later deride them as gullible and even "traitors."[14] But in fact, Hoboithle Miko and Neha Miko were men of moderation performing their assigned roles within traditional Creek diplomacy in the face of this strange new tactic, presenting a treaty as a fait accompli. This treaty confirmed the Oconee cession from the disputed 1783 Treaty of Augusta and added a new cession on the coast south of the Altamaha River, lands that were both Creek and within the claims of Spanish East Florida. In exchange, the Georgians pledged to keep settlement off the rest of Creek land.[15]

In late March 1786, the Creek National Council met to discuss what had happened and to decide whether to go to war against Georgia. Leaders from all the major Upper and Lower towns met at the Upper Creek town of Tuckabatchee with that town's Great Chief Mad Dog presiding. Lower Creeks described how when Georgia was a British colony, it was a two-week journey between there and the closest Creek town, but now there were settlements only two days away. Individual Creeks described continually running into Georgians as they hunted on their own lands. Creeks wanted to know from McGillivray if Spain would support them if they went to war. He assured them that the Spanish king "will afford us means of defense . . . of lands that our fathers have owned and possessed, ever since the first rising of the sun and the flowing of the waters." McGillivray also argued in the Council that, as the Indians closest to Georgia, the Creeks had a duty to the Southern Confederacy "to check the Americans in time before they got too strong for us."[16]

The longer that Georgians encroached on Creek hunting lands, the harder it would be to remove them. The Creeks had tried to live peacefully, but the Georgians strong-armed "every straggling Indian hunter" into signing "an instrument of writing, which they falsely call a grant, made them by the Nation." McGillivray deemed this practice of getting Hoboithle Miko and Neha Miko to sign treaties "as unjust as it is absurd." Creeks' "only alternative" was war. After lively discussion, the Creek National Council unanimously resolved "to take arms in our defense and repel those invaders of our lands." They agreed to drive off squatters and destroy their settlements but also to try to avoid bloodshed and not to cross into land they recognized as belonging to the United States. They sent word to the Spanish and other members of the Southern and Northern Confederacies to tell them of the resolution and their hope that they would all "consider the Americans as common enemies."[17]

War was on. After the council, Creek leaders dispersed to their towns to prepare. In mid-April, McGillivray and Mad Dog of Tuckabatchee sent the leaders red war clubs and bundles of sticks indicating

that "the broken days" had begun. The recipient was to make the announcement in his town and then break one stick each day at sunrise.
When the last stick was broken, the warriors were to ready themselves
for battle while their sisters and wives prepared their weapons and
provisions.[18] There were plenty of young men eager for war. Not only
did they support Creek goals of political independence and territorial
defense, they also wanted to fight for the same reasons young men
always had—for the reputation of their clan and town and individual
glory and prestige. When the time came, war parties rode to the
Oconee lands, where they destroyed houses and crops and killed any
squatters who put up a defense. Other war parties joined with Cherokees to raid the Cumberland settlements. By the following spring,
Shawnees joined in the Cumberland raids, and Northern Confederacy Indians renewed attacks in the Ohio Valley and Great Lakes. War
sent squatters fleeing and threw into doubt the claims of speculators.[19]

As the warriors went to war, McGillivray worked to make good on
his promises of Spanish support. In Pensacola he collected musket
balls and gunpowder from West Florida Governor Arturo O'Neill.
After sending those home on packhorses, McGillivray headed west to
New Orleans to meet with Louisiana Governor Esteban Miró. Lower
Creek representatives collected ammunition at Spanish St. Augustine. Creeks and Cherokees used the thousands of pounds of powder,
musket balls, and flints to inflict serious damage on the squatters.[20]

Georgians expressed surprise at the attacks. They had misinter-
preted the lack of Creek violence as a sign that the treaties were valid
and that the settlements were legitimate. According to the Georgia
Assembly, the Creek attacks came without provocation. Georgia
called on Congress for help, but Congress had no funds to support an
expedition and no mandate to send troops at the request of one state.
Similarly, states had no obligation to help one another in time of war,
so Georgia could only attempt to make military alliances with neighboring states. Georgia also sent Colonel Daniel McMurphy, the state's
superintendent of Indian affairs, to try to negotiate with the Lower
Creeks. In early August, the Creek National Council met at Tuckabatchee. Sick with fever, McGillivray fitfully sat through the negotiations. By then, McMurphy had returned home, perhaps fearing Creek

violence, but Neha Miko and Hoboithle Miko delivered his offer to withdraw to Georgia's old boundaries if the Creeks would cede "a small piece of land" on the Oconee.[21] Rather than consent to the peace proposal, the Creeks came to "very spirited resolutions" to continue the war until Georgia admitted that the "Treaty of Augusta" and "Treaty of Galphinton" were invalid.[22] The Council sent Hoboithle Miko and Neha Miko to try to persuade Georgia to, as McGillivray put it, "remove the cause of our dissatisfaction by recalling from the Oconee lands all the individuals settled there, renouncing all idea of pretension to the disputed lands, and by restraining the settlers within the boundaries established and agreed upon in the year 1773, when Georgia belonged to the British government."[23]

Two diplomatic meetings in the spring of 1787 left Creeks unsure whether to continue fighting or to wait and see if their violence thus far was enough to intimidate the United States. First, in April, Congressional Indian Superintendent James White arrived to meet with Creeks and Seminoles in the Lower Towns. Yaholla Miko of Coweta said that elderly Creeks could still remember granting the English permission to build a city on the Savannah River in the 1730s. The English had agreed not to expand beyond Savannah without Creek permission. Yet now "the descendants of a people that have so recently settled on our lands, and have been protected by us," had forgotten the Creeks' gift and were trying "to destroy a nation to which they and their Fathers are so much indebted." It was time for Congress to discipline Georgia.[24]

The Creeks were disgusted to hear from White that he had no authority to remove settlers. When he suggested making peace without removing the illegal settlers, his proposal was unanimously rejected. However, the Creeks agreed to a ceasefire while White explained their case to Congress.[25]

In their second diplomatic meeting that spring, Creeks convened in May and June at Little Tallassee to hear a call to war from a large deputation of Hurons, Mohawks, Oneidas, and Shawnees representing the Northern Confederacy. They advocated joining together "for a general defense against all invaders of Indian rights." Creeks agreed they should work together for the purpose of "restraining the Americans within proper bounds."[26] They gave their assent for the Northern Confederacy to notify the Americans that both confederacies had resolved as a Grand Confederacy of North and South "to attack the Americans in every place wherever they shall pass over their own proper limits, not never to grant them lands, nor suffer surveyors to roam about the country."[27]

Despite the insistence in the Articles of Confederation that "no State shall engage in any war without the consent of the United States in Congress assembled," Congress could not stop Georgia from provoking a war. A few weeks after the council with the Northern Confederacy representatives, several Lower Creeks from the town of Cussita were hunting near some Georgia settlements. They had every expectation of safety. Not only was there a truce, but Cussitas had friendly relations with those settlements. The Cussitas often sold meat to the Georgians before returning home from a hunt. Georgians knew that Cussita Headman Neha Miko had negotiated with them when few other Creeks would and had argued against the war in Creek councils. Despite these ties and the truce, a group of Georgians attacked the Cussita hunters and killed between six and twelve, according to various accounts, and scalped and hacked up the bodies with axes. The survivors attested that the victims had cried out that they were friends from Cussita.[28]

This attack was a serious escalation of a war in which few thus far had died. Creeks were shocked. A letter representing "the voice of the whole Lower Towns" and signed by Neha Miko demanded of Georgia Governor George Mathews to know why Georgians "have killed your friends."[29] Governor Mathews wrote back to Neha Miko apologizing for the "mistake" and trying to divide the Creeks by proposing a truce with only the Lower Creeks.[30] Having traveled to the Lower Towns to deal with the emergency, McGillivray was pleased to witness Neha Miko admonish Georgians for falling "upon our people your real friends."[31] Neha Miko and Hoboithle Miko were the Creeks' primary diplomats with Georgia, and it was within their role, indeed their mandate, to conduct diplomacy even when other Creeks had decided on war. But when Georgia proved itself unworthy of such efforts, Hoboithle Miko and Neha Miko decided it was time for Creek unanimity. They were not alone. From the north to the south, American violence pushed many a moderate Indian leader into thoughts of war.[32]

In September, the Creek National Council resolved "to take vengeance."[33] Hoboithle Miko and McGillivray went together to Pensacola to show their unanimity and collect munitions. Cussitas and Cowetas joined the fight. By November, Creeks had pummeled a force of 150 militia under Revolutionary War hero Brigadier General Elijah Clarke, destroyed multiple settlements, and killed thirty-one white Georgians.[34]

The Southern Confederacy and Chickasaw Independence

To protect the territorial sovereignty of all Indians, supporters of pan-Indian confederation urged Indians to commit resources to common defense. They believed that the best defense would be to protect the whole border around Indian country rather than individual Indian nations. It was a difficult case to make to separate sovereignties. The Creeks had tried to incorporate the Chickasaws into the Creek Confederacy earlier in the century, perhaps on the same terms as the Alabamas. Now McGillivray believed that the Chickasaws had finally agreed to surrender some of their national independence to a Southern Confederacy. A Creek and Cherokee delegation to London in 1791 told crown officials that the Creeks and Cherokees "are now united into one, and are governed by one Council" and that the Chickasaws and Choctaws were now "swayed in all their public measures" by this Council.[35] The Chickasaws and Choctaws, however, did not agree.

The Chickasaws wanted good relations with their Indian neighbors, but they did not believe that they had surrendered independent Chickasaw foreign policy-making to McGillivray and the Creeks. The Chickasaws, like the Choctaws, were far from the American states and were only beginning to experience pressure on their land. They already had direct access to the Spanish and did not need McGillivray's mediation. The Chickasaws even had an additional source of European trade, French traders in the Illinois country, who brought goods from British Canada. They continued Payamataha's strategy of peace.[36]

When Congress invited the Chickasaws to negotiations at Hopewell Plantation on the Seneca River in South Carolina, Chickasaw leaders followed their policy of peace and accepted. On the morning of January 9, 1786, Piomingo and Mingo Taski Etoka formally introduced themselves to Congressional Commissioners Andrew Pickens, Benjamin Hawkins, and Joseph Martin as well as North Carolina's representative, Congressman William Blount. The two Chickasaw headmen presented white strands of beads to signify peace and explained that "our two old leading men are dead," meaning Payamataha in 1785 and Mingo Houma in 1784. Piomingo had taken Payamataha's place as leading diplomat, and Mingo Taski Etoka had taken on the role of Mingo Houma as the Chickasaws' principal civil chief. The new leaders promised that they came "with the same friendly talks" as their predecessors.[37]

The Chickasaws were surprised when the Congressional commissioners presented a draft treaty, although the Creeks could have warned them. As the Chickasaws listened to the interpreter read the treaty, they heard a shocking lack of understanding of the region and its history. The first article declared that, now that the Revolutionary War had ended, "Chickasaws will free all American prisoners and return all negroes and other property." Piomingo protested that the Chickasaws had no American prisoners or property because they had not fought against the Americans. The second article declared the Chickasaws "under the protection of the United States of America, and of no other sovereign whosoever." This was the kind of white lie to which the Chickasaws did not mind agreeing, in the spirit of Payamataha's desire to please everyone. Then the third article began with "The boundary of the lands hereby allotted to the Chickasaw nation to live on and hunt on." Piomingo stood and halted the reading. Congress could not "allot" lands to the Chickasaws. Chickasaw land was Chickasaw land. Piomingo agreed to proceed only once the commissioners assured him that they "were not desirous of getting his land" and that Congress merely wanted "five or six miles square" for "a trading post" at Muscle Shoals on the Tennessee River (now the northwestern corner of Alabama).[38]

An American trading post was exactly what Chickasaws wanted. There had been a British post on Chickasaw land in the 1760s and 1770s, and they missed its convenience. With that assurance, Piomingo "readily acquiesced." Knowing the American reputation for interpreting agreements loosely, Piomingo used a map to mark out the allowed spot and offered that the traders could use some lands north of the Tennessee River to raise crops and livestock for their own use. Piomingo also agreed to the Americans' plea that the Chickasaws not aid ongoing Creek and Cherokee attacks on the Cumberland. Piomingo even let the Americans believe that Chickasaws might consider fighting against the Creeks if they persisted—a typical Chickasaw pledge meant for assisting good relations with the United States, not actually an offer of military action.[39]

Piomingo and Mingo Taski Etoka hoped that the meeting at Hopewell would help protect their lands. Chickasaws had heard tales from Delawares, Shawnees, and Cherokees of hordes of squatters, but they were just now seeing the beginnings of them. During the war, they had allowed loyalist refugees to live in Chickasaw country, but now Americans had joined them, and the hundreds of immigrants were starting to act entitled rather than indebted. Repeatedly, Chickasaws had to tell them that they could not simply build houses or pasture their cattle wherever they liked. At Hopewell, Piomingo complained to the Congressional commissioners that there were too many "white people in our land" ignoring Chickasaw sovereignty. When a new immigrant arrived, those already there would "without our permission, or even asking of it, build a house for him, and settle him among us." Their disrespect for property rights was such that, when a Chickasaw horse got loose, occasionally "they brand him and claim him." The Chickasaws had decided to kick out all of the white people living in the nation except for the most useful traders, but they needed pressure from Congress on its own citizens to make their policy function without bloodshed. The Commissioners agreed that Congress would warn against illegal settlement, and they approved the Chickasaw "right to punish" disobedient whites.[40]

In the past, the decision to give five square miles of Chickasaw land for a trading post or anything else was an exclusively Chickasaw decision. But McGillivray and those who agreed with him had adopted a new concept of pan-Indian confederation, one that Nativists in the Ohio Valley had promoted since the 1760s. McGillivray accused the Chickasaws of ceding land "which belongs to my Nation" and threatened to "chastise that people for their fault." McGillivray went personally to the Chickasaw Nation to try to bring them in line with Confederacy policy.[41]

Like the Chickasaws, the Choctaws and some Cherokees signed treaties with the United States at Hopewell, while Creek and Cherokee advocates of a Southern Confederacy believed it was their right to use violence to dissuade treaty-making without the approval of the Confederacy. Bands of Creeks and Cherokees tailed both the Chickasaws and Choctaws on their way to Hopewell and stole horses and supplies from their camps. Cherokees attacked Piomingo's delegation on their way home, taking the presents the Americans had just given them, while Creeks attacked the returning Choctaws. As soon as McGillivray learned of the Chickasaw cession of Muscle Shoals, a party of Creeks rode there and surprised the Americans who had begun building a post, sending them fleeing without time to collect their goods.[42]

McGillivray's claim was an audacious one, that the Chickasaws had joined a confederacy that now had jurisdiction over their land. To McGillivray and other proponents of the Southern Confederacy, Chickasaw land was now Confederacy land, at least vis-à-vis the Americans, and the whole point of the Confederacy was keeping the Americans out. If Piomingo continued "failing to keep faith with the general Confederation of the other Nations," they had the right to force him "to desist from his friendship" with the Americans. McGillivray informed the Spanish that the Creeks, "together with the other Nations of the Confederation, are resolved to exterminate these friends of the Americans among the Chickasaws."[43] Payamataha would have been shocked at Creek threats to assassinate Piomingo and other Chickasaw leaders for exercising their own nation's independent foreign policy.

As conflict with the Creeks grew, Chickasaws could no longer sustain Payamataha's policy of peace with everyone. Some Chickasaws wondered if it was time to jettison Payamataha's policy and take up arms with the Creeks against the Americans. Right after the convention with the Creeks and Cherokees in 1785, some Chickasaws had circulated a message to the Quapaws and their other allies about joint action if the Americans attacked. These Chickasaws had advised that if Northern and Southern Indians worked together and recruited both British and Spanish support, perhaps "they can destroy them or drive them from all these continents."[44] In 1786, some Chickasaws traveled to Creek country and to Spanish Natchez and Mobile to complain about Chickasaw leadership. The old policy of negotiating with multiple sides would not work if Chickasaw unanimity devolved into real factions and even intra-Chickasaw violence.[45]

While the Chickasaws maintained a tenuous peace, evidence of the need for anti-American action grew. In 1787, one group of American squatters floated down the Ohio and Mississippi rivers and formed a settlement at Wolf Creek, only a half day's journey from a Chickasaw town. Even Piomingo had to agree that "the Americans intend to take all our country before they are done."[46] Attempting to persuade the Americans to move farther away, Piomingo and Mingo Taski Etoka offered them a tract on Chickasaw Bluffs, but many Chickasaws objected to these concessions and were "murmuring that now the Americans had obtained one piece of land in the neighborhood of their Nation they might soon expect to hear of further encroachments."[47] Indeed, within three years, emigration agents were advertising in Maryland for settlers to come to Chickasaw Bluffs, where they could have one hundred acres for $13.50 plus traveling expenses. The advertisement claimed that the Chickasaws were "a peaceable, friendly, and humane people" who had made "repeated and pressing solicitations" for the settlement. If that stretch of the truth did not persuade immigrants, the agent added a big lie: Despite the name, the Chickasaws lived far away from Chickasaw Bluffs, "down in Georgia, about 120 miles distant."[48]

When faced with an American trading post in the heart of Chickasaw country, the Southern Confederacy employed violence to discipline the Chickasaws. In the spring of 1787, when Congress had not renewed its attempt to build a trading post, Piomingo invited Georgia Commissioner William Davenport to build one. As the Georgians were working on construction, a party of Creeks rode in. Not bothering to speak to the Chickasaws and Choctaws present, the Creeks killed Davenport and six others, dispersing the rest. Shocked at this violence on their own land, the Chickasaws "stood nearby speechless." The Creek party headed for home, making a point of riding through Chickasaw towns displaying the seven scalps and seventy rifles they had seized. Soon thereafter, McGillivray sent messages from the Southern and Northern Confederacies to the Chickasaws and Choctaws demanding that they "declare themselves openly, whether we are to consider [them] as friends or not."[49] Chickasaws continued to demand that Congress build a trading post, and a joint Chickasaw-Choctaw delegation traveled to New York in 1787 to press the point. President Washington would attempt again in 1790, in hopes that a military force at Muscle Shoals would "enable us either to intimidate the Creeks or strike them with success," but Creeks, Shawnees, and Cherokees drove off that attempt as well.[50]

McGillivray urged the Spanish to help him punish the Chickasaws. He suggested to Governor Miró that if war against the Chickasaws and Choctaws broke out, they should not receive any Spanish supplies. But he also recommended that if the Chickasaws and Choctaws fell in line, then the Spanish should send them more goods at better prices to prevent American recruitment. For McGillivray, effective violence and improved trade would ideally show the Chickasaws and Choctaws the power of the Southern Confederacy and confirm his position in charge of the Confederacy's foreign relations.[51]

The Spanish Empire and Its Dependencies

Louisiana Governor Esteban Miró agreed that the Chickasaws should not recruit American trade. At the 1784 Mobile congress, the Chickasaws had agreed not to admit any trader without a Spanish passport. Yet not only had they allowed Americans into northeastern

Chickasaw territory, they had also given William Davenport a spot for a trading post near the Mississippi River, clearly within Spanish dominion right across the Mississippi from the Spanish colonial town of Ste. Geneviève. Still, Spanish officials' vision of their alliance with southeastern Indians was not the same as Alexander McGillivray's. The Spanish believed they were in charge. Indian nations could govern themselves internally but should follow Spanish guidance in foreign relations. In fact, the Spanish view looked a lot like both Britain's wartime view of Indians and McGillivray's view of the Southern Confederacy, but with Spanish officials on top. Indians should be dependencies within a strong and expanding Spanish empire.[52]

Despite these differences of opinion, the Spanish relationship with southeastern Indians could work well as long as they maintained mutually compatible layers of sovereignty. The Upper, Lower, and Seminole towns, paths, and agricultural and hunting lands were Creek but within the claims of the Spanish empire. Although colonial officials pined for true control, they knew that the Creeks controlled their lands. The Creeks in turn did not mind if European mapmakers labeled their region Spanish. When an American emissary tried to persuade West Florida Governor Arturo O'Neill that the United States and Spain were on the same side against the "savage" nature of Indians, O'Neill saw this rhetoric for what it was, an attempt to get Spanish arms out of Creek hands. O'Neill's representative responded with Spain's own self-serving but more accurate principle of Indian sovereignty, claiming that the governor "makes it a rule never to direct or influence anything that the Assemblies of the Nations ought to decide." The Pensacola Congress, he explained, granted Creeks and others "the commerce and the protection of our Monarch . . . without encroaching on their laws or customs."[53]

Disputed lands on the edges of Creek country were more complicated for Spain. Spanish officials sympathized with the Creek argument that Georgians were squatting "on their hunting lands" and that Spain's treaties with southeastern Indians obligated it to protect them from the encroachments.[54] The responsibility was double if the lands also fell within Spain's colonial borders. Diego de Gardoqui and John Jay still had not rendered a treaty delineating the border between

Spanish colonies and the United States. If the Spanish empire extended as far east and north as King Carlos III maintained, then Georgians had settled on Spanish land without permission. However, if the border with the United States was west of Oconee, things got trickier. For their part, Georgians interpreted sovereignty unilaterally. To them, these lands were part of Georgia, and they could not be ruled by Spain, the Creeks, or even their own Congress. At least some Georgians extended their border claim to the Mississippi River and believed that all of Creek country was "within the State of Georgia." In these Georgians' view, Indians had no "rights at all but what are subservient to or dependent on the legislative will of the State claiming Jurisdiction over the lands they live and hunt on."[55]

Spain's policy was secretly to fund Creek action, making it impossible for Americans to settle beyond Spain's ideal borders and thereby persuading Congress to agree to Spain's treaty terms. Gálvez instructed Miró to give the Creeks powder, ball, and guns but "with the greatest secrecy and dissimulation." Miró was to pretend that they were regular trade goods for hunting, not war supplies. If the Americans retaliated against the Creeks on land that was either clearly within the Spanish empire or disputed between Spain and the United States, then Miró was authorized to force them all the way back across the Oconee.[56] Keeping thousands of pounds of muskets, powder, and ball secret was not actually possible, of course. The keepers of the royal warehouses in St. Augustine, Pensacola, Mobile, and New Orleans could try to hide the transfer, but they had to involve scores of clerks and laborers. More to the point, secrecy was not in the Creeks' interest. Creeks pointedly boasted to Americans of Spanish support, hoping to intimidate Americans into compliance.[57]

Hiding Spanish support and debating the exact line between the United States and Spanish West Florida mattered little to Creeks. It was all Creek country, and they had a right to defend it. If Spain was truly their ally, it should help protect all Creek lands against incursions that flew in the face of international diplomacy. Creeks had the sovereign right to defend their own territory and make alliances to assist in that defense.

For Spain, however, the path to imperial control over its colonies did not set a high value on the independence of Indians. In 1786, based on his experience on the Gulf Coast, Gálvez devised the official instructions for Indian relations in the northern part of the empire. Bernardo de Gálvez was soon in a position to implement his vision of expanding the Spanish empire with the help of Indian allies. Like British Indian Superintendent John Stuart in the 1760s and 1770s, Gálvez had come to believe that Indians held a vital place in European imperialism. If Indians agreed to exclusive trade and protected their interior lands from rival European empires and the United States, the relationship would work well. In the short term, faithful Indian allies should receive guns, gunpowder, ammunition, and other manufactured goods. But Gálvez's long-term goal was Indian dependence. "Accustomed to guns and powder," Indians would forget how to make and use bows and arrows and eventually be "unable to do without us." Then the Spanish could truly rule. Dependent on European goods, Indians might "possibly improve their customs by following our good example, voluntarily embracing our religion and vassalage." If not, Spain could disarm them and control them by force.[58]

Governor Miró tried to apply Gálvez's strategy of transforming the Creeks into dependent vassals. Aiming to rein in Creek independence and control their relations with the United States, Miró in March 1787 ordered that Creek supplies be cut off to encourage them to make a truce with the Americans. Miró figured that the Creek victories thus far would make Georgians agree to Creek terms. Stopping the war now would leave Georgians cowering on their side of the Creek border but prevent the war from drawing in the Spanish or other states. Miró ordered Governor O'Neill at Pensacola not to give the Creeks any more munitions unless the Georgians attacked them at home, a decision supported by Miró's superiors. The king agreed that the Creeks should be on the defensive and hold on to their munitions "in case they are invaded."[59] To the Spanish, this seemed a reasonable policy toward all concerned and the most likely to strengthen Spanish authority over its allies and to curb the United States without making it into an enemy. In the coming years, the decision to withhold arms would have disastrous consequences for both the Creeks and the Spanish.

The Independent Nations of
Kentucky, Cumberland, and Franklin?

Alongside the United States, Spanish and British colonies, and Indian nations, a new kind of polity arose in the decades right after the
Revolution: settlements of Americans who imagined futures outside
the United States. In the twenty-first century, after the United States
has prospered for more than two centuries, it is hard to imagine early
Americans who did not feel they needed to remain part of the United
States. Yet supporting American independence from Britain and the
creation of a kingless republic did not mean that all Americans believed that they should forever be part of the United States. There
could be more American republics on this vast continent if the U.S.
federal government did not suit all of their needs, and people might
reject republicanism completely if it could not keep them secure. Indeed, Kentucky and other settlements west of the Appalachians operated largely as independent republics in the 1780s and most of the
1790s. Yet the need for trade and security meant that these small settlements could not stand completely alone. They would need allies.
Spain offered these farmers, speculators, and merchants exactly the
kind of future that Oliver Pollock had imagined during the war but
now found himself too indebted to enjoy.[60]

Throughout the 1780s, Americans were moving west from the thirteen original states in droves. Before the Revolution, immigrants had
come through the Cumberland Gap from Virginia or down the Ohio
River from Pennsylvania, in violation of Britain's Proclamation of
1763 forbidding trans-Appalachian settlement. They founded the
"Watauga" or "Holston" settlements at the headwaters of the Tennessee River and "Kentucky" in and around Danville and Lexington
(named in 1775 for the victory over the British in Massachusetts).
Shawnee and Cherokee attacks during the Revolutionary War cleared
out these settlements, but immediately after the war, large numbers of
immigrants moved back, assuming that the peace included Indians.
Others even moved west of Holston to the Cumberland River Valley
around Nashville. By the end of 1785 some twenty-five thousand set-

tlers lived in the Kentucky region, growing corn, wheat, tobacco, hemp, and cotton, which they traded overland through Fort Pitt (Pittsburgh), much of the corn as distilled whiskey. Holston and Cumberland were smaller settlements, mostly hunting for the fur trade, but they were growing. Farther south than Kentucky, these communities could not develop commercial agriculture without access to the Mississippi.[61]

Settlers came for economic opportunities, which depended on access to land and markets, and they were likely to award their loyalty to whatever political entity could help them raise and sell cash crops. George Washington observed that "the Western States . . . stand as it were upon a pivot. The touch of a feather would turn them any way." He wanted Congress to invest in canals and roads that would give westerners access to East Coast port cities and keep them away from Spain's or Britain's promises. Oriented toward the U.S. economy, they would be not only loyal but also industrious and republican citizens, and their participation in turn would secure eastern merchants' commitment to an expanding interior.[62]

Congress had no funds to build an infrastructure linking east and west, so western settlements continued to protest that Congress and the states were endangering their lives and livelihoods. For example, Holston was part of North Carolina, but settlers there felt that the state was not protecting the interests of its citizens west of the Appalachians. They believed that their state had an obligation to defend them against Chickasaws, Cherokees, and Creeks who opposed the settlements. Small-scale settlers wanted their state to reduce the power of speculators, while speculators lobbied for state recognition of large land possessions, which they could then sell for a profit. Both expected either the North Carolina legislature or Congress to win them access to the Mississippi and the port of New Orleans, by diplomacy or force.

When their frustration with North Carolina reached the breaking point, the residents of Holston in 1784 declared their independence from North Carolina and constituted themselves as the State of Franklin, named in honor of Benjamin Franklin. At first, the State of Franklin asked Congress for admission back into the United States as the fourteenth state, but North Carolina wanted it back. In Congress, only seven states voted in favor of approving its statehood, when the Articles of Confederation required nine to admit a new state. Writing from Paris, Jefferson himself spoke for many Americans who feared that if Congress admitted this breakaway settlement, the "states will crumble to atoms by the spirit of establishing every little canton into a separate state."[63]

People in Franklin and the other western settlements found themselves dissatisfied with their status in the United States. They had many of the problems of the formerly British colonies, including insufficient representation in faraway legislative bodies and the sense that they received little benefit from those who claimed them. Indeed, in Franklin's deliberations over whether to secede from North Carolina, one delegate pulled a copy of the Declaration of Independence from his pocket and paralleled the grievances listed by Thomas Jefferson in 1776 with theirs in 1784. If the American republic could not give them access to markets and protection from Indians who opposed their land claims, perhaps an empire could.[64]

Believing that independent trans-Appalachian states would be too vulnerable and isolated from markets, some people imagined creating countries allied with Spain or even colonies within the Spanish empire. Men with plans for the trans-Appalachian West streamed into Diego de Gardoqui's New York City house at the southern end of Broadway, close to soldiers drilling at the Battery and Bowling Green, where there had once been a statue of King George III. Some of the visitors were Europeans, such as Pedro Wouver d'Arges and Prussian Revolutionary War hero Baron Friedrich von Steuben. Others were U.S. officials and officeholders going behind the back of their government.[65]

Representatives from the western part of North Carolina even considered independence. During the Congressional debates in the summer of 1786 over whether to change John Jay's instructions and accept a Spanish treaty that did not include access to the Mississippi, North Carolina Congressman James White (who would soon meet the Creeks as superintendent of Indian affairs in the Southern District) introduced himself to Gardoqui as a large landowner in the

Cumberland settlements and an Irish Catholic. White informed Gardoqui that if easterners in Congress managed to push through the bill to change Jay's instructions, the people of Cumberland "will consider themselves abandoned by the Confederation and will act independently." If Spain would offer Cumberland access to the Mississippi and the port of New Orleans, "His Catholic Majesty will acquire their eternal goodwill and they, as an Independent State, will draw closer to His Majesty." Allied with Spain, the independent state of Cumberland would "serve as a barrier" to U.S. expansion.[66] In later decades, this kind of negotiation between a U.S. Congressman and a foreign diplomat would obviously be treason, but in the 1780s, White could argue that the fate of the west was still unsettled. Just in case, though, he kept his negotiations secret.

Gardoqui was delighted to receive leaders from other western settlements who also proposed secret plans that involved independent states under Spain's protection. John Sevier was a militia commander who had fought Dragging Canoe's Chickamauga Cherokees during and after the Revolution and now had been elected governor of Franklin. He wrote to Gardoqui to request Spanish negotiation between Franklin and the Cherokees and the rest of the Southern Confederacy. In Franklin after his meeting with Gardoqui, James White (still a member of Congress) reported that Franklin's "leading men" were willing to swear an oath of allegiance to the Spanish king and "abjure the authority of and dependence on, any other power" as long as they could have their own independent "civil police, and internal government."[67] Virginia Congressman John Brown, who lived in Virginia's Kentucky counties, added to the chorus, assuring Gardoqui that "there was not the slightest doubt that the Kentucky assembly would resolve to set up an independent state, unless war with the Indians threatened them to such an extent that" they had to run back to Congress for help.[68] If Spain could help the western settlements obtain uncontested possession of the land and a market for their products and protect them from Indians, they might, as James White put it, "preserve their independence from the American Republics."[69]

While Diego de Gardoqui was hearing these plans in New York, other Spanish officials received similar offers. In London, displaced loyalists approached the Spanish ambassador to offer to establish towns on the northeastern edge of Spain's colonies "in order to form a strong barrier to check any aggression on the part of the United States of America."[70] Kentuckian James Wilkinson traveled to New Orleans to propose an alliance between Spain and an independent Kentucky. In July 1787, Wilkinson introduced himself to Louisiana Governor Esteban Miró as a U.S. brigadier general during the Revolution, not mentioning that he had been forced to resign his commission after being accused of corruption and plotting to remove George Washington as the Continental Army's commander-in-chief. Wilkinson declared that Kentucky's leading men had sent him to New Orleans "to open a negotiation" with Spain "to admit us under its protection as vassals." Wilkinson compared Kentucky's situation in 1787 to that of the thirteen rebellious colonies in 1776. Debts from the Revolutionary War had made Virginia into the same "oppressive" taxer that Britain had been. What good were governments that sacrificed western interests for eastern ones and levied high taxes without providing western settlers equal representation or "defense against the savages"? If westerners had access to New Orleans, their "forcible dependency" on manufactured goods "will cease, and with it all motives for the conjunction with the other side of Appalachian Mountains." Wilkinson predicted that Franklin and Cumberland would follow Kentucky and create "a distinct confederation of the inhabitants of the West" and "a friendly understanding with Spain."[71]

The following year, Miró heard similar proposals from a more familiar man: Oliver Pollock. Now out of jail, Pollock had begun to imagine that the postwar world he had worked for, one that tied the agricultural produce of Kentucky and the Ohio Valley to Spanish markets around the world, might happen without the United States. In Philadelphia, he met James Brown, a member of Virginia's Congressional delegation from the Kentucky counties. Brown told Pollock, as he also told James Madison and Thomas Jefferson, that Kentuckians were so upset with Congress's reluctance to let them separate from Virginia that they would soon declare themselves an independent republic with a commercial relationship with Spain. This move would open a lively Mississippi River trade in flour, tobacco, and slaves, and Pollock would be the ideal merchant to manage it. Brown had promised to send Pollock the independence resolution as soon as it passed so that Pollock could give it to Miró to pass up to the crown. Perhaps the Pollocks' future could lie with Spain and discontented Americans.[72]

As Pollock prepared to travel to New Orleans, he heard that a devastating fire in March 1788 had leveled New Orleans northwest of the Place d'Armes and destroyed the Cabildo from which Bernardo de Gálvez had inspired New Orleanians after the hurricane of 1779. As Pollock loaded his ship for the journey, he included building materials and a pump fire engine bought from Benjamin Franklin to give to Miró, in hopes of getting back on the governor's good side. In New Orleans, Pollock told Governor Miró of the Kentuckians' situation and proposed to import flour and tobacco from Kentucky, as well as Philadelphia if possible, free from duties, into New Orleans and to Spanish ports beyond. The income could go toward paying his debt to New Orleans merchants and the Spanish government. Miró granted Pollock's request but had to inform him that he had already extended the same privilege to James Wilkinson.[73]

Miró, Gardoqui, and other Spanish officials were too dazzled by the temptation of creating anti-American dependencies to remember that such rebellious citizens were unlikely to be dependable subjects or allies. Following Bernardo de Gálvez's wartime model of offering British West Floridians security, land, and markets, they eagerly welcomed American dissidents. While encouraging U.S. citizens to rebel against their government was not internationally acceptable, Miró wrote, "should it happen that they could obtain their absolute independence from the United States," then Spain might treat them like any other nation regardless of Congress's opinion.[74] And at least some of Franklin and Cumberland fell within Spain's land claims anyway. The time seemed right to take advantage of, as Governor Miró put it, "the state bordering on anarchy in which the Federative Government of the United States finds itself."[75]

Similarly, Gardoqui explained to the crown that there was danger ahead for the Spanish empire "if this rapidly-growing young Empire," the United States, "unites as it grows"; however, if Spain acted now, it could win them, not by force but "by tact and generosity, leaving them their customs, religion and laws, on the supposition that in time they will be imperceptibly drawn to ours," especially because their own government was so incompetent.[76] If Spain did not act, Britain surely would gobble up these places, adding them to Canada and perhaps eventually taking Louisiana, exactly what James Bruce and Lord Dunmore had proposed. Then the Gulf Coast victories would be lost, and Britain would "bless the day her colonies rebelled and thus brought her this opportunity."[77] Gardoqui hoped Congress might even let the west go willingly, realizing that spreading west would hurt the United States by draining its population and bringing down eastern property values with too much cheap land. King Carlos III wholeheartedly agreed. In 1788, he legalized the sale of Mississippi and Ohio Valley goods out of New Orleans, and he offered free trade to men working to separate from the United States.[78]

From Spain's perspective, it all could work out perfectly for Spain as well as for Indians and trans-Appalachian immigrants, all of whom should recognize that they needed a strong and benevolent sovereign to keep the peace and promote prosperity. Even some people on the ground envisioned cooperation. In the spring of 1788, emissaries from Cumberland traveled to Creek country to tell Alexander McGillivray "that Cumberland and Kentucky were determined to free themselves from a dependence on Congress, as that body could not or would not protect their persons and property nor encourage their commerce." The men from Cumberland said that they were willing to be allies of the Creeks and subjects to the Spanish king.[79]

In return for becoming dependents of Spain, western immigrants wanted Spain to prevent Indian attacks, thereby providing safety for their families and a secure possession of the land. James Robertson of Nashville informed Governor Miró that Cumberland was "daily plundered and its inhabitants murdered by the Creeks, and Cherokees, unprovoked." Surely the rumors were untrue that Spain was "encouraging the Indians to make war on us and furnishing them with ammunition." If Spain could provide the protection that Congress could not, the Cumberland settlers would "remain a grateful people."[80] Of course Miró had supplied Creek and Cherokee attacks in the past and knew both that the violence was not "unprovoked" and that he had little power to stop Indians from retaliating when Americans invaded their lands. Still, Miró urged McGillivray to make peace with settlements that were willing to ally with Spain.[81]

The problems in Spain's promise of protection and prosperity to both Indians and former Americans were evident in the State of Franklin's demand to "increase their territory by being allowed to extend along the Cherokee and Tennessee Rivers" to the headwaters of the Yazoo and Mobile rivers. These lands might or might not be within the Spanish empire, but they were indisputably within the purview of the Creeks and the Southern Confederacy. Spanish officials recognized that the land requests violated, as one official put it, "the equity with which the Indians should be treated, leaving them lands for hunting and cultivation."[82] But westward immigrants did not much care about that kind of equity, and neither did Indian nations, who completely rejected the idea of being *left* only some of their lands.

Ultimately the Spanish hoped to use their access to resources and the world beyond North America to create dependencies of Indians and former Americans, all under a rising empire. John Jay worried that they would succeed and split Americans "into three or four independent and probably discordant republics or confederacies, one inclining to Britain, another to France, and a third to Spain, and perhaps played off against each other by the three." Then, Jay concluded, "what a poor, pitiful figure will America make." Spaniards and Indians thought this future seemed just about right.[83]

Americans into Spaniards

Another group of Americans offered to become Spanish subjects directly, by immigrating to the Spanish Floridas and Louisiana. Moving one's family out of the U.S. republic and into a Catholic foreign colony seems like a step backward from Revolution and away from independence, but these families did not see it that way. Like other Americans, they sought land and access to markets, the building blocks of personal and familial independence. Seeking them in a stable colony seemed more promising than creating a new independent nation surrounded by more powerful colonies and Indian nations.

To Spain, inviting American immigration was less politically controversial than undermining the United States by arming Indians or encouraging regions to separate. Although Bernardo de Gálvez had warned Miró to "remain very cautious" about American immigrants and had even barred settlement by Protestants after the Treaty of Paris, by 1787 Miró believed that disappointment with Congress might turn immigrants into good Spanish subjects.[84] Surely "men who have lived under a precarious government, that did not give them any protection, surrounded by the peril of Indians, destitute of trade," would be loyal to a government that in contrast "protects them, facilitates an outlet for their products, decides their controversies with justice without exacting any tribute or molesting them in their domestic operations." Spain could win the affection of the immigrant generation, and future generations "will know no other fatherland than this one."[85]

Miró offered immigrants a deal designed to make them grateful subjects. Any "good inhabitant" was welcome to a land grant big enough for a family farm, from about two hundred acres for a small household to nearly seven hundred for a large one. Every head of a family must "take the due oath of allegiance to his most Catholic Majesty," agreeing "to take up arms in defense of this province against whatsoever enemy who could attempt to invade it." Once they swore allegiance, they would "enjoy the same franchises and privileges" as other subjects and "be governed by the same laws and customs." They would have a free market at New Orleans for their produce, exempt from all duties and taxes. They would not be required to convert to Catholicism or financially support the church, although "no public worship shall be allowed but that of the Roman Catholic Church." Some could have the plantations that James and Isabella Bruce and other fleeing loyalists had left behind on the Amite and surrounding rivers just west of the Mississippi.[86]

Thousands of Americans accepted Spain's offer. Some were speculators seeking to organize new settlements and sell off the land in smaller parcels or at least extract payments for transportation. Most were landless Americans hoping to find the family independence promised by the Revolution by owning their own small farms, even if those farms ended up within the Spanish empire. The typical immigrants looked like the Richards family of Kentucky: a husband, wife, and one child, who floated down the Ohio and Mississippi rivers to Natchez, bringing with them their only property: an ax. The immigrants floated downriver by the hundreds on ramshackle rafts. Miró noted that the boats had no keels or oars. They could only float downriver—it was "impossible to make them return."[87] Twentieth-century America saw many episodes of refugees piling into flimsy boats, trying to reach the promise of the United States. In the late eighteenth century, it was Americans who put all they owned on quickly constructed vessels to float toward Spanish opportunity.

Colonel George Morgan, who as Congress's Indian affairs agent during the Revolutionary War had proposed invading West Florida and making it the fourteenth state, chose Spanish over American opportunity. In 1788, he collected investors, including Oliver Pollock and Aaron Burr, into a New Jersey Land Society and received permission from Congress to buy a large tract of land in the Illinois country. Congress granted permission but at a higher price than Morgan had requested, two dollars for every three acres rather than one dollar. While Morgan was considering the terms, he was also discussing with Gardoqui a similar idea, but in Spanish Louisiana. In January 1789, Morgan left Pittsburgh with four boats carrying about sixty adults and children, many of whom were German immigrants, for a place on the Mississippi River that he called "New Madrid." Using his investors' funds, Morgan planned to sell the lands to the settlers and make a tidy profit since Spain was giving the land away.[88]

Part of Morgan's advertising to potential settlers was that "there is not a single nation or tribe of Indians, who claim, or pretend to claim a foot of the land." Indeed, while most of Spain's empire north of Mexico was owned and occupied by Indians, New Madrid, west of the Mississippi River, actually was Spain's to give away. Nearby Osages and Quapaws did not use that land and believed that a post would bring useful trade to the region. Morgan chose a site on the west bank of the Mississippi about forty-five miles downriver from where the Ohio met the Mississippi, where the settlers believed they could grow corn, tobacco, hemp, flax, cotton, and indigo. They began laying out a planned town with wide tree-lined streets, cabins surrounded by women's vegetable gardens, and farms for the men outside of town.[89]

Despite New Madrid's pro-Spanish name, its founder undermined Spanish authority. When Miró received Morgan's report, he charged him with trying to establish "a Republic within [Spain's] own domains." Morgan was not supposed to sell land that "His Majesty concedes gratis." Also, Morgan had distributed land in parcels from 320 to a shocking 4,800 acres, much larger than the king's allowance of two hundred to seven hundred acres. And Morgan had apparently neglected to inform the settlers that they needed to swear an oath of loyalty to Spain and refrain from public Protestant worship. Even the sycophantic name was offensive. Naming cities "is a right belonging only to the Sovereign."[90] Morgan promised to follow the rules in the future, but Miró glimpsed the independence these new supposed Spanish subjects might assume.[91]

While Spaniards weighed the benefits against the dangers, Indians saw no value at all in welcoming American immigration. These were the very people the Creeks wanted to push back to the Atlantic coast. McGillivray swore that "filling up your country with those accursed republicans is like placing a common thief as a guard on your door and giving him the key in his pocket." As trader William Panton tried to explain to Miró, the Creeks did not believe these recent Americans had really become Spanish subjects, "for it is a phenomenon quite beyond their comprehension to conceive it possible that a set of men who so wantonly throw away their natural sovereign can be serious in placing themselves under the Government of another."[92]

Much more troubling to the Creeks and Choctaws than the trans-Mississippi settlements was the one the Spanish allowed in the hunting lands right between Choctaw and Creek territories on the Tombigbee River north of Mobile. Many of these immigrants were refugees from Creek attacks on the Cumberland who had presented themselves in Spanish New Orleans and Mobile to ask for protection.

Choctaws attacked the Tombigbee settlements and recruited Alabamas and Creeks to help. McGillivray told the Spanish that he was urging Alabamas and Creeks not to join the attack, but he may in fact have supported it. He and his sister Sophia had a plantation not far from these new settlements to raise livestock to sell at Pensacola and had actually invited British traders and loyalist officers they had known during the war to settle there. But the new immigrants were far more numerous and soon began to spread beyond the lower Tombigbee, deeper into Creek and Choctaw country. During the winter of 1788-1789, Creek hunters came across surveyors marking lines ten miles from Little Tallassee itself. McGillivray explained that the uncontrolled spreading "is a thing that I always feared would happen ever since I first knew the intention of the government to introduce Americans." The Spanish now were seeing firsthand what Indians in the east already knew: "the disposition to usurp that the Americans have if once they are allowed to establish themselves."[93]

The Creeks Seek New Allies

The acceleration of Spanish-sponsored immigration at the same time that Governor Miró cut off supplies for the Creek war against Georgia shook the Spanish-Creek alliance to its core. The Spanish had hoped that both the Creeks and the Americans would be impressed by Spain's ability to bring peace and prosperity to its Indian and non-Indian dependents, but Indians felt betrayed and alarmed. While Miró claimed that the immigrants had become "true Spaniards," McGillivray believed they were still "Americans in their hearts."[94] He reminded Miró that the security of Spanish West Florida and Louisiana depended on "the security of our establishment as an Independent Nation."[95] Creek independence should not worry Spain. The strong allies could stand together against the disjointed American states. With Creeks united in the decision for war and "victorious over the Americans in every quarter," the best course now would be "following up the blows lately given to those turbulent people with vigour."[96]

Miró's decision then to cut off supplies was disastrous for McGillivray's position at home. His role was to nurture the connections that would provide economic and military security. Creeks demanded to know from him whether Spain was still committed to containing the Americans and providing arms and ammunition. McGillivray asked Miró for a copy of the Royal Order that King Carlos III had issued after the 1784 congress to prove to the Creeks that the Spanish had pledged to supply their war. But the Spanish continued to disappoint. Miró sent McGillivray a copy of the Royal Order but, fearing that it would fall into American hands, deleted the part that explicitly mentioned supplying "Alexander McGillivray all of the guns that he has requested for the Creek Indians to attack the Americans."[97]

Not only had McGillivray promised Spanish supplies to the Creeks, he was also supplying the Cherokees as part of trying to build the Southern Confederacy. Geographically on the other side of the Spanish from Creek country, the Cherokees expected McGillivray to funnel munitions to them. As he tried to persuade the Spanish to change their minds, McGillivray also pursued three means of reducing Creek dependence on Spanish supplies. He made overtures to selected Americans, frightened the Spanish with the specter of an alliance between the Southern Confederacy and the United States, and considered a proposal to renew the Creek-British alliance.

First, McGillivray built American connections. He wrote the Congressional commissioners that the Creeks were ready to "begin again on new ground." They would make peace if Georgia would "retire from the Oconee lands to within the limits prescribed to that State when it was a British province."[98] Although the Creeks and Georgia did not reach an agreement, McGillivray's overtures did lead to a new truce. McGillivray also welcomed peace offers from Cumberland and Franklin. James Robertson told McGillivray that Cumberland was devastated by Creek attacks and had sent him to seek good relations with the Creeks and the Spanish. McGillivray heard from Franklin Governor John Sevier that his state, "now in rebellion to Congress," desired friendship with the Creeks.[99]

McGillivray did not trust these "crafty, cunning, republicans." Rather, he used his negotiations with Congress, Georgia, Cumberland, and Franklin to remind the Spanish that they did not want the Creeks and the United States to get too friendly. He wrote West Florida Governor Arturo O'Neill that the Georgians and Congress seemed ready not only to "secure us in all our claims to our lands" but also to give the Creeks free access to American ports.[100] If the Americans bought the products of the Creek hunt for good rates and sold goods from London for prices that undercut Spain, the Creeks would revoke their pledge to trade exclusively with Spanish-approved traders, and Gálvez and Miró's goal of Indian dependence would be lost. Miró warned McGillivray to "refrain from making any commercial treaty."[101]

With Spain surprisingly unhelpful and the United States predictably so, a rumor that the British wanted to get involved again in the southeast was welcome news. The bearer was William Augustus Bowles, a young man from a Maryland loyalist family who had joined the Maryland Loyalists Battalion in 1777, at the age of fourteen. Sent to West Florida with the Maryland Loyalists the following year, Bowles had been dishonorably dismissed from British service for insubordination. After that, he lived for a year with a Lower Creek family, the Perrymans, near where the Chattahoochee and Flint rivers come together to form the Apalachicola River. Among the Creeks, Bowles found what he later described as "a situation so flattering to the independence natural in the heart of man."[102] Like many outsiders who visited Indian communities, he imagined that Indians were free to do as they liked, failing to see the obligations of community and labor that bound members of an Indian town just as surely as any other kind of polity. Compared with the British army, his status as a guest in Creek country certainly granted him new independence of movement. Bowles later claimed that the Lower Creeks had adopted him, which is possible. Many Indians of the eastern woodlands practiced adoption, allowing outsiders to join a clan and become one of their people if they gave up their old identity and fully embraced the new.[103]

After the war, Bowles would try to open trade between southeastern Indians and the British in the Bahamas. In 1781, Bowles had been reinstated in the British army, so he was among the troops evacuated from Pensacola after the Spanish victory, perhaps in the same ship as James and Isabella Bruce. Disinclined to return to Maryland as a traitor or to accept the British offer of land in snowy Acadia (which the British had taken from Amand Broussard's family), Bowles spent some time in the Bahamas and then returned to the Perrymans in the mid-1780s. There, Bowles heard his Lower Creek friends' new frustrations with Spanish trade—high prices for European goods, low payments for their furs, and Miró's recent decision to cut off military aid. As he listened, Bowles made a plan.[104]

By 1788, Bowles had returned once again to the Bahamas, where he exaggerated his influence in Creek country to John Miller, a member of His Majesty's Council for the Bahamas who operated a trading house. Bowles explained that Spain had licensed William Panton and John Leslie to provide the trade but that, with "his own influence," an ambitious trading house like Miller's would find that "nothing could be easier than to supplant them."[105] Miller had reason to believe him. In the 1770s, he was a trader in West Florida and a member of His Majesty's Council for West Florida, along with James Bruce. When the Spanish took over in 1781, Miller had fled to the Bahamas but was captured when the Spanish invaded there and until the war's end was imprisoned in Havana, where he had months to plot his return to West Florida. Miller introduced Bowles to Lord Dunmore, who became governor of the Bahamas after Britain lost Virginia and South Carolina. Bowles persuaded Dunmore that together they could enact Dunmore's earlier idea of recruiting loyalists, Indians, and slaves to take West Florida and Louisiana from Spain.[106]

When Bowles sent word to the Creeks of his new British connections, McGillivray and others were eager to trade. Although McGillivray quickly identified Bowles as one of the "vagrant and needy men, allured with prospects of mending broken fortunes by plunder to be gained in war," the times were right for a new military supplier in Creek country.[107] McGillivray knew that reestablishing trade with Britain would give the Creeks leverage over the Spanish, the United States, and other Indians of the Southern Confederacy. Trade from the Bahamas would particularly satisfy the Seminoles, who repeatedly complained to the Spanish and in the Creek National Council about insufficient trade at their closest port, Spanish San Marcos. Hearing that Bowles had promised to land on the Gulf's Apalachee Bay, not far from San Marcos, McGillivray sent fifty packhorses in the summer of 1788 to collect the anticipated goods. But contrary to rumors of abundant supplies, only two or three small vessels landed, and even those had scant supplies on them. Another promised vessel had either wrecked, been seized by the Spanish, or never actually existed.[108]

In Coweta for a council, McGillivray met with William Bowles, who gave him a sword and a regimental uniform on behalf of Governor Dunmore and the British crown. As McGillivray recorded, Bowles offered "to procure us a supply of arms and ammunition" and gather loyalist troops from around the British empire to join the Creeks and other Indians "in making war and defending our country from being seized upon by the Americans." The two men had a fruitful conversation about their shared experiences in the siege of Pensacola, their opposition to Americans, and their plans for a future of Creek prominence in regional trade.[109]

To each side, Bowles exaggerated his influence with the other, setting up both for disappointment. Bowles returned to the Bahamas in the fall of 1788 wearing a red turban and other Creek clothes and making the outrageous claim that McGillivray had "ceded" to him "all the authority and influence he possessed among the Creek Indians." Bowles claimed that he was now "effectually king and Commander in Chief of the Creek Nation, by virtue of McGillivray's cession to him of that power and dignity." Bowles and John Miller recruited men for an expedition to Creek country, pledging to give them Creek land to be worked by the slaves they would seize from Georgia. He said the job would be easy because the Creeks would help expel the Spanish. In late September, Bowles and his men landed two armed schooners at Mosquito Lagoon on Florida's Atlantic coast about eighty miles south of St. Augustine. Despite his promises, the Seminoles and Lower Creeks did not rush to their aid. Most of his followers deserted and fled to the Spanish. By the time Bowles stumbled into the Lower Creek Towns three months later with his five remaining followers, Creeks and Seminoles had come to doubt the

William Augustus Bowles wearing Creek attire, painted on his trip to London by Thomas Hardy, 1790–1791. (Image No. 1012620, Upton House, Warwickshire, British National Trust)

British connections he had claimed the previous summer. McGillivray sent his brother-in-law Louis LeClerc Milfort to accompany Bowles and a few Creeks and Chickamauga Cherokees to Apalachee Bay. As December turned into January, they waited, and still no ship came into sight.[110]

It had become clear that Bowles was not the key to a renewed Creek-British alliance. When a fishing boat finally arrived, weeks later, it only confirmed Creek and Cherokee doubts. The Indians could see by the boat's size as it approached that it could not contain "a tenth of the goods, flour, and munitions that he promised on his first journey."[111] When the vessel landed, it revealed another cargo of mostly heavy munitions: what Bowles wanted for bombarding Spanish posts but not the light arms and other goods that Creeks needed.

The Creeks and Cherokees packed the cannons and the few other goods on their horses and carried them away. Following McGillivray's instructions, Milfort ordered Bowles to "leave the Nation never to return to it."[112] Echoing West Floridians' opinion of James Willing, McGillivray concluded that Bowles's "backers have chosen an instrument not at all appropriate for such undertakings. . . . He does not seem to be suited for great things."[113]

Still, Bowles seemed to have the ear of important Britons, so a semi-official Creek and Chickamauga Cherokee delegation accompanied him to London to make their case to King George III. British officials were desperate enough for an insider in the southeast that high-level ministers including British Home Secretary William Grenville (son of the prime minister who instituted the Stamp Act back in 1765) met with them. Reluctant to anger Spain, King George did not receive them himself, but Grenville accepted their letter to the king.

In the letter, the Creeks and Cherokees reiterated a proposal that Creeks had been making to Spain and Britain since at least the 1770s: the right of independent Indian nations to trade on the same basis as other polities. They argued that Britain should include the Creek and Cherokee Nations in its Free Port Act, which had opened trade between Nassau in the Bahamas and ports in the Americas that were under the control of any European power. The letter sent by the Creeks and Cherokees pointed out that American ports under *Indian* control should count too. Creeks possessed shipping technology and controlled a long strip of the Gulf and Atlantic Coast, the southernmost part of it only 150 miles from Nassau, a long day's sail. Sailing their own vessels and flying their own flags, Creeks could import indigo, tobacco, dyes, saltpeter, furs, hides, tallow, wax, timber, and tar in exchange for manufactures.

Central to the argument for free trade was the independent sovereignty of "the united Nations of Creeks and Cherokees." The Creeks and Cherokees claimed their right to exist as independent nations on the world stage. While the Americans said "that we were now their people, and their subjects, and that we were to submit, as a conquered nation," these Indian nations were in fact "independent of, and allied

with, your Majesty, upon terms that implied no sovereignty over us."
The delegation apparently persuaded William Grenville to interpret
the Free Port Act as allowing free trade at Nassau from Creek ships
coming from Creek ports.[114]

While Bowles and his Creek and Cherokee friends were on their
way to London, his feckless trudge through the Florida wetlands had
further destabilized the Creek-Spanish alliance. For a time, each side
persuaded itself that the other was in league with Britain, the United
States, or both, and Bowles seemed to prove Spanish suspicions true.
Whereas East Florida Governor Vicente Manuel de Zéspedes dismissed Bowles as "an ignorant man" trying to lead "a band of vaga-
bonds ... to steal negroes and horses," West Florida Governor O'Neill
panicked.[115] He wrote his superiors that the British were combining
forces with Alexander McGillivray and William Panton to attack San
Marcos and perhaps Pensacola.[116]

In reaction to O'Neill's suspicions, panic spread through Creek
country, already full of worry that with Spain having cut off supplies
and the Bahamas connection apparently useless, they would be at the
mercy of the Georgians. Creeks feared going to Pensacola, where
they might be accused of plotting attack against either the Tombigbee
River settlements or Pensacola itself. Hoboithle Miko again began
urging peace and trade with Georgia. McGillivray tried "to settle
their minds" that Spanish trade would continue, but he was not so
sure anymore. Between Miró's orders to make peace with Georgia
and O'Neill's accusations of Creek aggression, McGillivray began to
worry that the Spanish were "engaged in a design to overthrow both
the authority and influence which I possess in this My Country."[117]

As relations between the Creeks and Spanish deteriorated, it became clear that Congress would do nothing to stop Georgia. In July
1788, the Congressional commissioners responded to the Creeks' desire that Congress force Georgians back east of the Oconee by offering instead to "write to the Governor of Georgia, requesting him to
issue his proclamation that no further trespasses be committed."[118] A
central government that could only make requests of its people was of
little use. That August, McGillivray wrote the commissioners to explain that removing the Georgians from the disputed lands was "an

indispensable preliminary" before the Creek National Council would even attend a treaty negotiation.[119] The commissioners in turn saw McGillivray's letters as evidence that the Creeks were being unreasonable. They responded that, although Congress was concerned about "full and ample redress" for the Creeks, it "will not lose sight of doing equal justice to the State of Georgia, whose claim to what you call the disputed lands, is confirmed by three different treaties, signed by your head-men and warriors," the fraudulent ones Hoboithle Miko and Neha Miko had signed.[120]

Unsure of British or Spanish supplies, the Creeks agreed to continue the truce with the United States until after the new federal government was set up under the Constitution, then in the process of ratification. McGillivray hoped "that a new Congress, acting on the principles of the new constitution of America, will set every thing to rights between us on the most equitable footing, so that we may become real friends to each other, settling on the same land, and having but one interest."[121] A central government with some power over the states would be easier for Indians to work with than the situation thus far. But solidifying U.S. power would itself be a danger.

Uniting the States

Like southeastern Indian nations, the thirteen states were attempting a new kind of confederation. In May 1787, delegates from the thirteen state legislatures assembled in Philadelphia to design what they would ultimately term "a more perfect union." Union under the Articles of Confederation had been far from perfect. Sharing the views of many, one Franklin settler observed that, "unless some measures are adopted to give more general satisfaction to the people throughout the Union, I think the affairs of America is on a tottering foundation."[122] The authors and supporters of the new Constitution hoped that it would create a confederation of united states strong enough to act as a nation and to establish its place as an independent power.

Because the Articles of Confederation rested primary sovereignty in the states, Congress had no more power to regulate Indian affairs or truly to make foreign policy than to collect revenue. The Articles gave Congress the power of "regulating the trade and managing all affairs with the Indians" who did not live within a state, but Virginia, North Carolina, and Georgia defined their states well past the Appalachians and into land claimed by Indians and the Spanish empire. Echoing British officials of the 1760s, the Congressional Committee on Southern Indians in 1787 concluded after much study that "the Indians, in general, within the United States want only to enjoy their lands without interruption, and to have their necessities regularly supplied by our traders." The cause of tension and violence seemed to be "an avaricious disposition in some of our people to acquire large tracts of land and often by unfair means."[123] Yet Congress could only ask the states and their citizens to comply, and the states had little incentive to surrender sovereignty to a central government that provided little in return.

Regarding the war between Georgia and the Creeks, for example, the secretary of the War Department, Henry Knox, wanted to end the war but saw that the Articles of Confederation might not allow Congressional interference. Knox recognized that the Creeks were "an independent tribe" and certainly not "members of the State of Georgia." On the other hand, Georgia claimed the Oconee lands, which meant that if Congress intervened, it would have to use the justification that the Oconee lands were part of the United States but not of Georgia, which meant siding with the Creek interpretation against Georgia's. Knox realized that the Articles left him in a bind "when land is the cause of the dispute." All he could do was recommend that Congress try to pressure Georgia to cede the territory to Congress, which then could settle the border dispute with the Creeks. As usual, Congress was left asking states for permission to act.[124]

The failure to gain access to the Mississippi, the absence of a commercial treaty with Spain, Indian attacks from the Ohio Valley to Georgia, a continuing currency crisis and postwar depression, and a rebellion in western Massachusetts over taxes and lack of credit led by Revolutionary War veteran Daniel Shays all increased fears that the republic could not represent the diverse interests of its people and was sure to break apart or lose its independence. Diego de Gardoqui called the United States "almost without Government, without a Treasury, or means of obtaining money, and torn between hope and fear of whether or not their Confederation can be consolidated."[125] The question was: Would the states surrender some of their independence to a national government for the sake of security, stability, and solvency?

In Philadelphia in May 1787, the delegates whom the state legislatures had empowered to draft commercial reforms to the Articles of Confederation shocked the country by starting from scratch and writing an entirely new constitution. If American voters had known this was the plan of James Madison and others there, other delegations would have come representing the opposition, and the plot to create a new government would have failed, leaving the United States still "almost without Government." But the convention approved the Constitution and agreed that it would require ratification by special conventions in only nine states to go into effect. Amendments to the Articles of Confederation required approval by all thirteen state legislatures, but the Constitution's supporters claimed that because it was entirely new, they could set new rules for its adoption.

Both the circumstances of the Constitution's creation and the substance of its more powerful centralized government were wildly controversial. On the other hand, Americans knew the Articles were not working, and the Constitution was at least a real plan. By working quickly before the opposition could organize, promising a Bill of Rights to protect liberties, and occasionally getting potential opponents drunk, by May 1788 the Constitution's proponents pushed it through eight states: Pennsylvania, Delaware, New Jersey, Connecticut, Massachusetts, Maryland, South Carolina, and Georgia, where continuing Creek raids had persuaded many of the need for a stronger national government. The addition of one more state would allow the nine to set up a new federal government, leaving the other four free to join or go off on their own.[126]

People inside and outside the union waited to see what New York and Virginia would do. A United States without those two populous and economically important states seemed unlikely to survive as an independent nation. In both states, people with land interests in the west were wary of a strong eastern government. Most of New York State opposed the Constitution, but commercial interests in New York City threatened to secede from the state to join the union alone. Still part of Virginia, Kentucky was represented at Virginia's ratifying convention. Although only fourteen of the over 150 delegates were from the Kentucky counties, the vote was likely to be close. They might decide which way Virginia would go and therefore perhaps the fate of the Constitution and the United States itself. Kentuckians still suspected that northeastern interests would sell them out for trade with Spain. Although James Madison assured them that the Constitution would protect the right of one-third of the states to deny ratification of a treaty, Kentuckians noticed that most of the Constitution's national supporters were northeasterners with commercial connections to Europe and the Caribbean out of New York and other Atlantic ports. After many long debates over whether the Constitution would make Mississippi access more or less likely, Virginia's convention voted for ratification 89 to 79, with most of the Kentucky delegates voting with Patrick Henry and against James Monroe.[127]

New York and New Hampshire also ratified the Constitution in mid-1788, so representatives began to set up a new government for the eleven United States; however, for now, the United States was smaller than in 1776. North Carolina and Rhode Island refused to join. Many people west of the Appalachians took the new government and the process of its creation as more evidence of eastern bullying. The New York *Morning Post and Daily Advertiser* reported in February 1789 that "many of the principal people" of Kentucky "are warmly in favor of a separation from the union, and contend that it is injurious to the interests of that country, to be connected with the Atlantic states." Naturally, if independent, they would ally with Spain and gain "free navigation of the Mississippi."[128] Indeed, after ratification, in early 1789, the Cumberland settlement renamed itself the "Miro District." James Robertson of Nashville wrote Governor Miró to inform him of the honor and the settlers' "wish to take every step in their power to cultivate the friendship of the subjects of his most Catholic Majesty."[129]

The qualities that had helped Americans throw off their empire could be their new nation's undoing. A nation of such independent folk was hard to govern. As José de Ezpeleta, now captain general in Havana, explained, "the United States of America fought for their liberty: they obtained it, but their very desire to enjoy it has caused dissensions among them for some time about the choice of a form of government." A majority of states had adopted a more effective Constitution, but some two hundred thousand Americans living west of the Appalachians were "feeling cramped now by this dependence" they had on the east. If Congress provided them no physical or economic security, what was its point? Ezpeleta believed that only the Spanish king "can help these people and stimulate them for their own interest to live quietly and apply themselves to the cultivation of the land and to other branches of industry," by giving them access to the Mississippi and Mobile rivers, "the only outlets that nature has left in so vast a Country."[130] As usual, the Spaniard neglected the implicit conflict with the Indians who already lived, farmed, hunted, and conducted business independently in that vast country.

While Spain wanted Indian and formerly American dependencies within the empire, the authors of the Constitution had quite a different framework in mind. Despite opponents' accusations that the new government would be tyrannical, the Federalists were not trying to make dependents of the states. Indeed, the framers argued that states would retain more independence than if they had to subordinate themselves to a European empire. To many Americans, the Constitution and the creation of a president, who would obviously be General George Washington, promised the security and order that could preserve American independence. At the same time, Indians were not invited to join the union, either as dependent nations or as individual citizens, not that many would have accepted the invitation anyway. It remained to be seen whether Americans themselves would agree to cede some independence to gain a somewhat more powerful union.

Conclusion: Shaky Confederacies

In spring 1789, in the western part of North Carolina, Creeks encountered "a considerable party of Americans." The Creeks believed that the Americans intended to attack Cherokee towns. Therefore, in keeping with Southern Confederacy obligations as they saw them, the Creeks "attacked and routed them." When the Creeks surveyed the bodies, they discovered that two of their victims were not Americans but Chickasaws. In looking through the papers that the men carried, the Creeks learned that the older man was Panssa Fallayah or Long Hair, brother to Payamataha's successor, Piomingo. The younger man was Long Hair's son and Piomingo's nephew. One of the papers the Creeks found was a letter from Piomingo expressing "the strongest professions of friendship to the Americans" and again offering land for a trading post at Chickasaw Bluffs. When McGillivray learned the news, he thought the Chickasaws had nothing to complain about. After all, the dead men had been "in the enemy's camp." If Chickasaws tried to take revenge, "they will be soon destroyed . . . for their defection from the general league."[131]

In response to the killings, Piomingo decided to recruit American "advice and assistance in carrying on a war against the Creeks." He led a delegation in the name of Chickasaws and Choctaws toward New York to meet President George Washington and his administration. On the way, they met with state officials in Kentucky and Virginia, who gave them enough munitions that Piomingo decided to head back home, writing Washington to ask him for help against their common enemy. His new Kentucky supporters forwarded his letter, adding their reminder that the Chickasaws were suffering because of trying to avoid "becoming dependent on the Spaniards, or joining the Creeks."[132] Despite the pro-American rhetoric, other delegations of Chickasaws traveled to Little Tallassee to smooth things over with McGillivray. As they had in the years of Payamataha, the Chickasaws worked on all fronts to keep the peace. But now both Indian and European allies were pushing them toward war, and their efforts lacked Payamataha's coordination.[133]

In 1789, neither the Southern Confederacy nor the confederation of United States was functioning particularly well. U.S. War Secretary Henry Knox believed that the Indian confederation effort might have a better chance than the American one. When Americans threatened their land, southeastern Indians might forget their differences and form a "union as firm as the six Northern nations." If the Northern and Southern Confederacies joined together and gained the backing of Britain and Spain, they might stop the United States. Although in Paris in 1783, the American delegates had claimed the right to Indians' lands east of the Mississippi, by the end of the decade federal officials had realized that the only way to avoid multiple Indian wars was to recognize Indian independence and negotiate with them as nations, the way the empires did.[134]

A vital question was how westward-bound Americans would react to the new, stronger federal government. In every state, there were Americans who believed that surrendering some of their independence to a stronger national government was a bad bargain. They argued that it would only return them to the problems they had with the British: taxation, lack of local control, and restriction on westward expansion. Would it be worth it for whatever protections the government could offer? And for Indians and Europeans, would the new national government create a nation that they could count on to control its people, perhaps driving some of them off in the process?

Kentuckian James Wilkinson assured Spanish officials that the Constitution would alienate westerners. While Americans at the moment were "captivated by the novelty of this Government to which they attribute all the force of a Powerful Monarchy," before long they would realize that even the new government could not provide the commercial benefits of a real empire. Soon the western United States would choose alignment with either Spanish Louisiana and West Florida or British Canada. Eventually, "the contrary and irreconcilable interests" of the eastern and western United States "will absolutely prevent any union between them, more so as the settlements of the west believe themselves to be in a condition to maintain their independence."[135]

Diego de Gardoqui too saw the Constitution as only a temporary

Jan Barend Elwe, *Amerique Septentrionale,* Amsterdam, 1792. (Lionel Pincus and Princess Firyal Map Division, The New York Public Library)

setback to Spanish ambitions. The godlike popularity of George Washington might have "saved this nation from the internal dissentions," but his influence could be no more than temporary "because it seems impossible that there could be found another man so beloved of all." After his presidency, the dissentions would surely pull the nation apart. Even during his rule, the United States might disintegrate because "the expectations of the people from this system are so gigantic that they cannot be fulfilled . . . disunion will follow."[136]

Republican Empires and Sovereign Dependencies

IN NOVEMBER 1814, Pensacola was preparing for another siege. White and black regulars and militia gathered with a few Indians in the old Fort George and newer forts at Red Cliffs and Santa Rosa Island to defend against enemy troops crossing the Perdido River from Mobile. But this time the defenders of Pensacola were both British and Spanish, the enemies from 1781 now (briefly) working together. At the head of the troops marching toward them was American General Andrew Jackson, determined to take West Florida from Spain. Creeks and Chickasaws provided even less defense of Pensacola than in 1781 but for different reasons. Few Creeks came this time, not because the fight was not in their interest but because a few months earlier Jackson's forces and Chickasaw warriors had fought alongside one Creek faction to defeat another in a disastrous civil war—the Red Stick War.[1]

The United States had grown in power in the previous two decades. In 1795, Northern Confederacy leaders ceded their rights to lands in present-day Ohio, Indiana, Michigan, Illinois, and Kentucky to the United States in the Treaty of Greenville. The same year, the

British finally evacuated their Great Lakes posts, and Spain, distracted by its fight against the French Revolution, attempted to save its possessions west of the Mississippi River and south of the Rio Grande by accepting the terms Congress had long tried to negotiate: the 31st parallel as West Florida's northern border and U.S. access to the Mississippi. By 1800, Napoleon Bonaparte had come to power in Europe, and he bullied Spanish King Carlos III's successor into returning Louisiana to France. Then in 1803, pressured by losses in Europe and a revolution in Haiti, Napoleon sold it to the United States, despite his promise to King Carlos IV never to allow the United States to have it. The Louisiana Purchase doubled the size of the United States and made it a trans-Mississippi nation.

Still, as the 1814 defense of Pensacola makes clear, the fight for the continent continued into the nineteenth century. The system of interdependence that Spain and southeastern Indians had established after the Revolution had been notably successful until the French Revolution threw Europe into turmoil. At the end of 1788, the Spanish had reversed their decision not to supply the Creeks with weapons, and they continued to supply Creek wars against the United States through the War of 1812 and beyond. As the threat of the United States grew, Indians and empires worked to put aside their differences. In 1792 on the Mississippi River just north of Natchez at a place the Spanish called Nogales (later renamed Vicksburg), the Spanish, Chickasaws, Creeks, Alabamas, Choctaws, and Cherokees came together again to pledge a mutual "offensive and defensive alliance" in which none would "decide any essential point which might affect the security and preservation of the others without consulting them."[2]

Together, Indians and Spaniards might have contained the United States, but conflicts in their long-term goals doomed the effort. Spanish officials certainly wanted to prevent American expansion, but they also envied its large population, which, at least in the Spanish view, enabled it to transcend the intricacies and expense of Indian politics. In the short run, depending on sovereign Native nations was better than standing alone, but Spanish officials longed for dependent European subjects and imperial control. Spain's attempt to make American immigrants into Spanish subjects supported this goal but undermined Native alliances. And Spanish America's own independence movements would ultimately throw Spain out of the Americas entirely.

Indians found themselves both wary of Spain's promises and too divided among themselves to agree on and follow a united foreign policy. Like the United States, they rejected dependence on an empire. They hoped to protect their sovereignty through wisely chosen alliances and carefully cultivated interdependence. Yet nothing in the histories of southeastern Indians had prepared them to unite under a single flag. They found it even harder to agree on a centralized authority than the states did.

Even if Indians could have overcome their differences, what unified policy should they have chosen? Follow Nativist prescriptions to unite against all Europeans and Euro-Americans? Ally with European empires but against the United States? Go on the offensive, or be prepared to defend if any of them were attacked? If war started, when should it stop? When Americans retreated to agreed-upon boundaries, or when all whites were expelled from the continent? Or should they avoid violence and follow Payamataha's strategy of security through peace? For southeastern Indians, the answer to complicated questions like what to do about Americans would never be simple or permanent. Policy needed to be dynamic enough to respond to changing exterior threats while remaining consensual within nations, clans, and towns. This diplomatic system had worked well in the past, both to deal with outside pressures and to allow full participation in community decisions. Yet change was coming too quickly this time with an adversary that was becoming more populous and less interested in continental networks of interdependence.

American immigrants crossed treaty lines, increasing Indian calls for unity while exposing Indian divisions. In 1790, Alexander McGillivray agreed to a treaty with Congress that set the Creek-Georgia border at the Oconee River, west of the Creeks' claim but well east of Georgia's. While McGillivray and George Washington's administration deemed the treaty a success, many Creeks thought that McGillivray had compromised too much, and Georgians thought the same about their president. As much as McGillivray wanted them to,

Creeks did not adopt a U.S. Constitution–style government that would strengthen the independence of the whole while reducing independence of the parts. The Alabamas never joined the Creeks completely, and the Seminoles separated to form their own nation. Worst of all, beginning in 1813, the Red Stick civil war broke out, in part over the question of how much to compromise with Americans.[3]

By then, years of debilitating headaches from near-constant travel and long nights of smoking and black drink had caught up with McGillivray. He died in 1793 in William Panton's house in Pensacola from pneumonia and complications from his longstanding gout. As his body was buried in Panton's garden, Creeks' "loud screams" of "unaffected grief" filled the air.[4] People mourned him at home too, including both his first wife, Elise Moniac, and another woman he had married around 1788, Levitia (Vicey) Cornells, the daughter of a Creek woman from Tuckabatchee. McGillivray had hoped to leave his plantations to his son, but his sisters instead followed Creek matrilineal traditions and distributed them among their children. Young Aleck would not have been able to profit from them long anyway—he died of pneumonia in Scotland in 1802. In the Red Stick War, McGillivray's nephew William Weatherford led attacks against other Creeks and American settlers north of Mobile, in and around the controversial Tombigbee settlements. After military victories by the U.S. Army in 1814, Creeks on both sides of the civil war lost most of their land. In an act unimaginable in 1793, the United States in 1834 forcibly removed most Creeks across the Mississippi. Having failed to cede independence to a central Creek government, the Creek people ultimately lost more independence as well as their homeland.[5]

Payamataha's way ultimately worked no better against the Americans' demographic onslaught and disdain for sharing the continent. Peace with everyone proved just as difficult as armed confederacy. Chickasaws found themselves drawn into violent conflict against the Creeks and Cherokees. Chickasaws even scouted and fought for the U.S. Army beginning in the 1790s. By then, many Chickasaws had decided that it was "a folly" to fight the United States.[6] Yet the decision to help the United States further undermined the long history of diplomacy that Payamataha had built. Not only was that peace impossible to keep without causing war against other Natives, it would not even keep the Chickasaws safe from the United States. The Chickasaws held out in the east only a few years longer than the Creeks before Americans decided they needed Chickasaw lands and forced them across the Mississippi too.[7]

The United States would be a new kind of empire, one that rejected imperial hierarchies of reciprocal dependencies and instead defined and advanced its own independence through exclusivist citizenship and military might. Its large population and commitment to farmland for all its citizens overrode networks of dependence and pushed Indians out of the way.[8]

Americans proved more able to resolve the paradox of independence for themselves than could Indians or Spain. In 1787, Diego de Gardoqui observed that "however strong the government of the United States may become, I do not believe that it will ever be sufficiently powerful to bring into subjection the people dwelling beyond the Mountains."[9] He was right, but leaders of the United States did not aim for "subjection," particularly after Thomas Jefferson's election in 1800. Jefferson's Republicans coopted westward immigrants and in doing so, established the legitimacy and strength of the federal government. Rather than offering white westerners dependent colonial status, as Spain had and as George Washington and the Federalists sometimes imagined, the nineteenth-century United States chose a course more fitting for a republic. Local citizens would rule locally, while the federal government promised military protection and economic opportunity and otherwise left them alone. New regions would have an apprenticeship as territories with a path to becoming states with the same rights and representation as the original thirteen. Like white male easterners, white male westerners would be citizens, not subjects. Local rule combined with national representation would decrease the urge to break away. By ceding some sovereignty to the new government created by the Constitution, the states established a framework for dominating the nineteenth-century west. The Constitution was controversial, but, with its Bill of Rights that explicitly protected certain liberties of individuals and states, it established a government with a better chance of lasting.[10]

Not all Americans agreed right away; some continued to envision alternative ways of preserving independence by dividing the continent. To many southerners, it seemed that the Washington administration was fighting Indians and building infrastructure for the northwest but leaving the southwest vulnerable to Indians and to Spain. As late as 1794, future president Andrew Jackson was threatening that unless Congress "lends us a more ample protection," Tennessee might leave the union and perhaps "seek a new protection from some other source."[11] After Kentucky became a state, Kentuckian James Wilkinson continued to spy for Spain and would conspire with Jefferson's vice president, Aaron Burr, to found their own independent republic west of the Mississippi.[12]

For a while, the regions west, north, and south of the United States retained multiple, interdependent sovereignties. Napoleon's 1800 takeover of Louisiana might have continued business as usual with his empire continuing the trade and alliance relationships that Payamataha's and McGillivray's people expected. In 1810, after Napoleon deposed Spain's king, people in Baton Rouge declared their independence as the "Republic of West Florida."[13] In the north, Indians, white and black former loyalists, and British officials found common cause against U.S. expansion, and in the negotiations after the War of 1812, Britain proposed to the United States that they mutually guarantee Indian possession in the northwest, although the U.S. delegates refused. After the War of 1812, a troop of former Gulf Coast slaves who had fought for the British settled a "Negro Fort" on the Apalachicola River in what was Spanish West Florida and Creek and Seminole country. This community of escaped slaves spoke French, Spanish, English, and various West African languages and lasted until 1816, when Andrew Jackson's forces destroyed their fort. Indeed, to Jackson, part of the appeal of the War of 1812 was the chance to seize the fruitful lands of West Florida and the Mississippi Valley and destroy the Indians and blacks armed by Spain and Britain. William Augustus Bowles returned to declare an independent "State of Muskogee" north of Apalachee Bay that would be allied with Britain and populated by Creeks, Cherokees, loyalists, runaway slaves, and disaffected Americans. Bowles attracted some support, including from Hoboithle Miko and Neha

Miko, although in general southeastern Indians were even less willing to surrender their local independence to join the State of Muskogee than Alexander McGillivray's Southern Confederacy.[14]

The U.S. ability to coopt both its own citizens and the subjects of neighboring colonies with land, security, and political rights would allow it to unite and expand despite Native, Spanish, and British opposition. That American republicans left the British empire and spread their slaveholding republic west ultimately worked out well for Amand Broussard and other Acadians. In the 1780s, Broussard became a prosperous planter, as Bernardo de Gálvez had promised would be possible under Spanish rule. But being a citizen in the American republic would prove even more profitable and secure than being a Spanish subject. After the Louisiana Purchase, Broussard and his French Louisiana neighbors came to see commonalities with American citizens. White colonists' fear of racial instability (heightened by runaway cimarrones and slave conspiracies at Pointe Coupée, Louisiana, in 1791 and 1795) and desire for economic development led them to support the American system of plantation slavery, the expulsion of Indians from valuable lands, and the exclusion of free people of color from citizenship.[15]

Joining the United States provided benefits to men like Broussard, and including these men in citizenship helped the United States to extend its power over this far-off region. In his midsixties, Amand Broussard again fought against Britain, this time for the United States under Andrew Jackson in the War of 1812's Battle of New Orleans. Broussard died in January 1818 and was buried in the parish cemetery, leaving a large estate to his many children. Four months later, Anne Benoît would stand in witness at the baptism of their latest grandchild, firm in the knowledge that the flight and exile that she and Amand had undertaken had resulted in wealth and security. Their house is now the largest one on display at the Vermilionville Living History Museum in Lafayette, Louisiana, a town named for the French hero of the Revolution. The prosperity that Broussard achieved reflected an American model of plantation slavery. The Broussard family's economic independence came at the expense of people who lost the land and the men and women forced to work it.[16]

Plantation slavery came to dominate the Gulf South. After the invention of the cotton gin in 1793, cotton plantations spread into the fertile lands north of the Gulf Coast. It was a sign of the times that Amand Broussard added a cotton mill to his plantation after 1793. The self-emancipations of the 1780s and 1790s would come to a screeching halt as the cotton boom took over Louisiana and the Floridas and the Haitian Revolution gave slaveholders a real example of an independent black republic. An imperial hierarchy of reciprocal dependencies in which most people were subordinated to others gave way to a slave society and a binary racial system. Antebellum planters defended slavery as the proper role for black Americans, not as an unfortunate economic necessity. Slaves who worked the South's cotton plantations would find a more brutal world with less chance for emancipation and less independence in daily life than in Petit Jean's enslavement.[17]

Most of the region's people would fare less well than French planters like Amand Broussard. Petit Jean and his wife lived free in Mobile, as the Gulf Coast became dominated by plantation slavery. Petit Jean's last appearance in the historical record was the 1786 Mobile census, which recorded him as a free mulatto. Despite the large numbers who had gained their freedom through the manumissions of the 1780s, free blacks became far outnumbered by slaves, mostly brought directly from West Africa. How distant these newly arrived West Africans must have seemed to this French-speaking Mobilian who had lived with locally born Afro-Floridians and Franco-Floridians all his life. But they were the way of the region's future. It would take more than half a century and a civil war to put an end to slavery in North America. Thanks to the Revolutionary War, people of African descent lost independence; some lost much, some the little they had.[18]

White women, too, lost ground as citizenship and property ownership became the American ideal. During and immediately after the Revolution, women in the thirteen colonies had played prominent roles in boycotts and patriotic displays. But white men in the early republic united around the argument that dependency was unmanly weakness. In this thinking, women's explicit legal ties of dependence rendered them incapable of the independent decision-making required of virtuous republican citizens. As political participation expanded to include more white men than under any monarch, Americans began to define citizenship as exclusively male and white. Under a monarchy, there were many kinds of subjects with varying rights and responsibilities, but American citizenship was binary. Either someone was a voting citizen or was not, and nonwhites and all women were excluded from voting and office-holding.[19]

Whether in empires or the new republic, white women's fortunes continued to depend almost entirely on marrying well. The Revolution could have abolished coverture, but instead it spread to former French and Spanish colonies, where women like Margaret Pollock and Anne Benoît had had the right to own property and operate businesses. While Isabella Bruce returned to Europe, Margaret Pollock and Anne Benoît remained with their husbands in lands that became part of the United States. Daughter and wife of prosperous New Orleans families, Margaret Pollock would see her fortunes decline with American independence, while the refugee Anne Benoît would rise to prominence along with her husband. But, like Margaret Pollock, her sex would prevent her and her daughters from becoming citizens in the republic.

Margaret Pollock's economic and social status declined because Oliver Pollock was never able to realize the opportunities he imagined in American independence. The United States adopted the symbol Oliver Pollock and his fellow merchants along the Gulf Coast used for Spanish and American dollars—the "$"—prompting later biographers to credit him as the inventor of the dollar sign. For a while his finances recovered. He ran enough trade through New Orleans that he was able to establish himself in the city again, to pay back his loans, and to begin to buy back his Mississippi Valley plantations. However, on a stop in Virginia in 1790, he was charged with defrauding two New Orleans merchants who had petitioned Virginia officials to arrest him. Their petition headed the Pollocks back toward penury. Oliver Pollock returned to Pennsylvania in 1791, where he and Margaret lived on their farm. Margaret Pollock died in 1799, memorialized in the local paper as "the faithful, the tender, the affectionate wife."[20]

Perhaps hoping to steer the country toward paying its debts, Pollock ran for Congress in 1797 and again in 1804. One of his endorsements praised "the many important public services rendered by Mr. Pollock during the Revolutionary war against Great Britain." Readers were advised to remember that "by his purse, his sword and counsel," he had "eminently contributed, in the Southern department of our country, to rescue the then United Colonies from the domination of a foreign Prince, and place them among the great Nations of the world as free and independent states." Despite his history, Pollock lost both times in large fields of candidates. Between the elections, he spent some time in debtors' prison in Philadelphia after signing the debt of a friend whose business failed. Congress paid its debt to Pollock by 1811, but Virginia still owed him nearly ten thousand dollars. He remarried in 1805, to a widow named Winifred Deady, and lived with her in Baltimore until her death in 1814. With little reason to remain in the east, he moved back to the Gulf Coast. He lived the rest of his life with his daughter Mary Robinson in and around Pinckneyville, Mississippi, a town named for the negotiator of the 1795 treaty that made the region part of the United States.[21]

Stretched thin by war in Europe and independence movements in Mexico and Central and South America, Spain agreed to part with the rest of the Floridas in 1819, yet the continent's struggles for independence and sovereignty were far from over. Although the United States tried to expel all other sovereignties from the continent, Canada and Mexico would remain the country's wary neighbors. Internally, of course, the Constitution had not resolved independence once and for all, as the secession crisis and civil war would show.

The movements to end slavery and to expand citizenship rights to all American men and women would take Enlightenment and Revolutionary ideals and rhetoric in quite different directions from the founding fathers' intent. In spite of early nineteenth-century republicanism's focus on white men, all kinds of Americans would seize on the Revolution to make such statements as the 1848 Seneca Falls Convention did in declaring, "We hold these truths to be self-evident: that all men and women are created equal." Nineteenth-century abolitionists to twentieth-century civil rights activists would call on

Americans to live up to their highest ideals and reject the exclusionary independence established in the early republic.[22]

American Indians' sovereignty did not end in the eighteenth century. The U.S. Supreme Court ruled in *Worcester v. Georgia* in 1832 that "Indian nations" are "distinct, independent political communities, retaining their original natural rights, as the undisputed possessors of the soil, from time immemorial," although it took until the 1930s for the United States to begin to be confident enough in its own sovereignty to tolerate other sovereignties within it. While most Americans stopped thinking of Indians as living in their own nations, most Indians remembered. For the Chickasaws and Creeks, removal from their homelands in the 1830s took their country but not their nationhood. Native American sovereignty has seen a resurgence in the past fifty years, and its association with American ideals of independence is in some ways a continuation of the projects that people like Payamataha and Alexander McGillivray were pursuing during the era of the Revolution.

The late eighteenth century saw the narrowing of the meaning of *independence* into simply the thirteen colonies' separation from Britain, and vast numbers of people and places were written out of the story of the American Revolution. Yet those people and places are central to the history of the United States that began in the 1770s and developed into a continental nation and a force around the world. The eventual victory of the revolutionaries and their new republic over those who opposed them has obscured the fact that the Revolution's outcome was not a foregone conclusion. The victory of the rebels over their empire was a surprise to the whole world, and it was only one surprise of the Revolution. Even at the end of the war, almost no one imagined that this republic would take over most of the continent. Europeans and Indians assumed that it would not last more than a few years. If states had insisted on the level of independence to which they aspired, they could not have won the war or survived against European and Indian powers in the region. But if the new nation had swung too far from state and local independence, the United States would have alienated its own people by replicating the tyranny of which they had accused the British. Striving for American independence really meant striving for the right balance of independence and dependence. Native Americans and European empires struck different balances, and ultimately both lost in North America. Only in the early nineteenth century did it become clear that this was a true revolution, one that had created a new player on the continent with new ambitions that would eventually bring dramatic change to the Gulf Coast and beyond.

ACKNOWLEDGMENTS

MY FATHER ONCE half-joked that historians are the kindest of academics, and I earnestly agree. I still cannot believe how lucky I am to have Alan Taylor and Dan Richter as my two great intellectual mentors, who have read my work for many years. They always offer praise and criticism when I need them and keep me grounded with their good humor and gentle teasing. Mike Green and Theda Perdue introduced me to the Native southeast in their books long before I met them. At UNC, I had the great fortune to gain them as colleagues and friends in time to write this book. Other mentors at UNC have shown me the very best path in life: Harry Watson, John Kasson, Joy Kasson, Jay Smith, Cynthia Radding, Bill Barney, Don Reid, Miles Fletcher, Don Raleigh, and Bill Ferris. I cannot imagine kinder or more supportive chairs than Lloyd Kramer and Fitz Brundage.

The book started in the loving incubator of my writing group: Jolie Olcott, Pete Sigal, Anna Krylova, and Dirk Bonker. Although they may not remember the conversations, Bob Lockhart, Chuck Grench, Susan Ferber, Lloyd Kramer, Chad Bryant, Fitz Brundage, Tol Foster, Colin Calloway, Andrew O'Shaughnessy, Nancy Shoemaker, Carla Gerona,

Sara Sundberg, and Alan Taylor helped shape the book early on. As I was beginning to write, I was fortunate to be at the National Humanities Center, just eight miles from my home, at the same time as three scholars who taught me that my book was a Caribbean and Atlantic story as well as a continental North American one: Bob DuPlessis, Laurent DuBois, and especially Trevor Burnard, who challenged my thinking with his rhetorical skill and long reading lists. A couple of years later, the National Humanities Center brought me Drew Cayton and Fred Anderson, who helped me see the book's implications for the nineteenth-century United States, among many other insights.

I received useful advice whenever I presented parts of the book, including the Triangle Early American History Seminar, the Triangle Working Group in Feminism and History, Southern Historians of the Piedmont, the Southern Intellectual History Circle, the McNeil Center for Early American Studies, the Omohundro Institute for Early American History and Culture, UNC, Duke, Wake Forest, the University of Miami, Brandeis, Indiana University, Princeton, the Filson Historical Society, the Huntington Library, and the annual meetings of the Organization of American Historians and the American Historical Association. I am particularly grateful for suggestions from Dallett Hemphill, Dan Richter, Ashli White, Richard Godbeer, Amy Bushnell, Holly Brewer, Glenn Crothers, Watson Jennison, Sarah Knott, Konstantin Dierks, Kirsten Sword, Peter Silver, Dan Usner, Jane Landers, Ed Gray, Elena Schneider, Eliga Gould, Kathryn Burns, Alan Gallay, Claudio Saunt, and Bertram Wyatt-Brown. Exchanges with Robin Fabel, José Manuel de Molina, Greg O'Brien, and especially David Nichols sharpened my thinking on particular subjects.

For sisterly companionship and serving as models of strong women, prestigious historians, and good human beings, I thank Malinda Maynor-Lowrey, Adriane Lentz-Smith, Sarah Pearsall, Christina Snyder, Michelle McDonald, Jane Kamensky, Karin Wulf, Sophie White, and Rhonda Lee. For their constant camaraderie and support, I thank Brett Rushforth, Seth Rockman, Roderick McDonald, and Ben Irvin as well as the friends who keep me looking forward to going to work: Chad Bryant, Brett Whalen, Wayne Lee, Michelle King, Miguel La Serna, Ben Waterhouse, Flora Cassen, Karen Auerbach, Emily Burrill,

Dan Cobb, Jean Dennison, Jenny Tone-Pah-Hote, Vin Steponaitis, Keith Richotte, Valerie Lambert, and Christian Lentz. Thanks also to supportive Duke colleagues present and past including Peter Wood, Lil Fenn, Reeve Huston, Phil Stern, Laura Edwards, Sally Deutsch, and Cynthia Brodhead, who several years ago suggested the title.

Undergraduate and graduate students at UNC kept me focused and energetic. Thanks to Katy Smith, Jonathan Hancock, Warren Milteer, Brooke Bauer, Liz Ellis, Garrett Wright, Tyler Will, Rachel Hynson, and Jeff Erbig for help on the manuscript. James Baynard, Kari Bussell, Amelia Kennedy, Chelsea Merritt, Nick Priore, and Keith Pulling were brave enough to give me wise advice in our undergraduate seminar, as were several generations of graduate seminars.

Many of the people mentioned above gave helpful comments on the project. Dan Dupre, Liam Riordan, Chris Hodson, Lisa Lindsay, Wayne Lee, Chad Bryant, Sarah Pearsall, Dan Richter, Dan Smith, and Michael McDonnell read key parts of the manuscript. I particularly thank those who read the whole thing and greatly improved it: Alan Taylor, Christina Snyder, Drew Cayton, Mike Green, Frank Asche, Marty Smith, John DuVal, and Kay DuVal (those last three several times each). Thanks to Sonya Rudenstine and Jack Davis for their hospitality as I conducted research at the P. K. Yonge Library, including introducing me to post-archive swims. Mackenzie Craig, Dan Papsdorf, and Nathaniel Millett provided essential source help. Thanks to Kay DuVal for writing the index to this book and the previous one.

I am deeply grateful for the work and support of librarians and other staff at the P. K. Yonge, UNC, Duke, the Library of Congress, the Historic New Orleans Collection, and the National Humanities Center, especially Bruce Chappell, James Cusick, Robert Dalton, Kent Mullikin, Jean Houston, Eliza Robertson, Josiah Drewry, Don Solomon, Lois Whittington, Carol Vorhaus, Sarah Payne, and James Getkin.

Researching and writing the book depended on funding from a number of sources at UNC, including the History Department, the Program in Medieval and Early Modern Studies, and the Institute for Arts and Humanities. Generous research grants included a Newberry

Library Short-Term Fellowship for Individual Research, a Filson Historical Society Fellowship, and an American Philosophical Society Phillips Fund for Native American Research Grant.

My agent, Jill Kneerim, has been everything she promised in our first conversation: editor, cheerleader, therapist, and friend, as has Katherine Flynn. At Random House, Jonathan Jao shaped the book in vital ways, and Molly Turpin was an insightful editor. All four steadfastly believed in my vision of the book and worked to make it the best it could be.

Dear friends outside my profession enrich my life. One of my earliest memories is laughing with Leslie Eichmann Harvey, and she and Shannon Mathis remain the funniest people I know. Whenever I need her, Dawn Sutter Madell drops everything in her own busy life. Shelagh Kenney has helped me through some tough days. Alice Mackenzie, Emily Bernhardt and Justin Wright, Malissa McLeod and Brett Whalen, Laura Moore and Brad Murray, Janice McCarthy and Martin Steinmeyer, and Silke Schmidt and Dan Phaneuf are family friends in the fullest meaning of both words. I do not have room to list all my beloved Trinity Park neighbors and George Watts Elementary friends, who contribute every day to my full and happy life in Durham.

As always, my family comes last in the acknowledgments and first in my heart. My parents, Kay and John DuVal, are wise, droll, and astonishingly uncritical of me. Everything is due to them. My brother, Niell DuVal, has been central to my life since I was four. I am amazed at the adults we have become together. I am grateful for the love and support of Frank DuVal, the Quigleys—Anne, Steve, Carol, Stephen, Michelle, Caroline, Katie, and Mary Kay—Dan Smith, Dave Smith, and Mary Lou Haller. Since my last book, Quentin DuVal-Smith has grown into a person with whom I can talk about history, which is one of the most wonderful things that has ever happened to me. Calvin DuVal-Smith sat on my lap as I drafted much of the manuscript. Any typos are his fault.

I dedicate the book to Marty Smith, my editor, personal chef, mixologist, running coach, closest friend, love of my life, partner in all things. He had to share my previous dedications with the rest of my family. This one is all for him.

NOTES

INTRODUCTION

1. For an overview of why scholarship on the American Revolution stagnated and how it is reviving today, see the introduction to *The Oxford Handbook of the American Revolution*, ed. Edward G. Gray and Jane Kamensky (New York, 2013).
2. See Gary B. Nash, *The Unknown American Revolution: The Unruly Birth of Democracy and the Struggle to Create America* (New York, 2005); Barbara Graymont, *The Iroquois in the American Revolution* (Syracuse, 1972); Colin G. Calloway, *The American Revolution in Indian Country: Crisis and Diversity in Native American Communities* (New York, 1995); Alan Taylor, *The Divided Ground: Indians, Settlers and the Northern Borderland of the American Revolution* (New York, 2006); Alfred F. Young, *Liberty Tree: Ordinary People and the American Revolution* (New York, 2006).
3. On individuals and families in historical writing, see Sarah M. S. Pearsall, *Atlantic Families: Lives and Letters in the Later Eighteenth Century* (New York, 2008), 145–8. On the importance of local affinities despite global connections, see Peter J. Kastor, *The Nation's Crucible: The Louisiana Purchase and the Creation of America* (New Haven, 2004), 28.
4. John Stuart to Henry Clinton, March 15, 1776, *Documents of the American Revolution, 1770–1783 (Colonial Office Series),* ed. K. G. Davies (Shannon, Ireland, 1972–1981), 12: 79. Throughout the book, I have corrected spelling in English-language quotations to make them parallel to my translations from Spanish and French. (Otherwise the British seem less literate than the Spanish and French.) Translations from Spanish and French are mine unless otherwise noted.
5. Thomas Jefferson to the Citizens of Washington, March 4, 1809, *The Writings of Thomas Jefferson: Being His Autobiography, Correspondence, Reports, Messages, Addresses, and*

Other Writings, Official and Private, ed. H. A. Washington (Washington, D.C., 1853), 8: 157.

6. For corrections to the declension model of the eighteenth-century Spanish empire, see Henry Kamen, *Empire: How Spain Became a World Power, 1492–1763* (New York, 2003); David J. Weber, *Bárbaros: Spaniards and Their Savages in the Age of Enlightenment* (New Haven, 2005); David J. Weber, *The Spanish Frontier in North America* (New Haven, 1992).

7. Jane Burbank and Frederick Cooper, *Empires in World History: Power and the Politics of Difference* (Princeton, 2010), 2–3; David A. Lake, *Hierarchy in International Relations* (Ithaca, 2009); Adam Watson, *The Limits of Independence* (New York, 1997).

8. Ned C. Landsman, *From Colonials to Provincials: American Thought and Culture, 1680–1760* (Ithaca, 1997), 3–4; Gordon S. Wood, *The Radicalism of the American Revolution* (New York, 1991), 6, 14, 19, 57; John E. Crowley, *The Privileges of Independence: Neo-mercantilism and the American Revolution* (Baltimore, 1993), 13–29; Ellen Hartigan-O'Connor, *The Ties That Buy: Women and Commerce in Revolutionary America* (Philadelphia, 2009); Serena R. Zabin, *Dangerous Economies: Status and Commerce in Imperial New York* (Philadelphia, 2009); Daniel Vickers, "Competency and Competition: Economic Culture in Early America," *William and Mary Quarterly* 47 (1990): 3–29; Margaret Ellen Newell, *From Dependency to Independence: Economic Revolution in Colonial New England* (Ithaca, 1998); Emma Rothschild, *The Inner Life of Empires: An Eighteenth-Century History* (Princeton, 2011).

9. Christina Snyder, *Slavery in Indian Country: The Changing Face of Captivity in Early America* (Cambridge, 2010), 5–7.

10. Edward Phillips, *The New World of Words, or, A Universal English Dictionary* (London, 1700).

11. On dependency theory, see Eric Wolf, *Europe and the People Without History* (Berkeley, 1982); Denys Delâge, *Bitter Feast: Amerindians and Europeans in Northeastern North America, 1600–64*, trans. Jane Brierley (Vancouver, 1993), 78; Richard White, *The Roots of Dependency: Subsistence, Environment, and Social Change among the Choctaws, Pawnees, and Navajos* (Lincoln, 1983), xvi–xvii. For critiques, see Kathleen DuVal, *The Native Ground: Indians and Colonists in the Heart of the Continent* (Philadelphia, 2006), 5–6; Richard White, *The Middle Ground: Indians, Empires, and Republics in the Great Lakes Region, 1650–1815* (New York, 1991), 94–6, 128–40, 482–5; Lauren Benton, *Law and Colonial Cultures: Legal Regimes in World History, 1400–1900* (New York, 2002); Gary Clayton Anderson, *The Indian Southwest, 1580-1830: Ethnogenesis and Reinvention* (Norman, 1999); Mark J. C. Crescenzi, *Economic Interdependence and Conflict in World Politics* (Lanham, 2005), 4.

12. Eliga H. Gould, *Among the Powers of the Earth: The American Revolution and the Making of a New World Empire* (Cambridge, 2012), 2, 112–4; David Armitage, *The Declaration of Independence: A Global History* (Cambridge, 2007), 30; Benjamin H. Irvin, *Clothed in Robes of Sovereignty: The Continental Congress and the People Out of Doors* (New York, 2011); Leonard J. Sadosky, *Revolutionary Negotiations: Indians, Empires, and Diplomats in the Founding of America* (Charlottesville, 2009).

13. Jefferson to George Rogers Clark, Dec. 25, 1780, *Papers of Thomas Jefferson*, ed. Julian P. Boyd (Princeton, 1951), 4: 237. On the United States as an empire, see, for example, Carroll Smith-Rosenberg, *This Violent Empire: The Birth of an American National Identity* (Chapel Hill, 2010).

14. For a synthesis of the new approach to colonial history, see Alan Taylor, *American Colonies* (New York, 2001). For scholarship that challenges the American Revolution as expanding liberty for all, see, for example, Betty Wood, "The Impact of the Revo-

lution on the Role, Status, and Experience of Women," in *A Companion to the American Revolution*, ed. Jack P. Greene and J. R. Pole (Malden, 2000), 419–26; Woody Holton, *Forced Founders: Indians, Debtors, Slaves, and the Making of the American Revolution in Virginia* (Chapel Hill, 1999); Terry Bouton, *Taming Democracy: "The People," the Founders, and the Troubled Ending of the American Revolution* (New York, 2007); Claudio Saunt, *West of the Revolution: An Uncommon History of 1776* (New York, 2014).

15. Liam Riordan, *Many Identities, One Nation: The Revolution and Its Legacy in the Mid-Atlantic* (Philadelphia, 2007).

PART I Introduction

1. Continental Congress to the Colony of West Florida, Oct. 22, 1774, *Journals of the Continental Congress, 1774–1789*, ed. Worthington C. Ford (Washington, 1904), 1: 103; J. Barton Starr, *Tories, Dons, and Rebels: The American Revolution in British West Florida* (Gainesville, 1976), 45–6; Andrew Jackson O'Shaughnessy, *An Empire Divided: The American Revolution and the British Caribbean* (Philadelphia, 2000).

CHAPTER 1

1. Weber, *Spanish Frontier in North America*, 147–203.

2. Martín Navarro, "Reflexiones Políticas sobre el estado actual de la provincia de la Luisiana," 1782, *Louisiana under the Rule of Spain, France, and the United States, 1785–1807*, ed. and trans. James Alexander Robertson (Cleveland, 1911), 1: 246.

3. George Johnstone to the Board of Trade, n.d. [received May 30, 1764], *Mississippi Provincial Archives: English Dominion*, ed. Dunbar Rowland (Nashville, 1911), 150; William Forbes to the Secretary of State, Jan. 29, 1764, *Mississippi Provincial Archives: English Dominion*, 141; Augustine Prevost to the Secretary of War, Sept. 7, 1763, *Mississippi Provincial Archives: English Dominion*, 136.

CHAPTER 2

1. For one recent example of shoehorning Indians into the "loyalist" category, see the otherwise sophisticated Maya Jasanoff, *Liberty's Exiles: American Loyalists in the Revolutionary World* (New York, 2011).

2. Thomas Nairne, *Nairne's Muskhogean Journals: The 1708 Expedition to the Mississippi River*, ed. Alexander Moore (Jackson, 1988), 38; Snyder, *Slavery in Indian Country*, 70–1; Arrell M. Gibson, *The Chickasaws* (Norman, 1971), 21–2; Robbie Ethridge, *From Chicaza to Chickasaw: The European Invasion and the Transformation of the Mississippian World, 1540–1715* (Chapel Hill, 2010), 74–5; Neal Salisbury, "The Indians' Old World: Native Americans and the Coming of Europeans," *William and Mary Quarterly* 53 (1996): 435–58. Archaeologists have in recent years been changing previous assumptions of an all-powerful Mississippian chief as they have found Mississippian societies with less hierarchal and dictatorial structures.

3. Daniel K. Richter, *Facing East from Indian Country: A Native History of Early America* (Cambridge, 2001), 175; Alan Gallay, *The Indian Slave Trade: The Rise of the English Empire in the American South, 1670–1717* (New Haven, 2002), 14, 70, 103, 129–30, 163, 170, 296; Snyder, *Slavery in Indian Country*, 51–76; David Brion Davis, *Challenging the Boundaries of Slavery* (Cambridge, 2003), 5–6.

4. Nairne, *Nairne's Muskhogean Journals*, 38, 47; Peter H. Wood, "The Changing Population of the Colonial South: An Overview by Race and Region, 1685–1790," in *Pow-*

hatan's Mantle: Indians in the Colonial Southeast, ed. Peter H. Wood, Gregory A. Waselkov, and M. Thomas Hatley, 2nd ed. (Lincoln, 2006), 84–5, 92–9; Snyder, *Slavery in Indian Country*, 46–72; Ethridge, *From Chicaza to Chickasaw*, 167–231, 237–8; Joseph M. Hall, *Zamumo's Gifts: Indian-European Exchange in the Colonial Southeast* (Philadelphia, 2009), 104–16; Wendy St. Jean, "Trading Paths: Mapping Chickasaw History in the Eighteenth Century," *American Indian Quarterly* 27 (2003): 765–6; Daniel K. Richter, *Before the Revolution: America's Ancient Pasts* (Cambridge, 2011), 320–1.

5. Feb. 26, 1747/8, *The Colonial Records of South Carolina: The Journal of the Commons House of Assembly*, ed. J. H. Easterby (Columbia, 1961), 70; Nairne, *Nairne's Muskhogean Journals*, 37; James Adair, *The History of the American Indians*, ed. Kathryn E. Holland Braund (Tuscaloosa, 2005), 197; Snyder, *Slavery in Indian Country*, 66–7, 78; Gibson, *Chickasaws*, 39–41; Claudio Saunt, "'Our Indians': European Empires and the History of the Native American South," in *The Atlantic in Global History, 1500–2000*, ed. Jorge Cañizares-Esguerra and Erik R. Seeman (Upper Saddle River, 2007), 61–75; White, *Roots of Dependency*, 50–61; R. S. Cotterill, *The Southern Indians: The Story of the Civilized Tribes before Removal* (Norman, 1954), 17–21; Kathleen DuVal, "Interconnectedness and Diversity in 'French Louisiana,'" in *Powhatan's Mantle*, 133–62. Thanks to Brooke Bauer for the Catawba reference.

6. Wendy Cegielski and Brad R. Lieb, "*Hina' Falaa,* 'The Long Path': An Analysis of Chickasaw Settlement Using GIS in Northeast Mississippi, 1650–1840," *Native South* 4 (2011): 33–5, 40–2; Wood, "Changing Population of the Colonial South," 93–5.

7. Adair, *History of the American Indians*, 118; Papers Relating to Congress with Choctaw and Chickasaw Indians, Dec. 31, 1771, "Peter Chester, Third Governor of the Province of West Florida under British Dominion, 1770–1781," *Publications of the Mississippi Historical Society*, ed. Mrs. Dunbar Rowland (Jackson, 1925), 5: 142; Bernard Romans, *A Concise Natural History of East and West Florida*, ed. Kathryn E. Holland Braund (Tuscaloosa, 1999), 124–8; Lyman C. Draper, "A Narrative Based on an Interview with Malcolm McGee," ed. James R. Atkinson, *Journal of Mississippi History* 66 (2004): 59; Pamela Munro, *Chickasaw: An Analytical Dictionary* (Norman, 1994), 327; Calloway, *American Revolution in Indian Country*, 220; Greg O'Brien, "Supplying Our Wants: Choctaws and Chickasaws Reassess the Trade Relationship with Britain, 1771–72," in *Coastal Encounters: The Transformation of the Gulf South in the Eighteenth Century*, ed. Richmond F. Brown (Lincoln, 2007), 63. Indian titles confused Europeans in the eighteenth century and historians ever since. Alexander Cameron wrote in frustration that he could not tell whether "the Great Chickasaw Warrior" whom people referred to "is Payamataha or not as I can find no person who can tell me. The Indians never ask names." Alexander Cameron to John Stuart, June 3, 1774, fr. 132, reel 7, Records of the British Colonial Office, Library of Congress, Washington, D.C.

8. Adair, *History of the American Indians*, 327, 337–9; Marquis de Vaudreuil to Antoine Louis Rouillé, Sept. 22, 1749, LO 185, box 4, Vaudreuil Papers, Loudoun Collection, Huntington Library, San Marino, Calif.; Louis Vivier to Father———, Nov. 17, 1750, *The Jesuit Relations and Allied Documents: Travels and Explorations of the Jesuit Missionaries in New France, 1610–1791*, ed. Reuben Gold Thwaites (Cleveland, 1896–1901), 69: 217; Nairne, *Nairne's Muskhogean Journals*, 42–4; John Richard Alden, *John Stuart and the Southern Colonial Frontier: A Study of Indian Relations, War, Trade, and Land Problems in the Southern Wilderness, 1754–1775* (New York, 1966), 92–3. On the history of scalping and selling scalps, see James Axtell and William C. Sturtevant, "The Unkindest Cut, or Who Invented Scalping," *William and Mary Quarterly* 37 (1980): 451–72.

9. Adair, *History of the American Indians*, 327, 337–9.

10. *Pennsylvania Gazette*, July 9, 1761.

11. Headmen and Warriors of the Chickasaw Nation to the King of Carolina and His Beloved Men, April 5, 1756, *Colonial Records of South Carolina: Documents Relating to Indian Affairs, 1754–1765*, ed. William L. McDowell Jr. (Columbia, 1970), 109–10; Receipts from the Headmen and Warriors of the Chickasaw Nation to Jerome Courtonne, March 30, 1756, *Colonial Records of South Carolina*, 114; Edward J. Cashin, *Guardians of the Valley: Chickasaws in Colonial South Carolina and Georgia* (Columbia, 2009), 58–62.

12. Because the details of eighteenth-century Chickasaw governance are unclear, we don't know how much influence Payamataha also had over domestic affairs, but he was clearly the Chickasaws' chief diplomat. *Journal of the Congress of the Four Southern Governors, and the Superintendent of That District, with the Five Nations of Indians, at Augusta, 1763* (Charles Town, 1764), 10–1, 20; Proceedings of the Treaty of Hopewell with the Chickasaws, Jan. 7, 1786, *Early American Indian Documents: Treaties and Laws, 1607–1789, Revolution and Confederation*, ed. Colin G. Calloway, gen. ed. Alden T. Vaughan (Bethesda, 1994), 18: 420; Nairne, *Nairne's Muskhogean Journals*, 38–9; Richard Green, *Chickasaw Lives* (Ada, 2007), 1: 49.

13. Payamataha speech at Mobile Congress, April 2, 1765, *Mississippi Provincial Archives: English Dominion*, 246; Papers Relating to Congress with Choctaw and Chickasaw Indians, Dec. 31, 1771, *Publications of the Mississippi Historical Society*, 5: 151–2. Wood, "Changing Population of the Colonial South," 95. Some Choctaws, Creeks, and Cherokees had begun to work for a pan-Indian peace during the Seven Years' War, while the Chickasaws were still fighting the French. Greg O'Brien, "The Great Choctaw-Chickasaw Peace and the War that Made It Possible," forthcoming; Wendy St. Jean, "Trading Paths: Chickasaw Diplomacy in the Greater Southeast, 1690–1790s" (Ph.D. diss., University of Connecticut, 2004), 126–52.

14. Chulustamastabe speech at Mobile Congress, April 2, 1765, *Mississippi Provincial Archives: English Dominion*, 244.

15. Charles Stuart to Cameron, Dec. 16, 1779, fr. 343–4, reel 8, Records of the British Colonial Office, Library of Congress.

16. *Journal of the Congress of the Four Southern Governors*, 13, 17, 19, 24–6.

17. Gregory Evans Dowd, *A Spirited Resistance: The North American Indian Struggle for Unity, 1745–1815* (Baltimore, 1992), 43, 47–8, 91.

18. For a movement with some similarities, see David J. Silverman, *Red Brethren: The Brothertown and Stockbridge Indians and the Problem of Race in Early America* (Ithaca, 2010), 7.

19. George Johnstone and John Stuart letter, June 12, 1765, *Mississippi Provincial Archives: English Dominion*, 184; Report of the Choctaw and Chickasaw Congress at Mobile, March 26, 1765, *Mississippi Provincial Archives: English Dominion*, 216–22.

20. Report of the Choctaw and Chickasaw Congress at Mobile, April 2, 1765, 243–7; Alden, *John Stuart and the Southern Colonial Frontier*, 200–2.

21. Report of the Choctaw and Chickasaw Congress at Mobile, March 27 and April 1–2, 1765, 224–43.

22. British officials complained that, as one Spanish official put it, "the Spaniards are sending subjects to draw away the tribes located in their domains." The Spanish official countered that Indians were the ones insisting on negotiating with the Spanish. Francisco Cruzat to Bernardo de Gálvez, Nov. 26, 1777, *The Spanish Régime in Missouri: A Collection of Papers and Documents Relating to Upper Louisiana*, ed. Louis Houck (New York, 1971), 1: 134–5; Johnstone speech, Report of the Choctaw and Chicka-

saw Congress at Mobile, March 26, 1765, 223; *Journal of the Congress of the Four Southern Governors,* 32–3.

23. François Desmazellières to Alejandro O'Reilly, June 2, 1770, fol. 96, leg. 107, Papeles de Cuba, Archivo General de Indies, Seville, Spain; Desmazellières to O'Reilly, June 4, 1770, fol. 97, leg. 107, Papeles de Cuba, Archivo General de Indias; Robert Farmar to Thomas Gage, Dec. 16, 1765, and May 9, 1766, Thomas Gage Papers, American Series, William L. Clements Library, University of Michigan, Ann Arbor, transcript at Indiana University, Bloomington. Thanks to Jacob Lee for the evidence of Chickasaw-Illinois peacemaking.

24. Desmazellières to O'Reilly, June 2, 1770, fol. 96, leg. 107, Papeles de Cuba, Archivo General de Indies; John Stuart to the Earl of Hillsborough, Feb. 7, 1772, *Documents of the American Revolution,* 5: 37; Enrique Grimarest, Report on the Mission of Paulous to the Chickasaws, Sept. 1782, *Spain in the Mississippi Valley, 1765–1794,* ed. and trans. Lawrence Kinnaird (Washington, D.C., 1946–49), 2: 57; Wendy St. Jean, "The Chickasaw-Quapaw Alliance in the Revolutionary Era," *Arkansas Historical Quarterly* 68 (2009): 274–5; St. Jean, "Trading Paths: Chickasaw Diplomacy," ch. 8; Kathleen DuVal, "The Education of Fernando de Leyba: Quapaws and Spaniards on the Border of Empires," *Arkansas Historical Quarterly* (2001): 1-29; Kathleen DuVal, "'A Good Relationship, & Commerce': The Native Political Economy of the Arkansas River Valley," *Early American Studies: An Interdisciplinary Journal* (Spring 2003): 61–89; Colin G. Calloway, *The Scratch of a Pen: 1763 and the Transformation of North America* (New York, 2006).

25. Edward Mease, "Narrative of a Journey Through Several Parts of the Province of West Florida in the Years 1770 and 1771," *Publications of the Mississippi Historical Society,* ed. Mrs. Dunbar Rowland, 5: 80; Charles Stuart to Peter Chester, n.d. [enclosed in letter of April 15, 1771], *Publications of the Mississippi Historical Society,* 5: 47; "Congress of the Principal Chiefs and Warriors of the Chickasaw and Choctaw Nations," Jan. 1, 1772, *Publications of the Mississippi Historical Society,* 5: 142; Desmazellières to O'Reilly, June 2, 1770, fol. 96, leg. 107, Papeles de Cuba, Archivo General de Indies; Romans, *Concise Natural History,* 123–4; Chester to Captain Dickson, May 5, 1771, B-13, Haldimand Papers, British Library, London, England; Frederick Haldimand to Thomas Gage, June 11, 1771, B-5, Haldimand Papers; *Pennsylvania Gazette,* July 16, 1772; St. Jean, "Trading Paths: Chickasaw Diplomacy," introduction and ch. 8; O'Brien, "Supplying Our Wants," 59–80.

26. John McIntosh to Charles Stuart, Sept. 3, 1772, *Documents of the American Revolution,* 5: 186; John Stuart to Hillsborough, Feb. 6, 1772, *Documents of the American Revolution,* 5: 34–5; Chester to Hillsborough, March 9, 1771, "Peter Chester, Third Governor," 5: 38; Calloway, *American Revolution in Indian Country,* 222.

27. Adair, *History of the American Indians,* 301–2; Papers Relating to Congress with Choctaw and Chickasaw Indians, Dec. 31, 1771, *Publications of the Mississippi Historical Society,* 5: 146; McIntosh to Charles Stuart, Sept. 3, 1772, *Documents of the American Revolution,* 5: 185–6; Report by Choctaw messenger on deputation to the Chickasaws, Oct. 24, 1782, *Spain in the Mississippi Valley,* 2: 61–2; Draper, "Narrative Based on an Interview with Malcolm McGee," 59, 65; Alden, *John Stuart and the Southern Colonial Frontier,* 209, 323.

28. John Stuart to Haldimand, Feb. 11, 1772, *Early American Indian Documents: Treaties and Laws, 1607–1789, Georgia and Florida Treaties, 1763–1776,* ed. John T. Juricek, gen. ed. Alden T. Vaughan (Bethesda, 2002), 12: 425–6; O'Brien, "Supplying Our Wants," 74–5; James R. Atkinson, *Splendid Land, Splendid People: The Chickasaw Indians to Removal* (Tuscaloosa, 2001), 95–6. Again in 1782, Mingo Houma insisted to Americans

that he was "King of this Nation." After his death, his successors called him "our old king." Chickasaw Message, July 9, 1782, *Early American Indian Documents*, 18: 271; Proceedings of the Treaty of Hopewell with the Chickasaws, Jan. 7, 1786, *Early American Indian Documents*, 18: 419.

29. Papers Relating to Congress with Choctaw and Chickasaw Indians, Dec. 31, 1771, "Peter Chester, Third Governor," 5: 142–5; Payamataha to Elias Durnford and Charles Stuart, April 23, 1770, fr. 611–2, reel 5, Records of the British Colonial Office, Library of Congress; Chester to Hillsborough, March 9, 1771, "Peter Chester, Third Governor," 5: 39–40; Charles Stuart to Chester, n.d., "Peter Chester, Third Governor," 5: 47; McIntosh to Richardson, April 15, 1766, *The New Régime, 1765–1767*, ed. Clarence Walworth Alvord and Clarence Edwin Carter (Springfield, 1916), 214; White, *Roots of Dependency*, 56–9.

30. Calloway, *American Revolution in Indian Country*, 220.

31. Romans, *Concise Natural History*, 124, 126, 128, 384n54; Cegielski and Lieb, "*Hina' Falaa*," 33–5, 42; Wood, "Changing Population of the Colonial South," 95; Atkinson, *Splendid Land, Splendid People*, 91.

CHAPTER 3

1. Alexander McGillivray to Esteban Miró, March 28, 1784, *McGillivray of the Creeks*, ed. John Walton Caughey (Columbia, 2nd ed., 2007), 74; Louis LeClerc Milfort, *Chef de guerre chez les Creeks*, ed. Christian Buchet (Paris, 1994), 180; Lachlan McGillivray, will, June 12, 1767, http://homepages.rootsweb.ancestry.com/~cmamcrk4/crkdox27.html; Michael D. Green, "Alexander McGillivray," in *American Indian Leaders: Studies in Diversity*, ed. R. David Edmunds (Lincoln, 1980), 42; Edward J. Cashin, *Lachlan McGillivray, Indian Trader: The Shaping of the Southern Colonial Frontier* (Athens, 1992), 73.

2. Calloway, *American Revolution in Indian Country*, 60; Colin G. Calloway, *White People, Indians, and Highlanders: Tribal Peoples and Colonial Encounters in Scotland and America* (New York, 2008), 20–33, 117–9; Cashin, *Lachlan McGillivray, Indian Trader*, 13–7; Robert Bain, *The Clans and Tartans of Scotland* (London, 1938, 1950), 208.

3. Kathryn E. Holland Braund, *Deerskins and Duffels: The Creek Indian Trade with Anglo-America, 1685–1815* (Lincoln, 1993), 3–25; Angela Pulley Hudson, *Creek Paths and Federal Roads: Indians, Settlers, and Slaves and the Making of the American South* (Chapel Hill, 2010), 3–4; J. Leitch Wright, *Creeks and Seminoles: The Destruction and Regeneration of the Muscogulge People* (Lincoln, 1986), 2–3.

4. Michael D. Green, "The Creek Confederacy in the American Revolution: Cautious Participants," in *Anglo-Spanish Confrontation on the Gulf Coast During the American Revolution*, ed. William S. Coker and Robert R. Rea (Pensacola, 1982), 57; Steven C. Hahn, *The Invention of the Creek Nation, 1670–1763* (Lincoln, 2004); Joshua Piker, *Okfuskee: A Creek Indian Town in Colonial America* (Cambridge, Mass., 2004), 91, 232–5, 243; Gallay, *Indian Slave Trade*, 33, 41–2; Michael D. Green, *The Politics of Indian Removal: Creek Government and Society in Crisis* (Lincoln, 1982); Charles Hudson, introduction, in *The Transformation of the Southeastern Indians, 1540–1760*, ed. Robbie Ethridge and Charles Hudson (Jackson, 2002), xx.

5. Gallay, *Indian Slave Trade*, 89, 133–4, 137, 161–2, 290–1; Hall, *Zamumo's Gifts*, 117–33; William L. Ramsey, *The Yamasee War: A Study of Culture, Economy, and Conflict in the Colonial South* (Lincoln, 2008); Steven C. Hahn, "The Mother of Necessity: Carolina, the Creek Indians, and the Making of a New Order in the American Southeast, 1670–1763," in *Transformation of the Southeastern Indians*, 79–81, 101–5; Green, *Politics*

of Indian Removal, 22; David H. Corkran, *The Creek Frontier, 1540–1783* (Norman, 1967), 61–81; Verner W. Crane, *The Southern Frontier, 1670–1732* (Tuscaloosa, 1929, 2004), 254–6; Hahn, *Invention of the Creek Nation,* 83–7, 96, 108–19

6. Green, "Creek Confederacy in the American Revolution," 58–9; Hahn, *Invention of the Creek Nation,* 4, 81–90, 96; Hahn, "Mother of Necessity," 79–80; Hudson, *Creek Paths and Federal Roads;* St. Jean, "Trading Paths: Chickasaw Diplomacy"; Cashin, *Lachlan McGillivray, Indian Trader,* 72. For similar patterns within the Iroquois Confederacy, see Daniel K. Richter, *The Ordeal of the Longhouse: The Peoples of the Iroquois League in the Era of European Colonization* (Chapel Hill, 1992), 190–254.

7. Richter, *Facing East from Indian Country,* 169–70, 178; Robert Paulett, *An Empire of Small Places: Mapping the Southeastern Anglo-Indian Trade, 1732–1795* (Athens, 2012), 66–99.

8. Milfort, *Chef de guerre,* 212; Theda Perdue, *"Mixed Blood" Indians: Racial Construction in the Early South* (Athens, 2003); Kathleen DuVal, "Indian Intermarriage and Métissage in Colonial Louisiana," *William and Mary Quarterly* 65 (2008): 267–304.

9. Adair, *History of the American Indians,* 273–5; Green, "Creek Confederacy in the American Revolution," 66.

10. It is possible that Sophia came later. Thomas Woodward to Albert Pickett, June 21, 1858, *Woodward's Reminiscences of the Creek, or Muscogee, Indians, Contained in Letters to Friends in Georgia and Alabama* (Montgomery, 1859; reprint Tuscaloosa, 1939), 60; Cashin, *Lachlan McGillivray, Indian Trader,* 74–5, 104–7, 156–8, 209; Claudio Saunt, *A New Order of Things: Property, Power, and the Transformation of the Creek Indians, 1733–1816* (New York, 1999), 83–4; Paulett, *Empire of Small Places,* 106-9.

11. Lachlan McGillivray built Vale Royal on lands that the famous Creek woman Mary Musgrove Bosomworth once claimed. Lachlan McGillivray, will, June 12, 1767, http://homepages.rootsweb.ancestry.com/~cmamcrk4/crkdox27.html; Cashin, *Lachlan McGillivray, Indian Trader,* 155, 209; Michael D. Green, "Mary Musgrove: Creating a New World," in *Sifters: Native American Women's Lives,* ed. Theda Perdue (New York, 2001), 29–47.

12. Atkin's speech to Eneah Mico, Sept. 29, 1759, qtd. in Hahn, *Invention of the Creek Nation,* 249; John T. Juricek, *Colonial Georgia and the Creeks: Anglo-Indian Diplomacy on the Southern Frontier, 1733–1766* (Gainesville, 2010); Jill Suzanne Hough, "Fathers and Brothers: Familial Diplomacy of the Creek Indians and Anglo-Americans, 1733 to Removal" (Ph.D. diss., University of California, Davis, 1999), 67–97; Hahn, *Invention of the Creek Nation,* 108, 206–7, 244–8, 250, 258–9; Fred Anderson, *Crucible of War: The Seven Years' War and the Fate of Empire in British North America, 1754–1766* (New York, 2000), 460–2; O'Brien, "Great Choctaw-Chickasaw Peace."

13. Augustine Prevost to the Wolf King and Other Creek Headmen, Oct. 12, 1763, *Early American Indian Documents,* 12: 201; Robert Farmar to the Secretary of War, Jan. 24, 1764, *Mississippi Provincial Archives: English Dominion,* 11.

14. George Johnstone and John Stuart, Report on Indian Congresses, June 12, 1765, *Mississippi Provincial Archives: English Dominion,* 185; *Journal of the Congress of the Four Southern Governors,* 27.

15. Farmar to the Creeks, Jan. 1764, *Mississippi Provincial Archives: English Dominion,* 80; Farmar to the Secretary of War, Jan. 24, 1764, *Mississippi Provincial Archives: English Dominion,* 11.

16. Johnstone and Stuart letter, June 12, 1765, *Mississippi Provincial Archives: English Dominion,* 185.

17. Adair, *History of the American Indians,* 274.

18. Johnstone and Stuart letter, June 12, 1765, *Mississippi Provincial Archives: English Do-*

minion, 187; Johnstone speeches, May 29 and 30, 1765, *Mississippi Provincial Archives: English Dominion,* 205, 208; Emistisiguo to Stuart, April 19, 1772, *Early American Indian Documents,* 12: 428; Meeting of Abekas, Tallapoosas, and Alibamas, Feb. 4, 1774, fr. 61, reel 7, Records of the British Colonial Office, Library of Congress, Washington, D.C.; Milfort, *Chef de guerre,* 191; David Andrew Nichols, *Red Gentlemen and White Savages: Indians, Federalists, and the Search for Order on the American Frontier* (Charlottesville, 2008); Daniel K. Richter, "Native Americans, the Plan of 1764, and a British Empire that Never Was," in *Cultures and Identities in Colonial British America,* ed. Robert Olwell and Alan Tully (Baltimore, 2006), 269–92. The 1768 Treaty of Fort Stanwix and the subsequent Lord Dunmore's War altered the Proclamation Line to the north, but it stayed basically the same on the Creeks' border. Taylor, *Divided Ground,* 40–5.

19. *Journal of the Congress of the Four Southern Governors,* 20; Johnstone and Stuart letter, June 12, 1765, *Mississippi Provincial Archives: English Dominion,* 185; Adair, *History of the American Indians,* 284–5; Wright, *Creeks and Seminoles,* 106; Helen Hornbeck Tanner, "Pipesmoke and Muskets: Florida Indian Intrigues of the Revolutionary Era," in *Eighteenth-Century Florida and Its Borderlands,* ed. Samuel Proctor (Gainesville, 1975), 19; Gregory Evans Dowd, *War under Heaven: Pontiac, the Indian Nations, and the British Empire* (Baltimore, 2002), 245–6; Richter, *Facing East from Indian Country,* 210; Green, "Creek Confederacy in the American Revolution," 61–4; Calloway, *American Revolution in Indian Country,* 44; Kathryn Holland, "The Anglo-Spanish Contest for the Gulf Coast as Viewed from the Townsquare," in *Anglo-Spanish Confrontation,* 91–2; Piker, *Okfuskee,* 66; Greg O'Brien, "Protecting Trade Through War: Choctaw Elites and British Occupation of the Floridas," in *Pre-Removal Choctaw History: Exploring New Paths,* ed. Greg O'Brien (Norman, 2008), 106–13; Starr, *Tories, Dons, and Rebels,* 16–7; Hahn, *Invention of the Creek Nation,* 1–3, 265–8, 271. Another reason for the Creek-Choctaw War may have been blaming one another for the smallpox outbreak of 1764. Paul Kelton, "Avoiding the Smallpox Spirits: Colonial Epidemics and Southeastern Indian Survival," *Ethnohistory* 51 (2004): 51.

20. Robert Middlekauff, *The Glorious Cause: The American Revolution, 1763–1789* (New York, rev. ed., 2005), 159–339.

21. Green, "Creek Confederacy in the American Revolution," 60; Watson W. Jennison, *Cultivating Race: The Expansion of Slavery in Georgia, 1750–1860* (Lexington, 2012), 42–3; Holton, *Forced Founders;* Cashin, *Lachlan McGillivray, Indian Trader,* 286–7; Jim Piecuch, *Three Peoples, One King: Loyalists, Indians, and Slaves in the Revolutionary South, 1775–1782* (Columbia, 2008), 57–60.

22. Woodward to Pickett, June 21, 1858, *Woodward's Reminiscences,* 60; Woodward to J. J. Hooper, Nov. 3, 1858, *Woodward's Reminiscences,* 108.

23. Cashin, *Lachlan McGillivray, Indian Trader,* 72–3; Braund, *Deerskins and Duffels,* 45.

CHAPTER 4

1. James Alton James, *Oliver Pollock: The Life and Times of an Unknown Patriot* (Freeport, 1937; 1970), 1–3, 57; Horace Brown Hayden, *Pollock Genealogy: A Biographical Sketch of Oliver Pollock, Esq., of Carlisle, Pennsylvania* (Harrisburg, 1883), frontispiece, 6.

2. Oliver Pollock, deposition, June 10, 1808, in James Wilkinson, *Memoirs of My Own Times* (Philadelphia, 1816), 2: appendix 1; James, *Oliver Pollock,* 3–4; Levi Marrero, "Charles III and Cuba," in *Charles III: Florida and the Gulf,* ed. Patricia R. Wickman (Miami, 1990), 49.

3. William Henry Egle, *Some Pennsylvania Women During the War of the Revolution* (Harrisburg, 1898), 160; Horace Edwin Hayden, "The Pollock Family of Pennsylvania," *Historical Register: Notes and Queries, Historical and Genealogical Relating to Interior Pennsylvania* 1 (1883): 96–8.

4. Pollock, deposition, June 8, 1808, in Wilkinson, *Memoirs*, 2: appendix 1; James, *Oliver Pollock*, 6–7, 44–5; Light Townsend Cummins, "Oliver Pollock and the Creation of an American Identity in Spanish Colonial Louisiana," in *Nexus of Empire: Negotiating Loyalty and Identity in the Revolutionary Borderlands, 1760s–1820s*, ed. Sylvia L. Hilton and Gene Allen Smith (Gainesville, 2010), 201; Weber, *Spanish Frontier in North America*, 200–2.

5. Cummins, "Oliver Pollock," 202; Peggy K. Liss, *Atlantic Empires: The Network of Trade and Revolution, 1713–1826* (Baltimore, 1983), 26–47.

6. Leroy E. Willie, *Oliver Pollock: Unsung Hero of the American Revolution* (Baton Rouge, 1998), 3.

7. Sherry Johnson, *Climate and Catastrophe in Cuba and the Atlantic World in the Age of Revolution* (Chapel Hill, 2011), 90–102; James, *Oliver Pollock*, 54–7.

8. John Fitzpatrick to Evan and James Jones, July 19, 1772, *The Merchant of Manchac: The Letterbooks of John Fitzpatrick, 1768–1790*, ed. Margaret Dalrymple Fisher (Baton Rouge, 1978), 124–5; Fitzpatrick to John McGillivray and William Struthers, Feb. 11, 1773, *Merchant of Manchac*, 141–2; Fitzpatrick to Pollock, May 21, 1777, *Merchant of Manchac*, 251; Fitzpatrick to Pollock, Jan. 10, 1778, *Merchant of Manchac*, 276; *English Land Grants in West Florida: A Register for the States of Alabama, Mississippi, and Parts of Florida and Louisiana, 1766–1776*, ed. Winston De Ville (Ville Platte, 1986), 24, 28; Light Townsend Cummins, "Oliver Pollock's Plantations: An Early Anglo Landowner on the Lower Mississippi, 1769–1824," *Louisiana History* 29 (1988): 35–48; Cummins, "Oliver Pollock," 201–6.

9. Pollock, deposition, June 8, 1808, in Wilkinson, *Memoirs*, 2: appendix 1; Fitzpatrick to Pollock, Jan. 23, 1777, *Merchant of Manchac*, 228; Light Townsend Cummins, "Oliver Pollock and George Rogers Clark's Service of Supply: A Case Study in Financial Disaster," in *Selected Papers from the 1985 and 1986 George Rogers Clark Trans-Appalachian Frontier History Conferences*, ed. Robert J. Holden (Vincennes, 1988), http://npshistory.com/series/symposia/george_rogers_clark/1985–1986; Kimberly S. Hanger, "Avenues to Freedom Open to New Orleans' Black Population, 1769–1779," in *The African American Experience in Louisiana*, ed. Charles Vincent (Lafayette, 1999), 1: 191; John Craig Hammond, "Slavery, Settlement, and Empire: The Expansion and Growth of Slavery in the Interior of the North American Continent, 1770–1820," *Journal of the Early Republic* 32 (2012): 183.

10. Lawrence Kinnaird, "The Western Fringe of the Revolution," *Western Historical Quarterly* 7 (1976): 256; Cummins, "Oliver Pollock," 206–8.

11. John W. Caughey, *Bernardo de Gálvez in Louisiana, 1776–1783* (Berkeley, 1934), 86–7.

12. Charles Stuart to John Stuart, Oct. 24, 1776, fr. 571–2, reel 7, Records of the British Colonial Office, Library of Congress, Washington, D.C.; Kathryn Trimmer Abbey, "Spanish Projects for the Reoccupation of the Floridas During the American Revolution," *Hispanic American Historical Review* 9 (1929): 266–7; James, *Oliver Pollock*, 61–6, 69–70; Kinnaird, "Western Fringe," 256–8.

13. Pollock to Andrew Allen and Robert Morris, Committee of Congress, Oct. 10, 1776, pp. 53–6, reel 64, Papers of the Continental Congress, 1774–1789, M247, National Archives and Records Service, Washington, D.C., microfilm at University of North Carolina, Chapel Hill; Pollock to the President of Congress, Sept. 18, 1782, in James, *Oliver Pollock*, appendix I, 347–8; Commercial Committee to Pollock, June 12, 1777,

pp. 29–33, reel 64, Papers of the Continental Congress; Commercial Committee to Pollock, Nov. 21, 1777, p. 41, reel 64, Papers of the Continental Congress; Hayden, "Pollock Family of Pennsylvania," 98; Caughey, *Bernardo de Gálvez in Louisiana,* 85–7, 98–100.

14. Pollock, invoice of merchandise shipped on the bateau *Providence,* Jan. 1, 1778, pp. 149–57, reel 64, Papers of the Continental Congress.

15. Holly A. Mayer, *Belonging to the Army: Camp Followers and Community during the American Revolution* (Columbia, 1996); Carol Berkin, *Revolutionary Mothers: Women in the Struggle for America's Independence* (New York, 2005); Mary Beth Norton, *Founding Mothers and Fathers: Gendered Power and the Forming of American Society* (New York, 1996).

CHAPTER 5

1. James Bruce Affidavit, June 21, 1765, *Mississippi Provincial Archives: English Dominion,* 499–500; Bruce, Memorial to the Lords of His Majesty's Treasury, Feb. 15, 1783, p. 137, T 1/582, British National Archives, Kew, England; Bruce Claim, March 1, 1783, p. 62, AO 12/99, British National Archives; Robin F. A. Fabel, "Boom in the Bayous: Land Speculation and Town Planning in the Florida Parishes under British Rule," in *A Fierce and Fractious Frontier: The Curious Development of Louisiana's Florida Parishes, 1699–2000,* ed. Samuel C. Hyde (Baton Rouge, 2004), 49. Thanks to Daniel Papsdorf for James Bruce's claims from London.

2. Patrick Griffin, *American Leviathan: Empire, Nation, and Revolutionary Frontier* (New York, 2007), 21.

3. James Grant to the Earl of Halifax, Sept. 1763, qtd. in Gabriel B. Paquette, *Enlightenment, Governance, and Reform in Spain and its Empire, 1759–1808* (New York, 2008), 118.

4. George Johnstone letter, Nov. 1, 1764, printed in *Georgia Gazette,* Jan. 10, 1765, p. 1; Linda Colley, *The Ordeal of Elizabeth Marsh: A Woman in World History* (London, 2007), 124; Gregory A. Waselkov and Bonnie L. Gums, *Plantation Archaeology at Rivière aux Chiens, ca. 1725–1848* (Mobile, 2000), 17, 25, 31, 72; Fabel, "Boom in the Bayous," 46, 48.

5. Microfilms 6902716, 6902816, 452086, Family History Library, Salt Lake City, Utah. I have found records of only one Isabella or Isabel who wedded a James Bruce in the British Isles between 1767 and 1769, the only years James went back after a decade in North America. Her name was Isabel Chrystie. Twenty-seven years earlier, an Isabel Cristy was christened in Nov. 1742 in Slains Parish, Aberdeenshire, to James Cristy, with no mother recorded. For a parallel Revolution-era story of a woman from Scotland who became a shopkeeper in Boston, see Patricia Cleary, *Elizabeth Murray: A Woman's Pursuit of Independence in Eighteenth-Century America* (Amherst, 2000).

6. It is possible but unlikely that James had already married Isabella and was returning for her. They had no children before 1770, and it is not clear that James had been back in Britain since he left to fight in the Seven Years' War. George Johnstone, letter of permission for leave of absence, Jan. 6, 1767, in *Minutes, Journals, and Acts of the General Assembly of British West Florida,* comp. Robert R. Rea with Milo B. Howard Jr. (Tuscaloosa, 1979), 73-4.

7. Carl Philipp Steuernagel, "A Brief Description of a Journey and about the Expedition of the Prince of Waldeck's Third Regiment in America from 20 May 1776 until the Return from America in the Year of 1783," in *Hessian Letters and Journals and a Memoir,* trans. Bruce E. Burgoyne, ed. Marie E. Burgoyne (Westminster, 2006), 94–6, 106, 153–4, 159, 167; German Officer, Dec. 14, 1778, *Letters from America, 1776-1779:*

Being Letters of Brunswick, Hessian, and Waldeck Officers with the British Armies During the Revolution, trans. Ray W. Pettengill (New York, 1924), 214–7; Philipp Waldeck, *Eighteenth Century America: A Hessian Report on the People, the Land, the War, as Noted in the Diary of Chaplain Philipp Waldeck (1776–1780),* trans. and ed. Bruce E. Burgoyne (Bowie, 1995), 94–5, 100–1, 113, 123–5; Philipp Waldeck, March 18, 1779, in *Letters from America, 1776–1779,* 226–7; Janet Schaw, *Journal of a Lady of Quality; Being the Narrative of a Journey from Scotland to the West Indies, North Carolina, and Portugal, in the Years 1774 to 1776,* ed. Evangeline Walker Andrews (New Haven, 1921), 104; Romans, *Concise Natural History,* 158; Peter Chester to Earl of Hillsborough, Aug. 29, 1771, *Publications of the Mississippi Historical Society,* 5: 90; Gould, *Among the Powers of the Earth,* 48–50.

8. George Johnstone to the Board of Trade, n.d. [received May 30, 1764], *Mississippi Provincial Archives: English Dominion,* 150; William Forbes to the Secretary of State, Jan. 29, 1764, *Mississippi Provincial Archives: English Dominion,* 141; Augustine Prevost to the Secretary of War, Sept. 7, 1763, *Mississippi Provincial Archives: English Dominion,* 136; Waldeck, *Eighteenth Century America,* 125; Town Plan of Pensacola under the British, 1766–1781, in Clinton N. Howard, *The British Development of West Florida, 1763–1769* (Berkeley, 1947), opposite p. 43; John J. Clune Jr. and Margo S. Springfield, *Historic Pensacola* (Gainesville, 2009), 102.

9. Peter Chester to George Germain, March 6, 1777, abstract, *Documents of the American Revolution,* 13: 49-50; Germain to John Stuart, May 15, 1778, fr. 780, reel 7, Records of the British Colonial Office, Library of Congress, Washington, D.C.; Waldeck, *Eighteenth Century America,* 125; Richard L. Campbell, *Historical Sketches of Colonial Florida* (Gainesville, 1975), 107–8; Clune and Springfield, *Historic Pensacola,* 140.

10. Hartigan-O'Connor, *Ties That Buy;* Cleary, *Elizabeth Murray,* 33; Pearsall, *Atlantic Families;* Colley, *Ordeal of Elizabeth Marsh,* xxix.

11. Anne Hulton, *Letters of a Loyalist Lady: Being the Letters of Anne Hulton, Sister of Henry Hulton, Commissioner of Customs at Boston, 1767–1776* (Cambridge, 1927), 54–5, 83; Romans, *Concise Natural History,* 159; T. H. Breen, "An Empire of Goods: The Anglicization of Colonial America, 1690–1776," *Journal of British Studies* 25 (1986): 496; Waselkov and Gums, *Plantation Archaeology,* 136-52, 175; Judith A. Bense, "Archaeology of Late Colonial Pensacola," in *Archaeology of Colonial Pensacola,* ed. Judith A. Bense (Gainesville, 1999), 125–30, 170–1, 175; Mary Beth Norton, *Separated by Their Sex: Women in Public and Private in the Colonial Atlantic World* (Ithaca, 2011), 165–7; Campbell, *Historical Sketches,* 84–5, 109.

12. Register of Births and Burials, June 24 to Dec. 24, 1770, *Publications of the Mississippi Historical Society,* 5: 42; Register of Christenings, June 24 to Dec. 24, 1770, *Publications of the Mississippi Historical Society,* 5: 43; Register of Burials, Dec. 24, 1770, to June 24, 1771, *Publications of the Mississippi Historical Society,* 5: 52; Register of Christenings, Dec. 24, 1770, to June 24, 1771, *Publications of the Mississippi Historical Society,* 5: 53.

13. Robin F. A. Fabel, "Ordeal by Siege: James Bruce in Pensacola, 1780–1781," *Florida Historical Quarterly* 66 (1988): 286; Hulton, *Letters of a Loyalist Lady,* 32, 58–9, 84. Thanks to Konstantin Dierks for pointing out the similar circumstances of Anne Hulton.

14. Judith A. Bense, *Unearthing Pensacola* (Pensacola, 2007), 240–5; Campbell, *Historical Sketches,* 85–8; Clune and Springfield, *Historic Pensacola,* 102, 113–4, 118.

15. Security put up by Bruce to Cadwallader Morris, April 13, 1776, appendix 4 of Robin F. A. Fabel, *The Economy of British West Florida, 1763–1783* (Tuscaloosa, 1988), 231; Longus, *Daphnis and Chloe: A Most Sweet, and Pleasant Pastorall ROMANCE for*

Young Ladies, trans. George Thornley (London, 1657); Daniel Defoe, *Roxana: The Fortunate Mistress* (London, 1724); Nathaniel Lee, *The Rival Queens, or The Death of Alexander the Great, Acted at the Theater-Royal, by Their Majesties Servants* (London, 1677); Elaine Forman Crane, "Political Dialogue and the Spring of Abigail's Discontent," *William and Mary Quarterly* 56 (1999): 745–69; Laurel Ulrich, *A Midwife's Tale: The Life of Martha Ballard, Based on Her Diary, 1785–1812* (New York, 1991), 43. Novelist Fanny Burney referred to a dog named Chloe and made a playful reference to the rivalry between Roxana and Statira all in the same short letter from 1781. Fanny Burney to Hester Lynch Thrale, July 28, 1781, *The Early Journals and Letters of Fanny Burney* (Oxford, 1988), 4: 194.

16. Felicity Nussbaum, "'Real, Beautiful Women': Actresses and *The Rival Queens,*" *Eighteenth-Century Life* 32 (2008): 138–58; Laurel A. Clark, "The Rights of a Florida Wife: Slavery, U.S. Expansion, and Married Women's Property Law," *Journal of Women's History* 22 (2010): 43; Deborah Rosen, "Women and Property Across Colonial America: A Comparison of Legal Systems in New Mexico and New York," *William and Mary Quarterly* 60 (2003): 355–82; Sara Brooks Sundberg, "A Female Planter from West Feliciana Parish, Louisiana: The Letters of Rachel O'Connor," *Louisiana History* 68 (2006): 47–8, 52; Amy Louise Erickson, *Women and Property in Early Modern England* (London, 1993); Norton, *Separated by Their Sex*; Karin A. Wulf, *Not All Wives: Women of Colonial Philadelphia* (Ithaca, 2000), 1–2.

17. Silvia Sebastiani, "Race, Women, and Progress in the Scottish Enlightenment," in *Women, Gender, and Enlightenment,* ed. Sarah Knott and Barbara Taylor (New York, 2005), 75–9; Wulf, *Not All Wives,* 72–3, 184–7.

18. Johnstone to the Board of Trade, Feb. 26, 1766, *Mississippi Provincial Archives: English Dominion,* 417; Starr, *Tories, Dons, and Rebels,* 38–9.

19. Edmund S. Morgan and Helen M. Morgan, *The Stamp Act Crisis: Prologue to Revolution* (Chapel Hill, 1953; 1995), 108–12; J. Barton Starr, "'The Spirit of What Is There Called Liberty': The Stamp Act in British West Florida," *Alabama Review* 29 (1976): 261–72; Cecil Johnson, *British West Florida, 1763–1783* (New Haven, 1943), 26; Howard, *British Development of West Florida,* 26; O'Shaughnessy, *An Empire Divided,* 81–104, 251.

20. Bruce Testimony, Jan. 13, 1766, *Mississippi Provincial Archives: English Dominion,* 366; Johnstone to the Board of Trade, Feb. 26, 1766, *Mississippi Provincial Archives: English Dominion,* 417; Stamp Act Testimony, Jan. 11, 1766, *Mississippi Provincial Archives: English Dominion,* 361; Wilfred B. Kerr, "The Stamp Act in the Floridas, 1765–1766," *Mississippi Valley Historical Review* 21 (1935): 465–9; John Shy, *Toward Lexington: The Role of the British Army in the Coming of the American Revolution* (Princeton, 1965), 282–5; Holton, *Forced Founders,* 41; Linda Colley, *Britons: Forging the Nation, 1707–1837,* rev. ed. (New Haven, 2009), 115–24; Douglas Hamilton, *Scotland, the Caribbean, and the Atlantic World, 1750-1820* (Manchester, 2005), 20–1; Pearsall, *Atlantic Families,* 157–8. On neighboring Georgia and East Florida and the Stamp Act, see Piecuch, *Three Peoples, One King,* 19–24; Robert M. Calhoon, *The Loyalists in Revolutionary America, 1760–1781* (New York, 1965, 1973), 3–15.

21. Ruma Chopra, *Choosing Sides: Loyalists in Revolutionary America* (Lanham, 2013).

22. Chester to Hillsborough, July 8, 1772, *Publications of the Mississippi Historical Society,* 5: 160–3.

23. Johnson, *British West Florida,* 155; William Nelson, *The American Tory* (Oxford, 1961), 3; J. Leitch Wright Jr., *Florida in the American Revolution* (Gainesville, 1975), 4, 13, 19; O'Shaughnessy, *Empire Divided*; Holton, *Forced Founders*; Robert Scott Davis, "Lessons

from Kettle Creek: Patriotism and Loyalism at Askance on the Southern Frontier," *Journal of Backcountry Studies* 1 (2006): 2; Campbell, *Historical Sketches,* 85-6, 90.

24. Lucille Griffith, "Peter Chester and the End of the British Empire in West Florida," *Alabama Review* 30 (1977): 18–20, 31; "1770-1773 British Land Grants," http://vidas. rootsweb.ancestry.com/brgrants.html.

25. Campbell, *Historical Sketches,* 85–6; Griffith, "Peter Chester and the End of the British Empire," 33; Andrew Jackson O'Shaughnessy, *The Men Who Lost America: British Leadership, the American Revolution, and the Fate of the Empire* (New Haven, 2013), 9–10.

26. Stuart to George Germain, Sept. 16, 1776, *Documents of the American Revolution,* 12: 223–4.

27. Charles Roberts, affidavit, March 28, 1777, abstract, *Documents of the American Revolution,* 13: 80.

CHAPTER 6

1. Sylvia Frey, *Water from the Rock: Black Resistance in a Revolutionary Age* (Princeton, 1991), 54-7, 77-9; Benjamin Quarles, *The Negro in the American Revolution* (Chapel Hill, 1961, 1996), xxviii, 119; Elizabeth Fenn, *Pox Americana: The Great Smallpox Epidemic of 1775–82* (New York, 2001), 55–61; Philip S. Foner, *Blacks in the American Revolution* (Westport, 1975), 54–74; Gary B. Nash, *The Forgotten Fifth: African Americans in the Age of Revolution* (Cambridge, 2006), 10–3; Barbara Clark Smith, *The Freedoms We Lost: Consent and Resistance in Revolutionary America* (New York, 2010), xi, 18–46; Peter H. Wood, "'The Dream Deferred': Black Freedom Struggles on the Eve of White Independence," in *In Resistance: Studies in African, Caribbean, and Afro-American History,* ed. Gary Y. Okihiro (Amherst, 1986), 166–87; Herbert Aptheker, *American Negro Slave Revolts* (New York, 1963), 21–3, 87–9.

2. Historians of slave participation in the American Revolution have noted the irony of slaves' seeking liberties within a rebellion for American independence. Peter H. Wood places the parallel within the context of its time, saying that African Americans in the Revolution were "trying to gain greater control of their own lives, trying to obtain what we would now crudely define as 'liberty and independence.'" Quarles, *Negro in the American Revolution,* xxvii; Peter H. Wood, "'Taking Care of Business' in Revolutionary South Carolina: Republicanism and the Slave Society," in *The Southern Experience in the American Revolution,* ed. Jeffrey J. Crow and Larry E. Tise (Chapel Hill, 1978), 276.

3. Gwendolyn Midlo Hall, *Africans in Colonial Louisiana: The Development of Afro-Creole Culture in the Eighteenth Century* (Baton Rouge, 1992), 29–45, 35, 171–2, 279–302; Ira Berlin, *Many Thousands Gone: The First Two Centuries of Slavery in North America* (Cambridge, 1998), 81-90; Gilbert C. Din, *Spaniards, Planters, and Slaves: The Spanish Regulation of Slavery in Louisiana, 1763–1803* (College Station, 1999), 147-9; Roderick A. McDonald, *The Economy and Material Culture of Slaves: Goods and Chattels on the Sugar Plantations of Jamaica and Louisiana* (Baton Rouge, 1993); James Thomas McGowan, "Creation of a Slave Society: Louisiana Plantations in the Eighteenth Century" (Ph.D. diss., University of Rochester, 1976), 97–109; James Benson Sellers, *Slavery in Alabama* (Tuscaloosa, 1950; 1994), 3–8; www.slavevoyages.org.

4. Some of Petit Jean's ancestors may have been cattle keepers on the savannahs of West Africa. Pedro Piernas to Bernardo de Gálvez, Jan. 15, 1781, doc. 21, reel 153, leg. 3, Papeles de Cuba, P. K. Yonge Library, University of Florida, Gainesville; William Dunbar, *Life, Letters, and Papers of William Dunbar of Elgin, Morayshire, Scotland, and*

Natchez, Mississippi, ed. Mrs. Dunbar Rowland (Jackson, 1930), 56; Waldeck, March 19, 1780, *Eighteenth Century America,* 152; Hall, *Africans in Colonial Louisiana,* 36, 143; David Wheat, "My Friend Nicolas Mongoula: Africans, Indians, and Cultural Exchange in Eighteenth-Century Mobile," in *Coastal Encounters,* 118; John D. Ware and Robert R. Rea, *George Gauld, Surveyor and Cartographer of the Gulf Coast* (Gainesville, 1982), 25.

5. Gilbert C. Din, "Slavery in Louisiana's Florida Parishes under the Spanish Regime, 1779–1803," in *Fierce and Fractious Frontier,* 62; Hammond, "Slavery, Settlement, and Empire," 180–90; www.slavevoyages.org. Similarly, in Spanish Louisiana, the slave trade reopened, and plantation slavery was increasing.

6. Johnson, *British West Florida,* 173–5.

7. Waselkov and Gums, *Plantation Archaeology,* 66-8; Mease, "Narrative of a Journey," 5: 88–9; Peter Chester to Earl of Hillsborough, Dec. 28, 1771, "Peter Chester," *Publications of the Mississippi Historical Society,* 5: 107; Daniel H. Usner Jr., "The Frontier Exchange Economy of the Lower Mississippi Valley in the Eighteenth Century," *William and Mary Quarterly* 44 (1987): 184–8; Wheat, "My Friend Nicolas Mongoula," 117–31; William Randolph Ryan, *The World of Thomas Jeremiah: Charles Town on the Eve of the American Revolution* (New York, 2010).

8. Dunbar, *Life, Letters, and Papers,* 26-8.

9. Dunbar, *Life, Letters, and Papers,* 29, 59.

10. Code Noir, 1724, *Interpreting a Continent: Voices from Colonial America,* ed. Kathleen DuVal and John DuVal (Lanham, 2009), 168. On the sometimes blurry line between degrees of unfreedom, see Seth Rockman, *Scraping By: Wage Labor, Slavery, and Survival in Early Baltimore* (Baltimore, 2009).

11. Hanger, "Avenues to Freedom," 1: 185; Martín Navarro to Enrique Grimarest, Feb. 18, 1782, p. 756, reel 442, leg. 83, Papeles de Cuba, P. K. Yonge; Jane Landers, *Black Society in Spanish Florida* (Urbana, 1999), 1–2; Daniel H. Usner Jr., *Indians, Settlers, and Slaves in a Frontier Exchange Economy: The Lower Mississippi Valley Before 1783* (Chapel Hill, 1992), 136–8; Hall, *Africans in Colonial Louisiana,* 202–36; Caughey, *Bernardo de Gálvez in Louisiana,* 144; Alan Taylor, *The Internal Enemy: Slavery and War in Virginia, 1772–1832* (New York, 2013); Linda M. Rupert, "'Henceforth All Slaves Who Seek Refuge in My Dominions Shall Be Free': The Development of Spanish Policy Towards Inter-Imperial Marronage in the Circum-Caribbean, 1664–1790," paper presented to the Triangle Early American History Seminar, Dec. 7, 2012.

12. The average loyalist applying for land in West Florida claimed over seven slaves. Usner, *Indians, Settlers, and Slaves,* 111–5; Wright, *Florida in the American Revolution,* 12, 21–3; Starr, *Tories, Dons, and Rebels,* 47–9, 228–32; Dunbar, *Life, Letters, and Papers,* 23; Bertram Wyatt-Brown, *The House of Percy: Honor, Melancholy, and Imagination in a Southern Family* (New York, 1994), 25-9; Berlin, *Many Thousands Gone,* 326–7; Jennifer K. Snyder, "Revolutionary Repercussions: Loyalist Slaves in St. Augustine and Beyond," in *The Loyal Atlantic: Remaking the British Atlantic in the Revolutionary Era,* ed. Jerry Bannister and Liam Riordan (Toronto, 2012), 165–84.

13. Berlin, *Many Thousands Gone,* 221, 325–7, 333; Hall, *Africans in Colonial Louisiana,* 277–9.

14. Christopher Alain Cameron, "To Plead Our Own Cause: African Americans in Massachusetts and the Making of the Antislavery Movement, 1630-1835" (Ph.D. diss., University of North Carolina at Chapel Hill, 2010), 121–7; Massachusetts Slave Petition to Thomas Gage, May 25, 1774, *Collections of the Massachusetts Historical Society* (Boston, 1877), 3: 432–3.

CHAPTER 7

1. "General Census of the Posts of Attakapas and Opelousas of 4 May 1777," in *Southwest Louisiana Families in 1777: Census Records of Attakapas and Opelousas Posts,* ed. Winston De Ville (Ville Platte, 1987), 12; *Southwest Louisiana Records: Church and Civil Records,* ed. Donald J. Hébert (Rayne, 1997), 1A: 127, 137.

2. *Southwest Louisiana Records,* 2A: 150; Geoffrey Plank, *An Unsettled Conquest: The British Campaign Against the Peoples of Acadia* (Philadelphia, 2001), 10–55; Bona Arsenault, *Histoire et genealogie des Acadiens* (Ottawa, 1978), 2: 431, 436, 471–2, 505–6, 524, 526, 753, 804, 807–8, 811, 816–7; Christopher Hodson, *The Acadian Diaspora: An Eighteenth-Century History* (New York, 2012), 4, 14–46; Warren A. Perrin, *Acadian Redemption: From Beausoleil Broussard to the Queen's Royal Proclamation* (Opelousas, 2004), 5–7, 14, 21; John Mack Faragher, *A Great and Noble Scheme: The Tragic Story of the Expulsion of the French Acadians from Their American Homeland* (New York, 2005), 241–2.

3. Plank, *Unsettled Conquest,* 140; Faragher, *Great and Noble Scheme,* 356.

4. Carl A. Brasseaux, *The Founding of New Acadia: The Beginnings of Acadian Life in Louisiana, 1765–1803* (Baton Rouge, 1987), 23, 27–30; Arsenault, *Histoire et genealogie des Acadiens,* 1: 207–10.

5. Brasseaux, *Founding of New Acadia,* 31–4; Carl A. Brasseaux, "A New Acadia: The Acadian Migrations to South Louisiana, 1764–1803," *Acadiensis* 15 (1985): 124; Christopher Hodson, "Exile on Spruce Street: An Acadian History," *William and Mary Quarterly* 67 (2010): 250; Hodson, *Acadian Diaspora,* 3.

6. Denis-Nicolas Foucault to Etienne-François, Duke of Choiseul-Stainville, Feb. 28, 1765, in "Arrival of Acadians from Santo Domingo," ed. and trans. Carl Brasseaux, *Attakapas Gazette* 10 (1975): 146; Hodson, *Acadian Diaspora,* 116, 198; Jacqueline Voorhies, "The Attakapas Post: The First Acadian Settlement," *Louisiana History* 17 (1976): 91; Brasseaux, "New Acadia," 124–5; Arsenault, *Histoire et genealogie des Acadiens,* 1: 292–4.

7. Charles-Philippe Aubry to Choiseul-Stainville, Feb. 25, 1765, in *Quest for the Promised Land: Official Correspondence Relating to the First Acadian Migration to Louisiana, 1764–1769,* ed. and trans. Carl A. Brasseaux, Emilio Fabian Garcia, and Jacqueline K. Voorhies (Lafayette, 1989), 31; Commission by Charles Philipe Aubry, qtd. in Dudley J. LeBlanc, *The True Story of the Acadians* (Lafayette, 1937), 163-4; Voorhies, "Attakapas Post," 91–6.

8. Foucault, statement of foodstuffs and munitions given to the refugee Acadian families, in "Aubry, Foucault, and the Attakapas Acadians: 1765," ed. Michael James Foret, *Attakapas Gazette* 15 (1980): 62; Aubry, Instructions for Louis Andry Regarding the Settlement of Acadian Families in the Attakapas Area, April 17, 1765, in *Quest for the Promised Land,* 33–7; "The Dauterive Compact," April 4, 1765, trans. Grover Rees, *Attakapas Gazette* 11 (1976): 91; Census and List of Militiamen and Acadian Householders Recently Established at the Attakapas According to the Survey of April 25, 1766, in *Some Late Eighteenth-Century Louisianans: Census Records of the Colony, 1758–1796,* trans. and comp. Jacqueline Voorhies (Lafayette, 1973), 125; *Louisiana Soldiers in the American Revolution,* ed. Winston De Ville (Ville Platte, 1991), 75–8; Brasseaux, "New Acadia," 125; Faragher, *Great and Noble Scheme,* 430–2.

9. Ulloa to Grimaldi, Oct. 26, 1768, *Spain in the Mississippi Valley,* 1: 78; Gilbert C. Din, "Spanish Control over a Multiethnic Society: Louisiana, 1763-1803," in *Choice, Persuasion, and Coercion: Social Control on Spain's North American Frontiers,* ed. Jesús F. de la Teja and Ross Frank (Albuquerque, 2005), 53–5.

10. Aubry to Choiseul-Stainville, Feb. 25, 1765, in *Quest for the Promised Land,* 31; *South-*

west Louisiana Records, 1A: 137; Brasseaux, "New Acadia," 126-8; Perrin, *Acadian Redemption,* 48; Jacqueline K. Voorhies, "The Acadians: The Search for the Promised Land," in *The Cajuns: Essays on Their History and Culture,* ed. Glenn R. Conrad (Lafayette, 1978), 107, 109.

11. *Attakapas Post: The Census of 1771,* ed. Winston De Ville (Ville Platte, 1986), 11; Inventories, Testaments, and Miscellaneous Instruments Pertaining to Heirship, 1760–1811, *Records of Attakapas District, Louisiana, 1739–1811,* comp. Mary Elizabeth Sanders (priv. pub., 1962; digitally published, Urbana, 2012), 38; Attakapas General Census, Oct. 30, 1774, in *Some Late Eighteenth-Century Louisianans,* 282; *Marriage Contracts of the Attakapas Post, 1760-1803,* vol. 5 of *Colonial Louisiana Marriage Contracts,* ed. Winston De Ville (St. Martinsville, 1966), 7; St. Martin Parish Marriage Index, 1760–1811, *Records of Attakapas District,* 27; *Southwest Louisiana Records,* 1A: 46; "General Census of the Posts of Attakapas and Opelousas of 4 May 1777," 12; "The Kelly-Nugent Report on the Inhabitants and Livestock in the Attakapas, Natchitoches, Opelousas and Rapides Posts, 1770," trans. Paulette Guilbert Martin, *Attakapas Gazette* 11 (1976): 192; Brasseaux, *Founding of New Acadia,* 123–4.

12. Duc de Praslin to Mistral, Sept. 13, 1766, in "Phantom Letters: Acadian Correspondence, 1766-1784," ed. Carl A. Brasseaux, *Acadiensis* 23 (1994): 128.

13. Voorhies, "Acadians," 108.

CHAPTER 8

1. David Taitt Journal to and through the Upper Creek Nation, Jan. 30–April 20, 1772, *Documents of the American Revolution,* 5: 254; Milfort, *Chef de guerre,* 70, 156–65; William Bartram, *William Bartram on the Southeastern Indians,* ed. Gregory A. Waselkov and Kathryn E. Holland Braund (Lincoln, 1995), 120–2; Steuernagel, "Brief Description," 159–61; Waldeck, *Eighteenth Century America,* 127–9; Braund, *Deerskins and Duffels,* 9–11, 16–7; Robbie Ethridge, *Creek Country: The Creek Indians and Their World* (Chapel Hill, 2003), 104–5.

2. Thomas Gage to John Stuart, Sept. 12, 1775, fr. 297, reel 7, Records of the British Colonial Office, Library of Congress.

3. John Stuart to the Great and Small Medal Chiefs and Rulers of the Cowetas, Tallapusas, Abekas, and Alibamas, Aug. 15, 1775, fr. 291, reel 7, Records of the British Colonial Office, Library of Congress; William Howe to John Stuart, Jan. 13, 1777, *Documents of the American Revolution,* 14: 28; John Stuart to Howe, April 13, 1777, *Documents of the American Revolution,* 14: 68; Howe to the Head Men, Kings, and Warriors of the Different Tribes of Indians in the Southern District of North America, May 9, 1777, reel 3, Guy Carleton, 1st Baron Dorchester, Papers, British National Archives, Kew, England, microfilm copy at University of North Carolina, Chapel Hill; John Stuart to Augustine Prevost, July 24, 1777, reel 3, Carleton Papers; Tanner, "Pipesmoke and Muskets," 20–1; Andrew K. Frank, *Creeks and Southerners: Biculturalism on the Early American Frontier* (Lincoln, 2005), 39–40; Green, "Creek Confederacy in the American Revolution," 66.

4. Alexander McGillivray's sister Sehoy married first Dutch trader Jacob Moniac and later British Deputy Indian Agent David Taitt. Elise Moniac was the daughter of Jacob Moniac and his first wife, Polly Colbert, who was probably the daughter of Scottish trader James Colbert and his Chickasaw wife. Sophia married French trader Benjamin Durant and had at least seven children with him. Louis Le Clerc Milfort later married their other sister, Jeannette. Thomas Woodward to J. J. Hooper, Nov. 3, 1858, *Woodward's Reminiscences,* 113; Milfort, *Chef de guerre,* 72–4, 213–5; Gregory A.

Waselkov, *A Conquering Spirit: Fort Mims and the Redstick War of 1813–1814* (Tuscaloosa, 2006), 39, kinship charts.

5. Milfort, *Chef de guerre*, 82, 171; Emistisiguo to John Stuart, Nov. 19, 1776, *Documents of the American Revolution*, 12: 250; David Taitt Journal, Jan. 30–April 20, 1772, *Documents of the American Revolution*, 5: 255; Cashin, *Lachlan McGillivray, Indian Trader*, 239, 275; Ethridge, *Creek Country*, 98–100; Christina Snyder, "Conquered Enemies, Adopted Kin, and Owned People: The Creek Indians and Their Captives," *Journal of Southern History* 73 (2007): 260.

6. Milfort, *Chef de guerre*, 161, 212–3; Upper Creeks to John Stuart, Feb. 4, 1774, *Early American Indian Documents*, 12: 441; Emistisiguo to John Stuart, March 2, 1776, *Early American Indian Documents*, 12: 180; John Stuart to George Germain, April 13, 1778, fr. 786–7, reel 7, Records of the British Colonial Office, Library of Congress; John Stuart to Germain, Aug. 10, 1778, *Documents of the American Revolution*, 15: 184; John Stuart to the Great and Small Medal Chiefs and Rulers of the Cowetas, Tallapusas, Abekas, and Alibamas, Aug. 15, 1775, fr. 290–2, reel 7, Records of the British Colonial Office, Library of Congress; Joshua A. Piker, "'White & Clean' & Contested: Creek Towns and Trading Paths in the Aftermath of the Seven Years' War," *Ethnohistory* 50 (2003): 315–48; Green, "Alexander McGillivray," 42–3, 48–50; Jack B. Martin and Margaret McKane Mauldin, *A Dictionary of Creek/Muskogee* (Lincoln, 2000).

7. Milfort, *Chef de guerre*, 72, 74; John Pope, *A Tour Through the Southern and Western Territories of the United States of North America* (Gainesville, 1792; 1979), 49–50; Green, "Alexander McGillivray," 41-2; J. H. O'Donnell, "Alexander McGillivray: Training for Leadership," *Georgia Historical Quarterly* 49 (1965): 175–6; Gilbert C. Din, "Louis LeClerc De Milford, a.k.a. General Francois Tastanegy: An Eighteenth-Century French Adventurer among the Creeks," in *Nexus of Empire*, 63–5.

8. Emistisiguo to John Stuart, Nov. 19, 1776, *Documents of the American Revolution*, 12: 250; David Taitt Journal, Jan. 30–April 20, 1772, *Documents of the American Revolution*, 5: 255; Snyder, "Conquered Enemies," 260.

9. Taitt to John Stuart, June 8, 1777, fr. 650–1, reel 7, Records of the British Colonial Office, Library of Congress.

10. John Stuart to Prevost, July 24, 1777, reel 3, Carleton Papers.

11. Milfort, *Chef de guerre*, 75–6.

12. John Stuart to William Knox, November 26, 1778, *Documents of the American Revolution*, 15: 214; DuVal, *Native Ground*, 19, 42.

13. Piecuch, *Three Peoples, One King*, 119–20.

14. McGillivray Report, Sept. 1, 1778, fr. 154–5, reel 8, Records of the British Colonial Office, Library of Congress; John Stuart to Germain, Dec. 4, 1778, fr. 114, reel 8, Records of the British Colonial Office, Library of Congress.

15. John Stuart to Germain, Jan. 23, 1777, *Documents of the American Revolution*, 14: 34–5; Taitt to Tonyn, May 23, 1777, *Documents of the American Revolution*, 13: 172; John Stuart to Germain, Nov. 24, 1776, *Documents of the American Revolution*, 12: 253–4; Michael D. Green, "The Expansion of European Colonization to the Mississippi Valley, 1780–1880," in *The Cambridge History of the Native Peoples of the Americas*, ed. Bruce G. Trigger and Wilcomb E. Washburn (New York, 1996), 1: 463; Dowd, *Spirited Resistance*, 52–6; Calloway, *American Revolution in Indian Country*, 57; Kathryn E. Holland Braund, "'Like to Have Made a War among Ourselves': The Creek Indians and the Coming of the War of the Revolution," in *Nexus of Empire*, 48–9; Snyder, *Slavery in Indian Country*, 162–3.

16. John Stuart to Germain, June 16, 1777, fr. 633, reel 7, Records of the British Colonial Office, Library of Congress.

17. Journal of a Conference Between the American Commissioners and the Creeks, May 16–19, 1776, *Early American Indian Documents,* 12: 183; Taitt to John Stuart, July 7, 1776, *Documents of the American Revolution,* 12: 159; Braund, "Like to Have Made a War among Ourselves," 46; Cashin, *Lachlan McGillivray, Indian Trader,* 106, 279–81; Cassandra Pybus, *Epic Journeys of Freedom: Runaway Slaves of the American Revolution and Their Global Quest for Liberty* (Boston, 2006), 38–40; Wright, *Creeks and Seminoles,* 108–9.

18. Feb. 6, 1777, *Journals of the Continental Congress,* 7: 96; John Stuart to Germain, March 10, 1777, *Documents of the American Revolution,* 14: 49; John Stuart to Howe, Oct. 6, 1777, reel 3, Carleton Papers; John Lewis Gervais to Henry Laurens, Aug. 16, 1777, *The Papers of Henry Laurens,* ed. David R. Chesnutt and C. James Taylor (Columbia, 1988), 11: 461; John Stuart to Howe, July 26, 1777, fr. 716, reel 7, Records of the British Colonial Office, Library of Congress; Speech to the Headmen and Warriors of the Creek Nation, June 17, 1777, *Early American Indian Documents,* 18: 221–3; Piecuch, *Three Peoples, One King,* 113–4; Braund, "Like to Have Made a War among Ourselves," 47, 52–3.

19. Lower Creek Indians to John Stuart, Oct. 19, 1777, reel 3, Carleton Papers.

20. John Stuart to Knox, Nov. 26, 1778, *Documents of the American Revolution,* 15: 214–5.

21. John Stuart to Howe, Oct. 6, 1777, reel 3, Carleton Papers.

22. Taitt to John Stuart, Aug. 13, 1777, reel 3, Carleton Papers; Piecuch, *Three Peoples, One King,* 334–5.

23. McGillivray to John Stuart, Sept. 21, 1777, fr. 765, reel 7, Records of the British Colonial Office, Library of Congress.

24. McGillivray to John Stuart, Sept. 21, 1777, fr. 766–7, reel 7, Records of the British Colonial Office, Library of Congress; Braund, "Like to Have Made a War among Ourselves," 53–4.

25. McGillivray to John Stuart, Sept. 21, 1777, fr. 767–8, reel 7, Records of the British Colonial Office, Library of Congress; John Stuart to Germain, Oct. 6, 1777, fr. 758+, reel 7, Records of the British Colonial Office, Library of Congress.

26. John Stuart to Howe, Oct. 6, 1777, reel 3, Carleton Papers; Green, "Creek Confederacy in the American Revolution," 66–7.

27. Wright, *Florida in the American Revolution,* 38–9, 42–4, 55–6.

28. McGillivray Report, Sept. 1, 1778, fr. 154–5, reel 8, Records of the British Colonial Office, Library of Congress; John Stuart to Germain, Dec. 4, 1778, fr. 114, reel 8, Records of the British Colonial Office, Library of Congress; Edward J. Cashin, *The King's Ranger: Thomas Brown and the American Revolution on the Southern Frontier* (Athens, 1989), 81–2. Taitt offered to lead them, but the Upper Creeks declined his help. Stuart suspected that Taitt "by his zealous exertions has rendered himself obnoxious to them" and called him back to Pensacola. John Stuart to Germain, Aug. 10, 1778, *Documents of the American Revolution,* 15: 180–2.

29. John Stuart to Knox, Nov. 26, 1778, *Documents of the American Revolution,* 15: 214–5; McGillivray to John Stuart, Aug. 6, 1778, fr. 40–3, reel 8, Records of the British Colonial Office, Library of Congress; Wright, *Florida in the American Revolution,* 55–6.

30. Martha Condray Searcy, *The Georgia-Florida Contest in the American Revolution* (Tuscaloosa, 1985), 164–8; Calhoon, *Loyalists in Revolutionary America,* 474; John Richard Alden, *The South in the American Revolution: 1763–1789* (Baton Rouge, 1957), 232–5.

31. Henry Hamilton to Frederick Haldimand, Dec. 30, 1778, *Documents of the American*

Revolution, 15: 291–2; Hamilton to Haldimand, Jan. 24, 1779, *Documents of the American Revolution,* 17: 48; Dowd, *Spirited Resistance,* 47, 56–8; Wright, *Creeks and Seminoles,* 120.

32. Archibald Campbell to Creeks, [Jan.] 1779, fr. 284, reel 8, Records of the British Colonial Office, Library of Congress; John Stuart to Upper and Lower Creeks, Feb. 1, 1779, fr. 282–3, reel 8, Records of the British Colonial Office, Library of Congress; John Stuart to Taitt, Feb. 1, 1779, fr. 291+, reel 8, Records of the British Colonial Office, Library of Congress; Germain to John Stuart, March 10, 1778, *Documents of the American Revolution,* 15: 67.

33. John Stuart to Upper and Lower Creeks, Feb. 1, 1779, fr. 282–3, reel 8, Records of the British Colonial Office, Library of Congress; Germain to John Stuart, Dec. 2, 1778, fr. 80, reel 8, Records of the British Colonial Office, Library of Congress.

34. Archibald Campbell to the Earl of Carlisle, Jan. 19, 1779, *B. F. Stevens's Facsimiles of Manuscripts in European Archives Relating to America, 1773–1783* (London, 1898), 1: 601; Archibald Campbell to Germain, Jan. 16, 1779, *Documents of the American Revolution,* 17: 39–40; Prevost to Henry Clinton, Feb. 14, 1779, *Documents of the American Revolution,* 17: 65–7; Archibald Campbell to Clinton, March 4, 1779, *Documents of the American Revolution,* 17: 73.

35. Charles Shaw to Germain, Aug. 7, 1779, *Documents of the American Revolution,* 17: 183–4.

36. Archibald Campbell to Creeks, [Jan.] 1779, fr. 284–5, reel 8, Records of the British Colonial Office, Library of Congress; Prevost to Clinton, March 1, 1779, *Documents of the American Revolution,* 17: 68–9; Archibald Campbell to Clinton, March 4, 1779, *Documents of the American Revolution,* 17: 74–5; Germain to Prevost, March 13, 1779, *B. F. Stevens's Facsimiles,* 12: 537–45; Kenneth Coleman, *The American Revolution in Georgia, 1763–1789* (Athens, 1958), 121–4; O'Donnell, "Alexander McGillivray," 176–7; Piecuch, *Three Peoples, One King,* 2–3, 6–7, 9–10, 137–9, 150–1; Snyder, "Conquered Enemies," 260–1; Calhoon, *Loyalists in Revolutionary America,* 474–6; Alden, *South in the American Revolution,* 232–5.

37. Shaw to Germain, Aug. 7, 1779, *Documents of the American Revolution,* 17: 183–4.

38. Commissioners for Indian Affairs to Germain, May 10, 1779, *Documents of the American Revolution,* 17: 118.

39. Germain to Prevost, March 13, 1779, *B. F. Stevens's Facsimiles,* 12: 537–45; Prevost to Clinton, March 15, 1779, reel 5, Carleton Papers; Commissioners for Indian Affairs to Germain, May 10, 1779, *Documents of the American Revolution,* 17: 118; Prevost to Clinton, Aug. 2, 1779, reel 6, Carleton Papers; Taitt to Germain, Aug. 6, 1779, fr. 267–71, reel 8, Records of the British Colonial Office, Library of Congress; O'Donnell, "Alexander McGillivray," 176–7; James H. O'Donnell, *Southern Indians in the American Revolution* (Knoxville, 1973), 80–1; Snyder, "Conquered Enemies," 260–1; Calhoon, *Loyalists in Revolutionary America,* 474–6; Piecuch, *Three Peoples, One King,* 156.

40. Germain to Prevost, March 13, 1779, *B. F. Stevens's Facsimiles,* 12: 543–4.

41. Germain to John Stuart, June 2, 1779, *Documents of the American Revolution,* 17: 138; Dowd, *Spirited Resistance,* 58.

42. Coleman, *American Revolution in Georgia,* 128–9.

43. John Stuart to Germain, January 23, 1778, *Documents of the American Revolution,* 15: 33; Cameron to Prevost, Oct. 15, 1779, reel 7, Carleton Papers; Cashin, *Lachlan McGillivray, Indian Trader,* 291–3; William S. Coker and Thomas D. Watson, *Indian Traders of the Southeastern Spanish Borderlands: Panton, Leslie & Company and John Forbes & Company, 1783–1847* (Gainesville, 1986), 53.

44. McGillivray to John Stuart, Aug. 6, 1778, fr. 40–3, reel 8, Records of the British Co-

lonial Office, Library of Congress; Return of Presents supplied in June 1779 to Alexander McGillivray for Upper Creeks, abstract, *Documents of the American Revolution,* 16: 196; McGillivray to John Stuart, March 9, 1778, reel 4, Carleton Papers; Snyder, "Conquered Enemies," 255–61.

45. McGillivray Report, Sept. 1, 1778, fr. 155, reel 8, Records of the British Colonial Office, Library of Congress; Milfort, *Chef de guerre,* 73.

46. Report of the Congress at Mobile, March 26, 1765, *Mississippi Provincial Archives: English Dominion,* 219.

47. John Stuart to Howe, March 18, 1777, fr. 609, reel 7, Records of the British Colonial Office, Library of Congress.

48. Howe to the Head Men, Kings, and Warriors of the Different Tribes of Indians in the Southern District of North America, May 9, 1777, reel 3, Carleton Papers; Adair, *History of the American Indians,* 301–2, 339; Calloway, *American Revolution in Indian Country,* 222; Wright, *Florida in the American Revolution,* 35.

49. Peter Chester to Howe, Aug. 30, 1776, reel 3, Carleton Papers.

50. Howe to the Head Men, Kings, and Warriors of the Different Tribes of Indians in the Southern District of North America, May 9, 1777, reel 3, Carleton Papers.

51. John Stuart to Chickasaws and Choctaws, May 14, 1777, fr. 644–5, reel 7, Records of the British Colonial Office, Library of Congress; John Stuart to Germain, June 16, 1777, fr. 629, reel 7, Records of the British Colonial Office, Library of Congress.

52. John Stuart to Chickasaws and Choctaws, May 14, 1777, fr. 644–5, reel 7, Records of the British Colonial Office, Library of Congress.

53. Charles Stuart to Chester, n.d., "Peter Chester, Third Governor," 5: 50; David Taitt Journal, March 12, 1772, *Documents of the American Revolution,* 5: 262; John Stuart to the Earl of Hillsborough, Feb. 7, 1772, *Documents of the American Revolution,* 5: 38; John Stuart to Frederick Haldimand, Feb. 3, 1774, *Documents of the American Revolution,* 8: 35; John Stuart to Germain, June 16, 1777, fr. 629, reel 7, Records of the British Colonial Office, Library of Congress; Villiers to Bernardo de Gálvez, Oct. 12, 1777, fol. 117, leg. 190, Papeles de Cuba, Archivo General de Indies; Calloway, *American Revolution in Indian Country,* 222–3.

54. July 19, 1777, *Journals of the Continental Congress,* 8: 566-7; Max Savelle, *George Morgan: Colony Builder* (New York, 1932), 73.

55. Benedict Arnold to Richard Peters, July 5, 1777, pp. 259–60, reel 157, Papers of the Continental Congress, 1774–1789, M247, National Archives and Records Service, Washington, D.C., microfilm at University of North Carolina, Chapel Hill; George Morgan to Arnold and Board of War, July 6, 1777, pp. 255–7, reel 157, Papers of the Continental Congress; Congressional Debates on Board of War Report, July 24 and 25, 1777, *Letters of Members of the Continental Congress,* ed. Edmund Burnett (Gloucester, 1963), 2: 421–2.

56. Congressional Debates on Board of War Report, July 24 and 25, 1777, in *Letters of Members of the Continental Congress,* 2: 421–3; Laurens to John Rutledge, Aug. 12, 1777, *Letters of Members of the Continental Congress,* 2: 446–7; Wright, *Florida in the American Revolution,* 45, 65-6; Starr, *Tories, Dons, and Rebels,* 81–2; Abbey, "Spanish Projects," 270–1; James, *Oliver Pollock,* 107–8.

57. Capitulation by delegates for the Natchez district to James Willing, Feb. 21, 1778, reel 3, Carleton Papers; Anthony Hutchins to Germain, May 21, 1778, *Documents of the American Revolution,* 15: 123; William Dunbar, journal entry for May 1, 1778, *Life, Letters, and Papers,* 61; Cummins, "Oliver Pollock," 204; Caughey, *Bernardo de Gálvez in Louisiana,* 103; John Caughey, "Willing's Expedition Down the Mississippi, 1778," *Louisiana Historical Quarterly* 15 (1932): 5–36; Burton Alva Konkle, *Thomas Willing and*

the First American Financial System (Philadelphia, 1937), 4, 14, 22, 136. On Willing's and Pollock's earlier business dealings, see John Fitzpatrick to Evan and James Jones, July 19, 1772; Fitzpatrick to Francis Poussett, Feb. 2, 1773; Fitzpatrick to Willing, Feb. 3, 1773; Fitzpatrick to Willing, June 16, 1775; all in *Merchant of Manchac,* 124–5, 141, 191; Robert E. Wright, "Thomas Willing (1731–1821): Philadelphia Financier and Forgotten Founding Father," *Pennsylvania History* 63 (1996): 527–8, 541, 543.

58. Commercial Committee to Edward Hand, Nov. 21, 1777, *Letters of Members of the Continental Congress,* 2: 565; Commercial Committee to Oliver Pollock, Nov. 25, 1777, pp. 194-5, reel 64, Papers of the Continental Congress; Caughey, *Bernardo de Gálvez in Louisiana,* 102-3, 107; Kinnaird, "Western Fringe," 259-60; Starr, *Tories, Dons, and Rebels,* 82, 86; James, *Oliver Pollock,* 81–3.

59. Hand to Peters, Dec. 24, 1777, p. 424, reel 178, Papers of the Continental Congress; Return of Volunteer Crew of *Rattletrap,* Dec. 22, 1777, *Frontier Defense on the Upper Ohio, 1777–1778,* ed. Reuben Gold Thwaites and Louise Phelps Kellogg (Madison, 1912), 302–3; Morgan to Willing, Jan. 1778, p. 435, reel 178, Papers of the Continental Congress; John Stuart to Germain, Jan. 23, 1778, *Documents of the American Revolution,* 15: 34; Hardy Perry to Farquar Bethune, Feb. 4, 1778, reel 3, Carleton Papers; Capitulation by delegates for the Natchez district to Willing, Feb. 21, 1778, reel 3, Carleton Papers; John Stuart to Germain, March 5, 1778, *Documents of the American Revolution,* 15: 56; Chester to Germain, March 25, 1778, *Documents of the American Revolution,* 15: 78; Willing Report to Congress, April 14, 1778, pp. 491–2, reel 104, Papers of the Continental Congress; John Stuart to Germain, May 2, 1778, *Documents of the American Revolution,* 15: 112; Declaration of Stephen Shakspear, May 6, 1778, *Spain in the Mississippi Valley,* 1: 273.

60. Germain to John Stuart, July 1, 1778, *Documents of the American Revolution,* 15: 152.

61. John Stuart to Charles Stuart, March 2, 1778, fr. 832, reel 7, Records of the British Colonial Office, Library of Congress.

62. Chester to Prevost, March 21, 1778, reel 4, Carleton Papers; Willing Report to Congress, April 14, 1778, pp. 491–2, reel 104, Papers of the Continental Congress; St. Jean, "Chickasaw-Quapaw Alliance," 276.

63. Charles Stuart to John Stuart, March 7, 1778, reel 4, Carleton Papers.

64. Of course, the logic worked in the opposite way for Indians who had allied with France in the Seven Years' War. Chickasaw Talk to the Rebels, May 22, 1779, fr. 41–2, reel. 65, Papers of the Continental Congress; Andrew Rainsford et al. to Germain, July 12, 1779, fr. 371–2, reel 8, Records of the British Colonial Office, Library of Congress; Calloway, *American Revolution in Indian Country,* 226; Dowd, *Spirited Resistance,* 48.

65. DuVal, *Native Ground,* 78, 128, 134–41.

66. John Stuart to Germain, Aug. 10, 1778, *Documents of the American Revolution,* 15: 183–4. Similarly, Nativists who advocated opposing "white people" sometimes exempted the French. See "Pontiac's Speech to an Ottawa, Potawatomi, and Huron Audience, 1763," *Interpreting a Continent,* 82. On "red" and "white" among eighteenth-century southeastern Indians, see Nancy Shoemaker, "How Indians Got to be Red," *American Historical Review* 102 (1997): 625–44.

67. John Stuart to Germain, Aug. 10, 1778, *Documents of the American Revolution,* 15: 183–4.

68. John Stuart to Germain, Jan. 11, 1779, *Documents of the American Revolution,* 17: 29–30.

69. Chickasaw Talk to the Rebels, May 22, 1779, fr. 41–2, reel 65, Papers of the Continental Congress; George C. Osborn, "Relations with the Indians in West Florida During the Administration of Governor Peter Chester, 1770–1781," *Florida Historical Quarterly* 31 (1953): 265–6.

70. Chickasaw Talk to the Rebels, May 22, 1779, fr. 41–2, reel 65, Papers of the Continental Congress; Andrew Rainsford et al. to Germain, July 12, 1779, fr. 371–2, reel 8, Records of the British Colonial Office, Library of Congress; Calloway, *American Revolution in Indian Country,* 226.

71. Mingo Houma, Payamataha, and other Chickasaws to Spaniards, March 8, 1779, CO5/80: 339–42, British National Archives, Kew, England. Thanks to Brandon Layton for this document.

72. Headmen and Warriors of the Chickasaw Nation to the King of Carolina and His Beloved Men, April 5, 1756, *Colonial Records of South Carolina,* ed. McDowell, 110.

CHAPTER 9

1. Piecuch, *Three Peoples, One King,* 86, 163–4; Quarles, *Negro in the American Revolution,* xxviii–xxx; Nash, *Forgotten Fifth,* 12–3; Pybus, *Epic Journeys of Freedom,* 40–1.

2. James Corbett David, *Dunmore's New World: The Extraordinary Life of a Royal Governor in Revolutionary America—with Jacobites, Counterfeiters, Land Schemes, Shipwrecks, Scalping, Indian Politics, Runaway Slaves, and Two Illegal Royal Weddings* (Charlottesville, 2013), 107.

3. Etienne de Périer to Jean Frédéric Phélypeaux, Compte de Maurepas, March 18, 1730, *Mississippi Provincial Archives: French Dominion,* ed. and trans. Dunbar Rowland and A. G. Sanders (Jackson, 1927), 1: 70; Carlos de Grand-Pre to Pedro Piernas, May 1, 1781, doc. 93, reel 153, leg. 3, Papeles de Cuba, P. K. Yonge Library, University of Florida, Gainesville; José de Ezpeleta to All of the Choctaw Chiefs, Aug. 26, 1780, fr. 2185, reel 167, leg. 2, Papeles de Cuba, P. K. Yonge; Francisco Cruzat to Bernardo de Gálvez, Nov. 11, 1780, fr. 75, reel 164, leg. 2, Papeles de Cuba, P. K. Yonge. Peter H. Wood, *Black Majority: Negroes in Colonial South Carolina from 1670 through the Stono Rebellion* (New York, 1974), 125–9; Frey, *Water from the Rock,* 48, 77–9; Landers, *Black Society in Spanish Florida,* 22, 202; Hall, *Africans in Colonial Louisiana,* 103, 173; Foner, *Blacks in the American Revolution,* 41.

4. William Dunbar, journal entry for May 1, 1778, *Life, Letters, and Papers,* 60–2; Oliver Pollock to Commercial Committee, April 1, 1778, p. 61, reel 64, Papers of the Continental Congress, 1774-1789, M247, National Archives and Records Service, Washington, D.C., microfilm at University of North Carolina, Chapel Hill.

5. John Stuart to Charles Stuart, March 2, 1778, fr. 831, reel 7, Records of the British Colonial Office, Library of Congress, Washington, D.C.; John Campbell to John Stuart, March 5, 1778, reel 3, Guy Carleton, 1st Baron Dorchester, Papers, British National Archives, Kew, England, microfilm copy at University of North Carolina, Chapel Hill; James Willing to Bernardo de Gálvez, April 5, 1778, *Spain in the Mississippi Valley,* 1: 263; Declaration of Stephen Shakspear, May 6, 1778, *Spain in the Mississippi Valley,* 1: 273–5; Anthony Hutchins to George Germain, May 21, 1778, *Documents of the American Revolution,* 15: 123–4; Kinnaird, "Western Fringe," 259; Caughey, *Bernardo de Gálvez in Louisiana,* 109-11, 142, 145–6; Starr, *Tories, Dons, and Rebels,* 78; James, *Oliver Pollock,* 118–20.

6. Willing to Bernardo de Gálvez, June 1, 1778, *Spain in the Mississippi Valley,* 1: 285.

7. Pollock to Bernardo de Gálvez, Aug. 29, 1778, *Spain in the Mississippi Valley,* 1: 304–5; Peter Chester to Bernardo de Gálvez, n.d., 1778, *Spain in the Mississippi Valley,* 1: 247; Berlin, *Many Thousands Gone,* 219–20.

8. Donald Campbell to John Stuart, March 5, 1778, reel 3, Carleton Papers; Alexander Ross to John Stuart, March 5, 1778, reel 3, Carleton Papers; Chester to Augustine Prevost, March 21, 1778, reel 4, Carleton Papers; Willing Report to Congress, April

14, 1778, p. 492, reel 104, Papers of the Continental Congress; Security put up by James Bruce to Cadwallader Morris, April 13, 1776, appendix 4 of Fabel, *Economy of British West Florida,* 231; Bruce, Additional Memorial to the Lords of His Majesty's Treasury, Feb. 15, 1783, p. 143, T 1/582, British National Archives; Schedule of Lands and Plantations of James Bruce, Feb. 15, 1783, p. 144, T 1/582, British National Archives; Bruce Claim, March 1, 1783, p. 62, AO 12/99, British National Archives; Fabel, "Ordeal by Siege," 285; Caughey, *Bernardo de Gálvez in Louisiana,* 108–11.

9. Robert R. Rea, "Planters and Plantations in British West Florida," *Alabama Review* 29 (1976): 224–5.

10. Schedule of Lands and Plantations of James Bruce, Feb. 15, 1783, p. 144, T 1/582, British National Archives.

11. *English Land Grants in West Florida,* 7, 10, 16–7, 20, 28–30; *Terms for Land Grants in New Colonies, 1763, in Royal Instructions to British Colonial Governors, 1670–1776,* ed. Leonard Woods Labaree (New York, 1935), 2: 528–9; "1770–1773 British Land Grants," http://vidas.rootsweb.ancestry.com/brgrants.html; Rothschild, *Inner Life of Empires,* 39; Johnson, *British West Florida,* 121, 131; Fabel, "Ordeal by Siege," 283–4; Fabel, "Boom in the Bayous," 44–59; Starr, *Tories, Dons, and Rebels,* 29–30.

12. Bruce, Additional Memorial to the Lords of His Majesty's Treasury, Feb. 15, 1783, p. 143, T 1/582, British National Archives; Schedule of Lands and Plantations of James Bruce, Feb. 15, 1783, p. 144, T 1/582, British National Archives; Romans, *Concise Natural History,* 169–72; Mease, "Narrative of a Journey," 5: 69; Dunbar, *Life, Letters, and Papers,* 23; Chester to Earl of Dartmouth, Jan. 21, 1775, *Documents of the American Revolution,* 9: 32–3; Rea, "Planters and Plantations," 224-5; Wright, *Florida in the American Revolution,* 14; Fabel, "Boom in the Bayous," 53–4; Waselkov and Gums, *Plantation Archaeology,* 64.

13. Chester to Earl of Hillsborough, Sept. 28, 1771, *Publications of the Mississippi Historical Society,* 5: 95–7; Chester to Dartmouth, Jan. 21, 1775, *Documents of the American Revolution,* 9: 32; Schedule of Lands and Plantations of James Bruce, Feb. 15, 1783, p. 144, T 1/582, British National Archives.

14. July 21, 1775, *Journals of the Continental Congress,* 2: 198.

15. Samuel Adams to James Warren, Nov. 3, 1778, *Letters of Members of the Continental Congress,* 3: 476.

16. George Morgan to Bernardo de Gálvez, April 26, 1778, *Spain in the Mississippi Valley,* 1: 266–8.

17. Alexander Cameron to Germain, July 18, 1780, fr. 444, reel 8, Records of the British Colonial Office, Library of Congress; Congressional Report, June 27, 1778, *Journals of the Continental Congress,* 11: 671; Fabel, "Boom in the Bayous," 50, 52; Eugene Lyon, "Demographic Trends: Florida and the Gulf," in *Charles III,* 43.

18. George Rogers Clark to Fernando de Leyba, Nov. 6, 1778, qtd. in Caughey, *Bernardo de Gálvez in Louisiana,* 133.

19. Henry Hamilton, "Address to the Inhabitants of Illinois," 1778, in *Virginia Gazette,* June 26, 1779, 1.

20. John Stuart to Germain, Jan. 23, 1778, *Documents of the American Revolution,* 15: 33–4; John Stuart to Germain, May 2, 1778, *Documents of the American Revolution,* 15: 112; John Stuart to Germain, May 19, 1778, *Documents of the American Revolution,* 15: 121–2; John Stuart to Germain, Aug. 10, 1778, *Documents of the American Revolution,* 15: 184.

21. John Stuart to William Howe, Feb. 4, 1778, reel 3, Carleton Papers; Waldeck, *Eighteenth Century America,* 125.

22. Germain to Chester, Feb. 7, 1777, abstract, *Documents of the American Revolution,* 13: 34;

Chester to Germain, March 25, 1778, *Documents of the American Revolution*, 15: 78–81; Peter Parker to Philip Stephens, April 19, 1778, abstract, *Documents of the American Revolution*, 13: 322; Chester to Germain, June 2, 1778, *Documents of the American Revolution*, 15: 129; John Stuart to Germain, Aug. 10, 1778, *Documents of the American Revolution*, 15: 183; Bettie Jones Conover, "British West Florida's Mississippi Frontier Posts, 1763–1779," *Alabama Review* 29 (1976): 184–5.

23. John Stuart to William Knox, Nov. 26, 1778, *Documents of the American Revolution*, 15: 213.

24. Chester to Germain, May 7, 1778, *Documents of the American Revolution*, 15: 119; Clune and Springfield, *Historic Pensacola*, 100–1. In England, militia reform had occasioned riots. Eliga H. Gould, *The Persistence of Empire: British Political Culture in the Age of the American Revolution* (Chapel Hill, 2000), 72–105; Ware and Rea, *George Gauld*, 207–10.

25. John Stuart to Knox, Nov. 26, 1778, *Documents of the American Revolution*, 15: 213–4.

26. *Minutes, Journals, and Acts*, 277–8.

27. Chester to Germain, March 25, 1778, *Documents of the American Revolution*, 15: 78–81; John Stuart to Germain, April 13, 1778, fr. 785–6, reel 7, Records of the British Colonial Office, Library of Congress; Cashin, *Lachlan McGillivray, Indian Trader*, 155–6; Conover, "British West Florida's Mississippi Frontier Posts," 184–5.

28. Donald Campbell to John Stuart, March 20, 1778, abstract, *Documents of the American Revolution*, 13: 269; John Stuart to Germain, April 13, 1778, fr. 781–2, reel 7, Records of the British Colonial Office, Library of Congress; Chester to Germain, April 14, 1778, *Documents of the American Revolution*, 15: 100; Chester to Germain, March 25, 1778, *Documents of the American Revolution*, 15: 79; Piecuch, *Three Peoples, One King*, 106, 108; Starr, *Tories, Dons, and Rebels*, 92, 103–8, 113–6.

29. Bethune Report, June 16, 1778, fr. 59–66, reel 8, Records of the British Colonial Office, Library of Congress; Anthony Hutchins to Germain, May 21, 1778, *Documents of the American Revolution*, 15: 124–5; John Stuart to Germain, April 13, 1778, fr. 781–7, reel 7, Records of the British Colonial Office, Library of Congress; Willing Report to Congress, April 14, 1778, p. 494, reel 104, Papers of the Continental Congress; Return of Indian Traders at Natchez, April 21, 1778, fr. 5, reel 8, Records of the British Colonial Office, Library of Congress; John Stuart to Germain, May 2, 1778, *Documents of the American Revolution*, 15: 112; Chester to Germain, May 7, 1778, *Documents of the American Revolution*, 15: 119; John Stuart to Knox, May 18, 1778, fr. 875, reel 7, Records of the British Colonial Office, Library of Congress; Bernardo de Gálvez to José de Gálvez, July 3, 1779, 3: 336–7, Bernardo de Gálvez Cartas al Josef de Gálvez, 1777–1781, Transcripts from the Archivo Nacional de Cuba, Ayer Collection, Newberry Library, Chicago; Greg O'Brien, *Choctaws in a Revolutionary Age, 1750–1830* (Lincoln, 2002), 40–1; Caughey, *Bernardo de Gálvez in Louisiana*, 125–6; Starr, *Tories, Dons, and Rebels*, 111–2.

30. David Taitt to Germain, Aug. 6, 1779, fr. 275, reel 8, Records of the British Colonial Office, Library of Congress.

31. Steuernagel, "Brief Description," 159; William Stiell to Germain, Oct. 15, 1778, abstract, *Documents of the American Revolution*, 13: 364; Waldeck, *Eighteenth Century America*, 124–5; John Stuart to Knox, Nov. 26, 1778, *Documents of the American Revolution*, 15: 213; John Stuart to Germain, Dec. 4, 1778, fr. 101, reel 8, Records of the British Colonial Office, Library of Congress; John Campbell to Henry Clinton, Feb. 10, 1779, Carleton Papers; Dunbar, journal entry for Oct. 28, 1778, *Life, Letters, and Papers*, 65–6; Starr, *Tories, Dons, and Rebels*, 124–5.

32. John Fitzpatrick to McGillivray, Struthers, & Company, April 10, 1778, *Merchant of Manchac*, 289; Fitzpatrick to John Miller, June 9, 1778, *Merchant of Manchac*, 294–5;

Fitzpatrick to Miller, Sept. 14, 1778, *Merchant of Manchac,* 306; Fitzpatrick to William Weir, Sept. 16, 1778, *Merchant of Manchac,* 307.

33. Diego Josef Navarro to Bernardo de Gálvez, June 17, 1778, fr. 1397, reel 186, leg. 1, Papeles de Cuba, P. K. Yonge; Germain to John Stuart, Aug. 5, 1778, *Documents of the American Revolution,* 15: 179; Starr, *Tories, Dons, and Rebels,* 123.

34. William Franklin to Germain, Dec. 20, 1778, *Documents of the American Revolution,* 15: 295; Irvin, *Clothed in Robes of Sovereignty,* 186, 196.

35. Germain to John Campbell, July 1, 1778, reel 4, Carleton Papers; Dunbar, journal entry for Dec. 13, 1778, *Life, Letters, and Papers,* 66.

36. Piers Mackesy, *The War for America, 1775–1783* (London, 1964), xiv, 182–3, 232–3, 318.

37. Clinton to Germain, October 8, 1778, *Documents of the American Revolution,* 15: 210.

38. German Officer, Oct. 31, 1778, *Letters from America, 1776–1779,* 205–6; Navarro to Antonio María Bucareli, Dec. 6, 1778, *Spain in the Mississippi Valley,* 1: 315–6; Clinton to Germain, Sept. 15, 1778, *Documents of the American Revolution,* 15: 201; Clinton to Prevost, Oct. 20, 1778, Carleton Papers; Clinton to John Campbell, Oct. 27, 1778, Carleton Papers; J. Barton Starr, "'Left as a Gewgaw': The Impact of the American Revolution on British West Florida," in *Eighteenth-Century Florida: The Impact of the American Revolution,* ed. Samuel Proctor (Pensacola, 1976), 18; Mackesy, *War for America,* 229–34; Daniel Krebs, *A Generous and Merciful Enemy: Life for German Prisoners of War during the American Revolution* (Norman, 2013), 3, 218; M. Christopher New, *Maryland Loyalists in the American Revolution* (Centreville, 1996), 82–3; Starr, *Tories, Dons, and Rebels,* 129–30; Wright, *Florida in the American Revolution,* 73; Caughey, *Bernardo de Gálvez in Louisiana,* 133–4.

39. John Campbell to Clinton, Feb. 10, 1779, Carleton Papers.

40. Mackesy, *War for America,* 275.

41. Cameron to Clinton, Dec. 15, 1779, reel 7, Carleton Papers; Germain to Cameron and Thomas Brown, June 25, 1779, *Documents of the American Revolution,* 17: 154; Cameron to Germain, May 1, 1780, fr. 433–5, reel 8, Records of the British Colonial Office, Library of Congress; James Campbell to Charles Stuart, Sept. 9, 1779, reel 7, Carleton Papers; Cameron to Prevost, Oct. 15, 1779, reel 7, Carleton Papers; Cameron to Clinton, Dec. 15, 1779, reel 7, Carleton Papers; Cameron to Germain, Dec. 18, 1779, reel 7, Carleton Papers; O'Donnell, "Alexander McGillivray," 177–8; Holland, "Anglo-Spanish Contest," 92; Cashin, *King's Ranger.*

CHAPTER 10

1. Oliver Pollock to President of Congress, Sept. 18, 1782, reel 64, Papers of the Continental Congress, 1774–1789, M247, National Archives and Records Service, Washington, D.C., microfilm at University of North Carolina, Chapel Hill; Pollock, deposition, June 8, 1808, in Wilkinson, *Memoirs,* 2: appendix 1; Hayden, "Pollock Family of Pennsylvania," 98; Caughey, *Bernardo de Gálvez in Louisiana,* 85–7, 98–100.

2. O'Reilly to Grimaldi, Sept. 30, 1770, *Spain in the Mississippi Valley,* 1: 185; Paquette, *Enlightenment, Governance, and Reform,* 117–23; Thomas E. Chávez, *Spain and the Independence of the United States: An Intrinsic Gift* (Albuquerque, N.M., 2002), 19.

3. The Count of Aranda to the Marquis of Grimaldi, Jan. 13, 1777, qtd. in Chávez, *Spain and the Independence of the United States,* 56; R. R. Palmer, *The Age of the Democratic Revolution: A Political History of Europe and America, 1760–1800* (Princeton, 1959), 85–107.

4. Reales Cédulas en que el Rey se sirve haver merced del Título de Castilla, con la

Denominacion de Conde de Gálvez (1783), photostat in *Tribute to Don Bernardo de Gálvez: Royal Patents and an Epic Ballad Honoring the Spanish Governor of Louisiana,* ed. Ralph Lee Woodward Jr., 9, 11–2; Stanley J. Stein and Barbara H. Stein, *Apogee of Empire: Spain and New Spain in the Age of Charles III, 1759–1789* (Baltimore, 2003); Paquette, *Enlightenment, Governance, and Reform;* Caughey, *Bernardo de Gálvez in Louisiana,* 68.

5. Paquette, *Enlightenment, Governance, and Reform,* 97; Chávez, *Spain and the Independence of the United States,* 20.

6. Peter Chester to Bernardo de Gálvez, June 10, 1777, *Documents of the American Revolution,* 14: 107; Bernardo de Gálvez to José de Gálvez (and attachments), Sept. 15, 1777, doc. 86, reel 13, leg. 2547, Audiencia de Santo Domingo, Archivo General de Indias, Historic New Orleans Collection, New Orleans, La.; Royal Decree to Extend Free Trade, Feb. 2, 1778, *Spain in the Mississippi Valley,* 1: 250–4; *Tribute to Don Bernardo de Gálvez,* xviii–xix; Caughey, *Bernardo de Gálvez in Louisiana,* 71, 91–2; Jack D. L. Holmes, *Honor and Fidelity: The Louisiana Infantry Regiment and the Louisiana Militia Companies, 1766–1821* (Birmingham, 1965), 23; Robin F. A. Fabel, "Anglo-Spanish Commerce in New Orleans During the American Revolutionary Era," in *Anglo-Spanish Confrontation,* 34.

7. Bernardo de Gálvez to Thomas Lloyd, May 11, 1777, reel 3, Guy Carleton, 1st Baron Dorchester, Papers, British National Archives, Kew, England, microfilm copy at University of North Carolina, Chapel Hill; "Commerce up the Mississippi and an account of the interruption to trade by the Spaniards," n.d. [May 1777], reel 3, Carleton Papers; William Stiell to William Howe, June 3, 1777, reel 3, Carleton Papers; Abbey, "Spanish Projects," 268–9.

8. Pollock to President of Congress, Sept. 18, 1782, p. 1, reel 64, Papers of the Continental Congress; James, *Oliver Pollock,* 75–6; Wright, *Florida in the American Revolution,* 70.

9. Bernardo de Gálvez to José de Gálvez, May 27, 1779, doc. 288, reel 14, leg. 2547, Audiencia de Santo Domingo, Historic New Orleans Collection; Landers, *Black Society in Spanish Florida,* 22, 202.

10. James Julian Coleman Jr., *Gilbert Antoine de St. Maxent: The Spanish-Frenchman of New Orleans* (New Orleans, 1968), 50–4; Coker and Watson, *Indian Traders,* 8–10.

11. James Bruce to John Pownall, Oct. 16, 1777, *Documents of the American Revolution,* 14: 225–7.

12. John Stuart to George Germain, April 13, 1778, fr. 784–5, reel 7, Records of the British Colonial Office, Library of Congress, Washington, D.C.; Charles Stuart Report, July 1, 1778, fr. 44–58, reel 8, Records of the British Colonial Office, Library of Congress; John Stuart to Germain, May 2, 1778, *Documents of the American Revolution,* 15: 113.

13. Bernardo de Gálvez to José de Gálvez, Sept. 19, 1777, doc. 90, reel 13, leg. 2547, Audiencia de Santo Domingo, Historic New Orleans Collection; John Stuart to Howe, Oct. 6, 1777, reel 3, Carleton Papers; John Blommart to John Stuart, Aug. 18, 1777, fr. 711, reel 7, Records of the British Colonial Office, Library of Congress; Henry Stuart to John Stuart, Aug. 11, 1777, abstract, *Documents of the American Revolution,* 13: 184; Bernardo de Gálvez to José de Gálvez, May 27, 1779, doc. 288, reel 14, leg. 2547, Audiencia de Santo Domingo, Historic New Orleans Collection.

14. Pollock to Diego Josef Navarro, May 13, 1778, fr. 1409–11, reel 186, leg. 1, Papeles de Cuba, P. K. Yonge Library, University of Florida, Gainesville; Pollock to Bernardo de Gálvez, n.d., 1778, Oliver Pollock Papers, Missouri Historical Society Archives, St. Louis, Missouri; Bernardo de Gálvez to Navarro, Sept. 2, 1778, 1: 125,

Bernardo de Gálvez Cartas al Capitán General de Habana, 1777–1781, Transcripts from the Archivo Nacional de Cuba, Ayer Collection, Newberry Library, Chicago, Ill.; Pollock to the President of Congress, Sept. 18, 1782, reel 64, Papers of the Continental Congress.

15. Pollock to Commercial Committee, April 1, 1778, p. 59, reel 64, Papers of the Continental Congress; William Dunbar, journal entry for May 1, 1778, *Life, Letters, and Papers,* 61–2.

16. Willing to Naval Committee, July 29, 1778, pp. 487–8, reel 104, Papers of the Continental Congress.

17. Pollock to Commercial Committee, July 6, 1778, pp. 80–1, reel 64, Papers of the Continental Congress.

18. Pollock to Commercial Committee, Oct. 5, 1778, pp. 90–3, reel 64, Papers of the Continental Congress; Pollock to Commercial Committee, Oct. 8, 1778, p. 93, reel 64, Papers of the Continental Congress; Commercial Committee to Pollock, July 19, 1779, p. 196, reel 64, Papers of the Continental Congress; Kinnaird, "Western Fringe," 262-4; Conover, "British West Florida's Mississippi Frontier Posts," 188-9; Caughey, *Bernardo de Gálvez in Louisiana,* 131–3.

19. Donald Campbell to John Stuart, March 5, 1778, reel 3, Carleton Papers; Pollock to Commercial Committee, March 6, 1778, p. 205, reel 64, Papers of the Continental Congress; Dunbar, journal entry for May 1, 1778, *Life, Letters, and Papers,* 62; Willing Report to Congress, April 14, 1778, p. 492, reel 104, Papers of the Continental Congress; Jean Baptiste Laffont, receipt to George Rogers Clark, July 15, 1778; Charles Charleville, receipt to Clark, July 18, 1778; Rapicault, receipt to Clark, July 24, 1778; Cerre, receipt to Clark, July 25, 1778; Simon Huberdau, receipt to Clark, July 25, 1778; Lauthe, receipt to Clark, July 25, 1778; D'Atchurut, receipt to Clark, Aug. 3, 1778; John Girault for Mrs. Bently, receipt to Clark, Aug. 14, 1778; Auguste Chouteau, two receipts to Clark, Nov. 19, 1778; all in George Rogers Clark Papers, Missouri Historical Society Archives; James Alton James, *The Life of George Rogers Clark* (Chicago, 1928), 123-6; Cummins, "Oliver Pollock and George Rogers Clark's Service of Supply"; Kinnaird, "Western Fringe," 260, 262; Caughey, *Bernardo de Gálvez in Louisiana,* 93–5, 105, 112–3; Starr, *Tories, Dons, and Rebels,* 90; "Clark-Leyba Papers," ed. Lawrence Kinnaird, *American Historical Review* 41 (1935): 92–112; William R. Nester, *George Rogers Clark: "I Glory in War"* (Norman, 2012), 64–77, 177. On colonial St. Louis, see Patricia Cleary, *The World, the Flesh, and the Devil: A History of Colonial St. Louis* (Columbia, 2011); J. Frederick Fausz, *Founding St. Louis: First City of the New West* (Charleston, 2011); William E. Foley, *The First Chouteaus, River Barons of Early St. Louis* (Urbana, 1983).

20. Pollock to Bernardo de Gálvez, May 2, 1778, *Spain in the Mississippi Valley,* 1: 270–1; Pollock to Commercial Committee, April 1, 1778, p. 61, reel 64, Papers of the Continental Congress; Pollock to Commercial Committee, Feb. 22, 1780, p. 129, reel 64, Papers of the Continental Congress; Starr, *Tories, Dons, and Rebels,* 92.

21. Bernardo de Gálvez to José de Gálvez, June 9, 1778, doc. 169, reel 13, leg. 2547, Audiencia de Santo Domingo, Historic New Orleans Collection; Bernardo de Gálvez to Patrick Henry, May 6, 1778, *Spain in the Mississippi Valley,* 1: 272; Pollock to Bernardo de Gálvez, Aug. 5, 1778, *Spain in the Mississippi Valley,* 1: 300; Bernardo de Gálvez to José de Gálvez, Oct. 24, 1778, doc. 202, reel 13, leg. 2547, Audiencia de Santo Domingo, Historic New Orleans Collection; Kinnaird, "Western Fringe," 263–4. The United States had adopted the Spanish dollar as its currency, but converting 1778 Spanish dollars to current U.S. dollars is no simple matter. In terms of purchasing power, $74,000 in 1778 would be nearly $1.3 million in 2013. But figured

in terms of how long a laborer would have to work to earn the same amount, $74,000 in 1778 would be over $35 million in 2013. The difference comes from the fact that goods have increased in price much more slowly than wages over the centuries. Historical data and a conversion tool are available on MeasuringWorth.com.

22. "General Census of the Posts of Attakapas and Opelousas of 4 May 1777," in *Southwest Louisiana Families in 1777*, 12; *Southwest Louisiana Records*, 1A: 127; Voorhies, "Acadians," 109.

23. José de Gálvez to Navarro, Aug. 29, 1779, *Spain in the Mississippi Valley*, 1: 355; Statement of Expenses of the Province of Louisiana, May 31, 1787, *Spain in the Mississippi Valley*, 2: 209.

24. Congressional Report, Jan. 31, 1780, *Journals of the Continental Congress*, 16: 114–5; Wright, *Florida in the American Revolution*, 70–1; Richard B. Morris, *The Peacemakers: The Great Powers and American Independence* (New York, 1965), 30–42; Eric Beerman, *España y la independencia de Estados Unidos* (Madrid, 1992), 41–2; René Chartrand, *Gibraltar 1779–83: The Great Siege* (Oxford, 2006), 32–6; Mackesy, *War for America*, 279–97.

25. José de Gálvez to Navarro, Aug. 29, 1779, *Spain in the Mississippi Valley*, 1: 355; Weber, *Spanish Frontier in North America*, 265–70.

26. Mackesy, *War for America*, 262–3, 436.

27. Bernardo de Gálvez to José de Gálvez, Aug. 17, 1779, 3: 345–6, Bernardo de Gálvez Cartas al Josef de Gálvez, 1777–1781, Transcripts from the Archivo Nacional de Cuba, Ayer Collection, Newberry Library; Arthur Lee to President of Congress, June 21, 1779, p. 272, reel 110, Papers of the Continental Congress.

28. John Stuart to Germain, March 5, 1778, *Documents of the American Revolution*, 15: 55.

29. Fred Anderson and Andrew Cayton, *The Dominion of War: Empire and Liberty in North America, 1500–2000* (New York, 2005), 166.

CHAPTER 11

1. Bernardo de Gálvez to José de Gálvez, October 16, 1779, 3: 357–66, Bernardo de Gálvez Cartas al Josef de Gálvez, 1777–1781, Transcripts from the Archivo Nacional de Cuba, Ayer Collection, Newberry Library, Chicago; Supplement to the *Gazeta de Madrid*, Jan. 14, 1780, in "Spain's Report of War with the British in Louisiana," ed. and trans. Jac Nachbin, *Louisiana Historical Quarterly* 15 (1932): 472.

2. Charles Phillipe Aubry to Etienne-François, Duke of Choiseul-Stainville, Feb. 25, 1765, in *Quest for the Promised Land*, 31; Bernardo de Gálvez to Diego Josef Navarro, Sept. 18, 1779, 8: 1075–8, leg. 1232, Dispatches of the Spanish Governors, 1766–1792, Photostats from the Archivo General de Indias, Ayer Collection, Newberry Library; Bernardo de Gálvez to José de Gálvez, Oct. 16, 1779, 3: 357–66, Gálvez Cartas al Josef de Gálvez; Gálvez Commendations of Francisco Collell, Vincente Rillieux, and Louis Paul LeBlanc, Oct. 16, 1779, *Confidential Despatches of Don Bernardo de Gálvez, Fourth Spanish Governor of Louisiana, Sent to His Uncle Don José de Gálvez, Secretary of State and Ranking Official of the Council of the Indies*, trans. Adolph Baum (Baton Rouge, 1938); State of the Militia Company of Attakapas, May 1, 1777, *Records of Attakapas District, Louisiana, 1739–1811*, comp. Mary Elizabeth Sanders (priv. pub., 1962; digitally published, Urbana, 2012), 45; *Louisiana Soldiers in the American Revolution*, 23–6; Kimberly S. Hanger, "A Privilege and Honor to Serve: The Free Black Militia of Spanish New Orleans," in *African American Experience in Louisiana*, 1: 235–6.

3. Bernardo de Gálvez to José de Gálvez, June 5, 1780, *Confidential Despatches of Don Bernardo de Gálvez*.

4. Bernardo de Gálvez to José de Gálvez, July 3, 1779, *Spain in the Mississippi Valley*, 1: 346; Bernardo de Gálvez to Navarro, Aug. 25, 1779, in *Yearbook of the Louisiana Society Sons of the American Revolution* (1921), 100–1.

5. On Concord, see Robert A. Gross, *The Minutemen and Their World* (New York, 1976).

6. Oliver Pollock to Commercial Committee, Aug. 25, 1779, pp. 112–3, reel 64, Papers of the Continental Congress, 1774–1789, M247, National Archives and Records Service, Washington, D.C., microfilm at University of North Carolina, Chapel Hill.

7. Bernardo de Gálvez to Navarro, Aug. 19, 1779, 8: 1055–9, leg. 1232, Dispatches of the Spanish Governors; Bernardo de Gálvez to José de Gálvez, Oct. 16, 1779, 3: 357–66, Gálvez Cartas al Josef de Gálvez; Supplement to the *Gazeta de Madrid*, Jan. 14, 1780, 472.

8. Pollock to Commercial Committee, Aug. 25, 1779, pp. 112–3, reel 64, Papers of the Continental Congress; Bernardo de Gálvez to José de Gálvez, Feb. 25, 1779, *Confidential Despatches of Don Bernardo de Gálvez;* Bernardo de Gálvez to Navarro, June 9, 1778, *Confidential Despatches of Don Bernardo de Gálvez;* Bernardo de Gálvez to Navarro, July 3, 1779, 2: 161–2, Bernardo de Gálvez Cartas al Capitán General de Habana, 1777–1781, Transcripts from the Archivo Nacional de Cuba, Ayer Collection, Newberry Library; James Dallas to John McGillivray, July 3, 1778, *Spain in the Mississippi Valley*, 1: 293; John Stuart to George Germain, Aug. 10, 1778, *Documents of the American Revolution*, 15: 182; Henry Atkins to Charles Stuart, Sept. 7, 1778, abstract, *Documents of the American Revolution*, 13: 351; Charles Stuart to John Stuart, Sept. 15, 1778, abstract, *Documents of the American Revolution*, 13: 351.

9. Johnson, *Climate and Catastrophe*, 143.

10. Bernardo de Gálvez to José de Gálvez, March 2, 1779, *Confidential Despatches of Don Bernardo de Gálvez*. On Bouligny, see Robert S. Weddle, *Changing Tides: Twilight and Dawn in the Spanish Sea, 1763–1803* (College Station, 1995), 91.

11. Bernardo de Gálvez to José de Gálvez, Oct. 16, 1779, 3: 357–66, Gálvez Cartas al Josef de Gálvez; Kastor, *Nation's Crucible*, 28.

12. Bernardo de Gálvez to José de Gálvez, Oct. 16, 1779, 3: 357–66, Gálvez Cartas al Josef de Gálvez.

13. Pollock to Commercial Committee, Aug. 25, 1779, pp. 112–3, reel 64, Papers of the Continental Congress; Supplement to the *Gazeta de Madrid*, Jan. 14, 1780, 473. In New Orleans, Acting Governor Pedro Piernas made the declaration of war public on Sept. 8. Holmes, *Honor and Fidelity*, 29–30.

14. Thomas Jefferson to Bernardo de Gálvez, Nov. 8, 1779, *Spain in the Mississippi Valley*, 1: 362; Resolution, Sept. 28, 1779, *Journals of the Continental Congress*, 15: 1119–20.

15. Jefferson to Bernardo de Gálvez, Nov. 8, 1779, *Spain in the Mississippi Valley*, 1: 363.

16. Resolution, Sept. 28, 1779, *Journals of the Continental Congress*, 15: 1119–20.

17. Philip Schuyler and Henry Marchant, Report to Congress, Dec. 7, 1779, *Journals of the Continental Congress*, 15: 1369–70; Juan de Miralles to Chevalier de La Luzerne, Nov. 24, 1779, p. 27, reel 123, Papers of the Continental Congress.

18. George Washington to Benjamin Lincoln, April 15, 1780, *The Writings of George Washington; Being His Correspondence, Addresses, Messages, and Other Papers, Official and Private*, ed. Jared Sparks (Boston, 1835), 7: 18; Abbey, "Spanish Projects," 274–9.

19. Bernardo de Gálvez to Jefferson, 1780, *Spain in the Mississippi Valley*, 1: 375.

20. Notes of Conference between John Jay and the Count of Floridablanca, Sept. 23, 1780, *The Correspondence and Public Papers of John Jay*, ed. Henry P. Johnson (New York, 1890–93), 1: 424–5.

21. Committee for Foreign Affairs to John Jay, Oct. 17, 1780, *Journals of the Continental Congress*, 18: 942.

22. Wright, *Florida in the American Revolution*, 115–7.

23. Pollock to Commercial Committee, Feb. 17, 1779, pp. 98–9, reel 64, Papers of the Continental Congress; Pollock to Commerce Committee, May 7, 1778, pp. 71, 73–4, reel 64, Papers of the Continental Congress; Pollock to Navarro, May 13, 1778, fr. 1409–11, reel 186, leg. 1, Papeles de Cuba, P. K. Yonge Library, University of Florida, Gainesville; Navarro to Pollock, June 21, 1778, fr. 1412–3, reel 186, leg. 1, Papeles de Cuba, P. K. Yonge; Pollock to Commercial Committee, Aug. 11, 1778, p. 84, reel 64, Papers of the Continental Congress; Pollock to Commercial Committee, Dec. 15, 1778, pp. 97–8, reel 64, Papers of the Continental Congress; Pollock to Commercial Committee, Sept. 30, 1779, p. 118, reel 64, Papers of the Continental Congress; Pollock to Bernardo de Gálvez, Oct. 15, 1779, p. 119, reel 64, Papers of the Continental Congress.

24. Pollock to Commercial Committee, Feb. 17, 1779, p. 101, reel 64, Papers of the Continental Congress; Pollock to Patrick Henry, July 17, 1779, pp. 105-8, reel 64, Papers of the Continental Congress; Kinnaird, "Western Fringe," 265–6.

25. Pollock to Henry, July 17, 1779, p. 108, reel 64, Papers of the Continental Congress.

26. Commercial Committee to Pollock, July 19, 1779, pp. 196–201, reel 64, Papers of the Continental Congress; Congressional Resolution, Jan. 14, 1779, *Journals of the Continental Congress*, 13: 65. By the end of the war, the Congress had printed over $240 million in paper currency with no taxation to back it up. Irvin, *Clothed in Robes of Sovereignty*, 75–7; Robert E. Wright, *One Nation Under Debt: Hamilton, Jefferson, and the History of What We Owe* (New York, 2008), 49–52; Jane Kamensky, *The Exchange Artist: A Tale of High-Flying Speculation and America's First Banking Collapse* (New York, 2008).

27. Pollock to Commerce Committee, May 7, 1778, p. 71, reel 64, Papers of the Continental Congress.

28. Report of the Board of War, Oct. 31, 1778, *Journal of the Continental Congress*, 12: 1083.

29. Pollock to Commercial Committee, July 19, 1780, pp. 133–4, reel 64, Papers of the Continental Congress; Bernardo de Gálvez to President of Congress, July 22, 1780, p. 171, reel 64, Papers of the Continental Congress; Nov. 29, 1780, *Journals of the Continental Congress*, 18: 1106–7.

30. George Morgan to Bernardo de Gálvez, April 26, 1778, *Spain in the Mississippi Valley*, 1: 266–8. The Spanish commandant at St. Louis had similar trouble finding a translator for Morgan's English letter. Francisco Cruzat to Morgan, Nov. 19, 1777, p. 120, reel 93, Papers of the Continental Congress.

31. Bernardo de Gálvez to Navarro, Dec. 12, 1778, 2: 133–4, Gálvez Cartas al Capitán General de Habana.

32. [David Rogers] to Henry, Oct. 4, 1778, reel 4, Guy Carleton, 1st Baron Dorchester, Papers, British National Archives, Kew, England, microfilm copy at University of North Carolina, Chapel Hill.

33. Henry to Bernardo de Gálvez, January 14, 1778, *Spain in the Mississippi Valley*, 1: 248–50; Bernardo de Gálvez to Henry, n.d. [Oct. 19, 1778], reel 4, Carleton Papers.

34. William Franklin to Germain, Nov. 2, 1778, *Documents of the American Revolution*, 15: 251.

35. Waldeck, Sept. 15–16, 1779, *Eighteenth Century America*, 132–3; John Campbell to Henry Clinton, Sept. 11, 1779, reel 7, Carleton Papers; John Campbell to Clinton, Sept. 14, 1779, reel 7, Carleton Papers; Bernardo de Gálvez to Navarro, Sept. 18, 1779, 8: 1075–8, leg. 1232, Dispatches of the Spanish Governors; Bernardo de Gálvez to José de Gálvez, Oct. 16, 1779, 3: 370–2, Gálvez Cartas al Josef de Gálvez; Alexander Dickson, Report, Sept. 22, 1779, reel 7, Carleton Papers; Caughey, *Bernardo de Gálvez in Louisiana*, 155.

36. Supplement to the *Gazeta de Madrid,* Jan. 14, 1780, 472; Pollock to Commercial Committee, Aug. 25, 1779, pp. 112–3, reel 64, Papers of the Continental Congress; Caughey, *Bernardo de Gálvez in Louisiana,* 72, 123–4.

37. John Campbell to Clinton, Sept. 14, 1779, reel 7, Carleton Papers; John Henderson to Commercial Committee, Sept. 17, 1779, pp. 114–5, reel 64, Papers of the Continental Congress; Statement of Inhabitants on Lake Pontchartrain, Oct. 16, 1779, in J. F. H. Claiborne, *Mississippi as a Province, Territory, and State: With Biographical Notices of Eminent Citizens* (Jackson, 1880), 122; Bernardo de Gálvez to José de Gálvez, Oct. 16, 1779, 3: 357–66, Gálvez Cartas al Josef de Gálvez; Bernardo de Gálvez to Navarro, Sept. 18, 1779, 8: 1075–8, leg. 1232, Dispatches of the Spanish Governors; Bernardo de Gálvez Commendations of Francisco Collell, Vincente Rillieux, and Louis Paul LeBlanc, Oct. 16, 1779, *Confidential Despatches of Don Bernardo de Gálvez;* John Campbell to Clinton, Nov. 7, 1779, reel 7, Carleton Papers; Supplement to the *Gazeta de Madrid,* Jan. 14, 1780, 476; Holmes, *Honor and Fidelity,* 30–1; Caughey, *Bernardo de Gálvez in Louisiana,* 161; James, *Oliver Pollock,* 199.

38. Bernardo de Gálvez to Navarro, Sept. 18, 1779, 8: 1075–8, leg. 1232, Dispatches of the Spanish Governors; Bernardo de Gálvez Commendation of Carlos Laveau Trudeau, Oct. 16, 1779, *Confidential Despatches of Don Bernardo de Gálvez;* Holmes, *Honor and Fidelity,* 30.

39. Bernardo de Gálvez to José de Gálvez, Oct. 16, 1779, 3: 357–66, 370–2, Gálvez Cartas al Josef de Gálvez; Supplement to the *Gazeta de Madrid,* Jan. 14, 1780, 474–5.

40. Bernardo de Gálvez Commendation of Carlos Laveau Trudeau, Oct. 16, 1779, *Confidential Despatches of Don Bernardo de Gálvez;* Bernardo de Gálvez to José de Gálvez, Oct. 16, 1779, 3: 357–66, Gálvez Cartas al Josef de Gálvez; John W. Wright, "Notes on the Siege of Yorktown in 1781 with Special Reference to the Conduct of a Siege in the Eighteenth Century," *William and Mary Quarterly* 12 (1932): 231–5; Caughey, *Bernardo de Gálvez in Louisiana,* 156, 180.

41. Baton Rouge Inhabitants to Dickson, Sept. 21, 1779, reel 7, Carleton Papers; Alexander Dickson, Report, Sept. 22, 1779, reel 7, Carleton Papers.

42. Navarro to Bernardo de Gálvez, Sept. 3, 1779, fr. 1671, reel 186, leg. 1, Papeles de Cuba, P. K. Yonge; Bernardo de Gálvez to Navarro, Sept. 18, 1779, 8: 1075–8, leg. 1232, Dispatches of the Spanish Governors; John Henderson to Commercial Committee, Sept. 17, 1779, p. 115, reel 64, Papers of the Continental Congress; Bernardo de Gálvez to José de Gálvez, Oct. 16, 1779, 3: 357–66, Gálvez Cartas al Josef de Gálvez; Supplement to the *Gazeta de Madrid,* Jan. 14, 1780, 474–5.

43. Bernardo de Gálvez to José de Gálvez, Oct. 16, 1779, 3: 357–66, 370–2, Gálvez Cartas al Josef de Gálvez; Bernardo de Gálvez to Navarro, Oct. 15, 1779, 8: 1079–81, leg. 1232, Dispatches of the Spanish Governors.

44. José Rodulfo Boeta, *Bernardo de Gálvez* (Madrid, 1977), 92–3.

45. Pollock to the Inhabitants of Natchez, Sept. 8, 1779, pp. 121-3, reel 64, Papers of the Continental Congress; Pollock to the Inhabitants of Natchez, Sept. 22, 1779, p. 122, reel 64, Papers of the Continental Congress; Kinnaird, *Spain in the Mississippi Valley,* 1: xxviii; Pollock to Bernardo de Gálvez, Aug. 6, 1779, qtd. in James, *Oliver Pollock,* 197.

46. Pollock to Commercial Committee, Jan. 20, 1780, p. 125, reel 64, Papers of the Continental Congress; July 10, 1780, *Journals of the Continental Congress,* 17: 600–1.

47. Inhabitants of the Settlements on Lake Pontchartrain to William Pickles, Oct. 16, 1779, p. 120, reel 64, Papers of the Continental Congress.

48. John Campbell, Commission for Jacob Winfree, March 17, 1781, *Spain in the Missis-*

sippi Valley, 1: 424; John Campbell to Germain, July 21, 1781, *Documents of the American Revolution*, 20: 194–5; Starr, *Tories, Dons, and Rebels*, 157; Wyatt-Brown, *House of Percy*, 30–2.

49. Waldeck, Sept. 26, 1779, Feb. 28, 1780, *Eighteenth Century America*, 134–50; James Bruce to Clarke and Milligan, Sept. 19, 1780, in Fabel, "Ordeal by Siege," 292–3; John Campbell to Clinton, Sept. 14, 1779, reel 7, Carleton Papers; Germain to Clinton, Sept. 27, 1779, *Documents of the American Revolution*, 17: 223; Bernardo de Gálvez to José de Gálvez, Oct. 16, 1779, 3: 357–66, Gálvez Cartas al Josef de Gálvez; Supplement to the *Gazeta de Madrid*, Jan. 14, 1780, 474–5; Fabel, "Ordeal by Siege," 285; Caughey, *Bernardo de Gálvez in Louisiana*, 159.

50. Waldeck, Sept. 19–20, 1779, *Eighteenth Century America*, 133–4; Campbell, *Historical Sketches*, 116.

51. Wright, *Florida in the American Revolution*, 73; Rothschild, *Inner Life of Empires*, 72; *Dictionary of National Biography*, ed. Leslie Stephen and Sidney Lee (London, 1885–1901), 7: 1113.

52. James Campbell to Dickson, Sept. 9, 1779, reel 7, Carleton Papers; Germain to Haldimand, June 17, 1779, *Documents of the American Revolution*, 17: 144; Germain to John Campbell, June 25, 1779, *Documents of the American Revolution*, 17: 153; Germain to Lords of Admiralty, June 25, 1779, *Documents of the American Revolution*, 17: 149; John Campbell to Peter Chester, Sept. 9, 1779, reel 7, Carleton Papers; Waldeck, Sept. 8, 1779, *Eighteenth Century America*, 132; John Campbell to Clinton, Nov. 7, 1779, reel 7, Carleton Papers.

53. J. P. MacLean, *An Historical Account of the Settlements of Scotch Highlanders in America Prior to the Peace of 1783* (Glasgow, 1900), 380-1.

54. John Campbell to Clinton, Feb. 10, 1779, reel 5, Carleton Papers; John Campbell to Germain, Dec. 26, 1778, abstract, *Documents of the American Revolution*, 13: 407; George C. Osborn, "Major-General John Campbell in British West Florida," *Florida Historical Quarterly* 27 (1949): 317-8; New, *Maryland Loyalists*, 84; Starr, *Tories, Dons, and Rebels*, 133–4.

55. John Campbell to Clinton, Dec. 15, 1779, reel 7, Carleton Papers; John Campbell to Clinton, Sept. 11, 1779, reel 7, Carleton Papers.

56. John Campbell to Clinton, Nov. 7, 1779, reel 7, Carleton Papers.

57. Memorial of Speaker and other members of Assembly of West Florida to the King, Nov. 25, 1778, abstract, *Documents of the American Revolution*, 16: 55; Commissioners for Trade and Plantations to Chester, March 12, 1779, abstract, *Documents of the American Revolution*, 16: 53; Petition of Freeholders and Principal Inhabitants of West Florida to the King, n.d. [May 1779], abstract, *Documents of the American Revolution*, 16: 99; Griffith, "Peter Chester and the End of the British Empire," 18–30; Fabel, "Boom in the Bayous," 51, 53.

58. Germain to Cameron, April 5, 1780, abstract, *Documents of the American Revolution*, 16: 299–300; Germain to John Campbell, April 4, 1780, abstract, *Documents of the American Revolution*, 16: 297.

59. Waldeck, Oct. 25, 1779, *Eighteenth Century America*, 138.

60. Clinton to Germain, Sept. 26, 1779, *Documents of the American Revolution*, 17: 222; Haldimand to Germain, Oct. 24, 1779, abstract, *Documents of the American Revolution*, 16: 198; Mackesy, *War for America*, 307–8, 315–8, 372.

61. John Campbell to Germain, Sept. 14, 1779, qtd. in Starr, *Tories, Dons, and Rebels*, 147; Chester to Germain, Nov. 15, 1779, abstract, *Documents of the American Revolution*, 16: 215; Starr, *Tories, Dons, and Rebels*, 146–7.

62. Waldeck, December 12, 1779, *Eighteenth Century America*, 144.

63. John Campbell to Germain, Dec. 15, 1779, *Documents of the American Revolution*, 17: 266–7; Starr, *Tories, Dons, and Rebels*, 187.

64. Pollock to Bernardo de Gálvez, Oct. 15, 1779, p. 119, reel 64, Papers of the Continental Congress; Pollock to Commercial Committee, Sept. 30, 1779, p. 118, reel 64, Papers of the Continental Congress; Krebs, *Generous and Merciful Enemy*, 218–25.

CHAPTER 12

1. James Campbell to Charles Stuart, Sept. 9, 1779, reel 7, Guy Carleton, 1st Baron Dorchester, Papers, British National Archives, Kew, England, microfilm copy at University of North Carolina, Chapel Hill.

2. Alexander Cameron to George Germain, Aug. 1780, fr. 589, reel 8, Records of the British Colonial Office, Library of Congress, Washington, D.C.

3. Bernardo de Gálvez to José de Gálvez, Oct. 16, 1779, 3: 366–70, Bernardo de Gálvez Cartas al Josef de Gálvez, 1777–1781, Transcripts from the Archivo Nacional de Cuba, Ayer Collection, Newberry Library, Chicago.

4. Payamataha Commission, Dec. 17, 1779, CO 5/81, British National Archives; Oliver Pollock to Commercial Committee, Sept. 30, 1779, pp. 117–8, reel 64, Papers of the Continental Congress, 1774-1789, M247, National Archives and Records Service, Washington, D.C., microfilm at University of North Carolina, Chapel Hill; Charles Stuart to Cameron, Dec. 16, 1779, fr. 342, reel 8, Records of the British Colonial Office, Library of Congress.

5. Bernardo de Gálvez to José de Gálvez, June 5, 1780, *Confidential Despatches of Don Bernardo de Gálvez*.

6. Bernardo de Gálvez to José de Gálvez, July 21, 1780, 3: 423–4, Gálvez Cartas al Josef de Gálvez; "Noticia de los efectos y géneros que se necesitan en los Almacenes de la Nueva Orleans para entretener la amistad de los Indios," Oct. 16, 1779, pp. 19–20 of back section, vol. 3, Gálvez Cartas al Josef de Gálvez.

7. Choctaw Six Towns talk to James Colbert, Nov. 19, 1779, reel 7, Carleton Papers; Cameron to Clinton, Dec. 15, 1779, reel 7, Carleton Papers; James Taylor Carson, *Searching for the Bright Path: The Mississippi Choctaws from Prehistory to Removal* (Lincoln, 1999), 37–9.

8. Charles Stuart to Cameron, Dec. 16, 1779, fr. 343–4, reel 8, Records of the British Colonial Office, Library of Congress; Campbell to Clinton, Dec. 15, 1779, reel 7, Carleton Papers; Campbell to Clinton, Feb. 10, 1780, reel 7, Carleton Papers.

9. Cameron to Germain, Dec. 20, 1779, fr. 335, 338, reel 8, Records of the British Colonial Office, Library of Congress; Campbell to Clinton, Dec. 15, 1779, reel 7, Carleton Papers.

10. O'Donnell, "Alexander McGillivray," 184n33; Dowd, *Spirited Resistance*, 58–9.

11. Campbell to Clinton, Feb. 10, 1779, reel 5, Carleton Papers; Fenn, *Pox Americana*, 15–20, 27–8, 114; Starr, *Tories, Dons, and Rebels*, 131–2; Green, "Creek Confederacy in the American Revolution," 69; Cynthia Radding, *Wandering Peoples: Colonialism, Ethnic Spaces, and Ecological Frontiers in Northwestern Mexico, 1700–1850* (Durham, 1997), 116.

12. The invention of the cowpox-based smallpox vaccine in 1798 was a huge advance. Adair, *History of the American Indians*, 274–5; Cameron to Augustin Prevost, Oct. 15, 1779, reel 7, Carleton Papers; Kelton, "Avoiding the Smallpox Spirits," 45–71; Fenn, *Pox Americana*, 3, 20–2, 29, 92–103, 115.

13. Cameron to Prevost, Oct. 15, 1779, reel 7, Carleton Papers.

14. Waldeck, *Eighteenth Century America*, 127–9; Fenn, *Pox Americana*, 115.

15. Bartram, *William Bartram on the Southeastern Indians,* 94; Campbell to Clinton, Feb. 10, 1779, reel 5, Carleton Papers; Holmes, *Honor and Fidelity,* 32.

16. Bernardo de Gálvez to Diego Josef Navarro, Oct. 16, 1779, *Confidential Despatches of Don Bernardo de Gálvez;* Luis Huet to Bernardo de Gálvez, Nov. 20, 1779, fr. 303, reel 186, leg. 1, Papeles de Cuba, P. K. Yonge Library, University of Florida, Gainesville; Bernardo de Gálvez to Esteban Miró, Dec. 31, 1779, *Spain in the Mississippi Valley,* 1: 366–8; Caughey, *Bernardo de Gálvez in Louisiana,* 173.

17. Pensacola and Mobile Accounts, Dec. 31, 1779, reel 7, Carleton Papers.

18. Piernas to Bernardo de Gálvez, Feb. 29, 1780, fr. 2257, reel 168, leg. 2, Papeles de Cuba, P. K. Yonge; Bernardo de Gálvez, "Journal of Don Bernardo de Galvez," English trans., *The Remembrancer; or, Impartial Repository of Public Events for the Year 1780* (London, 1780), 2: 91; Bernardo de Gálvez to Carlos de Grand-Pre, Jan. 2, 1780, fr. 5, reel 164, leg. 2, Papeles de Cuba, P. K. Yonge.

19. Bernardo de Gálvez to Miró, Dec. 31, 1779, *Spain in the Mississippi Valley,* 1: 366–8; Bernardo de Gálvez, "Journal of Don Bernardo de Galvez," *Remembrancer,* 2: 91, 99; Piernas to Bernardo de Gálvez, Feb. 28, 1780, fr. 498 reel 164, leg. 2, Papeles de Cuba, P. K. Yonge; Joseph Calvert to Congress, April 24, 1780, p. 357, reel 64, Papers of the Continental Congress; [Piernas] to José de Ezpeleta, Dec. 5, [1780], fr. 2228, reel 167, leg. 2, Papeles de Cuba, P. K. Yonge; Caughey, *Bernardo de Gálvez in Louisiana,* 72, 123–4, 174–5; James, *Oliver Pollock,* 202; Starr, " 'Left as a Gewgaw,' " 19-20; Starr, *Tories, Dons, and Rebels,* 168; Holmes, *Honor and Fidelity,* 32.

20. Pollock to Samuel Huntington, July 22, 1780, p. 134, reel 64, Papers of the Continental Congress.

21. Bernardo de Gálvez to José de Gálvez, Oct. 16, 1779, 3: 357–66, Gálvez Cartas al Josef de Gálvez; Nov. 23, 1780, *Journals of the Continental Congress,* 18: 1086; James, *Oliver Pollock,* 198, 200.

22. Campbell to Clinton, Feb. 12, 1780, reel 7, Carleton Papers; Waldeck, Feb. 8–13, 1780, *Eighteenth Century America,* 147.

23. Bernardo de Gálvez, "Journal," *Remembrancer,* 2: 92–3; Waldeck, Feb. 15–16, 1780, *Eighteenth Century America,* 147–8; Pollock to Commercial Committee, Feb. 22, 1780, p. 129, reel 64, Papers of the Continental Congress; Peter Chester to Patrick Tonyn, Feb. 18, 1780, reel 7, Carleton Papers. Accounts differ as to the date of the storm that did the most damage; the weather was generally stormy the first two weeks of that February.

24. Bernardo de Gálvez, "Journal," *Remembrancer,* 2: 92–5; Bernardo de Gálvez to Miró, Dec. 31, 1779, *Spain in the Mississippi Valley,* 1: 366–8; Agreement of Josef Navarro and Juan Baptista Bonet, Jan. 31, 1780, *Spain in the Mississippi Valley,* 1: 370–2; Caughey, *Bernardo de Gálvez in Louisiana,* 174, 177.

25. Campbell to Clinton, March 24, 1780, reel 8, Carleton Papers.

26. Steuernagel, "Brief Description," 170.

27. Waldeck, March 1–19, 1780, *Eighteenth Century America,* 151–3; Campbell to Clinton, March 24, 1780, reel 8, Carleton Papers; Starr, " 'Left as a Gewgaw,' " 19–20.

28. Articles of Capitulation, March 13, 1780, reel 8, Carleton Papers; Durnford to Campbell, March 14, 1780, reel 8, Carleton Papers; Piernas to Bernardo de Gálvez, Feb. 28, 1780, fr. 498 reel 164, leg. 2, Papeles de Cuba, P. K. Yonge; Bernardo de Gálvez, "Journal," *Remembrancer,* 2: 98–9; Starr, " 'Left as a Gewgaw,' " 19–20; Holmes, *Honor and Fidelity,* 33.

29. Campbell to Clinton, March 24, 1780, reel 8, Carleton Papers; Bernardo de Gálvez, "Journal," *Remembrancer,* 2: 99; Bernardo de Gálvez to José de Gálvez, March 20, 1780, *Remembrancer,* 2: 91.

30. Piernas to Bernardo de Gálvez, March 22, 1780, fr. 2268, reel 168, leg. 2, Papeles de Cuba, P. K. Yonge; Bernardo de Gálvez to Campbell, April 9, 1780, reel 8, Carleton Papers.

31. Martín Navarro, Report of the Troops Used in the Pensacola Expedition, Feb. 28, 1781, *Spain in the Mississippi Valley,* 1: 421–2; Hanger, "Privilege and Honor to Serve," 1: 228, 236; Starr, *Tories, Dons, and Rebels,* 190–1; William S. Coker and Hazel P. Coker, *The Siege of Mobile, 1780, in Maps* (Pensacola, 1982), 107–9.

32. Bernardo de Gálvez, "Journal," *Remembrancer,* 2: 94–5.

33. Enrique Grimarest to Bernardo de Gálvez, April 18, 1780, fr. 921, reel 165, leg. 2, Papeles de Cuba, P. K. Yonge; Grimarest to Bernardo de Gálvez, [April] 19, 1780, fr. 924, reel 165, leg. 2, Papeles de Cuba, P. K. Yonge; Bernardo de Gálvez to Grimarest, April 21, 1780, fr. 524, reel 165, leg. 2, Papeles de Cuba, P. K. Yonge; Ezpeleta to Bernardo de Gálvez, May 12, [1780], fr. 351, reel 186, leg. 1, Papeles de Cuba, P. K. Yonge; Ezpeleta to Bernardo de Gálvez, July 11, 1780, fr. 2482, reel 168, leg. 2, Papeles de Cuba, P. K. Yonge; Ezpeleta to Piernas, Aug. 4, 1780, fr. 2502, reel 168, leg. 2, Papeles de Cuba, P. K. Yonge; Wright, *Florida in the American Revolution,* 108–9; Chávez, *Spain and the Independence of the United States,* 182; Dunbar, *Life, Letters, and Papers,* 56. Peter H. Wood has shown how slaves entrusted with transporting goods by land and river might begin delivering messages from their masters as well and eventually become some of the most skilled guides and scouts around. Petit Jean and other Gulf Coast slaves likely went through a similar process. Wood, *Black Majority,* 117–8.

34. Grimarest to Bernardo de Gálvez, April 18, 1780, fr. 921, reel 165, leg. 2, Papeles de Cuba, P. K. Yonge; Bernardo de Gálvez to Grimarest, April 21, 1780, fr. 524, reel 165, leg. 2, Papeles de Cuba, P. K. Yonge; Grimarest to Bernardo de Gálvez, April 24, 1780, fr. 2439, reel 168, leg. 2, Papeles de Cuba, P. K. Yonge; Ezpeleta to [Bernardo de Gálvez], July 18, [1780], fr. 2491, reel 168, leg. 2, Papeles de Cuba, P. K. Yonge; Sellers, *Slavery in Alabama,* 7–9, 11. On enslaved messengers and spies elsewhere in the war, see Pybus, *Epic Journeys of Freedom,* 21, 25, 27–8, 37, 41, 44.

35. Grimarest to Bernardo de Gálvez, April 18, 1780, fr. 921, reel 165, leg. 2, Papeles de Cuba, P. K. Yonge; Bernardo de Gálvez to Grimarest, April 21, 1780, fr. 527, reel 165, leg. 2, Papeles de Cuba, P. K. Yonge; Usner, *Indians, Settlers, and Slaves,* 107.

36. Bernardo de Gálvez to Grand-Pre, May 27, 1780, fr. 7, reel 164, leg. 2, Papeles de Cuba, P. K. Yonge; Berlin, *Many Thousands Gone,* 329.

37. Gálvez ordered that the slaves be returned to New Orleans and instructed their masters not to punish them. Nonetheless, they managed to stay in Mobile at least three more months, and perhaps longer. Ezpeleta to Bernardo de Gálvez, May 22, 1780, fr. 1005, reel 165, leg. 2, Papeles de Cuba, P. K. Yonge; Bernardo de Gálvez to Ezpeleta, May 30, 1780, fr. 1006, reel 165, leg. 2, Papeles de Cuba, P. K. Yonge; Ezpeleta to Piernas, Aug. 31, 1780, fr. 2203, reel 167, leg. 2, Papeles de Cuba, P. K. Yonge.

38. Ezpeleta to Piernas, Aug. 6, 1780, fr. 1043, reel 165, leg 2, Papeles de Cuba, P. K. Yonge.

39. John Adams to Samuel Huntington, May 9, 1780, p. 35, reel 111, Papers of the Continental Congress; Francis D. Cogliano, *Revolutionary America, 1763–1815: A Political History* (New York, 2009), 107–8; Middlekauff, *Glorious Cause,* 444–56; Don Higginbotham, *George Washington and the American Military Tradition* (Athens, 1985), 55–7. Washington's forces did mutiny in Jan. 1781. Nash, *Unknown American Revolution,* 357–65.

40. Huntington to George Washington, June 5, 1780, p. 17, reel 24, Papers of the Continental Congress.

41. Adams to Huntington, July 7, 1780, p. 173, reel 111, Papers of the Continental Congress; *Journals of the Continental Congress,* 17: 490; Pollock to Commercial Committee, July 19, 1780, pp. 133–4, reel 64, Papers of the Continental Congress; Bernardo de Gálvez to President of Congress, July 22, 1780, p. 171, reel 64, Papers of the Continental Congress; Nov. 29, 1780, *Journals of the Continental Congress,* 18: 1106–7.

42. James Wright to Clinton, March 18, 1780, reel 8, Carleton Papers; Piecuch, *Three Peoples, One King.*

43. Alexander McGillivray to Thomas Brown, March 28, 1780, fr. 420–1, reel 8, Records of the British Colonial Office, Library of Congress; William McIntosh to Brown, March 20, 1780, fr. 418–9, reel 8, Records of the British Colonial Office, Library of Congress.

44. John Campbell to Clinton, Feb. 10, 1780, reel 7, Carleton Papers.

45. McGillivray Account, March 28, 1780, reel 8, Carleton Papers.

46. Campbell to Clinton, Feb. 12, 1780, reel 7, Carleton Papers; Cameron to Germain, Feb. 19, 1780, fr. 425, reel 8, Records of the British Colonial Office, Library of Congress; Cameron to Germain, July 18, 1780, fr. 441, reel 8, Records of the British Colonial Office, Library of Congress; Waldeck, March 27–30, April 1-6, 1780, *Eighteenth Century America,* 154–9; O'Donnell, "Alexander McGillivray," 178–9.

47. Waldeck, April 12, 1780, *Eighteenth Century America,* 160–2.

48. Cameron to Germain, Oct. 31, 1780, *Documents of the American Revolution,* 18: 221–2.

49. McGillivray to Brown, May 13, 1780, fr. 462, reel 8, Records of the British Colonial Office, Library of Congress.

50. Cameron to Germain, July 18, 1780, fr. 436–47, reel 8, Records of the British Colonial Office, Library of Congress; James, *Oliver Pollock,* 204.

51. Bernardo de Gálvez to Campbell, April 9, 1780, reel 8, Carleton Papers; Ezpeleta to Campbell, Aug. 26, 1780, reel 167, leg. 2, Papeles de Cuba, P. K. Yonge; McGillivray to Brown, May 13, 1780, fr. 462, reel 8, Records of the British Colonial Office, Library of Congress.

52. Bernardo de Gálvez to José de Gálvez, Oct. 16, 1779, 3: 370–2, Gálvez Cartas al Josef de Gálvez.

53. Campbell to Clinton, May 13, 1780, reel 8, Carleton Papers; Green, "Creek Confederacy in the American Revolution," 69.

54. McGillivray to Brown, May 13, 1780, fr. 463, reel 8, Records of the British Colonial Office, Library of Congress.

55. Cameron to Germain, July 18, 1780, fr. 436–7, reel 8, Records of the British Colonial Office, Library of Congress.

56. McGillivray to Brown, May 13, 1780, fr. 463, reel 8, Records of the British Colonial Office, Library of Congress; William Knox to Philip Stephens, July 1, 1780, abstract, *Documents of the American Revolution,* 16: 355; Milfort, *Chef de guerre,* 165.

57. Cameron to Brown, June 16, 1780, fr. 456–7, reel 8, Records of the British Colonial Office, Library of Congress; O'Donnell, "Alexander McGillivray," 178-9; Green, "Creek Confederacy in the American Revolution," 68.

58. Campbell to Clinton, May 13, 1780, reel 8, Carleton Papers.

59. McIntosh to Brown, May 6, 1780, fr. 460–1, reel 8, Records of the British Colonial Office, Library of Congress; McGillivray to Brown, May 13, 1780, fr. 463, reel 8, Records of the British Colonial Office, Library of Congress.

60. Ezpeleta to [Bernardo de Gálvez], July 12, [1780] , fr. 2483, reel 168, leg. 2, Papeles

de Cuba, P. K. Yonge; Ezpeleta to Bernardo de Gálvez, July 8, 1780, fr. 2480, reel 168, leg. 2, Papeles de Cuba, P. K. Yonge; Grimarest to Bernardo de Gálvez, April 23, 1780, fr. 2437, reel 168, leg. 2, Papeles de Cuba, P. K. Yonge; Grimarest to Bernardo de Gálvez, April 20, 1780, fr. 2431, reel 168, leg. 2, Papeles de Cuba, P. K. Yonge.

61. Bernardo de Gálvez to José de Gálvez, July 20, 1780, 3: 422, Gálvez Cartas al Josef de Gálvez.

62. Ezpeleta to [Bernardo de Gálvez], July 12, [1780], fr. 2483, reel 168, leg. 2, Papeles de Cuba, P. K. Yonge; Cameron to Germain, July 18, 1780, fr. 436–7, reel 8, Records of the British Colonial Office, Library of Congress; Ezpeleta to Bernardo de Gálvez, Nov. 19, 1780, fr. 2310, reel 168, leg. 2, Papeles de Cuba, P. K. Yonge Library.

63. Piernas to Bernardo de Gálvez, March 28, 1780, fr. 2275, reel 168, leg 2, Papeles de Cuba, P. K. Yonge.

64. Waldeck, Aug. 14, 1780, *Eighteenth Century America,* 168; Piernas to Bernardo de Gálvez, April 6, 1780, fr. 2281, reel 168, leg. 2, Papeles de Cuba, P. K. Yonge Library; Piernas to Bernardo de Gálvez, May 3, 1780, fr. 980, reel 165, leg. 2, Papeles de Cuba, P. K. Yonge.

65. Steuernagel, "Brief Description," 171–2; Waldeck, *Eighteenth Century America,* 173; Cameron to Germain, Nov. 30, 1780, fr. 635–6, reel 8, Records of the British Colonial Office, Library of Congress; Ezpeleta to Bernardo de Gálvez, Jan. 20, 1781, reel 153, leg. 3, Papeles de Cuba, P. K. Yonge; Cameron to Germain, Feb. 10, 1781, *Documents of the American Revolution,* 20: 58–9; Casualty Report, Jan. 8, 1781, reel 9, Carleton Papers.

66. Waldeck, April 13, 1780, *Eighteenth Century America,* 162–3; Payamataha to Cameron, 1780, fr. 451–2, reel 8, Records of the British Colonial Office, Library of Congress.

67. Thomas Jefferson to George Rogers Clark, Jan. 29, 1780, *Kaskaskia Records, 1778–1790,* ed. Clarence Walworth Alvord (Springfield, 1909), 144–9; Cameron to Germain, Nov. 30, 1780, fr. 633–40, reel 8, Records of the British Colonial Office, Library of Congress; James, *Oliver Pollock,* 205; Gibson, *Chickasaws,* 72–3; Nester, *George Rogers Clark,* 199–202; Robert S. Cotterill, "The Virginia-Chickasaw Treaty of 1783," *Journal of Southern History* 8 (1942): 483–4. Chickasaws also participated in an offensive in the spring of 1779 against Americans venturing too close to Chickasaw country. Commissioners for Indian Affairs to Germain, May 10, 1779, *Documents of the American Revolution,* 17: 121–2.

68. Francisco Cruzat to Miró, March 19, 1782, *Spanish Régime in Missouri,* 1: 209–10; Payamataha Commission, Dec. 17, 1779, CO 5/81, British National Archives; Payamataha to Cameron, n.d. [1780], fr. 451–2, reel 8, Records of the British Colonial Office, Library of Congress.

69. Payamataha to Cameron, 1780, fr. 451–2, reel 8, Records of the British Colonial Office, Library of Congress; Waldeck, Aug. 26–28, 1780, *Eighteenth Century America,* 168–9.

70. Campbell to Clinton, Sept. 18, 1780, in N. Orwin Rush, *The Battle of Pensacola, March 9 to May 8, 1781: Spain's Final Triumph over Great Britain in the Gulf of Mexico* (Tallahassee, 1966), 22.

71. Payamataha to Cameron, 1780, fr. 451–2, reel 8, Records of the British Colonial Office, Library of Congress.

72. Colbert to Cameron, June 30, 1780, fr. 596, reel 8, Records of the British Colonial Office, Library of Congress.

73. Cameron to Germain, July 18, 1780, fr. 437–8, reel 8, Records of the British Colonial Office, Library of Congress; Bethune to Cameron, Aug. 24, 1780, fr. 601–7, reel 8,

Records of the British Colonial Office, Library of Congress; Waldeck, Aug. 14, 1780, *Eighteenth Century America,* 168.

74. José de Gálvez to Bernardo de Gálvez, Jan. 15, 1782, *Spanish Régime in Missouri,* 1: 207; Act of Possession of the East Bank of the Mississippi River North of the District of Natchez, Nov. 22, 1780, *Spain in the Mississippi Valley,* 1: 401; Act of Possession of the Valleys of the St. Joseph and Illinois Rivers, Feb. 12, 1781, *Spain in the Mississippi Valley,* 1: 418; Wright, *Florida in the American Revolution,* 114; Holmes, *Honor and Fidelity,* 35; Susan Sleeper-Smith, "Women, Kin, and Catholicism: New Perspectives on the Fur Trade," *Ethnohistory* 47 (2000): 437–8.

75. Royal Order, March 13, 1780, fr. 210, reel 164, leg. 2, Papeles de Cuba, P. K. Yonge.

76. [Pedro Piernas to Bernardo de Gálvez], January 15, 1781, doc. 21, reel 153, leg. 3, Papeles de Cuba, P. K. Yonge.

CHAPTER 13

1. James Bruce to Clarke and Milligan, Nov. 1, 1780, in Fabel, "Ordeal by Siege," 293–4; Bruce to Clarke and Milligan, Feb. 22, 1781, in Fabel, "Ordeal by Siege," 294; Bruce to Clarke and Milligan, Feb. 24, 1780, in Fabel, "Ordeal by Siege," 295; Wright, *Florida in the American Revolution,* 92; Kate Haulman, *The Politics of Fashion in Eighteenth-Century America* (Chapel Hill, 2011), 68–73.

2. José de Ezpeleta to Bernardo de Gálvez, March 14, 1781, doc. 44a, reel 153, leg. 3, Papeles de Cuba, P. K. Yonge Library, University of Florida, Gainesville; Bernardo de Gálvez, *Diario de las operaciones de la expedicion contra la Plaza de Panzacola concluida por las armas de S. M. Católica, baxo las órdenes del mariscal de campo D. Bernardo de Galvez* (n.p. [Havana?], n.d. [1781?]), 2–3; "Bernardo de Gálvez's Combat Diary for the Battle of Pensacola, 1781," ed. and trans. Maury Baker and Margaret Bissler Haas, *Florida Historical Quarterly* 56 (1977): 181; Campbell to Clinton, April 9, 1781, in Rush, *Battle of Pensacola,* 95; William S. Coker and Hazel P. Coker, *The Siege of Pensacola, 1781, in Maps* (Pensacola, 1981), 42; Robert Farmar, "Bernardo de Galvez's Siege of Pensacola in 1781 (As Related in Robert Farmar's Journal)," ed. James A. Padgett, *Louisiana Historical Quarterly* 26 (1943): 315; Cameron to Germain, May 27, 1781, *Documents of the American Revolution,* 20: 149–50.

3. *Parliamentary Debates,* ed. T. C. Hansard (London, 1829–91), 22: 291–302.

4. Allan J. Kuethe, *Cuba, 1753–1815: Crown, Military, and Society* (Knoxville, 1986), 113–4; J. H. Elliott, *Empires of the Atlantic World: Britain and Spain in America, 1492–1830* (New Haven, 2007), 325–6, 355–63; Charles F. Walker, *The Tupac Amaru Rebellion* (Cambridge, 2014).

5. "Bernardo de Gálvez's Combat Diary," 196; Rush, *Battle of Pensacola,* 7; Starr, *Tories, Dons, and Rebels,* 184-5; Jacinto Panis to Bernardo de Gálvez, April 29, 1779, *Spain in the Mississippi Valley,* 1: 337; *Journal of Don Francisco Saavedra de Sangronis, 1780–1783,* ed. Francisco Morales Padrón, trans. Aileen Moore Topping (Gainesville, 1989), 174; Stanley Faye, "British and Spanish Fortifications of Pensacola, 1781–1821," *Florida Historical Quarterly* 20 (1942): 278-9; Norman Simons, "The Pensacola Fortifications," in *Siege! Spain and Britain: Battle of Pensacola, March 9–May 9, 1781,* ed. Virginia Parks (Pensacola, 1981), 45; Frederick Cubberly, "Fort George (St. Michael), Pensacola," *Florida Historical Quarterly* 6 (1928): 221.

6. John Campbell to Thomas Brown, Nov. 15, 1780, reel 9, Guy Carleton, 1st Baron Dorchester, Papers, British National Archives, Kew, England, microfilm copy at University of North Carolina, Chapel Hill; John Campbell to Clinton, Sept. 18,

1780, in Rush, *Battle of Pensacola,* 22. On contemporary siege tactics, see Wright, "Notes on the Siege of Yorktown," 229–52; on the siege of Fort William Henry in the Seven Years' War, see Louis-Antoine de Bougainville, *Écrits sur le Canada: Mémoires, journal, lettres* (Québec, 2003), 198–233.

7. Navarro to José de Gálvez, March 1, 1781, doc. 40, reel 71, leg. 2609, Audiencia de Santo Domingo, Archivo General de Indias, Historic New Orleans Collection; Steuernagel, "Brief Description," 173; Starr, *Tories, Dons, and Rebels,* 196; Carmen de Reparaz, *Yo Solo: Bernardo de Gálvez y la toma de Panzacola en 1781: una contribución española a la independencia de los Estados Unidos* (Madrid, 1986), 3; John Campbell to George Germain, May 7, 1781, *Documents of the American Revolution,* 20: 136; Gálvez, *Diario de las operaciones,* 1; *Journal of Don Francisco Saavedra,* 112–7, 127–8; *The Log of H.M.S. Mentor, 1780-1781: A New Account of the British Navy at Pensacola,* ed. James A. Servies (Gainesville, 1982), 163.

8. Fabel, "Ordeal by Siege," 286.

9. Bruce to Clarke and Milligan, Sept. 19, 1780, in Fabel, "Ordeal by Siege," 292–3.

10. Virginia Parks, "The Siege of Pensacola," in *Siege! Spain and Britain,* 57; Farmar, "Bernardo de Galvez's Siege," 318; Gálvez, *Diario de las operaciones,* 34; *Journal of Don Francisco Saavedra,* 173.

11. O'Donnell, "Alexander McGillivray," 179-80; Green, "Creek Confederacy in the American Revolution," 69–70; Holland, "Anglo-Spanish Contest," 94, 98–9; Calloway, *American Revolution in Indian Country,* 227–8; Cameron to Germain, Nov. 30, 1780, fr. 635, reel 8, Records of the British Colonial Office, Library of Congress, Washington, D.C.; Waldeck, Nov. 19, 1780, *Eighteenth Century America,* 171; Starr, *Tories, Dons, and Rebels,* 177–9.

12. Cameron to Germain, Sept. 20, 1780, fr. 599–600, reel 8, Records of the British Colonial Office, Library of Congress; John Ferling, *Almost a Miracle: The American Victory in the War of Independence* (Oxford, 2007), 212–3; John Brewer, *The Sinews of Power: War, Money, and the English State, 1688–1783* (London, 1989), 114–5.

13. Germain to Brown, July 8, 1780, fr. 422, reel 8, Records of the British Colonial Office, Library of Congress.

14. Cameron to Campbell, Nov. 8, 1780, fr. 643–4, reel 8, Records of the British Colonial Office, Library of Congress.

15. Cameron to Brown, June 16, 1780, fr. 456–7, reel 8, Records of the British Colonial Office, Library of Congress.

16. Green, "Creek Confederacy in the American Revolution," 70–1.

17. Cameron to Germain, May 27, 1781, *Documents of the American Revolution,* 20: 149–50; Carson, *Searching for the Bright Path,* 38–9; Holland, "Anglo-Spanish Contest," 99; O'Brien, *Choctaws in a Revolutionary Age.*

18. Rush, *Battle of Pensacola,* 6–7, 26.

19. Gálvez, *Diario de las operaciones,* 7–8; Campbell to Clinton, Jan. 5, 1781, in Rush, *Battle of Pensacola,* 27; Panis to Bernardo de Gálvez, April 29, 1779, *Spain in the Mississippi Valley,* 1: 337; Campbell to Clinton, April 9, 1781, in Rush, *Battle of Pensacola,* 93.

20. Cameron to Germain, March 20, 1781, in Holland, "Anglo-Spanish Contest," 99–100; Farmar, "Bernardo de Galvez's Siege," 316; Gálvez, *Diario de las operaciones,* 8–9, 12; Campbell to Germain, May 7, 1781, *Documents of the American Revolution,* 20: 136.

21. Greg O'Brien, "The Choctaw Defense of Pensacola in the American Revolution," in *Pre-Removal Choctaw History,* 142.

22. Cameron to Campbell, March 20, 1781, in Holland, "Anglo-Spanish Contest," 99–100.

23. Gálvez, *Diario de las operaciones,* 8; "Bernardo de Gálvez's Combat Diary," 180–1; Camp-

bell to Germain, May 7, 1781, *Documents of the American Revolution*, 20: 136; Steuernagel, "Brief Description," 175–6; *Journal of Don Francisco Saavedra*, 142–3; Farmar, "Bernardo de Galvez's Siege," 315.

24. Farmar, "Bernardo de Galvez's Siege," 316; Francisco de Miranda, "Diario de lo mas particular ocurrido desde el dia de nuestra salida del puerto de la Havana," in *Archivo del General Miranda* (Caracas, 1929), 1: 144–5.

25. Ezpeleta to Bernardo de Gálvez, March 14, 1781, doc. 44a, reel 153, leg. 3 Papeles de Cuba, P. K. Yonge; Bernardo de Gálvez, *Diario de las operaciones*, 6, 12; "Bernardo de Gálvez's Combat Diary," 181; Miranda, "Diario," 1: 143–6; Coker and Coker, *Siege of Pensacola*, 42; Francisco de Borja Medina Rojas, "José de Ezpeleta and the Siege of Pensacola," in *Anglo-Spanish Confrontation*, 115–6.

26. Report of Troops Used in the Pensacola Expedition, Feb. 28, 1781, attached to doc. 40, reel 71, leg. 2609, Audiencia de Santo Domingo, Historic New Orleans Collection.

27. Farmar, "Bernardo de Galvez's Siege," 317; Campbell to Germain, May 7, 1781, *Documents of the American Revolution*, 20: 136.

28. Gálvez, *Diario de las operaciones*, 9–11; Farmar, "Bernardo de Galvez's Siege," 317; Campbell to Germain, May 7, 1781, *Documents of the American Revolution*, 20: 136.

29. Bruce to Clarke and Milligan, April 26, 1781, in Fabel, "Ordeal by Siege," 296.

30. Wright, *Florida in the American Revolution*, 132.

31. Fabel, "Ordeal by Siege," 290; Holland, "Anglo-Spanish Contest," 99–100.

32. Gálvez, *Diario de las operaciones*, 14–5; "Bernardo de Gálvez's Combat Diary," 182; Francisco de Borja Medina Rojas, *José de Ezpeleta, Gobernador de La Mobila, 1780–1781* (Sevilla, 1980), 747.

33. Gálvez, *Diario de las operaciones*, 15; "Bernardo de Gálvez's Combat Diary," 182; Medina Rojas, *José de Ezpeleta*, 747.

34. Miranda, "Diario," 1: 161.

35. Gálvez, *Diario de las operaciones*, 15–6; "Bernardo de Gálvez's Combat Diary," 182; Farmar, "Bernardo de Galvez's Siege," 317.

36. Gálvez, *Diario de las operaciones*, 16; "Bernardo de Gálvez's Combat Diary," 182–3.

37. Gálvez, *Diario de las operaciones*, 16–7; "Bernardo de Gálvez's Combat Diary," 183.

38. Holland, "Anglo-Spanish Contest," 100.

39. Ezpeleta to Bernardo de Gálvez, April 5, 1781, fr. 1365, reel 166, leg. 2, Papeles de Cuba, P. K. Yonge; Steuernagel, "Brief Description," 173–4; Medina Rojas, *José de Ezpeleta*, 760–1.

40. Farmar, "Bernardo de Galvez's Siege," 319; Cameron to Germain, May 27, 1781, *Documents of the American Revolution*, 20: 150; Braund, *Deerskins and Duffels*, 3.

41. Draper, "Narrative Based on an Interview with Malcolm McGee," 44–5.

42. *Journal of Don Francisco Saavedra*, 181.

43. *Journal of Don Francisco Saavedra*, 178; Gálvez, *Diario de las operaciones*, 20, 22; "Bernardo de Gálvez's Combat Diary," 187; O'Brien, "Choctaw Defense of Pensacola," 126–7, 150; Carson, *Searching for the Bright Path*, 38–9.

44. Campbell to Clinton, April 9, 1781, in Rush, *Battle of Pensacola*, 95–6.

45. *Journal of Don Francisco Saavedra*, 163-4.

46. Gálvez, *Diario de las operaciones*, 17–21; "Bernardo de Gálvez's Combat Diary," 184, 186–7.

47. Miranda, "Diario," 1: 161, 168; "Bernardo de Gálvez's Combat Diary," 185–6, 191–2; Farmar, "Bernardo de Galvez's Siege," 319–20; *Journal of Don Francisco Saavedra*, 154–6, 164; Gálvez, *Diario de las operaciones*, 22, 28.

48. *Journal of Don Francisco Saavedra*, 153–4, 168; Miranda, "Diario," 1: 160.

49. Miranda, "Diario," 1: 158; Gálvez, *Diario de las operaciones,* 21–3; "Bernardo de Gálvez's Combat Diary," 187; Farmar, "Bernardo de Galvez's Siege," 320–1; Campbell to Clinton, May 12, 1781, in Rush, *Battle of Pensacola,* 101.

50. Farmar, "Bernardo de Galvez's Siege," 318; Gálvez, *Diario de las operaciones,* 23–4; "Bernardo de Gálvez's Combat Diary," 187; *Journal of Don Francisco Saavedra,* 154; Campbell to Clinton, May 12, 1781, in Rush, *Battle of Pensacola,* 101.

51. Gálvez, *Diario de las operaciones,* 23–4; Miranda, "Diario," 1: 150; *Journal of Don Francisco Saavedra,* 144–6, 154; Kuethe, *Cuba, 1753–1815,* 111–2.

52. Victorio de Navia to José de Gálvez, March 3, 1781, John B. Stetson Collection, P. K. Yonge; Piernas to Ezpeleta, March 9, 1781, fr. 1301, reel 166, leg. 2, Papeles de Cuba, P. K. Yonge; Navia to José de Gálvez, April 8, 1781, Stetson Collection, P. K. Yonge; *Journal of Don Francisco Saavedra,* 144.

53. Germain to Campbell, March 7, 1781, quoted in Osborn, "Major-General John Campbell," 337; *The Annual Register, or a View of the History, Politics, and Literature, for the Year 1781* (London, 1800), 98, 101–2; Mackesy, *War for America,* 275, 416; Johnson, *Climate and Catastrophe,* 144.

54. Campbell to Clinton, April 9, 1781, in Rush, *Battle of Pensacola,* 94–5; Wright, *Florida in the American Revolution,* 90; O'Shaughnessy, *Empire Divided,* 213–25; James W. Raab, *Spain, Britain, and the American Revolution in Florida, 1763–1783* (Jefferson, 2008), 135, 137.

55. Farmar, "Bernardo de Galvez's Siege," 320, 322; James A. Matthews Journal, April 24, 1781, in Claiborne, *Mississippi as a Province, Territory, and State,* 126; Gálvez, *Diario de las operaciones,* 25–6; Germain to Campbell, March 7, 1781, abstract, *Documents of the American Revolution,* 19: 59; Germain to Campbell, April 12, 1781, abstract, *Documents of the American Revolution,* 19: 87; Bruce to Clarke and Milligan, April 26, 1781, in Fabel, "Ordeal by Siege," 296.

56. *Journal of Don Francisco Saavedra,* 151, 153–6; Campbell to Germain, May 7, 1781, *Documents of the American Revolution,* 20: 137; Farmar, "Bernardo de Galvez's Siege," 321–2; Gálvez, *Diario de las operaciones,* 24–5; "Bernardo de Gálvez's Combat Diary," 189; Miranda, "Diario," 1: 157, 159–61.

57. Bruce to Clarke and Milligan, April 26, 1781, in Fabel, "Ordeal by Siege," 296–6.

58. Bruce to Clarke and Milligan, May 7, 1781, in Fabel, "Ordeal by Siege," 297.

59. Miranda, "Diario," 1: 169.

60. Farmar, "Bernardo de Galvez's Siege," 324–6; Gálvez, *Diario de las operaciones,* 30–1; Miranda, "Diario," 1: 169–71; Campbell to Clinton, May 12, 1781, in Rush, *Battle of Pensacola,* 103; *Journal of Don Francisco Saavedra,* 166; Matthews Journal, May 4, 1781, 126.

61. Gálvez, *Diario de las operaciones,* 31; Miranda, "Diario," 1: 171; Campbell to Germain, May 7, 1781, *Documents of the American Revolution,* 20: 138; Campbell to Germain, May 12, 1781, *Documents of the American Revolution,* 20: 141; Campbell to Clinton, May 12, 1781, in Rush, *Battle of Pensacola,* 103; *Journal of Don Francisco Saavedra,* 168–9.

62. Gálvez, *Diario de las operaciones,* 32–3; "Bernardo de Gálvez's Combat Diary," 193; Miranda, "Diario," 1: 174–5; *Authentic Memoirs of William Augustus Bowles, Esquire, Ambassador from the United Nations of Creeks and Cherokees to the Court of London* (London, 1791), 35–6; *Journal of Don Francisco Saavedra,* 170–1; Campbell to Clinton, May 12, 1781, in Rush, *Battle of Pensacola,* 104–5; *Log of H.M.S. Mentor,* 186.

63. Gálvez, *Diario de las operaciones,* 33–4; Miranda, "Diario," 1: 175; Farmar, "Bernardo de Galvez's Siege," 327; "Bernardo de Gálvez's Combat Diary," 195–6; Cameron to Germain, May 27, 1781, *Documents of the American Revolution,* 20: 150.

64. *Spain in the Mississippi Valley,* 1: 421–2; Roland C. McConnell, *Negro Troops of Antebellum Louisiana: A History of the Battalion of Free Men of Color* (Baton Rouge, 1968), 20.

65. Gálvez, *Diario de las operaciones,* 34, 46–7; "Bernardo de Gálvez's Combat Diary," 196–7; Miranda, "Diario," 1: 176; Starr, *Tories, Dons, and Rebels,* 211–2.

66. Pollock to Bernardo de Gálvez, July 7, 1781, Oliver Pollock Papers, Missouri Historical Society Archives, St. Louis; Gálvez, *Diario de las operaciones,* 33–4; Miranda, "Diario," 1: 175; Farmar, "Bernardo de Galvez's Siege," 327; James, *Oliver Pollock,* 230.

67. Cameron to Germain, May 27, 1781, *Documents of the American Revolution,* 20: 150; *Journal of Don Francisco Saavedra,* 171.

68. Cameron to Germain, May 27, 1781, *Documents of the American Revolution,* 20: 150.

69. Cameron to Germain, Aug. 1780, fr. 591–2, reel 8, Records of the British Colonial Office, Library of Congress.

CHAPTER 14

1. John Campbell to George Germain, May 12, 1781, *Documents of the American Revolution,* 20: 140.

2. James McNamara to Nisbet Balfour, March 12, 1781, abstract, *Documents of the American Revolution,* 19: 71; Thomas Brown to Alexander Leslie, December 5, 1781, reel 11, Guy Carleton, 1st Baron Dorchester, Papers, British National Archives, Kew, England, microfilm copy at University of North Carolina, Chapel Hill.

3. Cogliano, *Revolutionary America,* 110; Piecuch, *Three Peoples, One King,* 175, 204, 207–8; Mackesy, *War for America,* xiv.

4. Mackesy, *War for America,* 435–6, 444, 506; Morris, *Peacemakers,* 252–3, 284–6, 311–40.

5. John Martin to Anthony Wayne, Sept. 7, 1782, "Official Letters of Governor John Martin, 1782–1783," *Georgia Historical Quarterly* 1 (December 1917): 327.

6. Middlekauff, *Glorious Cause,* 606; Gould, *Among the Powers of the Earth,* 133.

7. Dowd, *Spirited Resistance,* 59–61; Elliott, *Empires of the Atlantic World,* 325–6, 355–63; Palmer, *Age of the Democratic Revolution,* 127–39, 285–320, 358–64.

8. John L. O'Sullivan, "Annexation," in *United States Magazine and Democratic Review* 17 (1845): 5–10; Katharine Lee Bates, "America the Beautiful," *America the Beautiful and Other Poems* (New York, 1911), 3.

9. Kathleen DuVal, "Independence for Whom? Expansion and Conflict in the South and Southwest," in *The World of the Revolutionary American Republic: Land, Labor, and the Conflict for a Continent,* ed. Andrew Shankman (Routledge, 2014), 97–115.

10. Bernardo de Gálvez to José de Gálvez, July 19, 1781, *Confidential Despatches of Don Bernardo de Gálvez;* Caughey, *Bernardo de Gálvez in Louisiana,* 221–5; Wright, *Florida in the American Revolution,* 130.

11. De la Villebeuvre to Miró, April 25, 1780, *Spain in the Mississippi Valley,* 1: 376.

12. Royal Cedula, Jan. 22, 1782, *Spain in the Mississippi Valley,* 2: 1–5; Bernardo de Gálvez to José de Gálvez, Aug. 5, 1784, *Spain in the Mississippi Valley,* 2: 107; Caughey, *Bernardo de Gálvez in Louisiana,* 250–1.

13. Wright, *Florida in the American Revolution,* 93–4.

14. Brown to Carleton, October 9, 1782, reel 14, Carleton Papers; Braund, *Deerskins and Duffels,* 313.

15. John Grahame to Carleton, July 20, 1782, reel 14, Carleton Papers; Piecuch, *Three Peoples, One King,* 301–5.

16. Brown to Leslie, Sept. 30, 1782, reel 14, Carleton Papers.

17. Wright, *Florida in the American Revolution,* 114.

18. Patrick Henry to Bernardo de Gálvez, January 14, 1778, *Spain in the Mississippi Valley,* 1: 249.

19. John Jay, notes, *Correspondence and Public Papers of John Jay,* 1: 328–9.

20. John Hancock to Bernardo de Gálvez, Aug. 15, 1781, *Spain in the Mississippi Valley,* 1: 434.

21. James, *Oliver Pollock,* 250–5, 263–4; Morris, *Peacemakers,* 235–40.

22. Oliver Pollock to Commercial Committee, Feb. 17, 1779, p. 100, reel 64, Papers of the Continental Congress, 1774–1789, M247, National Archives and Records Service, Washington, D.C., microfilm at University of North Carolina, Chapel Hill; Pollock to Henry, July 17, 1779, p. 108, reel 64, Papers of the Continental Congress.

23. July 10, 1780, *Journals of the Continental Congress,* 17: 600; Resolution, March 8, 1782, *Journals of the Continental Congress,* 22: 121; James, *Oliver Pollock,* 261–2.

24. Jay to Robert Livingston, Nov. 17, 1782, *Correspondence and Public Papers of John Jay,* 2: 390; Wright, *Florida in the American Revolution,* 121.

25. Benjamin Franklin to Livingston, April 12, 1782, *The Private Correspondence of Benjamin Franklin* (London, 1817), 2: 114; Franklin to Jay, Jan. 19, 1782, p. 61, reel 135, Papers of the Continental Congress; James, *Oliver Pollock,* 245–6, 267.

26. Samuel Flagg Bemis, *A Diplomatic History of the United States* (New York, 5th ed., 1965), 54.

27. Wright, *Florida in the American Revolution,* 117; Morris, *Peacemakers,* 441–3, 552.

28. Congressional Resolution, Jan. 14, 1779, *Journals of the Continental Congress,* 13: 62–3.

29. March 18, 1783, *Journals of the Continental Congress,* 24: 928; March 22, 1783, *The Debates in the Several State Conventions on the Adoption of the Federal Constitution,* ed. Jonathan Elliot (Philadelphia, 1861), 5: 73–4; Adams, entry for Sept. 15, 1775, *Diary of John Adams,* 2: 173.

30. The Count of Floridablanca to the Count of Aranda, January 2, 1783, *Documents from East Florida, 1783–1785: A File of Documents Assembled, and Many of Them Translated,* comp. and trans. Joseph Byrne Lockey, ed. John Walton Caughey (Berkeley, 1949), 42; Starr, *Tories, Dons, and Rebels,* 223–4; Morris, *Peacemakers,* 435–7; Mackesy, *War for America,* 506–9.

31. Alexander McGillivray for the Chiefs of the Creek, Chickasaw, and Cherokee Nations, July 10, 1785, *McGillivray of the Creeks,* 90–3; Bernardo de Campo to Floridablanca, August 9, 1783, *Documents from East Florida,* 139; James H. Merrell, "Declarations of Independence: Indian-White Relations in the New Nation," in *American Revolution: Its Character,* 197–223.

32. Report of the Congressional Committee on Indian Affairs in the Southern Department, May 28, 1784, *Early American Indian Documents,* 18: 380–2; Nichols, *Red Gentlemen and White Savages,* 21–5.

33. John Stuart to Lower Creeks, Oct. 20, 1777, reel 3, Carleton Papers.

34. Report from the Yazoo River, March 9, 1783, *Spain in the Mississippi Valley,* 2: 71–3.

35. Brown to Carleton, Jan. 12, 1783, reel 17, Carleton Papers; Brown to Carleton, April 28, 1783, reel 19, Carleton Papers; John Douglass to Carleton, Jan. 20, 1783, reel 18, Carleton Papers.

36. Indian Talks to Patrick Tonyn, May 16, 1783, fr. 679–80, reel 8, Records of the British Colonial Office, Library of Congress, Washington, D.C.

37. McGillivray to Miró, March 28, 1784, *McGillivray of the Creeks,* 73; Tonyn to Carleton, Dec. 23, 1782, reel 17, Carleton Papers; Townshend to Brown, Feb. 14, 1783, reel 18, Carleton Papers; Brown to Carleton, Feb. 23, 1783, reel 18, Carleton Papers; Piecuch, *Three Peoples, One King,* 306; Wright, *Florida in the American Revolution,* 126–7.

38. Miró to [Juan Manuel de Cagigal], June 5, 1782, 9: 1305–6, leg. 1304, Dispatches of the Spanish Governors, 1766–1792, Photostats from the Archivo General de Indias, Ayer Collection, Newberry Library, Chicago; Statement of Expenses of the Province of Louisiana, May 31, 1787, *Spain in the Mississippi Valley*, 2: 209.

39. Martín Navarro to Enrique Grimarest, Feb. 28, 1782, p. 759, reel 442, leg. 83, Papeles de Cuba, P. K. Yonge Library, University of Florida, Gainesville; Miró to Grimarest, Feb. 27, 1782, doc. 202, reel 153, leg. 3, Papeles de Cuba, P. K. Yonge; Miró to [Cagigal], June 5, 1782, 9: 1305–6, leg. 1304, Dispatches of the Spanish Governors; Arturo O'Neill to Cagigal, Sept. 23, 1782, *Spain in the Mississippi Valley*, 2: 58; Gilbert de St. Maxent to Miró, Dec. 5, 1782, *Spain in the Mississippi Valley*, 2: 67–8; Council of War Held at St. Louis, July 8, 1782, *Spain in the Mississippi Valley*, 2: 40; Ygnacio Delino to Miró, [Dec.?] 31, 1782, doc. 355, reel 153, leg. 3, Papeles de Cuba, P. K. Yonge; Vicente Zéspedes to Bernardo de Gálvez, Aug. 16, 1784, *Spain in the Mississippi Valley*, 2: 109.

40. Francisco Cruzat to Miró, March 19, 1782, *Spanish Régime in Missouri*, 1: 209–10.

41. Charles Stuart to John Stuart, Dec. 26, 1770, *Documents of the American Revolution*, 2: 303; Testimony of Madame Cruzat to Miró, May 30, 1782, *Spanish Régime in Missouri*, 1: 211–34; John Stuart to Charles Stuart, March 2, 1778, fr. 832, reel 7, Records of the British Colonial Office, Library of Congress; John Stuart to John McGillivray, March 28, 1778, fr. 789–90, reel 7, Records of the British Colonial Office, Library of Congress; Campbell to Colbert, Nov. 23, 1780, fr. 435, reel 104, Papers of the Continental Congress; Adair, *History of the American Indians*, 369; Gibson, *Chickasaws*, 65, 80; Calloway, *American Revolution in Indian Country*, 222–5, 229; St. Jean, "Trading Paths: Chickasaw Diplomacy," ch. 6; Gilbert C. Din, "Loyalist Resistance after Pensacola: The Case of James Colbert," in *Anglo-Spanish Confrontation*, 158; Green, *Chickasaw Lives*, 1: 68.

42. Colbert to Miró, October 6, 1782, *Spain in the Mississippi Valley*, 2: 60.

43. Nicanora Ramos, Testimonio, May 30, 1782, copy attached to Bernardo de Gálvez to José de Gálvez, Aug. 5, 1782, Archive of the Indies Collection, Missouri Historical Society, St. Louis; English translation available *Spanish Régime in Missouri*, 1: 221–31; Testimony of Silvestre L'Abbadie, July 5, 1782, *Spain in the Mississippi Valley*, 2: 24–5.

44. Testimony of L'Abbadie, 2: 21–4; Ramos, Testimonio; Holmes, *Honor and Fidelity*, 104, 175. Marie Andrée is the only female black slave belonging to the Cruzats whom I have found in the records. She appears in the St. Louis parish records at the right times, and she was an appropriate age. Basilica of St. Louis Old Cathedral Baptisms, 1769–1840, item 11 on microfilm reel US/CAN 1902829, pp. 17, 28, Family History Library, Salt Lake City, Utah.

45. Testimony of L'Abbadie, 2: 26, 32; Ramos, Testimonio; Council of War Held at St. Louis, July 8, 1782, *Spain in the Mississippi Valley*, 2: 40.

46. Miró to Villiers, May 21, 1782, reel 153, leg. 3, Papeles de Cuba, P. K. Yonge; Miró to Nicolas Delassize, May 29, 1782, reel 153, leg. 3, Papeles de Cuba, P. K. Yonge; Miró to Enrique Grimarest, June 3, 1782, reel 153, leg. 3, Papeles de Cuba, P. K. Yonge.

47. Francisco Cruzat to Miró, Aug. 8, 1782, *Spain in the Mississippi Valley*, 2: 50–3; Din, "Loyalist Resistance after Pensacola," 164–5.

48. Miró to Balthazár de Villiers, May 22, 1782, reel 153, leg. 3, Papeles de Cuba, P. K. Yonge.

49. Miró to [Cagigal], June 15, 1782, 9: 1316–8, leg. 1304, Dispatches of the Spanish

Governors; Miró to Cagigal, July 6, 1782, 9: 1320–4, leg. 1304, Dispatches of the Spanish Governors; Miró to Luis Villars, July 9, 1782, reel 153, leg. 3, Papeles de Cuba, P. K. Yonge; Navarro to José de Gálvez, June 4, 1782, *Spain in the Mississippi Valley*, 2: 19; Pedro Piernas to Bernardo de Gálvez, June 22, 1782, reel 153, leg. 3, Papeles de Cuba, P. K. Yonge.

50. Miró to Bernardo de Gálvez, June 5, 1782, *Spanish Régime in Missouri*, 1: 214–5; Bernardo de Gálvez to José Gálvez, Aug. 5, 1782, Archive of the Indies Collection, Missouri Historical Society.

51. Miró to Bernardo de Gálvez, June 5, 1782, *Spanish Régime in Missouri*, 1: 214–5; Miró to Villars, Oct. 3, 1782, reel 153, leg. 3, Papeles de Cuba, P. K. Yonge.

52. Jacobo Du Breuil to Miró, May 5, 1783, fol. 403, leg. 107, Papeles de Cuba, Archivo General de Indias, Seville, Spain; Du Breuil to Miró, Aug. 26, 1783, fol. 464, leg. 107, Papeles de Cuba, Archivo General de Indias; Report by Choctaw messenger on deputation to the Chickasaws, Oct. 24, 1782, *Spain in the Mississippi Valley*, 2: 61–2; Grimarest, Report on the Mission of Paulous to the Chickasaws, Sept. 1782, *Spain in the Mississippi Valley*, 2: 57; DuVal, *Native Ground*, 153–8. Oddly enough, James Willing apparently showed up at Spain's Arkansas Post in Quapaw country with rumors that American troops were coming to take the Mississippi Valley. Partly through the efforts of his well-connected sister, Mary Willing Byrd, Willing had been freed in a prisoner exchange. Council of War Held at St. Louis, July 8, 1782, *Spain in the Mississippi Valley*, 2: 39–40; Thomas Jefferson to Mary Willing Byrd, Oct. 24, 1779, William H. English Collection, Special Collections Research Center, University of Chicago Library, Chicago, accessed online at Library of Congress American Memory Project; Charles Moore, *The Northwest Under Three Flags, 1635–1796* (New York, 1900), 312; Konkle, *Thomas Willing*, 136.

53. Du Breuil to Miró, Nov. 8, 1783, *Spain in the Mississippi Valley*, 2: 89–91; Nairne, *Nairne's Muskhogean Journals*, 40–1; Nancy Shoemaker, *A Strange Likeness: Becoming Red and White in Eighteenth-Century North America* (New York, 2004), 40; St. Jean, "Trading Paths: Chickasaw Diplomacy," introduction and ch. 8.

54. Chickasaw Message, July 9, 1782, *Early American Indian Documents*, 18: 270–1; J. Donne to James Wilkinson, Jan. 17, 1784, fr. 439–49, reel 104, Papers of the Continental Congress; William Clark to Benjamin Harrison, Oct. 18, 1782, *George Rogers Clark Papers, 1781–1784*, ed. James Alton James (Springfield, 1926), Virginia Series 4 (1926), 136; Draper, "Narrative Based on an Interview with Malcolm McGee," 50; Cotterill, "Virginia-Chickasaw Treaty," 485–6.

55. Cherokees to Evan Shelby, April 1782, *Calendar of Virginia State Papers and Other Manuscripts*, ed. William P. Palmer (Richmond, 1875–93), 3: 171–2; Chief of the Chickasaws to the Americans, April 1782, *Calendar of Virginia State Papers*, 3: 172–3.

56. Mingo Houma, Payamataha, and other Chickasaw Chiefs to the President of Congress, July 28, 1783, *Early American Indian Documents*, 18: 370–1.

57. Nichols, *Red Gentlemen and White Savages*, 11, 19.

58. Council between Virginians and the Chickasaws, Oct. 25, 1782, *Early American Indian Documents*, 18: 275–7.

59. Harrison to Virginia Indian Commissioners, Jan. 11, 1783, *Early American Indian Documents*, 18: 364–5; Cotterill, "Virginia-Chickasaw Treaty," 489–90.

60. Mingo Houma, Payamataha, and other Chickasaw Chiefs to the President of Congress, July 28, 1783, *Early American Indian Documents*, 18: 370–1.

61. Benjamin Hawkins and Andrew Pickens to Richard Henry Lee, Dec. 2, 1785, *American State Papers: Indian Affairs*, ed. Walter Lowrie (Washington, 1832–1834), 1: 39;

Abernethy, *South in the New Nation*, 75; Cegielski and Lieb, "*Hina' Falaa*," 33–4; Wood, "Changing Population of the Colonial South," 95; Cotterill, "Virginia-Chickasaw Treaty," 492–3.

62. Snyder, *Slavery in Indian Country*, 163, 176.

63. Testimony of L'Abbadie, July 5, 1782, *Spain in the Mississippi Valley*, 2: 27–9.

64. Testimony of L'Abbadie, 2: 26–9, 32; Ramos, Testimonio; Du Breuil to Miró, May 5, 1783, fol. 403, leg. 107, Papeles de Cuba, Archivo General de Indias.

65. McGillivray to McLatchy, Dec. 25, 1784, *McGillivray of the Creeks*, 86; McGillivray to John Leslie, Dec. 10, 1785, *Documents from East Florida*, 744.

66. O'Neill to Ezpeleta, Oct. 19, 1783, *McGillivray of the Creeks*, 62–3; Zéspedes to Diego de Gardoqui, May 24, 1786, *McGillivray of the Creeks*, 112n58.

67. McGillivray to Miró, March 24, 1784, "Papers Relating to the Georgia-Florida Frontier, 1784–1800," ed. D. C. Corbitt, *Georgia Historical Quarterly* 20 (1936): 360; McGillivray to O'Neill, March 26, 1784, *McGillivray of the Creeks*, 73; Pope, *Tour Through the Southern and Western Territories*, 48–9; Waselkov, *Conquering Spirit*, kinship charts.

68. Taylor, *Divided Ground*, 113–7; Martin and Mauldin, *A Dictionary of Creek/Muskogee*, 236.

69. McGillivray to Miró, March 28, 1784, *McGillivray of the Creeks*, 74; McGillivray to O'Neill, March 26, 1784, *McGillivray of the Creeks*, 72–3; McGillivray to O'Neill, Feb. 5, 1784, *McGillivray of the Creeks*, 69–70.

70. Ezpeleta to Bernardo de Gálvez, Feb. 8, 1784, p. 57, doc. 15, reel 2, Mississippi Provincial Archives: Spanish Dominion, 1759–1804, comp. Dunbar Rowland, Jackson, Miss.

71. Miró to Ezpeleta, Aug. 1, 1784, 10: 1474–1502, leg. 1394, Dispatches of the Spanish Governors.

72. Zéspedes to Bernardo de Gálvez, Aug. 16, 1784, *Spain in the Mississippi Valley*, 2: 108–10; Miró to McGillivray, July 13, 1787, 11: 84; McGillivray to Miró, July 25, 1787, "Papers from the Spanish Archives Relating to Tennessee and the Old Southwest," ed. and trans. D. C. and Roberta Corbitt, *East Tennessee Historical Society's Publications*, 11: 89; Milfort, *Chef de guerre*, 207; Landers, *Black Society in Spanish Florida*, 34. On the continuing divisions, see Wright, *Creeks and Seminoles*, 115–7.

73. Saunt, *New Order of Things*, 73.

74. Snyder, *Slavery in Indian Country*, 21–2, 26–8, 129–38; Saunt, *New Order of Things*, 62, 70–3; Green, *Politics of Indian Removal;* Thomas D. Watson, "Strivings for Sovereignty: Alexander McGillivray, Creek Warfare, and Diplomacy, 1783–1790," *Florida Historical Quarterly* 58 (1980): 400–14. On contemporaneous economic and political changes among the Cherokees and Choctaws, see Theda Perdue, *Slavery and the Evolution of Cherokee Society, 1540–1866* (Knoxville, 1979).

75. McGillivray to O'Neill, Feb. 5, 1784, *McGillivray of the Creeks*, 69–70; O'Neill to Bernardo de Gálvez, May 20, 1783, pp. 7–12, reel 2, Mississippi Provincial Archives: Spanish Dominion.

76. John Martin to Creeks, Jan. 11, 1782, "Official Letters of Governor John Martin, 1782–1783," 282, 284–5; Georgia Assembly Resolution, January 11, 1783, *The Revolutionary Records of the State of Georgia* (Atlanta, 1908), 3: 207.

77. Martin to Greene, April 10, 1782, "Official Letters of Governor John Martin," 303–4.

78. Meeting with the Lower Creeks, April 10, 1789, *Early American Indian Documents*, 18: 507; Green, "Expansion of European Colonization," 1: 470.

79. McGillivray to James White, April 8, 1787, *Early American Indian Documents*, 18: 445; Treaty of Augusta with the Creeks, Nov. 1, 1783, *Early American Indian Documents*, 18: 372–3; McGillivray to Thomas Pinckney, February 26, 1789, *Early American Indian Documents*, 18: 504; Meeting with the Lower Creeks, April 10, 1789, *Early American Indian Documents*, 18: 507; Milfort, *Chef de guerre*, 122; Nichols, *Red Gentlemen and White Savages*, 11, 19; Hough, "Fathers and Brothers," 109–12.

80. Benjamin Hawkins, "A Sketch of the Creek Country in the Years 1798 and 1799," *The Collected Works of Benjamin Hawkins, 1796–1810*, ed. Thomas Foster (Tuscaloosa, 2003), 9s; John Stuart to Lower Creeks, Oct. 20, 1777, reel 3, Carleton Papers.

81. McGillivray to O'Neill, Jan. 1, 1784, *McGillivray of the Creeks*, 65; McGillivray to O'Neill, Feb. 5, 1784, *McGillivray of the Creeks*, 70; McGillivray to McLatchy, Sept. 18, 1784, *McGillivray of the Creeks*, 81; Hough, "Fathers and Brothers," 114–7; Coleman, *American Revolution in Georgia*, 240.

82. McGillivray to O'Neill, July 6, 1785, *McGillivray of the Creeks*, 90; Frank Lambert, *The Barbary Wars: American Independence in the Atlantic World* (New York, 2005), 4–5, 52–60; Thomas Bender, *A Nation Among Nations: America's Place in World History* (New York, 2006), 62.

83. McGillivray to O'Neill, Feb. 5, 1784, *McGillivray of the Creeks*, 70.

84. McGillivray to O'Neill, Jan. 1, 1784, *McGillivray of the Creeks*, 64; Braund, *Deerskins and Duffels*, 170–1; Wright, *Creeks and Seminoles*, 116–7.

85. A Gentleman in Cherokee Country to His Friend in Virginia, August 2, 1787, *Calendar of Virginia State Papers*, 4: 333–4; Kevin T. Barksdale, *The Lost State of Franklin: America's First Secession* (Lexington, 2009), 84–5.

86. O'Neill to José de Gálvez, Feb. 20, 1787, *McGillivray of the Creeks*, 144.

87. Navarro Account, July 27, 1784, p. 145, reel 2, Mississippi Provincial Archives: Spanish Dominion; Green, "Alexander McGillivray," 48–50. Alexander McGillivray's brother-in-law Louis Le Clerc Milfort claimed that the Creeks made McGillivray supreme chief of the whole nation, but Milfort also claimed that he persuaded them to, so something may have been lost in the translation. McGillivray did not act as a chief, although he did have a tremendous amount of influence both within and beyond the Creek Nation. Milfort, *Chef de guerre*, 77–81, 212–3. For an example of Creek diplomats who inflated their titles, see Joshua Piker, "The Empire, the Emperor, and the Empress: The Interesting Case of Mrs. Mary Bosomworth," in *European Empires in the American South*, ed. Joseph P. Ward (Oxford, Miss., forthcoming).

88. McGillivray to O'Neill, April 18, 1787, *McGillivray of the Creeks*, 149–50; John Galphin to Henry Osborn, June 1, 1789, *American State Papers: Indian Affairs*, 1: 36.

89. Green, "Expansion of European Colonization," 1: 471; Waselkov, *Conquering Spirit*, 12.

90. On mutual hatred to the north, see Richter, *Facing East From Indian Country*, 189–206; Peter Silver, *Our Savage Neighbors: How Indian War Transformed Early America* (New York, 2008).

91. Agreement for gifts and commerce with the Indians, March 18, 1782, *Confidential Despatches of Don Bernardo de Gálvez*.

92. Spanish dollars, American dollars, and Spanish pesos were all the same value. Congress in 1776 adopted the peso as its currency under the name *dollar*, the English word for the German Thaler. José de Gálvez to Viceroy of New Spain, Oct. 30, 1782, *Confidential Despatches of Don Bernardo de Gálvez*; José de Gálvez to Martín de Mayorga Ferrer, Oct. 30, 1782, *Confidential Despatches of Don Bernardo de Gálvez*; Miró to Grimarest, March 26, 1783, doc. 400–1, reel 153, leg. 3, Papeles de Cuba, P. K. Yonge; Elliott, *Empires of the Atlantic World*, 255.

93. Miró to Navarro, April 15, 1784, reel 1, Panton, Leslie, and Company Papers, Library of Congress.

94. McGillivray to O'Neill, May 1, 1784, *McGillivray of the Creeks,* 75; McGillivray to Miró, May 1, 1784, *Spain in the Mississippi Valley,* 2: 101.

95. Treaty of Augusta with the Creeks, Nov. 1, 1783, *Early American Indian Documents,* 18: 372–3; Treaty of Pensacola, June 1, 1784, *McGillivray of the Creeks,* 75–6.

96. Miró to Ezpeleta, Aug. 1, 1784, 10: 1474–1502, leg. 1394, Dispatches of the Spanish Governors; Treaty of Pensacola, June 1, 1784, *McGillivray of the Creeks,* 75–6.

97. Treaty of Pensacola, June 1, 1784, *McGillivray of the Creeks,* 76.

98. *Recopilación de leyes,* libro 4, capítulo 12, ley 5, qtd. in William B. Taylor, *Landlord and Peasant in Colonial Oaxaca* (Stanford, 1972), 67.

99. Miró to Ezpeleta, Aug. 1, 1784, 10: 1474-1502, leg. 1394, Dispatches of the Spanish Governors.

100. Miró to Navarro, April 15, 1784, reel 1, Panton Leslie Papers; Treaty of Pensacola, June 1, 1784, *McGillivray of the Creeks,* 76; Miró, Navarro, O'Neill, and McGillivray Agreement, June 1, 1784, reel 1, Panton Leslie Papers.

101. Miró to Ezpeleta, Aug. 1, 1784, 10: 1474–1502, leg. 1394, Dispatches of the Spanish Governors; Miró to Bernardo de Gálvez, April 30, 1784, doc. 598, reel 154, leg. 3, Papeles de Cuba, P. K. Yonge; Coker and Watson, *Indian Traders.*

102. O'Neill to Morales, April 16, 1784, pp. 91–6, doc. 16, reel 2, Mississippi Provincial Archives: Spanish Dominion. On McGillivray's thinking on the trade agreement, see McGillivray to Miró, March 24, 1784, "Papers Relating to the Georgia-Florida Frontier, 1784-1800," 360–1.

103. Navarro to José de Gálvez, Aug. 18, 1784, Audiencia de Santo Domingo, Archivo General de Indias, leg. 2609, doc. 255, reel 72, Historic New Orleans Collection; McGillivray to O'Neill, Jan. 1, 1784, *McGillivray of the Creeks,* 66; [Miró] to McGillivray, June 7, 1784, *McGillivray of the Creeks,* 77; Zéspedes to Bernardo de Gálvez, Aug. 16, 1784, *Spain in the Mississippi Valley,* 2: 108–10; McGillivray to Charles McLatchy, Oct. 4, 1784, *McGillivray of the Creeks,* 82–3; McGillivray to McLatchy, Dec. 25, 1784, *McGillivray of the Creeks,* 85–6; McGillivray to Zépedes, May 22, 1785, *McGillivray of the Creeks,* 88; McGillivray to O'Neill, July 24, 1785, *McGillivray of the Creeks,* 93–4; Saunt, *New Order of Things,* 76–7.

104. McGillivray letter, n.d. [June 1784], *McGillivray of the Creeks,* 77–8.

105. Memorandum of the [Tallassee] King's Proposals and Complaints, Nov. 1783, "Indian Treaties and Cessions of Land in Georgia, 1705–1837," comp. and ed. J. E. Hays, typescript manuscript, Georgia Dept. of Archives and History, Atlanta. Many thanks to David Nichols for this document.

106. McGillivray to O'Neill, Nov. 20, 1784, *McGillivray of the Creeks,* 84.

107. McGillivray to William Clark, April 24, 1785, reel 2, Panton Leslie Papers.

108. Nichols, *Red Gentlemen and White Savages,* 69; Snyder, *Slavery in Indian Country,* 165–6.

109. Treaty of French Lick between Virginia and the Chickasaws, Nov. 5–6, 1783, *Early American Indian Documents: Treaties and Laws,* 18: 374–6; Cotterill, "Virginia-Chickasaw Treaty," 494–5.

110. Treaty of Peace between Spain and the Chickasaw Nation, June 22 and 23, 1784, reel 1, film 663, leg. 2360, Papeles de Cuba, U.S. Library of Congress Microfilm of transcripts of selected manuscript documents pertaining to Arkansas, at the University of Arkansas, Fayetteville; O'Brien, *Choctaws in a Revolutionary Age,* 150.

111. Treaty of Peace between Spain and the Chickasaw Nation, June 22 and 23, 1784, reel 1, film 663, leg. 2360, Papeles de Cuba, U.S. Library of Congress Microfilm, University of Arkansas.

112. Rations Given to Indians at the Congress of Mobile, June 24, 1784, *Spain in the Mississippi Valley*, 2: 102–7; Miró to Ezpeleta, Aug. 1, 1784, 10: 1474–1502, leg. 1394, Dispatches of the Spanish Governors.

113. P. Mulenberg to Thomas Milton, July 5, 1784, fr. 113–6, reel 69, Papers of the Continental Congress; Cruzat to Miró, Aug. 13, 1785, *Spain in the Mississippi Valley*, 2: 133–4.

114. Cruzat to Miró, Aug. 23, 1784, *Spain in the Mississippi Valley*, 2: 117–9; Dowd, *Spirited Resistance*, 93.

115. May 8, 1783, *Journals of the Continental Congress*, 24: 333; Elias Boudinot to Pollock, May 9, 1783, p. 186, reel 24, Papers of the Continental Congress.

116. Navarro, "Reflexiones Políticas sobre el estado actual de la provincia de la Luisiana," 1782, *Documentos históricos de la Florida y la Luisiana, siglos XVI al XVIII*, ed. Manuel Serrano y Sanz (Madrid, 1913), 361, 365, 368.

117. Livingston to Jay, June 23, 1782, p. 451, reel 105, Papers of the Continental Congress.

118. [James Madison], Oct. 17, 1780, *Journals of the Continental Congress*, 18: 937–8.

119. [Madison], Oct. 17, 1780, *Journals of the Continental Congress*, 18: 945–6.

120. Aug. 20, 1782, *Journals of the Continental Congress*, 23: 476; Taylor, *Divided Ground*, 237–8.

121. Aug. 20, 1782, *Journals of the Continental Congress*, 23: 476; Wright, *Florida in the American Revolution*, 122–3.

122. Miró to Cruzat, March 8, 1785, doc. 717, reel 154, leg. 3, Papeles de Cuba, P. K. Yonge; José de Gálvez to Miró, June 26, 1784, doc. 622, reel 154, leg. 3, Papeles de Cuba, P. K. Yonge; Thomas Patterson to Pollock, May 1, 1784, p. 433, reel 64, Papers of the Continental Congress; Caughey, *Bernardo de Gálvez in Louisiana*, 247.

123. Miró to Bernardo de Gálvez, Aug. 20, 1783, doc. 494, reel 154, leg. 3, Papeles de Cuba, P. K. Yonge; Miró to Cruzat, July 13, 1785, doc. 771, reel 154, leg. 3, Papeles de Cuba, P. K. Yonge.

124. Thomas Green to Col. Bledsoe, Sept. 10, 1785, *Spain in the Mississippi Valley*, 2: 147–8; [Miró] to Nicolas Long, Nathaniel Christmas, and William Davenport, Sept. 7, 1785, doc. 912, reel 154, leg. 3, Papeles de Cuba, P. K. Yonge; Miró to José de Gálvez, June 14, 1785, doc. 82, reel 17, leg. 2550, Audiencia de Santo Domingo, Historic New Orleans Collection; Miró to Pedro Piernas, June 17, 1785, doc. 750, reel 154, leg. 3, Papeles de Cuba, P. K. Yonge; Miró to José de Gálvez, June 25, 1785, doc. 83, reel 17, leg. 2550, Audiencia de Santo Domingo, Historic New Orleans Collection; James, *Oliver Pollock*, 310–4; Abernethy, *South in the New Nation*, 75–6.

125. Miró to McGillivray, June 14, 1785, doc. 747, reel 154, leg. 3, Papeles de Cuba, P. K. Yonge; Miró to Pedro Piernas, June 17, 1785, doc. 750, reel 154, leg. 3, Papeles de Cuba, P. K. Yonge; O'Neill to Bernardo de Gálvez, July 8, 1785, "Papers from the Spanish Archives Relating to Tennessee and the Old Southwest," 9: 121–3.

126. O'Neill to Bernardo de Gálvez, July 21, 1785, "Papers from the Spanish Archives Relating to Tennessee and the Old Southwest," 9: 123; Bouligny to Miró, July 24, 1785, "Papers from the Spanish Archives Relating to Tennessee and the Old Southwest," 9: 125–8; Miró to Bernardo de Gálvez, Jan. 28, 1786, doc. 1148, reel 155, leg. 3, Papeles de Cuba, P. K. Yonge.

127. Bouligny to Miró, Aug. 22, 1785, *Spain in the Mississippi Valley*, 2: 136–41.

128. Congressional Resolution, Oct. 13, 1785, *Journals of the Continental Congress*, 29: 829–30.

129. Bernardo de Gálvez to Gardoqui, n.d., qtd. in Boeta, *Bernardo de Gálvez*, 124–5; Savelle, *George Morgan*, 202. On imperial officials' difficulties interpreting American

geography, see Paul W. Mapp, *The Elusive West and the Contest for Empire, 1713–1763* (Chapel Hill, 2011).

130. Pollock to Lee, July 6, 1785, p. 485, reel 64, Papers of the Continental Congress; Pollock to Jay, June 3, 1785, p. 481, reel 64, Papers of the Continental Congress; Firm of Willing, Morris to Jay, April 7, 1785, p. 519, reel 104, Papers of the Continental Congress.

131. Report by Jay, Aug. 3, 1786, *Journals of the Continental Congress,* 31: 472–84; Gardoqui to Jay, May 25, 1786, *Journals of the Continental Congress,* 31: 469–72; Samuel Flagg Bemis, *Pinckney's Treaty: A Study of America's Advantage from Europe's Distress, 1783–1800* (Baltimore, 1926), 87–8.

132. Bemis, *Pinckney's Treaty,* 94–102; James, *Oliver Pollock,* 311–3. On early U.S. diplomatic bumbling, see Bemis, *Diplomatic History of the United States,* 65–84; George C. Herring, *From Colony to Superpower: U.S. Foreign Relations since 1776* (New York, 2008), 11–92.

133. Gould, *Persistence of Empire,* 210–2; Burbank and Cooper, *Empires in World History.*

CHAPTER 15

1. Thomas Jefferson, *Notes on the State of Virginia* (Paris, 1782), 251–2; Vicente Manuel Zéspedes to the Governor of Georgia, December 12, 1784, *Journals of the Continental Congress,* 34: 459; Jane G. Landers, *Atlantic Creoles in the Age of Revolutions* (Cambridge, 2010), 34–5.

2. Woody Holton, *Black Americans in the Revolutionary Era. A Brief History with Documents* (Boston, 2009), 15; Pybus, *Epic Journeys of Freedom,* 60–2.

3. Cameron, "To Plead Our Own Cause," 121–7, 101, 135–6.

4. Jefferson, *Notes on the State of Virginia,* 301; Nash, *Forgotten Fifth,* 71–122.

5. Bernardo de Gálvez, certificate of service for Pedro, July 1, 1781, fr. 1187, reel 166, leg. 2, Papeles de Cuba, P. K. Yonge Library, University of Florida, Gainesville (and similar certificates in the same legajo); Piernas to Bernardo de Gálvez, January 9, 1782, fr. 1728, reel 167, leg. 2, Papeles de Cuba, P. K. Yonge; Bernardo de Gálvez to José de Gálvez, Jan. 18, 1782, John B. Stetson Collection, P. K. Yonge.

6. Starr, *Tories, Dons, and Rebels,* 202; Landers, *Black Society in Spanish Florida,* 7–8, 202.

7. Peter Bestes et al. to the Representative of the Town of Thompson, April 20, 1773, *A Documentary History of the Negro People in the United States,* ed. Herbert Aptheker (Secaucus, 1951), 1: 7; Hanger, "Avenues to Freedom," 1: 186-7; Berlin, *Many Thousands Gone,* 210–3; Cameron, "To Plead Our Own Cause," 118.

8. Gálvez, *Diario de las operaciones,* 80–1; Berlin, *Many Thousands Gone,* 221.

9. Royal Cedula, Jan. 22, 1782, *Spain in the Mississippi Valley,* 2: 1–5; Caughey, *Bernardo de Gálvez in Louisiana,* 250–1; Hall, *Africans in Colonial Louisiana,* 213; James A. McMillen, *The Final Victims: Foreign Slave Trade to North America, 1783–1810* (Columbia, 2004); Hammond, "Slavery, Settlement, and Empire," 183–6.

10. Berlin, *Many Thousands Gone,* 221; Robin Blackburn, "Introduction," *Paths to Freedom: Manumission in the Atlantic World,* ed. Rosemary Brana-Shute and Randy J. Sparks (Columbia, 2009), 1–13.

11. Recensement General, Dec. 10, 1781, ed. Mr. and Mrs. Lionel Theriot, *Attakapas Gazette* 20 (1985): 29.

12. *Southwest Louisiana Records,* 1A: 119-20, 122, 125, 128-30, 136-9, 144, 148-9, 1B: 119, 125, 2B: 150-1; *Marriage Contracts of the Attakapas Post, 1760–1803,* vol. 5 of *Colonial Louisiana Marriage Contracts,* ed. Winston De Ville (St. Martinsville, 1966), 57, 65.

13. Esteban Miró to Francisco Bouligny, May 28, 1784, doc. 609, reel 154, leg. 3, Papeles de Cuba, P. K. Yonge; Dunbar, *Life, Letters, and Papers,* 26–9, 46–7, 59; Usner, *Indians, Settlers, and Slaves,* 136–41; Hall, *Africans in Colonial Louisiana,* 97–9, 202–36, 306–7.

14. Miró, Orders, May 1, 1784, doc. 668-a, reel 154, leg. 3, Papeles de Cuba, P. K. Yonge; Sophie White, "Slaves and Poor Whites' Informal Economies in an Atlantic Context," in *Louisiana: Crossroads of the Atlantic World,* ed. Cécile Vidal (Philadelphia, 2014), 89–102.

15. Miró to habitants de la Côte des Chapitoulas, April 24, 1784, doc. 591, reel 154, leg. 3, Papeles de Cuba, P. K. Yonge; Miró, Orders, May 1, 1784, doc. 668-a, reel 154, leg. 3, Papeles de Cuba, P. K. Yonge; Hall, *Africans in Colonial Louisiana,* 221–2; McGowan, "Creation of a Slave Society," 233–45. The *Code Noir* had included most of these restrictions for French Louisiana, and the Spanish had repeatedly tried to crack down on commerce conducted by slaves, but the traveling passes for slaves and the requirement that free black Louisianans carry papers were new. The crown soon loosened those back to prewar restrictions. Louis Sala-Molins, *Le Code Noir, ou le calvaire de Canaan* (Paris, 1987), 120, 122, 129, 146; O'Reilly, proclamation, Aug. 24, 1769, *Spain in the Mississippi Valley,* 1: 89–90; Berlin, *Many Thousands Gone,* 221, 339.

16. Miró to Bouligny, May 28, 1784, doc. 609, reel 154, leg. 3, Papeles de Cuba, P. K. Yonge; Miró to Bernardo de Gálvez, July 31, 1784, doc. 638, reel 154, leg. 3, Papeles de Cuba, P. K. Yonge; Miró to Bernardo de Gálvez, October 1, 1784, doc. 668, reel 154, leg. 3, Papeles de Cuba, P. K. Yonge; Miró to Delassize, October 3, 1784, doc. 673, reel 154, leg. 3, Papeles de Cuba, P. K. Yonge; Miró to Mr. Dreux, October 7, 1784, doc. 641-a, reel 154, leg. 3, Papeles de Cuba, P. K. Yonge; Hall, *Africans in Colonial Louisiana,* 212-35; Gilbert C. Din, "'Cimarrones' and the San Malo Band in Spanish Louisiana," *Louisiana History* 21 (1980): 237–62.

17. José de Ezpeleta to Bernardo de Gálvez, May 22, 1780, fr. 1005, reel 165, leg. 2, Papeles de Cuba, P. K. Yonge.

18. Martín Navarro to Enrique Grimarest, Feb. 18, 1782, p. 756, reel 442, leg. 83, Papeles de Cuba, P. K. Yonge; Hanger, "Avenues to Freedom," 1: 186.

19. McGowan, "Creation of a Slave Society," 193–201; Berlin, *Many Thousands Gone,* 331–3, 340; Jennifer M. Spear, *Race, Sex, and Social Order in Early New Orleans* (Baltimore, 2008), 7, 100–3, 109–28; Elliott, *Empires of the Atlantic World,* 107–8.

20. McGowan, "Creation of a Slave Society," 202–3.

21. Bernardo de Gálvez to José de Gálvez, Jan. 14, 1782, pp. 861–2, reel 2, Mississippi Provincial Archives: Spanish Dominion, 1759–1804, comp. Dunbar Rowland, Jackson, Miss.; Miró to Bernardo de Gálvez, December 12, 1785, doc. 1100, reel 155, leg. 3, Papeles de Cuba, P. K. Yonge; Waldeck, *Eighteenth Century America,* 173; Census of Pensacola, 1784, *The Spanish Censuses of Pensacola, 1784–1820,* ed. William S. Coker and G. Douglas Inglis (Pensacola, 1980), 33–44; Fabel, "Ordeal by Siege," 291; Wright, *Florida in the American Revolution,* 92–3; Starr, *Tories, Dons, and Rebels,* 236–7.

22. Waldeck, *Eighteenth Century America,* 173; Wright, *Florida in the American Revolution,* 118.

23. James Bruce Claim, March 1, 1783, p. 62, AO 12/99, British National Archives, Kew, England; Piecuch, *Three Peoples, One King,* 283, 298–9, 315–6; Wright, *Florida in the American Revolution,* 117–24; J. Leitch Wright, "Lord Dunmore's Loyalist Asylum," *Florida Historical Quarterly* 49 (1971): 371–5; David, *Dunmore's New World,* 123–5, 135.

24. Bruce to [Lord Shelburne], Aug. 22, 1782, Earl of Shelburne Papers, William L. Clements Library, University of Michigan, Ann Arbor.

25. Bruce to [Lord Shelburne], Aug. 22, 1782, Shelburne Papers, Clements Library;

Bruce, "Materials for Ship Building in West Florida," Dec. 10, 1782, Shelburne Papers, Clements Library.

26. Bruce, Memorial to the Lords of His Majesty's Treasury, Feb. 15, 1783, p. 137, T 1/582, British National Archives; Bruce, Additional Memorial to the Lords of His Majesty's Treasury, Feb. 15, 1783, p. 143, T 1/582, British National Archives; Bruce Claim, March 1, 1783, p. 62, AO 12/99, British National Archives; Bruce, Memorial to the Lords of His Majesty's Treasury, April 12, 1783, p. 141, T 1/582, British National Archives; Pearsall, *Atlantic Families,* 188–92; David, *Dunmore's New World,* 136–8.

27. Starr, *Tories, Dons, and Rebels,* 238.

28. Bruce Claim, March 1, 1783, p. 62, AO 12/99, British National Archives; Bruce Claim, March 4, 1783, p. 62, AO 12/99, British National Archives; Decision on Bruce Claim, [March] 1783, p. 63, AO 12/99, British National Archives; Fabel, "Ordeal by Siege," 291.

29. Bruce, Memorial to the Lords of His Majesty's Treasury, April 12, 1783, p. 141, T 1/582, British National Archives.

30. West Florida Proprietors to Lord North, n.d. [1783], and West Florida Proprietors to the House of Commons, March 16, 1787, both in "The Case and Petition of His Majesty's Loyal Subjects, Late of West Florida," ed. J. Barton Starr, *Florida Historical Quarterly* 59 (1980): 199–212; Starr, *Tories, Dons, and Rebels,* 238.

31. Edmund Rush Wegg became Attorney General of the Bahamas, despite his leadership of the Stamp Act protests in Pensacola three and a half decades earlier. Wright, *Florida in the American Revolution,* 139–41; Thelma Peters, "The American Loyalists in the Bahama Islands: Who They Were," *Florida Historical Quarterly* 40 (1962): 232 3; *Genealogica and Heraldica: Proceedings of the 22nd International Congress of Genealogical and Heraldic Sciences in Ottawa, August 18–23, 1996* (Ottawa, 1998), 259; A. Talbot Bethell, *Early Settlers of the Bahamas and Colonists of North America* (Nassau, 1937), 130, 190–1; David, *Dunmore's New World,* 154.

32. Thelma Peters, "The Loyalist Migration from East Florida to the Bahama Islands," *Florida Historical Quarterly* 40 (1961): 137; Wright, *Florida in the American Revolution,* 148.

33. Sarah M. S. Pearsall, "'Citizens of the World': Men, Women, and Country in the Age of Revolution," in *Old World, New World: America and Europe in the Age of Jefferson,* ed. Leonard J. Sadosky, Peter Nicolaisen, Peter S. Onuf, and Andrew J. O'Shaughnessy (Charlottesville, 2010), 62; Judith M. Bennett, *History Matters: Patriarchy and the Challenge of Feminism* (Philadelphia, 2006), 63, 78.

34. Bernardo de Gálvez to José de Gálvez, July 19, 1781, *Confidential Despatches of Don Bernardo de Gálvez.*

35. Robert Morris to Bernardo de Gálvez, draft, November 21, 1781, *The Revolutionary Diplomatic Correspondence of the United States,* 4: 852–3; *Journals of the Continental Congress,* 21: 883, 1028, 1046–7, 1107; James, *Oliver Pollock,* 270-1.

36. Oliver Pollock request to Miró, April 20, 1782, *Spain in the Mississippi Valley,* 2: 8–11; James, *Oliver Pollock,* 272, 280, 354; Cummins, "Oliver Pollock's Plantations," 43; Cummins, "Oliver Pollock and George Rogers Clark's Service of Supply."

37. Margaret Pollock to Miró, Oct. 29, 1782, *Spain in the Mississippi Valley,* 2: 63.

38. Margaret Pollock to Miró, Nov. 12, 1782, *Spain in the Mississippi Valley,* 2: 64–5.

39. Hayden, "Pollock Family of Pennsylvania," 98-100.

40. Margaret Pollock to Miró, [Sept.] 1783, *Spain in the Mississippi Valley,* 2: 79.

41. Miró to Margaret Pollock, Sept. 13, 1783, *Spain in the Mississippi Valley,* 2: 79–80.

42. Margaret Pollock to Miró, Sept. 13, 1783, *Spain in the Mississippi Valley,* 2: 80.

43. Clark to Harrison, Jan. 17, 1782, *Calendar of Virginia State Papers,* 3: 25, 29; James, *Oliver Pollock,* 274.

44. Oliver Pollock to the President of Congress, Sept. 18, 1782, in James, *Oliver Pollock,* appendix I, 354.

45. *Journals of the Continental Congress,* Oct. 22, 1782, 23: 680–1.

46. John Hanson to Miró, Oct. 31, 1782, Oliver Pollock Papers, Missouri Historical Society Archives; James, *Oliver Pollock,* 278–9; Bruce H. Mann, *Republic of Debtors: Bankruptcy in the Age of American Independence* (Cambridge, 2002), 169–70, 176.

47. Oliver Pollock to President of Congress, Feb. 24, 1783, pp. 389–90, reel 64, Papers of the Continental Congress, 1774–1789, M247, National Archives and Records Service, Washington, D.C., microfilm at University of North Carolina, Chapel Hill; Resolution of Virginia House of Delegates, Dec. 27, 1782, *Spain in the Mississippi Valley,* 2: 68–9; Virginia Congressional Delegates to Bernardo de Gálvez, May 4, 1783, *Spain in the Mississippi Valley,* 2: 76; James, *Oliver Pollock,* 279–80.

48. Miró to Oliver Pollock, Oct. 8, 1783, *Spain in the Mississippi Valley,* 2: 87–8.

49. Oliver Pollock to Miró, Oct. 24, 1783, *Spain in the Mississippi Valley,* 2: 89.

50. Congressional Commission, June 2, 1783, *Journals of the Continental Congress,* 24: 376–7; Elias Boudinot to Bernardo de Gálvez, June 3, 1783, p. 187, reel 24, Papers of the Continental Congress.

51. Luís de Unzaga y Amezaga to Oliver Pollock, Aug. 22, 1783, p. 191, reel 150, Papers of the Continental Congress; Oliver Pollock to Morris, Sept. 10, 1783, p. 185, reel 150, Papers of the Continental Congress; Unzaga to Oliver Pollock, Dec. 27, 1783, p. 367, reel 64, Papers of the Continental Congress; Oliver Pollock to Morris, March 16, 1784, p. 865, reel 150, Papers of the Continental Congress; Oliver Pollock to Unzaga, May 31, 1784, p. 450, reel 64, Papers of the Continental Congress; Oliver Pollock to Morris, July 7, 1784, p. 469, reel 64, Papers of the Continental Congress; James, *Oliver Pollock,* 283–6.

52. Crowley, *Privileges of Independence,* 55–60; Peter S. Onuf, introduction, *Old World, New World,* 2.

53. Oliver Pollock to Morris, Aug. 28, 1784, p. 445, reel 64, Papers of the Continental Congress; James, *Oliver Pollock,* 288–9.

54. Oliver Pollock to Unzaga, Aug. 17, 1784, p. 457–8, reel 64, Papers of the Continental Congress.

55. Unzaga to Oliver Pollock, Aug. 26, 1784, p. 459, reel 64, Papers of the Continental Congress.

56. Oliver Pollock to Morris, Aug. 28, 1784, p. 445, reel 64, Papers of the Continental Congress.

57. Oliver Pollock to Bernardo de Gálvez, March 1, 1785, p. 473, reel 64, Papers of the Continental Congress; Oliver Pollock to Richard Henry Lee, July 6, 1785, p. 485, reel 64, Papers of the Continental Congress; Bernardo de Gálvez to Oliver Pollock, April 27, 1785, p. 77, reel 73, Papers of the Continental Congress.

58. Oliver Pollock to Jay, June 3, 1785, p. 481, reel 64, Papers of the Continental Congress; James, *Oliver Pollock,* 292–3; Jay to Bernardo de Gálvez, Sept. 21, 1785, General Records of the Department of State, RG 59, National Archives and Records Service, Washington, D.C., http://research.archives.gov/description/6705687.

59. List of Marriages and Baptisms Registered at St. Joseph's Church, Philadelphia, 1771-1786, microfilm 496869, Family History Library, Salt Lake City, Utah. Next Oliver Pollock had to defend himself against humiliating Congressional accusations of smuggling in the summer of 1785. Congress eventually found no basis for the ac-

cusations and pledged the reimbursements, again without paying. Congressional Report, July 8, 1785, *Journals of the Continental Congress,* 29: 522–3; Committee Report, July 12, 1785, *Journals of the Continental Congress,* 29: 531–2; Oliver Pollock to Lee, July 6, 1785, p. 485, reel 64, Papers of the Continental Congress; James, *Oliver Pollock,* 297–306.

60. Oliver Pollock to President of Congress, Sept. 22, 1785, p. 507, reel 64, Papers of the Continental Congress; Oliver Pollock to President of Congress, Sept. 28, 1785, p. 511, reel 64, Papers of the Continental Congress; Hayden, *Pollock Genealogy,* frontispiece; James, *Oliver Pollock,* 304–6.

CHAPTER 16

1. Nairne, *Nairne's Muskhogean Journals,* 38.

2. Alexander McGillivray to Esteban Miró, Oct. 4, 1787, *McGillivray of the Creeks,* 160, 162; Snyder, *Slavery in Indian Country,* 163–4.

3. Alan Taylor, *Liberty Men and Great Proprietors: The Revolutionary Settlement on the Maine Frontier, 1760–1820* (Chapel Hill, 1990).

4. John Quincy Adams, "An Oration upon the Importance and Necessity of Public Faith, to the Well-Being of a Community," July 18, 1787, *Diary of John Quincy Adams,* ed. David Grayson Allen et al. (Cambridge, 1981), 2: 258.

5. McGillivray for the Chiefs of the Creek, Chickasaw, and Cherokee Nations, July 10, 1785, *McGillivray of the Creeks,* 90–3; McGillivray to Arturo O'Neill, July 24, 1785, *McGillivray of the Creeks,* 93; Milfort, *Chef de guerre,* 125–6; Vicente Manuel de Zéspedes to O'Neill, June 15, 1785, *Documents from East Florida,* 559; Zéspedes to Bernardo de Gálvez, June 12, 1785, *Documents from East Florida,* 557.

6. McGillivray to O'Neill, May 12, 1786, "Papers from the Spanish Archives Relating to Tennessee and the Old Southwest," 10: 139; O'Neill to Bernardo de Gálvez, May 20, 1786, "Papers from the Spanish Archives Relating to Tennessee and the Old Southwest," 10: 137; McGillivray for the Chiefs of the Creek, Chickasaw, and Cherokee Nations, July 10, 1785, *McGillivray of the Creeks,* 91–2; McGillivray to Vicente Folch, May 14, 1789, *McGillivray of the Creeks,* 232; Nichols, *Red Gentlemen and White Savages,* 69–70; Dowd, *Spirited Resistance,* 94; Taylor, *Divided Ground,* 116.

7. P. Mulenberg to Thomas Milton, July 5, 1784, fr. 113–6, reel 69, Papers of the Continental Congress, 1774-1789, M247, National Archives and Records Service, Washington, D.C., microfilm at University of North Carolina, Chapel Hill.

8. McGillivray to John Leslie, Nov. 20, 1788, *McGillivray of the Creeks,* 206–8.

9. McGillivray to James White, April 8, 1787, *Early American Indian Documents,* 18: 445–6.

10. Green, "Alexander McGillivray," 51–2.

11. Milfort, *Chef de guerre,* 194–5; Cashin, *Lachlan McGillivray, Indian Trader,* 298–302, 308.

12. Benjamin Hawkins, Andrew Pickens, and Joseph Martin to the Creeks, June 10, 1785, *McGillivray of the Creeks,* 95–6; McGillivray to Pickens, Sept. 5, 1785, *Early American Indian Documents,* 18: 387–8; McGillivray to Halloing, King of the Cowetas, Sept. 2, 1785, "Papers from the Spanish Archives Relating to Tennessee and the Old Southwest," 10: 145; McGillivray to O'Neill, Oct. 10, 1785, *McGillivray of the Creeks,* 98n46; O'Neill to Bernardo de Gálvez, Oct. 31, 1785, reel 2, Panton, Leslie, and Company Papers, Library of Congress, Washington, D.C.

13. McGillivray to O'Neill, Feb. 10, 1786, *McGillivray of the Creeks,* 103; McGillivray to

Miró, May 1, 1786, *McGillivray of the Creeks,* 107; McGillivray to O'Neill, April 18, 1787, *McGillivray of the Creeks,* 150; Report of U.S. Indian Commissioners to Congress, Nov. 17, 1785, *Early American Indian Documents,* 18: 392.

14. McGillivray to Zéspedes, Nov. 15, 1786, *McGillivray of the Creeks,* 139.

15. Hawkins to McGillivray, Jan. 8, 1786, *McGillivray of the Creeks,* 101; Hawkins to McGillivray, Jan. 11, 1786, "Papers from the Spanish Archives Relating to Tennessee and the Old Southwest," 10: 129; McGillivray to Miró, May 1, 1786, *McGillivray of the Creeks,* 106–10; Report of U.S. Indian Commissioners to Congress, Nov. 17, 1785, *Early American Indian Documents,* 18: 392; Nichols, *Red Gentlemen and White Savages,* 45–7; Treaty at Galphinton, Nov. 12, 1785, *Early American Indian Documents,* 18: 390-1; Coleman, *American Revolution in Georgia,* 243.

16. McGillivray to O'Neill, March 8, 1786, *McGillivray of the Creeks,* 103–4; Talk between Zéspedes and Yntipaya Masla, May 29, 1786, *McGillivray of the Creeks,* 115; McGillivray to Miró, May 1, 1786, *McGillivray of the Creeks,* 108-9; McGillivray to Halloing, King of the Cowetas, April 14, 1786, "Papers from the Spanish Archives Relating to Tennessee and the Old Southwest," 10: 143–4.

17. McGillivray to O'Neill, March 28, 1786, *McGillivray of the Creeks,* 104–6; McGillivray to Miró, May 1, 1786, *McGillivray of the Creeks,* 109; Nichols, *Red Gentlemen and White Savages,* 55.

18. Milfort, *Chef de guerre,* 175–7. For an earlier example, see the Natchez War against France. "Antoine Simon Le Page Du Pratz Describes French Conflict with the Natchez, 1729," in *Interpreting a Continent,* 264.

19. McGillivray to Hallowing King of the Cowetas, April 14, 1786, "Papers from the Spanish Archives Relating to Tennessee and the Old Southwest," 10: 143–4; McGillivray to Miró, May 1, 1786, *McGillivray of the Creeks,* 109; McGillivray to O'Neill, May 12, 1786, "Papers from the Spanish Archives Relating to Tennessee and the Old Southwest," 10: 138; O'Neill to Bernardo de Gálvez, May 20, 1786, "Papers from the Spanish Archives Relating to Tennessee and the Old Southwest," 10: 137–8; McGillivray to O'Neill, March 4, 1787, *McGillivray of the Creeks,* 145; McGillivray to O'Neill, April 4, 1787, *McGillivray of the Creeks,* 147; Nichols, *Red Gentlemen and White Savages,* 70; Green, "Expansion of European Colonization," 1: 472; Barksdale, *Lost State of Franklin,* 84.

20. McGillivray to Miró, May 1, 1786, *McGillivray of the Creeks,* 110; O'Neill to Bernardo de Gálvez, May 20, 1786, "Papers from the Spanish Archives Relating to Tennessee and the Old Southwest," 10: 137–8; Zéspedes to José de Ezpeleta, May 24, 1786, *McGillivray of the Creeks,* 113n60; McGillivray to O'Neill, Aug. 12, 1786, *McGillivray of the Creeks,* 127–8; O'Neill to Miró, Sept. 18, 1786, "Papers from the Spanish Archives Relating to Tennessee and the Old Southwest," 10: 146–7; O'Neill to Bernardo de Gálvez, Oct. 11, 1786, "Papers from the Spanish Archives Relating to Tennessee and the Old Southwest," 10: 149; McGillivray to Zéspedes, Nov. 15, 1786, *McGillivray of the Creeks,* 138.

21. O'Neill to Bernardo de Gálvez, May 30, 1786, "Papers from the Spanish Archives Relating to Tennessee and the Old Southwest," 140.

22. McGillivray to William Panton, August 3, 1786, *McGillivray of the Creeks,* 123; Creek Indians to the Georgia Governor and Legislature, Aug. 3, 1786, *McGillivray of the Creeks,* 123–4.

23. McGillivray to Habersham, Sept. 18, 1786, *McGillivray of the Creeks,* 131. Hoboithle Miko and Neha Miko signed the "Treaty of Shoulderbone" with Georgia in November, which included the same provisions as the "Treaty of Galphinton." Treaty of Shoulderbone, Nov. 3, 1786, *Early American Indian Documents,* 18: 433–6.

24. McGillivray to a Person in New Providence, June 30, 1787, "Papers from the Spanish Archives Relating to Tennessee and the Old Southwest," 14: 95–6; McGillivray to O'Neill, April 18, 1787, *McGillivray of the Creeks,* 149–50; Coleman, *American Revolution in Georgia,* 246–7.

25. McGillivray to Miró, June 20, 1787, "Papers from the Spanish Archives Relating to Tennessee and the Old Southwest," 11: 82–3; Fat King to George Mathews and Council of Georgia, July 27, 1787, p. 359, reel 87, Papers of the Continental Congress.

26. McGillivray to Miró, June 20, 1787, "Papers from the Spanish Archives Relating to Tennessee and the Old Southwest," 11: 82–4.

27. McGillivray to O'Neill, June 20, 1787, *McGillivray of the Creeks,* 153–4; Dowd, *Spirited Resistance,* 104. One of McGillivray's first proposals for the Southern Confederacy was to prevent any Americans from passing through their lands at all while Congress and Spain still had not made a treaty to set their border. O'Neill to Bernardo de Gálvez, Sept. 4, 1785, "Papers from the Spanish Archives Relating to Tennessee and the Old Southwest," 9: 130.

28. Fat King to George Mathews and Council of Georgia, July 27, 1787, p. 359, reel 87, Papers of the Continental Congress; Coleman, *American Revolution in Georgia,* 247.

29. Creek Indians to George Mathews, June 14, 1787, p. 349, reel 87, Papers of the Continental Congress.

30. George Mathews to the Headmen and Warriors of the Lower Creeks, June 29, 1787, p. 355, reel 87, Papers of the Continental Congress.

31. Fat King to Governor George Mathews and Council of Georgia, July 27, 1787, p. 359, reel 87, Papers of the Continental Congress.

32. Dowd, *Spirited Resistance,* 95.

33. O'Neill to Miró, Sept. 8, 1787, "Papers from the Spanish Archives Relating to Tennessee and the Old Southwest," 12: 101.

34. O'Neill to Miró, Sept. 17, 1787, "Papers from the Spanish Archives Relating to Tennessee and the Old Southwest," 12: 101; McGillivray to Miró, Oct. 4, 1787, *McGillivray of the Creeks,* 160–1; O'Neill to Miró, Oct. 6, 1787, "Papers from the Spanish Archives Relating to Tennessee and the Old Southwest," 12: 111; O'Neill to Ezpeleta, Nov. 10, 1787, fol. 178, leg. 1393, reel 329, Papeles de Cuba, P. K. Yonge Library, University of Florida, Gainesville; McGillivray to O'Neill, Nov. 20, 1787, *McGillivray of the Creeks,* 163–4; O'Neill to Miró, Nov. 28, 1787, "Papers from the Spanish Archives Relating to Tennessee and the Old Southwest," 12: 113–4; Coleman, *American Revolution in Georgia,* 248–9.

35. William Augustus Bowles to King George III, Jan. 3, 1791, FO 4-09-003, British National Archives, Kew, England; Milfort, *Chef de guerre,* 196; St. Jean, "Trading Paths: Mapping Chickasaw History," 766.

36. Nichols, *Red Gentlemen and White Savages,* 44, 53.

37. Proceedings of the Treaty of Hopewell with the Chickasaws, Jan. 7, 1786, *Early American Indian Documents,* 18: 419–20; Draper, "Narrative Based on an Interview with Malcolm McGee," 58–9.

38. Proceedings of the Treaty of Hopewell with the Chickasaws, Jan. 7, 1786, *Early American Indian Documents,* 18: 420.

39. Proceedings of the Treaty of Hopewell with the Chickasaws, Jan. 7, 1786, *Early American Indian Documents,* 18: 420–2; Atkinson, *Splendid Land, Splendid People,* 91; Green, *Chickasaw Lives,* 1: 69–70. North Carolina ultimately disavowed this treaty anyway, claiming that it gave the Chickasaws lands that actually belonged to North Carolina, which Congress had no right to do. North Carolina House of Commons Resolution, Jan. 6, 1787, *Early American Indian Documents,* 18: 442.

40. Proceedings of the Treaty of Hopewell with the Chickasaws, Jan. 7, 1786, *Early American Indian Documents,* 18: 421–2; Francisco Bouligny to Miró, Aug. 28, 1785, *Spain in the Mississippi Valley,* 2: 143; Louis Chacheré to Philipe Treviño, Sept. 5, 1785, *Spain in the Mississippi Valley,* 2: 146; Chacheré to [Bouligny], Nov. 7, 1785, *Spain in the Mississippi Valley,* 2: 151.

41. McGillivray to O'Neill, May 12, 1786, "Papers from the Spanish Archives Relating to Tennessee and the Old Southwest," 10: 138–9.

42. Hawkins and Pickens to Charles Thomson, Dec. 10, 1785, *American State Papers: Indian Affairs,* 1: 49; Proceedings of the Treaty of Hopewell with the Chickasaws, Jan. 7, 1786, *Early American Indian Documents,* 18: 418, 422; McGillivray to O'Neill, May 12, 1786, "Papers from the Spanish Archives Relating to Tennessee and the Old Southwest," 138; Nichols, *Red Gentlemen and White Savages,* 52.

43. O'Neill to Bernardo de Gálvez, May 20, 1786, "Papers from the Spanish Archives Relating to Tennessee and the Old Southwest," 10: 137–8; O'Neill to Bernardo de Gálvez, May 30, 1786, "Papers from the Spanish Archives Relating to Tennessee and the Old Southwest," 10: 140; Draper, "Narrative Based on an Interview with Malcolm McGee," 51.

44. Francisco Cruzat to Miró, Dec. 4, 1785, *Spain in the Mississippi Valley,* 2: 157; Miró to Cruzat, March 5, 1786, *Spain in the Mississippi Valley,* 2: 170. Peorias rumored that the Chickasaws were recruiting against the Spanish, but, as Illinois Indians, the Peorias had reason to set Spain against the Chickasaws.

45. Green, *Chickasaw Lives,* 1: 70–1.

46. O'Neill to Miró, Aug. 3, 1787, "Papers from the Spanish Archives Relating to Tennessee and the Old Southwest," 11: 91; Piomingo to Martin, Feb. 15, 1787, *Early American Indian Documents,* 18: 443; Gibson, *Chickasaws,* 80–1; Samuel Cole Williams, *History of the Lost State of Franklin* (New York, 1933), 141–2.

47. Alexander Frazer to O'Neill, June 12, 1787, "Papers from the Spanish Archives Relating to Tennessee and the Old Southwest," 11: 85; McGillivray to Miró, July 25, 1787, "Papers from the Spanish Archives Relating to Tennessee and the Old Southwest," 11: 88–9.

48. An Invitation to Emigrate to the Western Country, April 3, 1790, *Spain in the Mississippi Valley,* 2: 317–21.

49. McGillivray to Miró, July 25, 1787, "Papers from the Spanish Archives Relating to Tennessee and the Old Southwest," 11: 88–9; Miró to José de Gálvez, June 1, 1787, "Papers from the Spanish Archives Relating to Tennessee and the Old Southwest," 11: 76; McGillivray to O'Neill, July 25, 1787, *McGillivray of the Creeks,* 159; Carlos de Grande-Pré to Miró, Oct. 26, 1787, *Spain in the Mississippi Valley,* 2: 236–7; John Doughty, "Up the Tennessee in 1790: The Report of Major John Doughty to the Secretary of War," ed. Colton Storm, *East Tennessee Historical Society's Publications* 17 (1945): 125–6.

50. Henry Knox to Arthur St. Clair, Dec. 19, 1789, *The Territorial Papers of the United States,* ed. Clarence E. Carter (Washington, 1934), 2: 224–6; Knox, Report on the Causes of Existing Hostilities between the United States, and Certain Tribes of Indians Northwest of the Ohio, Jan. 26, 1792, *Territorial Papers,* 2: 360.

51. McGillivray to Miró, July 25, 1787, "Papers from the Spanish Archives Relating to Tennessee and the Old Southwest," 11: 88–9; McGillivray to Miró, June 20, 1787, "Papers from the Spanish Archives Relating to Tennessee and the Old Southwest," 11: 84; McGillivray to Miró, Oct. 4, 1787, *McGillivray of the Creeks,* 160, 162.

52. Treaty of Peace between Spain and the Chickasaw Nation, June 22 and 23, 1784, reel 1, film 663, leg. 2360, Papeles de Cuba, U.S. Library of Congress Microfilm of

transcripts of selected manuscript documents pertaining to Arkansas, at University of Arkansas Library, Fayetteville; Miró to José de Gálvez, June 1, 1787, "Papers from the Spanish Archives Relating to Tennessee and the Old Southwest," 11: 76.

53. Daniel McMurphy to O'Neill, July 11, 1786, *McGillivray of the Creeks*, 120; Enrique Roche to McMurphy, July 23, 1786, "Papers from the Spanish Archives Relating to Tennessee and the Old Southwest," 10: 146; O'Neill to Bernardo de Gálvez, Oct. 11, 1786, "Papers from the Spanish Archives Relating to Tennessee and the Old Southwest," 10: 149.

54. Bernardo de Gálvez to Miró, Aug. 23, 1786, pp. 699-70, reel 2, Mississippi Provincial Archives: Spanish Dominion, 1759–1804, comp. Dunbar Rowland, Jackson, Miss.; Bernardo de Gálvez to José de Gálvez, Aug. 26, 1786, doc. 113, leg. 2551, Audiencia de Santo Domingo, Historic New Orleans Collection; Instructions to Diego de Gardoqui, September 1, 1786, *Documentos Históricos de La Florida y La Luisiana, Siglos XVI al XVIII*, 380.

55. Hawkins to McGillivray, Jan. 8, 1786, *McGillivray of the Creeks*, 101; Hawkins to McGillivray, Jan. 11, 1786, "Papers from the Spanish Archives Relating to Tennessee and the Old Southwest," 10: 129; McMurphy to O'Neill, July 11, 1786, *McGillivray of the Creeks*, 118–20.

56. Bernardo de Gálvez to Miró, May 20, 1786, "Papers from the Spanish Archives Relating to Tennessee and the Old Southwest," 10: 136–7; Miró to José de Gálvez, June 1, 1787, "Papers from the Spanish Archives Relating to Tennessee and the Old Southwest," 11: 78–9; Miró to Gardoqui, June 28, 1786, attached to Miró to José de Gálvez, June 28, 1786, doc. 136, reel 18, leg. 2551, Audiencia de Santo Domingo, Historic New Orleans Collection.

57. O'Neill to Miró, Aug. 3, 1787, "Papers from the Spanish Archives Relating to Tennessee and the Old Southwest," 11: 90.

58. Bernardo de Gálvez, *Instructions for Governing the Interior Provinces of New Spain*, 1786, ed. and trans. Donald E. Worcester (Berkeley, 1951), 41; Weber, *Spanish Frontier in North America*, 227–30.

59. Ezpeleta to José de Gálvez, Oct. 11, 1787, doc. 1, leg. 2552, Audiencia de Santo Domingo, Historic New Orleans Collection; Miró to O'Neill, March 24, 1787, *McGillivray of the Creeks*, 145–6; Miró to José de Gálvez, March 24, 1787, doc. 7, reel 19, leg. 2552, Audiencia de Santo Domingo, Historic New Orleans Collection; [the Count of Floridablanca] to [Antonio Valdés], July 31, 1787, reel 3, Panton Leslie Papers; Miró to O'Neill, April 1, 1788, reel 3, Panton Leslie Papers.

60. Roger H. Brown, *The Republic in Peril: 1812* (New York, 1964), 3–7; Gould, *Among the Powers of the Earth*, 111–2.

61. Chacheré to Bouligny, [Dec. 1785], "Papers from the Spanish Archives Relating to Tennessee and the Old Southwest," 9: 140; Bouligny to Miró, Aug. 22, 1785, *Spain in the Mississippi Valley*, 2: 136–42.

62. George Washington to Benjamin Harrison, Oct. 10, 1784, *Writings of George Washington*, 9: 63; Daniel H. Usner Jr., "Remapping Boundaries in the Old Southwest, 1783–1795," in *George Washington's South*, ed. Tamara Harvey and Greg O'Brien (Gainesville, 2004), 26–8; Stephen Aron, *How the West Was Lost: The Transformation of Kentucky from Daniel Boone to Henry Clay* (Baltimore, 1996), 73–8, 119–22; Anderson and Cayton, *Dominion of War*, 182–4; Drew R. McCoy, *The Elusive Republic: Political Economy in Jeffersonian America* (New York, 1980). For Washington's longer reflections after a visit to the west, see diary entry for October 4, 1784, *George Washington's Diaries: An Abridgement*, ed. Dorothy Twohig (Charlottesville, 1999), 264–6.

63. Thomas Jefferson to Richard Henry Lee, July 12, 1785, *Papers of Thomas Jefferson*, 8:

287; David Campbell to Arthur Campbell, Dec. 27, 1784, folder 3, State of Franklin, Arthur Campbell Papers, Filson Historical Society, Louisville, Ky.; Barksdale, *Lost State of Franklin*, 73–4.

64. Chacheré to [Bouligny], Nov. 7, 1785, *Spain in the Mississippi Valley*, 2: 152–4; Barksdale, *Lost State of Franklin*, 3, 18–21, 34, 53–4; Dale Van Every, *Ark of Empire: The American Frontier, 1784–1803* (New York, 1963), 9–10. Settlers were often at odds with speculators over land claims and the Revolution's meaning for small farmers. See Taylor, *Liberty Men and Great Proprietors*.

65. Gardoqui to Floridablanca, Dec. 6, 1787, "Papers from the Spanish Archives Relating to Tennessee and the Old Southwest," 16: 93; Gardoqui to Floridablanca, April 18, 1788, "Papers from the Spanish Archives Relating to Tennessee and the Old Southwest," 17: 10; Pedro Wouver d'Arges to Miró, Aug. 12, 1788, Pontalba Papers, trans. Gilbert Pemberton, Temple Bodley Collection, Filson Historical Society.

66. Summary of a Conversation between James White and Gardoqui, Aug. 26, 1786, "Papers from the Spanish Archives Relating to Tennessee and the Old Southwest," 16: 83–4; Gardoqui to Floridablanca, Oct. 28, 1786, "Papers from the Spanish Archives Relating to Tennessee and the Old Southwest," 16: 86–7, 90; Andrew McMichael, *Atlantic Loyalties: Americans in Spanish West Florida, 1785–1810* (Athens, 2008).

67. White to Miró, April 18, 1789, *Spain in the Mississippi Valley*, 2: 267–8; White to Ezpeleta, Dec. 24, 1788, "Papers from the Spanish Archives Relating to Tennessee and the Old Southwest," 18: 143–5; John Sevier to Gardoqui, Sept. 12, 1788, "Papers from the Spanish Archives Relating to Tennessee and the Old Southwest," 15: 103; Gardoqui to Miró, Oct. 10, 1788, "Papers from the Spanish Archives Relating to Tennessee and the Old Southwest," 18: 133; McGillivray to Miró, Sept. 20, 1788, *McGillivray of the Creeks*, 201; Nichols, *Red Gentlemen and White Savages*, 66–7; Van Every, *Ark of Empire*, 85–96.

68. Gardoqui to Miró, Oct. 2, 1788, "Papers from the Spanish Archives Relating to Tennessee and the Old Southwest," 18: 131–2.

69. White to Ezpeleta, Dec. 24, 1788, "Papers from the Spanish Archives Relating to Tennessee and the Old Southwest," 18: 143–5.

70. Bernardo de Campo to Floridablanca, August 9, 1783, *Documents from East Florida*, 139.

71. Wilkinson, Memorial to Miró and Martín Navarro, [Sept. 3, 1787], Pontalba Papers; Wilkinson to Miró and Navarro, May 15, 1788, Pontalba Papers; Miró to Antonio Valdés, June 15, 1788, "Papers from the Spanish Archives Relating to Tennessee and the Old Southwest," 15: 89–90; Miró and Navarro to Valdés, Sept. 25, 1787, Pontalba Papers; Wilkinson to Gardoqui, Jan. 1, 1789, Pontalba Papers; John Anthony Caruso, *The Appalachian Frontier: America's First Surge Westward*, (Knoxville, 2nd ed., 2003), 315.

72. John Brown to James Madison, May 12, 1788, *Documentary History of the Constitution of the United States of America, 1786–1870* (Washington, 1905), 1: 611–2; Brown to Jefferson, Aug. 10, 1788, *Documentary History of the Constitution*, 2: 9–11; Oliver Pollock Memorial, February 10, 1789, doc. 164, leg. 2553, reel 21, Audiencia de Santo Domingo, Historic New Orleans Collection; James, *Oliver Pollock*, 326, 330.

73. Pollock Memorial, February 10, 1789, doc. 164, leg. 2553, reel 21, Audiencia de Santo Domingo, Historic New Orleans Collection; Charles Gayarré, *History of Louisiana: Spanish Dominion* (New Orleans, 3rd ed., 1885), 3: 222–3; James, *Oliver Pollock*, 327–9, 31–2; Cummins, "Oliver Pollock's Plantations," 44.

74. Gardoqui to Floridablanca, April 18, 1788, "Papers from the Spanish Archives Relating to Tennessee and the Old Southwest," 17: 107–8; Miró, Offer to Western Americans, April 20, 1789, *Spain in the Mississippi Valley*, 2: 269–71.

75. Miró and Navarro to Valdés, Sept. 25, 1787, Pontalba Papers; Cummins, "Oliver Pollock," 202.
76. Gardoqui to Floridablanca, April 18, 1788, "Papers from the Spanish Archives Relating to Tennessee and the Old Southwest," 17: 107–8.
77. Miró and Navarro to Valdés, Sept. 25, 1787, Pontalba Papers.
78. Gardoqui to Floridablanca, Oct. 24, 1788, "Papers from the Spanish Archives Relating to Tennessee and the Old Southwest," 18: 133–8; Floridablanca to Gardoqui, May 24, 1788, "Papers from the Spanish Archives Relating to Tennessee and the Old Southwest," 16: 95–6; Miró and Navarro to Wilkinson, Sept. 6, 1787, Pontalba Papers; Miró to Valdés, June 15, 1788, "Papers from the Spanish Archives Relating to Tennessee and the Old Southwest," 15: 89–90; Miró to Valdés, Aug. 28, 1788, Pontalba Papers; Miró, Offer to Western Americans, April 20, 1789, *Spain in the Mississippi Valley,* 2: 269–71.
79. McGillivray to O'Neill, April 25, 1788, *McGillivray of the Creeks,* 178.
80. James Robertson to Miró, Jan. 29, 1789, "Papers from the Spanish Archives Relating to Tennessee and the Old Southwest," 19: 81; Robertson to Miró, Sept. 2, 1789, *Spain in the Mississippi Valley,* 2: 279; Daniel Smith to Gardoqui, March 11, 1789, "Papers from the Spanish Archives Relating to Tennessee and the Old Southwest," 19: 97
81. Miró to McGillivray, May 10, 1789, "Papers from the Spanish Archives Relating to Tennessee and the Old Southwest," 20: 111; Miró to Smith, Sept. 15, 1789, "Papers from the Spanish Archives Relating to Tennessee and the Old Southwest," 21: 91.
82. Ezpeleta to Valdés, Dec. 29, 1788, "Papers from the Spanish Archives Relating to Tennessee and the Old Southwest," 18: 141–2.
83. John Jay, Federalist no. 4, *The Federalist Papers,* ed. Clinton Rossiter (New York, 1961), 49; Gould, *Among the Powers of the Earth,* 130–4; James E. Lewis Jr., *The American Union and the Problem of Neighborhood: The United States and the Collapse of the Spanish Empire, 1783–1829* (Chapel Hill, 1998), 6.
84. Bernardo de Gálvez to Miró, Jan. 26, 1786, p. 696, reel 2, Mississippi Provincial Archives: Spanish Dominion.
85. Miró and Navarro to Valdés, Sept. 25, 1787, Pontalba Papers. Britain was doing much the same thing in Upper Canada. Alan Taylor, "The Late Loyalists: Northern Reflections of the Early American Republic," *Journal of the Early Republic,* 27 (2007), 1–34.
86. McMichael, *Atlantic Loyalties,* 17–20.
87. Miró to Bernardo de Gálvez, April 20, 1786, "Papers from the Spanish Archives Relating to Tennessee and the Old Southwest," 10: 130; Miró to José de Gálvez, Jan. 17, 1787, "Papers from the Spanish Archives Relating to Tennessee and the Old Southwest," 11: 63; Grand-Pré, Report of Americans Arriving at Natchez, July 5, 1788, *Spain in the Mississippi Valley,* 2: 257–8; Gardoqui to Floridablanca, March 4, 1789, "Papers from the Spanish Archives Relating to Tennessee and the Old Southwest," 19: 87–8, 91–2; Miró to Valdés, June 18, 1789, "Papers from the Spanish Archives Relating to Tennessee and the Old Southwest," 20: 113–4; Nichols, *Red Gentlemen and White Savages,* 58–9.
88. George Morgan memorial, June 25, 1788, *Kaskaskia Records, 1778–1790,* 483; Report of Committee on the Memorial of George Morgan, July 15, 1788, *Territorial Papers,* 2: 129–30; Thomas Hutchins to Gardoqui, Jan. 25, 1789, "Papers from the Spanish Archives Relating to Tennessee and the Old Southwest," 19: 93–5; Gardoqui to George Morgan, Oct. 4, 1788, Pontalba Papers; Gardoqui to Floridablanca, Oct. 24, 1788, "Papers from the Spanish Archives Relating to Tennessee and the Old Southwest," 18: 133–8; "List of the persons who have subscribed to Colonel George Morgan their acceptance of the plots of land, which he has promised to allot them in his

projected settlement of New Madrid," Pontalba Papers; Savelle, *George Morgan*, 200–3.

89. George McCully et al. to John Morgan, April 14, 1789, "Account of the Settlement of New Madrid," *American Museum* 6 (1789): 69–71; John Dodge et al. to John Turnbull, April 14, 1789, *Spanish Régime in Missouri*, 1: 279–83.

90. Miró to George Morgan, May 23, 1789, Pontalba Papers. New Madrid would be the epicenter of a major set of earthquakes in 1811 and 1812. See Jonathan Todd Hancock, "A World Convulsed: Earthquakes, Authority, and the Making of Nations in the War of 1812 Era" (Ph.D. diss., University of North Carolina, Chapel Hill, 2013).

91. George Morgan to Miró, May 24, 1789, Pontalba Papers; Savelle, *George Morgan*, 203–8.

92. Panton to Miró, July 3, 1789, reel 5, Panton Leslie Papers; Miró to Robertson, April 20, 1789, *Spain in the Mississippi Valley*, 2: 268–9.

93. McGillivray to Folch, April 22, 1789, *McGillivray of the Creeks*, 227–8; McGillivray to Panton, May 20, 1789, "Papers Relating to the Georgia-Florida Frontier, 1784–1800," 283, 285–6; Miró to Folch, May 10, 1789, reel 5, Panton Leslie Papers; Waselkov, *Conquering Spirit*, 16–23; Karl Davis, "The Founding of Tensaw: Kinship, Community, Trade, and Diplomacy in the Creek Nation," in *Coastal Encounters*, 81–98. In May 1789, McGillivray persuaded the Alabama chiefs to go to Mobile "to ensure the commandant of their peaceable intentions." After that, he entirely blamed the Choctaws rather than the Alabamas in discussions with Miró. McGillivray to Miró, May 26, 1789, *McGillivray of the Creeks*, 234; McGillivray to Miró, June 9, 1789, *McGillivray of the Creeks*, 236.

94. Miró to José de Gálvez, May 20, 1789, doc. 38, reel 20, leg. 2553, Audiencia de Santo Domingo, Historic New Orleans Collection; McGillivray to O'Neill, March 1, 1788, *McGillivray of the Creeks*, 168.

95. McGillivray to Miró, Aug. 12, 1788, *McGillivray of the Creeks*, 193–4.

96. McGillivray to Zéspedes, Jan. 5, 1788, *McGillivray of the Creeks*, 165; McGillivray to Miró, Jan. 10, 1788, *McGillivray of the Creeks*, 167; Leslie to Zéspedes, Jan. 28, 1788, *McGillivray of the Creeks*, 167n116; McGillivray to Zéspedes, Oct. 6, 1787, *McGillivray of the Creeks*, 162–3; McGillivray to O'Neill, April 15, 1788, *McGillivray of the Creeks*, 176.

97. Miró to Valdés, July 13, 1788, doc. 22, reel 10, leg. 2544, Audiencia de Santo Domingo, Historic New Orleans Collection; McGillivray to Miró, Oct. 4, 1787, *McGillivray of the Creeks*, 160–1; Miró to McGillivray, Oct. 16, 1787, p. 176, reel 3, Mississippi Provincial Archives: Spanish Dominion; McGillivray to Miró, June 12, 1788, *McGillivray of the Creeks*, 183–4.

98. McGillivray to Hawkins, April 14, 1788, p. 621, reel 85, Papers of the Continental Congress; McGillivray to Pickens and Mathews, June 4, 1788, *McGillivray of the Creeks*, 181–3.

99. McGillivray to O'Neill, Aug. 12, 1788, *McGillivray of the Creeks*, 192; McGillivray to Anthony Bledsoe and Robertson, April 14, 1788, p. 620, reel 85, Papers of the Continental Congress; McGillivray to O'Neill, April 25, 1788, *McGillivray of the Creeks*, 178; McGillivray to Leslie, Nov. 20, 1788, *McGillivray of the Creeks*, 206–8; Coleman, *American Revolution in Georgia*, 249–50.

100. McGillivray to O'Neill, March 1, 1788, *McGillivray of the Creeks*, 170; McGillivray to Miró, March 15, 1788, *McGillivray of the Creeks*, 171; McGillivray to O'Neill, March 28, 1788, *McGillivray of the Creeks*, 173; McGillivray to Miró, June 12, 1788, *McGillivray of the Creeks*, 184.

101. Miró to McGillivray, July 8, 1788, *McGillivray of the Creeks*, 188.

102. *Authentic Memoirs of William Augustus Bowles,* 13.

103. *Life of General W. A. Bowles: A Native of America, Born of English Parents in Frederic County, Maryland, in the Year 1764* (New York, 1803), 4–9; J. Leitch Wright Jr., *William Augustus Bowles, Director General of the Creek Nation* (Athens, 1967), 6–24; *Authentic Memoirs of William Augustus Bowles,* 1–27; New, *Maryland Loyalists,* 49–54, 58–64, 88, 99–100, 105, 115; J. Leitch Wright Jr., "The Queen's Redoubt Explosion in the Lives of William A. Bowles, John Miller and William Panton," in *Anglo-Spanish Confrontation,* 181–2; Bowles to King George III, Jan. 3, 1791, FO 4-09-003, British National Archives.

104. *Authentic Memoirs of William Augustus Bowles,* 22–3; Bowles to King George III, Jan. 3, 1791, FO 4-09-003, British National Archives; Wright, *William Augustus Bowles,* 13, 21, 24.

105. McGillivray to Leslie, Feb. 8, 1789, *McGillivray of the Creeks,* 222–3.

106. John Fitzpatrick to John Miller, May 5, 1772, *Merchant of Manchac,* 118; McGillivray to Zéspedes, Jan. 5, 1788, *McGillivray of the Creeks,* 166; Wright, *William Augustus Bowles,* 26–7; Wright, "Lord Dunmore's Loyalist Asylum," 377–8; Jasanoff, *Liberty's Exiles,* 235–7; David, *Dunmore's New World,* 144–62.

107. McGillivray to Leslie, Nov. 20, 1788, *McGillivray of the Creeks,* 205–7.

108. Lower Creeks and Seminoles, talk to Zéspedes, Dec. 8, 1784, *Documents from East Florida,* 430; O'Neill to Miró, Oct. 28, 1788, *McGillivray of the Creeks,* 204; O'Neill to Miró, Sept. 10, 1788, "Papers from the Spanish Archives Relating to Tennessee and the Old Southwest," 15: 102.

109. McGillivray to Miró, Feb. 1, 1789, "Papers from the Spanish Archives Relating to Tennessee and the Old Southwest," 19: 82; McGillivray to O'Neill, June 22, 1788, *McGillivray of the Creeks,* 186; McGillivray to Miró, Aug. 12, 1788, *McGillivray of the Creeks,* 194–5; McGillivray to O'Neill, Aug. 12, 1788, *McGillivray of the Creeks,* 192–3; Zéspedes to McGillivray, Oct. 8, 1788, *McGillivray of the Creeks,* 202–3; McGillivray to Leslie, Nov. 20, 1788, *McGillivray of the Creeks,* 205–7; O'Neill to Miró, Dec. 22, 1788, *McGillivray of the Creeks,* 211–2; McGillivray to Panton, Feb. 1, 1789, *McGillivray of the Creeks,* 218–9; Wright, *William Augustus Bowles,* 28–9.

110. Panton to Miró, Aug. 5, 1788, reel 4, Panton Leslie Papers; Bowles to Howard, Nov. 15, 1788, reel 4, Panton Leslie Papers; Statement of McDonald, Lovern, Duir, and Maiben, Nov. 21, 1788, reel 4, Panton Leslie Papers; Leslie to McGillivray, Dec. 11, 1788, "Papers Relating to the Georgia-Florida Frontier, 1784-1800," 21: 282; O'Neill to Miró, Jan. 28, 1789, reel 4, Panton Leslie Papers; McGillivray to Miró, Feb. 1, 1789, "Papers from the Spanish Archives Relating to Tennessee and the Old Southwest," 19: 82; McGillivray to Zéspedes, Feb. 6, 1789, *McGillivray of the Creeks,* 221; McGillivray to Leslie, Feb. 8, 1789, *McGillivray of the Creeks,* 222–3; *Lucayan Royal Herald,* Aug. 15, 1789, *McGillivray of the Creeks,* 219n177; Bowles to *Lucayan Royal Herald,* Nassau, Aug. 19, 1789, reel 5, Panton Leslie Papers; Wright, *William Augustus Bowles,* 29–31.

111. Zéspedes to Ezpeleta, December 2, 1788, *McGillivray of the Creeks,* 208–9.

112. McGillivray to Panton, January 12, 1789, *McGillivray of the Creeks,* 214–5; McGillivray to Miró, Feb. 1, 1789, "Papers from the Spanish Archives Relating to Tennessee and the Old Southwest," 19: 83; McGillivray to Charles Howard, Feb. 10, 1789, reel 4, Panton Leslie Papers; McGillivray to Panton, Feb. 1, 1789, *McGillivray of the Creeks,* 217–9; Milfort, *Chef de guerre,* 115-7; Green, "Alexander McGillivray," 57–8.

113. McGillivray to Leslie, Feb. 8, 1789, *McGillivray of the Creeks,* 223; *Authentic Memoirs of William Augustus Bowles,* 54–6; Frank, *Creeks and Southerners,* 113.

114. [Marquis de la Torre] to Julián de Arriaga, Sept. 28, 1775, "Official Spanish Correspondence Pertaining to Relations with the Uchiz Indians, 1771–1783," Florida His-

tory Online, www.unf.edu/floridahistoryonline/Projects/uchize/, University of North Florida, Jacksonville; McGillivray to Miró, Feb. 1, 1789, "Papers from the Spanish Archives Relating to Tennessee and the Old Southwest," 19: 83n6; David Craig to William Blount, March 15, 1792, *American State Papers: Indian Affairs,* 1: 264; *Authentic Memoirs of William Augustus Bowles,* 65–7; McGillivray to Panton, Oct. 28, 1791, *McGillivray of the Creeks,* 299; Bowles to Zéspedes, Aug. 21, 1789, reel 5, Panton Leslie Papers; Bowles to Floridablanca, Aug. 30, 1789, reel 5, Panton Leslie Papers; Milfort, *Chef de guerre,* 80, 117; Caughey, *McGillivray of the Creeks,* 47–50; Wright, *William Augustus Bowles,* 36–55.

115. Zéspedes to McGillivray, Oct. 8, 1788, *McGillivray of the Creeks,* 202–3.

116. O'Neill to Diego de Vegas, June 26, 1788, *McGillivray of the Creeks,* 191n137; O'Neill investigation, Aug. 11–12, 1788, *McGillivray of the Creeks,* 191n140.

117. McGillivray to Leslie, Nov. 20, 1788, *McGillivray of the Creeks,* 206–8; McGillivray to O'Neill, Aug. 22, 1788, *McGillivray of the Creeks,* 196–7.

118. U.S. Commissioners to McGillivray and Others, the Chief Men and Warriors of the Creek Nation, July 16, 1788, *Early American Indian Documents,* 18: 465.

119. McGillivray to the U.S. Commissioners, Aug. 12, 1788, *Early American Indian Documents,* 18: 466.

120. Richard Winn, Pickens, and Mathews to McGillivray and the Headmen and Warriors of the Creek Nation, Nov. 28, 1788, *Early American Indian Documents,* 18: 479.

121. McGillivray to Winn, Pickens, and Mathews, Sept. 15, 1788, *Early American Indian Documents,* 18: 471.

122. David Campbell to Arthur Campbell, Aug. 14, 1787, folder 4, Arthur Campbell Papers, Filson Historical Society.

123. Report of Committee on Southern Indians, Aug. 3, 1787, *Early American Indian Documents,* 18: 454–5; Sadosky, *Revolutionary Negotiations,* 118–22.

124. Knox, Report on the Southern Indians, July 18, 1787, *Early American Indian Documents,* 18: 449–50; Green, "Expansion of European Colonization," 1: 466.

125. Gardoqui to Ezpeleta, Nov. 12, 1787, "Papers from the Spanish Archives Relating to Tennessee and the Old Southwest," 13: 103–5; Zéspedes to Valdés, March 24, 1788, "Papers from the Spanish Archives Relating to Tennessee and the Old Southwest," 14: 88; Mann, *Republic of Debtors,* 171–82.

126. James MacGregor Burns, *The Vineyard of Liberty: The American Experiment* (New York, 1981), 47–57.

127. Pauline Maier, *Ratification: The People Debate the Constitution, 1787–1788* (New York, 2011), 237–40, 276–8, 286.

128. New York *Morning Post and Daily Advertiser,* Feb. 17, 1789, "Papers from the Spanish Archives Relating to Tennessee and the Old Southwest," 19: 92.

129. Robertson to Miró, Jan. 29, 1789, "Papers from the Spanish Archives Relating to Tennessee and the Old Southwest," 19: 81.

130. Ezpeleta to Valdés, Dec. 29, 1788, "Papers from the Spanish Archives Relating to Tennessee and the Old Southwest," 18: 139–41.

131. McGillivray to Miró, June 24, 1789, *McGillivray of the Creeks,* 239–40.

132. Martin to Washington, Sept. 25, 1789, *The Papers of George Washington, Presidential Series,* ed. W. W. Abbot and Dorothy Twohig (Charlottesville, 1993), 4: 85; Piomingo to Washington, Oct. 30, 1789, abstract, *Papers of George Washington, Presidential Series,* 4: 260–1; Inhabitants of Kentucky to [Washington], Sept. 8, 1789, *Papers of George Washington, Presidential Series,* 4: 2–3; Knox to Inhabitants of Kentucky, Dec. 15, 1789, *Papers of George Washington, Presidential Series,* 4: 3.

133. McGillivray to Folch, May 14, 1789, *McGillivray of the Creeks,* 232; Folch to Miró, June 12, 1789, "Papers from the Spanish Archives Relating to Tennessee and the Old Southwest," 20: 112; Panton to Miró, July 3, 1789, reel 5, Panton Leslie Papers; McGillivray to Panton, Aug. 10, 1789, *McGillivray of the Creeks,* 248.

134. Knox to Washington, July 7, 1789, *American State Papers: Indian Affairs,* 1: 52–4; Dorothy V. Jones, *License for Empire: Colonialism by Treaty in Early America* (Chicago, 1982), 147–8.

135. Wilkinson to Miró, Sept. 17, 1789, Pontalba Papers.

136. Gardoqui to Floridablanca, March 4, 1789, "Papers from the Spanish Archives Relating to Tennessee and the Old Southwest," 19: 88–9.

CONCLUSION

1. Faye, "British and Spanish Fortifications," 287–9; Waselkov, *Conquering Spirit;* J. C. A. Stagg, *The War of 1812: Conflict for a Continent* (New York, 2012), 151.

2. Treaty of Nogales, Oct. 28, 1793, *Spain in the Mississippi Valley,* 3: 223–7; Esteban Miró to Alexander McGillivray, Dec. 13, 1788, *McGillivray of the Creeks,* 209–10; Charles A. Weeks, *Paths to a Middle Ground: The Diplomacy of Natchez, Boukfouka, Nogales, and San Fernando de las Barrancas, 1791–1795* (Tuscaloosa, 2005).

3. Milfort, *Chef de guerre,* 128–9; Caughey, *McGillivray of the Creeks,* 42–4; Green, "Alexander McGillivray," 55–6; Green, "Expansion of European Colonization," 1: 474–5; Braund, *Deerskins and Duffels,* 175–6.

4. McGillivray to George Galphin Jr., May 18, 1789, *American State Papers: Indian Affairs,* 1: 35; McGillivray to William Panton, May 20, 1789, "Papers Relating to the Georgia-Florida Frontier, 1784–1800," 286–7; McGillivray to Miró, May 26, 1789, *McGillivray of the Creeks,* 235; Galphin to Andrew Pickens and Henry Osborn, May 27, 1789, *American State Papers: Indian Affairs,* 1: 35–6; Panton to François Luis Hector, Barón de Carondelet, Feb. 16, 1793, *McGillivray of the Creeks,* 353; Panton to Carondelet, Feb. 20, 1793, *McGillivray of the Creeks,* 354; Obituary Notice in the *Gentleman's Magazine, McGillivray of the Creeks,* 362.

5. Waselkov, *Conquering Spirit,* 27, 39; Cashin, *Lachlan McGillivray, Indian Trader,* 310.

6. J. F. Hamtramck to Henry Knox, March 31, 1792, *Territorial Papers,* 2: 382; Winthrop Sargent to Edmund Randolph, Sept. 13, 1794, *Territorial Papers,* 3: 423–4; Knox to William Blount, May 14, 1793, *American State Papers: Indian Affairs,* 1: 430; Wendy St. Jean, "How the Chickasaws Saved the Cumberland Settlement in the 1790s," *Tennessee Historical Quarterly* 68 (2009), 2–20.

7. Piomingo to Joseph Martin, Sept. 28, 1789, MS 722, Edward E. Ayer Collection, Newberry Library, Chicago; Doughty, "Up the Tennessee in 1790," 121–5; Knox to Piomingo, February 17, 1792, *American State Papers: Indian Affairs,* 1: 249; Nichols, *Red Gentlemen and White Savages,* 140; Green, *Chickasaw Lives,* 1: 71–3; Gibson, *Chickasaws,* 86–90.

8. Carroll Smith-Rosenberg, "Dis-Covering the Subject of the 'Great Constitutional Discussion,' 1786-1789," *Journal of American History* (1992): 847–8; Taylor, *Divided Ground,* 80–1.

9. Diego de Gardoqui to José Moñino y Redondo, the Count of Floridablanca, Dec. 6, 1787, "Papers from the Spanish Archives Relating to Tennessee and the Old Southwest," 92.

10. Anderson and Cayton, *Dominion of War,* 188–91, 212; Lewis, *American Union,* 13–6; Eric Hinderaker, *Elusive Empires: Constructing Colonialism in the Ohio Valley, 1673–1800*

(New York, 1997); Edward Countryman, "Indians, the Colonial Order, and the Social Significance of the American Revolution," *William and Mary Quarterly* 53 (1996): 360.

11. Andrew Jackson to John McKee, May 16, 1794, *The Papers of Andrew Jackson,* ed. Sam B. Smith and Harriet Chappell Owsley (Knoxville, 1980), 1: 49; Andrew R. L. Cayton, "'Separate Interests' and the Nation-State: The Washington Administration and the Origins of Regionalism in the Trans-Appalachian West," *Journal of American History* (1992): 39–67; Gould, *Among the Powers of the Earth,* 112.

12. Nancy Isenberg, *Fallen Founder: The Life of Aaron Burr* (New York, 2007), 286–371; Thomas Perkins Abernathy, *The Burr Conspiracy* (New York, 1954), 4–5; Weber, *Spanish Frontier in North America,* 282. On other conspiracies of the era, see Harry Ammon, *The Genet Mission* (New York, 1973); Jennison, *Cultivating Race,* 89–125; Andrew R. L. Cayton, "'When Shall We Cease to Have Judases?' The Blount Conspiracy and the Limits of the 'Extended Republic,'" in *Launching the "Extended Republic": The Federalist Era,* ed. Ronald J. Hoffman and Peter J. Albert (Charlottesville, 1996), 156–89.

13. Kathleen DuVal, "Choosing Enemies: The Prospects for an Anti-American Alliance in the Louisiana Territory," *Arkansas Historical Quarterly* (Autumn 2003): 233–52; Kathleen DuVal, "Cross-Cultural Crime and Osage Justice in the Western Mississippi Valley," *Ethnohistory* (Fall 2007): 697–722; McMichael, *Atlantic Loyalties,* 1; Gould, *Among the Powers of the Earth,* 192–7.

14. Alan Taylor, *The Civil War of 1812: American Citizens, British Subjects, Irish Rebels, and Indian Allies* (New York, 2010); A. T. Mahan, "The Negotiations at Ghent in 1814," *American Historical Review* 11 (1905): 73–4; Nathaniel Millett, *The Maroons of Prospect Bluff and their Quest for Freedom in the Atlantic World* (Gainesville, 2013); Anderson and Cayton, *Dominion of War,* 223; Wright, *William Augustus Bowles,* 23, 55–7, 66-95, 157–60, 166; Wright, *Creeks and Seminoles,* 118; Jennison, *Cultivating Race,* 127–55.

15. Return of Certificates, Sept. 1811, *American State Papers: Public Lands,* 2: 707; Land Claims in the Western District of Louisiana, April 8, 1816, *American State Papers: Public Lands,* 3: 161-2, 165-6, 209; Trevor Burnard, "Freedom, Migration, and the American Revolution," in *Empire and Nation: The American Revolution in the Atlantic World,* ed. Eliga H. Gould and Peter S. Onuf (Baltimore, 2005), 295–314; Taylor, *Internal Enemy.*

16. *Southwest Louisiana Records,* 2A: 150, 324; Kastor, *Nation's Crucible;* Fausz, *Founding St. Louis,* 193–4; La Maison Broussard, Vermilionville, Lafayette, La.

17. Berlin, *Many Thousands Gone,* 99, 342–4; Edward E. Baptist, *Creating an Old South: Middle Florida's Plantation Frontier Before the Civil War* (Chapel Hill, 2002); Adam Rothman, *Slave Country: American Expansion and the Origins of the Deep South* (Cambridge, 2005); Hanger, "Avenues to Freedom," 1: 185; Shawn Cole, "Capitalism and Freedom: Manumissions and the Slave Market in Louisiana, 1725–1820," *Journal of Economic History* 65 (2005): 1008–27; Ashli White, *Encountering Revolution: Haiti and the Making of the Early Republic* (Baltimore, 2010).

18. Census of the Mobile District, 1786, http://vidas.rootsweb.com/1786cen.html.

19. Harry L. Watson, *Liberty and Power: The Politics of Jacksonian America* (New York, 1990, 2006); Elaine F. Crane, "Dependence in the Era of Independence," in *American Revolution: Its Character,* 253–75; Wulf, *Not All Wives,* 184–7; Smith-Rosenberg, *This Violent Empire,* 137–67; Wood, *Radicalism of the American Revolution,* 104, 178–9; Smith, *Freedoms We Lost;* Sarah M. S. Pearsall, "Gender," in *The British Atlantic World, 1500–1800,* ed. David Armitage and Michael J. Braddick (New York, 2009), 129; Joan Gunderson, "Independence, Citizenship, and the American Revolution," *Signs* 13

(1987): 59–77; Linda K. Kerber, "The Paradox of Women's Citizenship in the Early Republic: The Case of *Martin vs. Massachusetts,* 1805," *American Historical Review* 97 (1992): 349–78.

20. Carlisle *Weekly Gazette,* Jan. 23, 1799, in Hayden, "Pollock Family of Pennsylvania," 95–8; Eric P. Newman, "The Dollar $ign: Its Written and Printed Origins," *America's Silver Dollars: Proceedings of the 1993 Coinage of the Americas Conference,* ed. John M. Kleeberg (New York, 1995), 1–49; James, *Oliver Pollock,* 329–36; Cummins, "Oliver Pollock's Plantations," 44–7.

21. James, *Oliver Pollock,* 338–44; Cummins, "Oliver Pollock," 209; Liss, *Atlantic Empires,* 119; Mann, *Republic of Debtors,* 190–208.

22. Rosemarie Zagarri, "The Rights of Man and Woman in Post-Revolutionary America," *William and Mary Quarterly* 60 (1998): 200–27.

INDEX

ABOUT THE AUTHOR

Kathleen DuVal is a professor of Early American History at the University of North Carolina at Chapel Hill. She is the recipient of many fellowships, including a National Humanities Center Fellowship and the Andrew W. Mellon Postdoctoral Fellowship from the McNeil Center for Early American Studies at the University of Pennsylvania. DuVal is the author of *The Native Ground: Indians and Colonists in the Heart of the Continent* and more than forty articles and reviews. She is also co-editor of *Interpreting a Continent: Voices from Colonial America*. She lives in Durham, North Carolina, with her husband and sons.